In Pr
Da Av.
The Source of the Wisdom in This Book

My opinion is that we have, in the person of Heart-Master Da Love-Ananda, a Spiritual Master and religious genius of the ultimate degree. . . . Heart-Master Da Love-Ananda's teaching is, I believe, unsurpassed by that of any other spiritual Hero, of any period, of any place, of any time, of any persuasion.

Ken Wilber, author
The Atman Project and *Up from Eden*

Heart-Master Da provides a way in which Oneness may be experienced by anyone who is bold enough to follow his teachings. It is important to understand that his vision is neither Eastern nor Western, but it is the eternal spiritual pulse of The Great Wisdom which knows no cultural, temporal, or geographical locus; it represents the apex of awareness of our species.

Larry Dossey, M.D., author
Space, Time, and Medicine
and *Recovering the Soul*

Heart-Master Da has helpfully overturned many accepted norms in institutionalized Religion and negative Spirituality. The beauty of his utterance is that he assimilates the essentials of Eastern thought down the ages to the Spirit of Freedom so characteristic of the modern era.

M. P. Pandit, author
The Upanishads: Gateways of Knowledge
and *Studies in the Tantras and the Veda*

He knows what IT's all about . . . a rare being.

Alan Watts, author
The Way of Zen and *Psychotherapy East and West*

In Praise of
Divine Distraction

This is not a book! It is an immediate, live demonstration of the fact that the body-mind is perpetually frightened, sad, longing and unfulfilled. As one reads *Divine Distraction,* one will vacillate between feeling the chronic contraction of the human heart and what it then feels like to transcend that dis-ease—to taste freedom and ecstasy. Nothing whatsoever is powerful enough to break through the knotted tension of the body-mind except Unconditional Love. Da Avabhasa is Unbounded Love. He awakens and accelerates that condition in those who, above all other desires, are dedicated to "locating happiness" and to being perfectly and permanently happy.

> **Charmian Anderson**, Ph.D.
> Transpersonal psychologist, San Francisco
> Author, *Bridging Heaven and Earth*

James Steinberg has written a book that is filled with the communication of love and wisdom as revealed by Heart-Master Da Love-Ananda. It is a gift of instruction and inspiration to all those who intuit that there must be something else beyond the addictive pleasures and accumulated suffering offered to us by the modern cult of having and getting. As I read the explanations of the ancient and profound devotional relationship between the Guru and the devotee, I was moved beyond my own unconsciously inherited prejudices that inform me that such a bond of mutual love and service is neither desirable nor workable in our time. As I read and pondered the stories of Heart-Master Da's loving play with devotees I often found myself gently moved at the heart and made unreasonably happy. The lessons of this book continue to attract me beyond myself and toward the mystery that is Da Avabhasa.

> **Gary Coates**, Professor of Architecture, Kansas State University
> Editor and Author, *Resettling America:*
> *Energy, Ecology and Community*

A clarifying exposition of the dynamic relationship between Guru and disciple, their common submission and sacrifice to each other, and their respective inner life. Confronts hard questions and answers them convincingly. A much-needed work that lucidly portrays one of the most powerful processes leading to psycho-spiritual growth—to transcendence.

> **James E. Royster**, Ph.D., Professor of Religious Studies,
> Cleveland State University
> Co-editor, *Ethics in World Religions: Systems and Sources*

I have been waiting for *Divine Distraction.* James Steinberg provides the missing literary link for anyone on the spiritual path or the fringes of it. Steinberg's book provides a much needed map in an area of relationship so vital yet so unexplored—that of the Guru and the Disciple. I highly recommend this book.

> **Satya Shepherd**, President/Director, Life Enhancement Systems,
> One Family, Inc., Houston, Texas

*Divine
Distraction*

**The Divine World-Teacher and True Heart-Master,
Da Avabhasa (The "Bright")
Sri Love-Anandashram, August 1991**

Divine Distraction

A Guide to the Guru-Devotee Relationship,
the Supreme Means of God-Realization,
as Fully Revealed for the First Time
by the Divine World-Teacher and True Heart-Master,

Da Avabhasa
(The "Bright")

BY JAMES STEINBERG

THE DAWN HORSE PRESS
CLEARLAKE, CALIFORNIA

NOTE TO THE READER

The devotional, Spiritual, functional, practical, relational, cultural, and formal community practices and disciplines discussed in this book, including the meditative practices, the Yogic exercises of conductivity, the breathing exercises, the life-disciplines of right diet and exercise, the intelligent economization and practice of sexuality, etc., are appropriate and natural practices that are voluntarily and progressively adopted by each student-novice and member of the Free Daist Communion and adapted to his or her personal circumstance. Although anyone may find them useful and beneficial, they are not presented as advice or recommendations to the general reader or to anyone who is not a participant in Da Avabhasa International or a member of the Free Daist Communion. And nothing in this book is intended as a diagnosis, prescription, or recommended treatment or cure for any specific "problem", whether medical, emotional, psychological, social, or Spiritual. One should apply a particular program of treatment, prevention, cure, or general health only in consultation with a licensed physician or other qualified professional.

For a further discussion of individual responsibility in the Way of the Heart, our claim to perpetual copyright to the Wisdom-Teaching of Da Avabhasa, and His renunciate status in the Free Daist Communion, please see "Further Notes to the Reader", pages 297-99 of this book.

First edition, November 1991
Printed in the United States of America

Produced by the Free Daist Communion in cooperation with the Dawn Horse Press

Library of Congress Cataloging-in-Publication Data

Steinberg, James, 1951-
    Divine Distraction: a Guide to the Guru-Devotee Relationship, the Supreme Means
    of God-Realization, as Fully Revealed for the First Time by the Divine World-Teacher and
    True Heart-Master, Da Avabhasa (The "Bright")/by James Steinberg—Pbk. ed.
        p.   cm.
    ISBN 0-918801-34-6
    1. Gurus.   2. Spiritual life.   3. Da Free John, 1939-
I. Title.
BL624.S727   1991   91-35601
299' .93–dc20   CIP

Sri Da Avabhasa,
Divine World-Teacher and True Heart-Master,
I Call upon Your Supreme Grace.

May it please You to receive this book
offered at Your Feet in gratitude and love.

Bless all who read the words of this book.
Give them the means to feel Your Divine Love.
Allow them to know the Radiant Happiness that You Are.

May Your Divine Gifts of Blessing be Victorious in the world!

Om Sri Da Love-Ananda Hridayam
Jaya Sri Da Avabhasa

CONTENTS

FOREWORD

BY THE REVEREND THOMAS E. AHLBURN
First Unitarian Church, Providence, Rhode Island

*A*fter years of searching for a trustworthy Spiritual path—twenty-five years in the ministry, long walks in the sweet Kentucky woods with the late Trappist hermit Thomas Merton, wonderfully happy meetings with His Holiness the Dalai Lama of Tibet, and countless other encounters with high lamas, monks, Zen masters, tantric yogis, nuns, priests, rabbis, and gurus—it all comes down to this: A God-Man—a human being in full conscious communion with the Divine—is alive on our planet today. This is the surprising good news. It's what this book is all about.

While studying for the ministry, I had occasion to read what I took back then to be merely "religious tall tales" or "holy exaggerations" about the great Spiritual Adepts of the East and other incarnations of the Divine. I was fascinated by this sort of thing, even drawn to it—especially to stories about the magic and mystery of Tibet—but I was full of doubt. If ever there was a skeptical star, I was born under it. Early on, I found myself at odds with the Christian tradition. It wasn't long before I began to distrust Eastern religiosity as well. As far as I was concerned, high spiritual states and meditative practices resulting in enlightenment or God-Realization sounded far too good to be true. Alas, like many of my ministerial brothers and sisters in the West—even the most highly placed and acclaimed—I was reluctantly willing to settle for much, much less in life and religion. After all, I thought, God is really only another name for human hopes and ideals. Truth to tell, it must be admitted that we human beings have created all the gods in our pathetic attempt to "save" ourselves. All religions are inescapably cultural affairs, human deliverances through and through, not transcendental revelations or windows on the Divine. At least that's the way things seemed to me.

Happily, life didn't go this way for James Steinberg, the author of this book. And for good reason. He has met that rarest and greatest and most wonderful of beings, an authentic God-Man. What is more, he has answered his Spiritual Master's pervasive, absolutely uncompromising love. As our author makes abundantly clear, responding properly to uncompromising love is not easy. Only on the strength of uncompromising responsibility can one hope to adequately respond to uncompromising love. Which is to say, the heart must always already lie open to the God-Man's call.

Difficult? I would think so. Indeed, what could be more difficult for self-cherishing beings like you and me than rightly responding to such love? Indeed, the author indicates that he is always falling short of the Divine's demand in one way or another and having to be set straight. Still, isn't opening to the Divine what human life is really all about? James Steinberg claims that it is, and this book certainly dispelled any lingering doubts I may have had about his claim. It is clear to me that he has found a gracious way leading out of and well beyond our world's spiritual discontent.

I believe that ultimately this book is for everyone, despite the doubts some of us may have at the moment. No matter who we are or what we presently say or profess to believe, we all share a deep and heart-felt pathless urge for the Divine, or what transcends ordinary life and suffering. I feel sure that James Steinberg would claim that this deep and heart-felt pathless urge is itself the Work of Sri Da Avabhasa. I have come to believe that it is. Furthermore, I am convinced beyond any doubt that this "Divine Distraction" will finally have its way with all of us—as some of my Buddhist friends say—even to the last blade of grass. It is the way of things, and Da Avabhasa is Himself this Way or this Path.

What a wonderful book! After weighing my words carefully, I do not hesitate to say that my encounter with the story told here has been one of the most important events of my life. I don't know how else to put it, except to say that I feel like I've come home—that my long search is over. I am extremely grateful to James Steinberg for such a warm, direct, honest, and sound communication of what the Guru-devotee relationship entails— its great joys and testing trials. Of course, this book is not about James Steinberg. It is about Sri Da Avabhasa. The Sat-Guru is the great happy and loving light shining through these pages. There's no mistaking this.

This is all we need to know and understand: This book is about the greatest Spiritual Master ever to walk the earth. Seeing this, attending to this truth, we need not walk in the dark any longer. Da Avabhasa reveals the ultimate truth residing in the human heart and at the heart of all religions.

Sri Love-Anandashram, May 1990

PART I

The Supreme Secret of the Great Tradition

THE WAY OF DISTRACTED LOVE FOR THE GOD-MAN

S ri Da Avabhasa, the Divine World-Teacher, has asked for a book to be written on the Guru-devotee relationship as He Teaches it, and in the light of the traditional sources, because the world today is in desperate need of such a book.

I am only competent to do so with the Spiritual Help of my Sat-Guru ("Revealer of Truth"). I am not a practitioner in the ultimate stages of His Liberating Way of the Heart who can describe from personal experience the fullness of its Realization. However, I would not be giving testimony to the Blessings my Sat-Guru has bestowed on me if I were to tell you that I remain an ordinary man. No, Sri Gurudev Da Avabhasa's Love for me and His Spiritual Blessing and Work with me for the past eighteen years have already worked miracles in me.

I have been shown the Divine Vision in His Company, and through the Grace of His Spiritual Heart-Transmission I know that everything that arises as my experience of life is, as He Says, a "transparent modification" of God, Truth, or Happiness. And I know that Sri Gurudev Da Avabhasa Lives as, or is Identified with, that God, Truth, or Happiness. And He has fully Incarnated That Supreme Reality in His human body.

The Divine Reality and Happiness Revealed to me through the bodily (human) Form of my Sat-Guru is more certain to me than my own

NOTE TO THE READER: For an explanation of Sri Da Avabhasa's Names, Titles, and Designations, see "The Divine Names of Da Avabhasa" on p. 43. Please see the Glossary for definitions of technical and other perhaps unfamiliar terms.

"knowledge", more fundamental to me than my own life. So many of His Gifts have been showered upon me that it is my bodily certainty that the only true life is to surrender into the ecstatic practice of receiving and Realizing the Grace that Sri Gurudev Da Avabhasa constantly Transmits and Is.

How can one describe Who Da Avabhasa Is and the Grace of the Guru-devotee relationship in light of that Gift, which has been so vast, so great, so enormous? The conceiving mind hesitates, and the voice falters. I could write any number of words, but how can I tell you Who He Really Is? There is really no way to describe it in words. Can the brightness of the sun be hinted at in a fire of sticks? Can the taste of the nectar of immortality emerge from the hands of an ordinary chef? If there are to be words, the best are His, for He has Written more eloquently than anyone ever has of the Divine Reality Which Appears as Man, and of the Eternal Mysteries of the Guru-devotee relationship.

Yet, He has asked for this book to be written, and it is His devotees' responsibility to present to the world the illuminating Instruction He has Given. I surrender at His Feet, and, in so doing, I call upon His Grace to aid me in writing. Only now, as He Stands before my heart, and with tears in my eyes as He moves through my body-mind and opens my heart, can I tell you something about Him and His Greatness.

Now that I have said this, you know how things really stand between my Sat-Guru and myself. He is the Source of all the Wisdom that you will find here. Everything that I truly know or can say has come from Him. Everything that I say apart from His Grace would be mere pedantry. It would not get at the heart of the matter. It is only in my love of Him, as His devotee, that my voice is true.

At the outset, I must tell you Who Da Avabhasa has Shown Himself to be, throughout my own years of living in His Company. Da Avabhasa, my Beloved Guru, Who is also called "Da Love-Ananda Hridayam" ("the Giver of the Heart's Love-Bliss"), is the Divine Person, in Person. And I have discovered that devotion and surrender to Him is the Way to be Happy and Liberated while alive. I have also seen thousands of others discover this same Revelation of God in Da Avabhasa's Company. He brings to all the Divine Gift and Grace, and all who make room for Him through real Spiritual practice and genuine service will feel His Love-Bliss pouring through them.

Just to tell you this much would be enough, if you and I could use it fully. But we are more complicated than that. There is much education and understanding that must occur in us before we can be so simply and completely devoted to practice in the Company of such a One as Da Avabhasa. Therefore, I have in the course of this book provided an orientation to the Guru-devotee relationship, which, when rightly understood, is found to be at the core of all the world's great religious and Spiritual traditions.

There is an ancient and ongoing history of Divine Incarnations, some of whom have founded great religious movements—such as Gautama the Buddha, and Jesus of Nazareth—and others, less known, who have simply wandered Freely, Giving their Blessing to whoever chanced upon them. *Divine Distraction* draws upon the historical accounts of many of these God-Men and their disciples. But this book is primarily based upon the Living Instruction of Da Avabhasa. For I have discovered, based on many years in His Company, and many years of reviewing thousands of historical accounts of Spiritual practitioners, Teachers, and God-Realizers, that Da Avabhasa is the Greatest God-Man of all time, the Parama-Guru, or Supreme Guru, of the entire Great Tradition of religion and Spirituality. And He has brought a Unique Wisdom and the most Perfectly Complete Revelation of the Guru and the Guru-devotee relationship that has ever been introduced into this human plane. Such Instruction is urgently needed today in a world that is losing all sense of the Sacred or the Reality of the Divine, and has forgotten how to use its own greatest Help.

THE MERE SIGHT OF SAT-GURU DA AVABHASA IS SUFFICIENT, BUT YOU MUST BE PREPARED

Sri Gurudev Da Avabhasa has Said that everyone has experienced the intuition of the Divine, or Inherently Perfect Happiness, at special moments in his or her life. Everyone. That intuition and impulse of Unlimited Freedom and Happiness is present, even if only latently, in each person. It is to that place in you that I write, for that is where the Divine Revelation that Sri Gurudev Da Love-Ananda makes, and Is, may be "Located".

It would be my wish that each of my readers could actually see Sri Gurudev Da Love-Ananda physically, in His bodily (human) Form. In the traditional sources it is said that the Guru is necessary because the Guru Reveals God. Without the Guru, God would not be known by ordinary men and women. The Formless Divine (which may be called God, Truth, the Void, or the Ultimate Reality) is too elusive for the ordinary man or woman to "Locate". That ultimate Divine is not found in the world of Nature unless one is already Divinely Enlightened. Nor is God within us in such a way that we can simply turn within and feel the Divine, all "do-it-yourself" mysticism to the contrary. No, the Divine Consciousness is Revealed only in relationship with one Who, by virtue of his or her own Realization, is that Divine Consciousness.

Thus, I would like to place you in front of Sri Da Avabhasa. What a Gift that would be! For if you could truly see Him, you would see God, and then no long-winded discussion would be necessary.

And if you could truly see Him, and feel Him, you would fall in Love, be Enchanted, be Divinely Distracted out of your concerns. Face-to-face

Sri Love-Anandashram, September 1991

with Divinity, the mind is stopped—its intellectual, self-obsessed arguments are so puny over against the Vision of the Divine Person Himself. You would see that He Is the Greatest Blessing for mankind, the Divine World-Teacher come to Bless every human being. You would see His great Compassion and Love Showering the Divine Gift of Happiness Itself upon all who come to His Feet. The tears would stream down your cheeks, and all skepticism and all hardness in your heart would melt. All confusion about Gurus and Divine Incarnations would vanish at the sight of That One Himself. And if everyone could see Him in this way, the entire world would rejoice.

The difficulty in this plan is that we men and women of this day and age are too wedded to the material dimension itself to be able to see Da Avabhasa in the fullness of His Divine Perfection. Even if He could be Present in His bodily (human) Form before everyone, all too many would only see His physical Features, and only see their own reflections on His Face, oblivious to His Ecstasy, even reacting and recoiling in their egoic "self-possession", or self-absorption.[1] And so it was for me when I first heard of His Appearance and saw His picture. I could not acknowledge Him at first, and only saw His boldness. It was only when I read His Instructive criticism of the futility of my and every person's search for happiness that I saw that He was to be cherished as the Divine Being.

Thus, preparation is necessary before the encounter with the Sat-Guru. We must learn how to make use of him (or her) first, before coming to his

---

1. Conventionally, "self-possession" means possession of oneself—or full control (calmness, or composure) of one's feelings, impulses, habits, and actions. Heart-Master Da uses the term in a "radical" sense, to indicate the state of being possessed by oneself, or controlled by chronically self-referring (or egoic) tendencies of attention, feeling, thought, desire, and action.

feet. Every great Spiritual culture has had within it cultural processes that have instructed its members on how to use the genuine Realizers and their Spiritual Guidance. Sadly, such wisdom is not commonly available in our day. And, even in the best of times—but especially today—Saints and Sages and Realizers have all too often been unacknowledged, misused, or misunderstood.

Thus, it is not only my intention that this book be a means to prepare the reader to rightly approach the God-Man; an additional purpose of this book is to counter the misinformation that exists in the popular mind about Gurus and about minority or alternative religions in general. Because the modern news and information media are themselves so uninformed, and misinformed, about the real nature of the Guru-devotee relationship (and in fact about any religious practices outside the mainstream), suspicion and even condemnation are often directed at any alternative religious Teacher or practitioner. This suspicion and this condemnation are simply a currently "acceptable" form of prejudice that, like racism and sexism, should no longer be tolerated. I will speak very directly to this matter in chapter five. It should be said here, however, by way of introduction, that this book is also a call for open-mindedness and tolerance relative to the Guru-devotee relationship and religious minorities, and is a means for contributing to the genuine education that can be the foundation of that tolerance.

THE APPEARANCE OF DA AVABHASA, THE DIVINE WORLD-TEACHER, WHOSE WORD AND ACTS ARE THE SUPREME HELP FOR MEN AND WOMEN OF THE MODERN AGE

Da Avabhasa comes as the Divine World-Teacher. I say this as His devotee with full conviction. I say this based on my clear Vision of Him and my full study of His Word and my full understanding of His Work. I say this based on my Intuition of Who He Is and why He has Incarnated. It is said in the *Bhagavad Gita* (4:7): "Whenever there is a decline of righteousness and rise of unrighteousness, O Bharata (Arjuna), then I . . . incarnate myself."[2] The Divine Consciousness Appears in the bodily (human) Form of the Heart-Master, who comes to accomplish the righteous realignment of all of humanity with God.

Traditionally, in a genuine Spiritual culture, it was understood that the Sat-Gurus were the greatest wealth, the most valuable Treasures of the realm, to be protected and honored above all. The Realizers were acknowledged as the Source of true Wisdom and of the Transmission of the Living Force of the Divine. In these settings, the need for the Sat-Guru himself was not in doubt. Today the need for the Wisdom-Influence of a Sat-Guru is even greater.

2. S. Radhakrishnan, trans., *The Bhagavad-Gita* (New York: Harper and Row, 1973), pp. 154-55.

Sri Gurudev Da Love-Ananda Wrote of this matter in the late 1970s:

If you want to learn about the Truth when Truth has become corrupted, then go to an Adept. Go to one who has Realized the Truth. Go to one who has already fulfilled the process completely. If you live in a moment in time when there is no Enlightened Tradition, when all the cults are corrupt, you can be certain that somewhere on Earth an Adept is alive. Such a person appears under exactly those conditions, when Truth is no longer visible in the cults, and when religions have become so corrupted by history and fetishism that they are about to become extinct.

. . . Only the Adepts, who are God-Realized, through whom the living Power of God manifests, can make a difference in human time. Such individuals are the instruments for the acculturation of humanity.

Periodically, such individuals must appear, and they must be influential. There is a notion that Adepts should be hiding in caves in the wilderness. This is not true. If the Adepts do not speak, the only voice that will be heard is that of ordinary people who are not God-Realized. The Adepts are the Sources of spiritual life. Such individuals must therefore enter into the stream of society, to purify the culture and reestablish the process of God-Realization. If they do not speak and become influential, there is no hope at all for humanity.

We exist in a moment in time when the cults are universally corrupted. Thus, it is a time for Adepts and true devotees to appear if there is to be any hope for the future of human beings. (The Enlightenment of the Whole Body, *pp. 155-56)*

Because the old ways and paths needed to be refreshed and reformed, because the world has dramatically changed and stands in need of fresh and direct means to its connection with the Living God, Da Avabhasa has come. He has come not as the leader or representative of any of the established religions of the world. He has come, in Full Enlightenment, as the Master of all Ways, which collectively He describes as the "Great Tradition". He is not only a Great One in the Ways of the past. He is the freshly Appearing Master come for every man and woman in Spiritual need.

In ages past, in cultures in which individuals acknowledged their tangible relationship with the Spiritual Reality, a supreme value was placed on the God-Realizer. It was completely obvious that those who themselves had incarnated or were alive in the Realization of the Spiritual Process itself were the authorities in all matters pertaining to Spiritual Life. It was clear that the best thing one devoted to Divine Self-Realization could do was to submit to the Guidance and authority of such a being, just as in other areas of life such submission to great masters is made—as a great orchestra submits to its conductor, or athletes to their coach. Submission to true Spiritual authority is naturally associated with freedom, based on intelligent evaluation of the Supreme Gifts of that relationship, Gifts which associate one with the Free State of Being of the Realizer, and ultimately duplicate that

Free Divine Realization in the devotee.

In a gathering with His devotees in 1987 Sri Da Avabhasa addressed the matter of true Spiritual Authority:

SRI DA AVABHASA: Just as freedom is associated with tolerance and cooperation, it is also naturally associated with authority—not suppressive authority, not the so-called true believer's fundamentalism, not cultism. The exercise of true intelligence and freedom, in other words, naturally or natively associates itself with true authority, honors and makes good use of the signs and representations, demonstrations, and Blessings of true Realizers. Such authority has traditionally been made the context of human culture, but it has unfortunately been adulterated, and almost eliminated, made taboo even, in the twentieth century. This has produced a process of subhuman acculturation wherein everybody as an ego is presumed to be a self-sufficient authority, anti-authority is the accepted disposition, and rebellion is regarded as the basis of freedom or liberty. You should be able to see, then, how important it is that there be such a Revelation, such an authority, and that it should be intelligently approached, but ultimately honored. My devotees should not be calling for indiscriminate fascination and affirmation, but for right honoring and intelligent "consideration"[3] of the Revelation that is the Way of the Heart. (April 6, 1987)

In this book I will from time to time quote traditional texts and points of view. But they are not the final authority that this book proclaims. As I have described above, I write not as a scholar, but as a devotee of Da Avabhasa. And to me, His is the ultimate Authority among all the sacred authorities, for I have seen His Supreme Divinity, and I acknowledge His Instruction as Divine Revelation. It has always been the voice of the Living Adept that is the supreme source of Wisdom, because that one directly addresses the men and women of his or her time.

I have quoted traditional sources as an aid in understanding Sri Gurudev Da Love-Ananda's Wisdom-Teaching on the Guru-devotee relationship, so that the connections between Him and other great Spiritual figures can be seen, and Who He Is and What He Offers may be made plain. Heart-Master Da Love-Ananda has always recommended that His own devotees study the representative literature of the entire Great Tradition to provide a context for understanding His own Revelation-Work. Through this study it can be seen that Da Avabhasa's Wisdom-Teaching is paralleled by Great Realizers of the past, even if the Revelations of the past are only partial in comparison with the uniquely complete and refreshed Revelation that is the Way of the Heart. But engaging in exhaustive comparisons with Teachers of the past is not the point. The point is to realize that Sri Gurudev Da Love-Ananda is an extraordinary Gift and Revelation. He is

3. The technical term "consideration" in Sri Da Avabhasa's Wisdom-Teaching means a process of one-pointed but ultimately thoughtless concentration and exhaustive contemplation of something until its essence or its ultimate obviousness is clear.

none other than the Divine Appearing in a Form to Serve the entire World.

Many times in this book I will use such expressions as, "Traditionally, devotees would have done this", or "In the genuine Spiritual cultures it would have been understood." When I make such references, it must be understood that such genuine cultures have existed only rarely, even in the most auspicious settings of India and Tibet. The world does not have a history of rightly honoring Realized beings. Krishna is reported in the *Bhagavata Purana* to have said that most people, not knowing his true Nature, looked down on him. The tragic fate of Jesus speaks volumes on humankind's wrong relationship to the Adept. Gautama the Buddha commented that very few people of his time understood his true Nature. And many other, less well-known Adepts also reported that they were not rightly addressed or served. Thus, when I speak of "the traditions", know that I am referring to those esoteric enclaves in which the right relationship to the Adept was understood and lived. And even in such cultures, it has generally been left to the Adepts or Realizers themselves to Reveal the secrets of how to relate to the incarnate God-Man.

My Own Graceful Instruction at the Feet of My Sat-Guru

I must testify from my own experience that the Truth Given directly by the Living Realizer is by far the most useful Instruction about the relationship to the Guru and about every aspect of practice. The total transformation and conversion of the body-mind is required in the process of God-Realization. The Spiritual Way is a concrete process that requires breaking through every obstruction in body, emotion, mind, and the higher aspects of the being. The Living Sat-Guru Instructs in an Immediate, Forceful manner in each of these dimensions. Measured against this Instruction, the traditional sources pale.

My own Instruction from Da Avabhasa has required an address to my tendency to become "fascinated" with Realizers, great Saints, and Yogis of the past. Traditional Teachers and Ways can become a fantasy world for me, where everything is safe and people are benign, and the Great and Difficult Ordeal that is Spiritual practice is "romantically" idealized.

Da Avabhasa calls this fantasy approach a version of the "talking" school[4] orientation, and time and again He has had to purify this in me,

---

4. "Talking" school is a phrase coined by Da Avabhasa to characterize those whose approach to sacred life is dominated by talking, thinking, reading, and philosophical analysis and debate, or even meditative enquiry or reflection without a concomitant and foundation discipline of every aspect of body, emotion, and mind. He contrasts this ineffectual—and often very presumptuous—"talking" school approach with that of what He terms the "practicing" school. Those who belong to a "practicing" school in any tradition are committed to the ordeal of self-transcending discipline in every area of life, under the guidance and challenging Mastery of a true Guru. Their sacred life is dominated by practical action in responsive obedience (or sympathetic conformity) to their Guru and self-transcending service to Guru, God, and all beings, and their use of mind and speech—like their use of all other bodily functions—is conserved or economized strictly to those uses that foster the fulfillment of their Guru's Admonitions and Instructions.

telling me that I was making the library my Guru . Understanding this has been a great Gift in my own practice, and has allowed me to serve others rightly. On one occasion, having just returned from India, I gave a presentation to fellow devotees on a long-dead Indian Teacher. And, in the midst of what was otherwise useful, I drew my audience into my own fantasy world. In Graceful response to hearing about this, Sri Gurudev sent me the message, "The Teaching is not in books. It is on your backside, placed there by My Foot on the day of your Initiation."

This is completely true. Nothing that I have learned in all of the random books that I have read has done more than to get me ready for Spiritual life, to arouse my interest in real practice. The process of Spiritual practice itself is the one lived in direct relationship to the Realizer. Endless reading and discussion is only dilettantism, a delay in taking up the real Spiritual Process. For the Realizer, the ego is an illusion, but for the ordinary aspirant it must be dealt with in the most practical and energetic terms. The difficult Sacred Ordeal of real sadhana, or Spiritual practice, cannot be avoided. And the living relationship to the Adept is the only thing that makes a difference.

Merely to provide a scholarly description of the Guru-devotee tradition is not the point of this book. The worth of this book does not come from my superior scholarship in the traditions, but from the lessons Given by my Heart-Master during my years of practice. Everything that I know about the Spiritual Process has come from training at His Feet. And it was not a conventional training. It has come through my relationship to Him, through the countless lessons that He has Given me and continues to Give me, and through His endless Instruction to me—in thousands of ways. He has Held me and Kissed me, Shouted at me and Slapped me. I have been in His Company when He "turned the Wheel of the Dharma" (the true Teaching, or Way of life) and Revealed the most profound Wisdom. I have been Graced to be with Him when He was most humanly vulnerable. I have watched Him dancing Ecstatically. He has Drawn me to Him and (apparently) held me away. He has Gracefully allowed me to become re-molded more and more in the likeness and ecstasy of His Divine Inherence. I have lived virtually all of my adult life in His Company, and in the Guru-devotee relationship with Him. That relationship, lived day after day, is the basis from which I write.

My particular Instruction and Lessons often came in the context of my service as Sri Da Avabhasa's librarian. In this service, I assisted Him in finding materials for His Divine Work with the literature of the Great Tradition. He has brought His Own Realization to the "consideration" of all of the traditional Ways, and, through His Commentary and the creation of carefully arranged reading lists, He has Revealed both the inherent relationships between the Spiritual traditions and their place in the overall Great and Single Way of God-Realization.

As issues relating specifically to the Great Tradition arose, I was called upon to research or "consider" them first from a traditional perspective and then in relationship to the Way of the Heart and the seven stages of life.[5] And through the process of this service at the Feet of Sri Gurudev Da Love-Ananda, He has Instructed me with great clarity and patience, and with a passionate Demand that I myself incarnate the Wisdom that He is always Revealing as part of my total practice in my relationship to Him.

During my nearly two decades in this special service, I presented more than one hundred thousand books to my Sat-Guru for His examination, and I pored over many thousands more. I have studied these books and Heart-Master Da Love-Ananda's Commentary on them. I have prepared lectures and articles about them. But this is not the source of my understanding of the Great Tradition.

Da Avabhasa has on occasion described how, by simply glancing at a paragraph in a book, He becomes intimate with the entire point of view (or scope of the subject) being represented. The mind cannot really grasp such a process, yet seeing Him enter into this psycho-physical process with the traditional sources (and through receiving the brief verbal Instruction that He has Given to me on these occasions), I have received an understanding of the Great Tradition that is prior to the conceptual mind. Thus, His Transmission is the source of my understanding of the Great Tradition. It is a mysterious process, and I do not know how to describe it altogether, but in working with Sri Gurudev Da Love-Ananda, and Contemplating Him in His Work with the Great Tradition, spending many hours with Him while He looked at books, following His Instructions in serving His own Work in this area—through all of this I received an understanding or clarity relative to the Spiritual traditions. Their nature became obvious.

But even this understanding is secondary to Spiritual practice itself. For in the end, of course, the Spiritual Process is not generated from the mind. In the Company of the Sat-Guru, and through genuine practice, the thinking mind can be clarified and released of its compulsiveness and confusion. But at last, the mind itself must be surrendered, let go. Only the direct Spiritual practice of surrender at the Feet of the Sat-Guru avails. Only feeling His Love, and allowing oneself to be absorbed in that Love, is the Great Way Itself.

---

5. Da Avabhasa has Described seven stages of growth and development that map the progression of human and Spiritual growth culminating in Divine Self-Realization. For a detailed summary of Da Avabhasa's Wisdom-Teaching on the seven stages of life, please see the Glossary entry, "stages of life".

THE LIVING GOD-MAN AND THE TRANSCENDENCE
OF THE UNIVERSAL DISEASE OF EGO-ADDICTION

Da Avabhasa Appears with the unique Function of Divine World-Teacher. He comes for all at a time when all are in need. Every individual is bound to the action and activity of suffering. Da Avabhasa has Revealed the critical understanding whereby every man and woman may see the self-created, chronic action that is the root of suffering and see the futility of trying to relieve that suffering through self-effort. It is only on the basis of such insight that one may embrace the great Means for Realization that is the Sat-Guru.

As Da Avabhasa has described, every man or woman is natively Free, always already Happy, in his or her inherent Nature. However, we do not live or feel this way. Instead, we all add the action of self-contraction—evidenced by our endless sense of dilemma, problem, and concern—to our native Happiness. This added contraction is the very action that is the ego-"I", the sense of being a separate, un-Happy self. Da Avabhasa has used the metaphor of pinching oneself to describe this activity. Feeling the "pinch" (which, at the level of the body, can be felt as a persistent cramp or contraction in the region of the navel), we try to do something about it. We distract ourselves with ordinary pursuits in the areas of money, or food, or sex, or we take up Spiritual seeking. But none of it really undoes the original problem.

At last, we realize that the pain is not caused by anything outside of us, but it is our own activity, our own "pinch". And when we see that we are pinching ourselves, that we are in fact addicted to the activity of self-contraction, then we become serious about Spiritual life and acknowledge the need to surrender at the Feet of the Sat-Guru.

Sri Da Avabhasa tells us that every ego-"I" is an addict of self-contraction. In the context of the devotional relationship with Sri Da Avabhasa, the practitioner of the Way of the Heart directly observes, understands, and transcends the inherent suffering of this activity that is the conditional self, or the ego-"I". Through this process of self-understanding, the mature condition of Happiness is allowed to manifest.

Writes Heart-Master Da Love-Ananda in *The Basket of Tolerance* (forthcoming):

The ego-"I" is (inherently and entirely) an addict, a seeker in pursuit of utter self-fulfillment and self-release. . . . The ego-"I" is an addict (or a seeker) in everything he or she does. That search is always a lust for objects and effects (whether apparently external or apparently internal). And the search itself is always founded upon "Narcissus", the basic self-contraction, the alienated, separate, and separative ego-"I". Therefore, to understand (and confess) the ego-"I" is to understand (and confess) all seeking (or every kind of addiction). And to discipline (and relinquish) any kind of seeking (or addiction) is, necessarily, to relinquish egoity, self-contraction, alienation, separation, separateness, and separativeness. Thus, to understand, and dis-cipline, and transcend seeking (or addiction) and the ego-"I" requires (and more and more becomes) a re-Union with (and, Ultimately, the Perfect Realization of) the (necessarily Divine) Source-Condition of human (and egoic) existence.

True and complete religious life (such as is practiced in the Way of the Heart, which I have Revealed) is a comprehensive discipline of separate and separative self (or egoity) that is committed to utterly transcend (rather than merely to fulfill or release) the ego-"I" (or all of self-contraction and seeking). Such a Way of life necessarily begins with (and must, with the help of the religious community of exemplary others, constantly and consistently re-establish) right and comprehensive self-appraisal (or growing self-understanding). Also, even though true religion is a practice that functions as a thoroughly personal, individual, and often private process, it is, as a real and effective practice and process, not an independent enterprise car-ried out and fulfilled by the separate (and inherently separative) ego-"I". Therefore, true religion (in any and every stage of life) is always and neces-sarily and inherently a practice and a process that originates, develops, and continues to develop only in the context of a living and effectively functioning religious community (which, as a "culture of expectation and inspiration", must nurture, stimulate, support, guide, and direct, and thus both inform and test, the individual's religious practice and process). Likewise, especially if true religious life is to develop in the advanced and the ultimate stages of life, an Adept Guru (or Sat-Guru) is required at every stage (to Guide and Inspire the practice, and to Bless the process, and to Transmit and Awaken every necessary stage of Realization). And such true (and truly human, or humanly mature) religious life progressively (and necessarily) requires the relinquishment of all seeking and all mere self-indulgence, or (via the pro-gressive development of the seven stages of life) the discipline and the tran-scendence of the total egoic life.

Sri Gurudev Da Avabhasa's Wisdom-Teaching is a source of great potential Help for every man and woman, because it directs every individual to see how he or she is bound to the drama of self-enclosure, which is his or her own activity of suffering. It provides the means by which in every moment one can observe and understand the activity of "Narcissus", or the separate and separative ego-"I", and be released from that bondage. Da Avabhasa's Wisdom on the negative effect of this chronic activity brings Liberating insight to every aspect of life and culture, including all conven-tional religious and Spiritual Ways.

Every individual is in need of such Instruction, and Da Avabhasa's Wisdom-Teaching is a Blessing for all, whether an individual ever directly takes up practice in His Way of the Heart or not. For everyone, the study and application of Sri Da Avabhasa's Wisdom-Teaching brings refreshment, clarification, and right understanding of his or her own life and religious or Spiritual practice.

Because His Wisdom-Teaching is universally applicable, Sri Da Avabhasa is the Divine World-Teacher. This term, as used in describing Da Avabhasa, has a number of meanings. It indicates that He has come to Serve an entire world in need. He has come to re-establish the Dharma, or True Teaching, in a world in which it has been lost. He is thus what is known as a "Dharma-Bearer". His World-Teaching is not simply a teaching of words. His Wisdom-Teaching is filled with Divine Siddhi, the Living Power of the Divine, brought freshly to this place to re-assert, in the world-plane, Divinity once more. He does not come to assert the primacy of traditions established in the past. He has re-established and re-authenticated the One, Ancient, and Eternal Great Way of which all previous traditions are partial Revelations. It is in this fullest sense that He is the World-Teacher.

It is not that other beings alive today are not Teaching in ways that are useful or benign. It is not that individuals practicing in any other traditional context must abandon their Way in order to make use of the Appearance of the Divine World-Teacher. Rather, what Heart-Master Da Avabhasa Brings is that Gift of Divine Wisdom that will, if heard and seen and applied, refresh and realign all traditions and every Teacher and Way. He has come not just for a single group but for all—in other words, not just for the priests, or the rich, or the learned, or a particular sect, but for every individual.

The Way of the Heart which Da Avabhasa has Revealed is based on the Graceful process of Love or feeling-Contemplation[6] of the Divine in the manifest Form of the God-Man. The entire Spiritual Process is about Divine Feeling or Love. Yet even though the Guru's Love is Given as a Free Gift, to feel and receive this Love requires a complementary self-understanding. As Da Avabhasa has Taught, there must be understanding of the ways in which one turns away or apparently separates from that Love, or the Real Divine Condition. Why is this so? Because God cannot be felt or intuited by one who has not become open to That Which transcends the conditional self. You will not have any free attention for the very Divine Reality if you are not fed up with your own addictive tendencies toward (illusory) self-fulfillment. You can only be fully receptive to the Transmission of the Adept after your heart is opened by the "Lesson of life": that nothing conditional can ultimately make you Happy, that the search for Happiness and fulfillment can never be finally successful, but you can Realize the native Happiness that is already the case. In other words, you cannot become Happy, you can only be Happy.

---

6. "Feeling-Contemplation" is Heart-Master Da Love-Ananda's term for the essential devotional and meditative practice that all devotees in the Way of the Heart engage in relationship to Him. Feeling-Contemplation of Heart-Master Da is Awakened by Grace through Darshan, or feeling-sighting of Him, and it is then practiced under all conditions, as the basis and epitome of all other practices in the Way of the Heart.

"WHAT IS TO BE REALIZED?":
THE UNIQUE WORLD-VIEW FOUNDED UPON DIVINE SELF-REALIZATION

The Appearance of the God-Man who has Realized Identity with the Divine Self makes possible a unique understanding of the world. Sri Da Avabhasa Describes this understanding in the Essay "What Is to Be Realized?", which appears in the book *Scientific Proof of the Existence of God Will Soon Be Announced by the White House!*:

> There is only the Radiant Transcendental Being, Who is One. All beings and things and worlds are ultimately and Really only identical to That One, Who is God, the Divine Person.

> Only God is Alive as everyone and everything. All beings and things and worlds are arising as spontaneous transformations or modifications of That One. God eternally Transcends the world and all beings, and yet the world and all beings are nothing but God. It is a Great and Passionate Mystery.

> The individual being, manifest as the body-mind, is only a transformation or modification of the Radiant Transcendental Being or Divine Person. Wherever or whenever there is a psycho-physical being, the Radiant Transcendental Being is conscious as that limitation and feels Itself to be a particular being. . . .

> As the being adapts and evolves and achieves Ecstasy in the Divine, it Realizes its eternal inherence in That One and, ultimately, its Identity as That One. Such is Enlightenment, Liberation, or Salvation. Therefore, Enlightenment, Liberation, Salvation, or That which is to be Realized, is not a form of "status" or egoic achievement in this world, the after-death world, or the next lifetime, but it is the Condition of Love and Happiness, which transcends the body-mind, its experiences, its relations, and the world, even as the world continues. . . .

> The Living God, the Beloved of all beings, has, from eternity, become a Great Sacrifice. The Radiant One has become the process of all possibilities. We are not merely the creatures or victims of God, created and set apart to suffer for some inexplicable reason. We are the very Sacrifice of God. God is Alive as us. Our lives are the creative ordeal to which God is eternally submitted. We need only Realize the Living One and thus become capable of this Divine Sacrifice, which is an eternal creative ordeal of Love that leads, step by step, toward a Most Wonderful Transformation. Once we transcend the illusion of our dark separate selves and enter into the Divine Process, we see clearly that the existence and destiny of the world and every being is the Fullness of Love-Bliss in a perfectly Transformed state that has become One with the Person and the Domain of the Transcendental Divine.

> This is my Testimony and my Confession. And it is the same Testimony and Confession proclaimed by all the Adepts who have appeared to serve mankind on Earth. (pp. 396-97)

This Great Testimony restores faith, for what Sri Da Avabhasa Proclaims is the possibility of Divine Realization in the case of each man and woman. And, more than just speaking about it, Da Avabhasa Embodies this Realization. He Lives as it.

A basic principle of all life is that we all communicate or "transmit" to others who come into our company the present state of our consciousness. If we are happy, others feel that happiness, no matter what we are doing or discussing. Likewise, if we are disturbed, others feel that anxiety. The communication of our state is instant, immediate. Just so, and to a magnified degree, in the case of the Divine Realizer. When we come into the Company of such a Being, we immediately, and to whatever degree we are open to it, feel his or her Transmission of the Divine, naturally and spontaneously. This is the process of Spiritual Transmission described in many traditions. It is the great Gift of the Guru to the devotee.

Anyone who truly gives the Divine Realizer his or her attention may receive a profound intuition of the God-Man's Realization. In fact, because the process of Spiritual Transmission transcends time and space, the devotee of the God-Man, who understands Who he Is, who has "found out" the God-Man, may live in direct relationship to him all the time, receiving his Blessing Transmission continuously. To do so is to make use of another great principle of the Guru-devotee relationship: You become, or Realize, what you meditate on, or contemplate, or yield your attention to. If one contemplates any ordinary thing, then one takes on its qualities. The great possibility and advantage made available by the Appearance of the God-Man, is to contemplate him. To grant the God-Man one's feeling-attention is to more and more receive His Grace, and to Realize His Divine Condition. This simple principle, that one becomes what one meditates on, allows the devotee to feel, receive, and be transformed by the Transmission of the Guru. This process is a secret that has been understood by Spiritual practitioners through history, and it has made the principle of Satsang, or living in direct contemplation of or Communion with the God-Man, the supreme method of Spiritual life.

THE WAY OF DISTRACTED LOVE FOR THE GOD-MAN

The principal Revelation of the Divine has always come in the Form of the God-Man, who is the Embodiment of the Divine Itself. In the Form of the God-Man, the Divine Makes the first Gesture by showing Love for men and women. He (or She) Embraces them with Divine Love. He Reveals to them the ultimate Nature of existence, which is felt as Love, a Love which transcends the world and the body-mind. And He Reveals Love by Loving. He Is that Love in bodily (human) Form.

There are those traditions that make God or the Divine a thing apart, to be addressed and felt and admired and surrendered to, but not to be literally Realized or Identified with. In this exoteric conception of the Divine, there may be a great Prophet or Incarnation who temporarily brings the Message of God to beings, or Serves as a link between beings and the Divine, but the state of that Prophet or Incarnation can never be duplicated by his followers.

In the esoteric, or fullest, Way, the Divine is to be Realized by every individual through the Grace of the Guru. As Da Avabhasa has described it, the Divine birthright and Great and Ultimate Destiny of every man or woman is to "duplicate" or Realize that same Divine Condition in which the Realizer Inheres. Thus, the True God-Man comes to Draw all others into his or her Realization Itself. This is the Gospel or Good News of the Siddhas, the "perfected ones", who call all to enter into the Divine in this moment, and not to wait for some hopeful happiness after death.

The Divine Adepts have Realized that Divinity in life. They speak ecstatically because they have transcended egoity, or identification with the body-mind. And the reason they come is to Reveal Divine Love to born beings.

Such Love is not conventional emotion. It is feeling to Infinity. It is unobstructed feeling, Prior to the body-mind or the ego. Such Love heals and frees one. It does not bind. It is the Love that the God-Man brings, and with which He Blesses. It is the heart of the Spiritual Process. Such compassionate Love is the essence of all that Sri Da Avabhasa Reveals to His devotees. They Realize that there is Only God, and that God is Love. God is not merely a good feeling, or conventional fulfillment. The Divine is the One Feeling that is Reality Itself.

The God-Man Da Avabhasa exists to Offer the Transmission of this Love, the Transmission of the Infinite Feeling that is God. This is the only purpose of the God-Man. He does not see humanity as a collection of "poor other people" who need to be Helped by Him from His superior position as the Realizer. He ecstatically Proclaims, "My Devotee Is The God I Have Come To Serve." He sees that ordinary beings are not experiencing or enjoying Who they Are, their own Divine Status. He Transmits to them the Real Nature of Love. It is not something that He must try to do. He Is that Love.

The primary "method" of Liberation used by the God-Man Da Avabhasa (as well as by the Great Beings who have come before Him) is His sheer Attractiveness. He is the Divine Form, and His Love is His Attractive Power. Heart-Master Da is the most Radiant, Most Distracting Object in the universe. For to truly see Him is to see no mere fleshy personality, but to see the Divine, the Self-Radiant and Self-Existing Consciousness, which Outshines even the Heart-Master's own body-mind.

The traditional literature describes Krishna as lustrous blue, and the Buddha and Christ with halos around them. How can a devotee describe what Sri Gurudev Da Love-Ananda looks like, or what it feels like to be in His Company? The Divine Quality has been metaphorically described—more lustrous than a thousand moons, more brilliant than if suns filled the sky, more dazzling than lightning in a darkened sky, more embracing than a lover's arms. But nothing can match the Divine Vision Itself. It is only this that the Sat-Guru brings. And if his devotee is too hardened to receive it, then the Sat-Guru is helpless. He (or she) has no trickery or gimmicks to offer. He can only try to find ways to open the eyes of his devotees so they can see What is before them.

And for the Sat-Guru, one way to awaken the devotee is to raise his (or her) voice. Like the Prophets of the *Old Testament,* he may have to rail at the turning away of men and women. He may use penetrating words to show the devotee his or her own turning away, or distraction by the separate and separative self. He may create lessons to show his devotee the fruitlessness of seeking Happiness in the objects and events of the worlds of experience. But this he does only to call those he Loves to turn to him, to see him, to receive his Love, to have eyes that can see the Divine Vision That he Is.

When the Sat-Guru is at last truly seen, then the devotee falls in love. The devotee turns his or her attention to What is Attractive. The love of the devotee naturally draws him or her beyond the things of the world. The distracting power of his or her love for the God-Man is simply greater than anything else. The rest of the world dims by comparison. Who cares for anything else once one has tasted that sweetness, that "unmortal and unimaged Grace"? The devotee does not love the Sat-Guru on the basis of a great effort. He or she simply responds. Only such Divine Love and Attraction, and no self-based motive, can hold the devotee to the Sat-Guru.

The body-mind will unwind its egoic tendencies, and that may take months or years, but it does not matter anymore. The devotee is "in love"—not simply loving, but "in love", a state beyond memory or conception. It is Joy, "Even Beyond Every Reason For It". It is Heart-Master Da Love-Ananda, the Giver of Love-Bliss, Who comes only to Love all beings and Who Transforms all beings if they will only receive Him and devote their lives to reception of His Love.

As the eye naturally turns to what is lustrous, and the fingers gravitate to what is soft, so the heart of every man and woman is spontaneously drawn to the Supremely attractive God-Man. One surrenders oneself naturally and easily to Contemplate that Beauty, for the God-Man is "Bright"[7] with a Shine that only the Divine Emanates. This I have seen with my own eyes. I have been Graced to view Da Avabhasa, and that Vision is the Ultimate Gift bestowed on any man or woman. Once it has been received deeply in one's heart, it can never be forgotten. Then, spontaneously,

---

7. By the word "Bright" (and its variations, such as "Brightness"), Sri Da Avabhasa refers to Self-Luminous Divine Being, eternally, infinitely, and inherently Self-Radiant. The "Bright" is not other than the Heart, or Transcendental (and Inherently Spiritual) Divine Self-Consciousness.

naturally, and more and more perfectly, one is diverted from all of one's suffering, all of one's problems, and a mortal life. One becomes absorbed and occupied in Remembrance and Contemplation of that Divine Being, that Transcendental God-Man. His Love-Filled Glance never leaves one's consciousness. And His breath-stealing Visage provides a never-ending Divine Icon for Contemplation. To hear His Joyous Laughter cuts through all despair and bewilderment. To listen to the Accounts of His Actions gladdens the heart.

Just as one thinks often of one's closest intimates, even more so does one's attention remain with the Supreme Sat-Guru, Who is Love Incarnate. In the ecstasy of contemplating him, more and more the Divine God-Man possesses one's attention, granting an enjoyment that cannot be matched by any worldly pleasure. More and more one is occupied with thoughts of him. Tears naturally well up in the eyes to feel him and his Always Given Gifts. When there is such Grace, what need for fame, wealth, or conventional pursuits? In such ecstatic Distraction the devotee more and more only feels the Divinity that is his or her Divine Sat-Guru. Yes, the ordinary life remains, and in fact the devotee becomes more able to fulfill its demands with great energy and intensity. But in the fullness of that Distraction, as Da Avabhasa Describes, everything that arises is understood as "simply the Intoxicated Play of the Absolute Divine Personality, Who is the Radiant Life and Consciousness of all beings and things." (*The Enlightenment of the Whole Body,* p. 542)

It is such Distraction that makes it possible for the devotee to undergo the full transformation required in genuine Spiritual practice. It is such Attraction to the God-Man that is the foundation of love that gives the devotee the capability to endure all the trials that are encountered in the course of God-Realizing sadhana.

So the title of this book is a description of the Guru-devotee relationship as Revealed by Da Avabhasa, the Supremely Attractive Lover of His devotees, the "God of Happiness while Alive". And that Distraction from all suffering is what He has Revealed to His devotees. As He has described it:

SRI DA AVABHASA: The Guru is not simply present to rap out a philosophy or distribute techniques that you may apply depending on your intelligence. The Guru is present to enjoy a Divine relationship with all those who are willing to assume such a relationship, with all those who have the capability for distraction by the Guru in an absolute love-relationship that is more and more distracting. But if that distraction is not present, if that love-desire distraction is not present in an individual's life, then the form of his or her sadhana is not initiated. It cannot begin. There is no point in even discussing the sadhana until the individual has begun to enjoy an ecstatic relationship with Me, a Spiritual relationship, not one that is in the air, but one that includes the whole of life, that draws the emotion, that awakens the love, that awakens the heart. That distracting relationship that is the principle of this sadhana must be established. (December 16, 1975)

The Message of This Book Is Ultimately the Appearance and Gift That Is Sri Da Avabhasa Himself

For me, one of the most creative challenges of the sadhana of presenting *Divine Distraction* is the sheer richness of Sri Gurudev Da Avabhasa's Work with His devotees and the magnitude of the Instruction He has Given. The essential points are certainly here, and even more material is presented in *Love of the God-Man*, a much larger work from which *Divine Distraction* has been excerpted. But even in *Love of the God-Man*, I had to omit countless details of Da Avabhasa's Wisdom-Teaching on the Guru-devotee relationship, and likewise numberless Leelas (Spiritual stories) of His Blessing Instruction, simply because of the limitations of space.

How can we ordinary beings make sense of this world, where every pleasure is followed by pain and where there is no ultimate security, and where, no matter how much you do to improve your life, you and all those you love are going to die in any case? In this place of bewilderment and suffering, where is the Means and Opportunity to Realize the Happiness that is beyond ordinary pleasures and pains, that transcends death itself? It has always been said that the greatest Opportunity for anyone is the Way of the Incarnate God-Man, Who has Already Realized that Grace, and Who is Alive with the Power to Draw others into His Freedom. The test of your use of this book is the extent to which you really examine, test, and use its wisdom. The Spiritual traditions always speak of reading sacred texts with heart-openness and receptivity, truly allowing them to influence you with their greater Wisdom, and allowing yourself to be moved by the Liberating Teaching of the Great Saints and Realizers. In this book, full of the Stories and Instruction of Da Avabhasa's Work with His devotees, there is a Blessing-Transmission. Allow it to Work in you, and you will be profoundly moved and transformed by its Grace.

Surrendering myself at Sat-Guru Da Love-Ananda's Feet and holding Him before my heart, I say to you, drink deeply of His Instruction as found in this book. Allow yourself to receive His Blessings, so you may be Illumined by what is "Bright" beyond belief. Be gladdened by His Freedom. Be transformed by His Appearance. And may you be Given the Grace to practice a genuine Spiritual relationship in the Company of this Supreme Realizer of the Heart, and so come to taste and at last to Realize His Sweetness beyond description.

In gratitude and Remembrance of that Supreme Being Whom I know as Sri Gurudev Da Love-Ananda Hridayam, I proclaim His Sat-Guru-Naama Mantra:

Om Sri Da Love-Ananda Hridayam

PART II

"I Am the Person of Love"

THE DIVINE LIFE AND WORK
OF DA AVABHASA

I Am the Person of Love, Who has spontaneously taken on human form for the sake of this world of beings. I am here to Be Love and to Do the Work of Love. Therefore, give Me your attention and feel My Regard.

Commune with the Person of Love in every moment. By this Means, always feel Love. Give Love. Receive Love. Be Love. This is the First Discipline, the Origin of the Way. (Da Avabhasa, November 30, 1983)

The appearance of a God-Man with the full capability to initiate men and women into His own Divine Condition is the greatest Blessing in all the worlds. The Divine World-Teacher and True Heart-Master, Da Avabhasa (The "Bright") is such a Living God-Man. His entire Life and Work have been undertaken with the Purpose of making the means to live a Divine life available to every man and woman.

Just as the stories of the life of Jesus the Christ, Gautama the Buddha, and Krishna the Avatar have been retold down through the ages to inspire humankind to Spiritual life, so every detail of the Life of Da Avabhasa has the potency to inspire us to genuine Spiritual practice. Is it any wonder that the Great Adept of this time would be born in the midst of the Spiritual wasteland of the West, where He was needed most? And is it not a Divine Gift that, being born and raised in the West, He is fitted to Instruct every being in what has increasingly become a "Westernized" world?

Da Avabhasa was born in Jamaica, New York, on November 3, 1939. The Miracle of His Birth is that it was the result of a Conscious Intention, a Compassionate Gesture by One Who was already in the God-Realized

Condition. For the first two years following His Birth, He lived in a State He called "the 'Bright'"—the Divinely Free and Radiant Condition of Unlimited Happiness and Love. Then, in response to the Spiritual needs of men and women, He assumed a human persona, identifying with a human personality in order to experience firsthand and to demonstrate in human terms the means by which every ordinary man and woman may Realize the Divine Self. He became Franklin Jones.

In outward terms, His Life over the next many years appeared conventional in many respects. His father was a salesman and His mother a Long Island housewife. Da Avabhasa went through a conventional course of education and participated in the pastimes typical of a youth in mid-twentieth century America. Through all of this the Great Adept was learning the mechanisms that bind the ordinary man and woman to a life of un-Happiness. But for Da Avabhasa the tangible Influence of the Divine was always in the background: Even in His childhood, Da Avabhasa experienced occasional Breakthroughs of the "Bright", remarkable Spiritual awakenings, and experiences of the kundalini (ascending Spiritual life-energies).

While attending Columbia College in 1957, His Sadhana, or conscious Spiritual practice, began, whereby He would demonstrate, in the modern world, the Way of Divine Enlightenment. He lived as an Avadhoot (one who wanders, free of all binding attachments), seeking answers to fundamental Spiritual questions in the "jungles" of the New York City streets. Then, as a graduate student at Stanford University, in California, He began a profound process of "listening" to every aspect of what arose to His consciousness. And He became awakened to an awareness of reality as a

psycho-physical, rather than a merely physical, process, while living on the beaches of
nearby San Gregorio. Mysteriously Guided by
the "Bright" Condition that He had enjoyed
from Birth, each phase of Da Avabhasa's life
culminated in a fundamental Spiritual insight
that spontaneously led Him to the next
phase.

Rudi (Swami Rudrananda)

Da Avabhasa's first human Teacher was
the Western kundalini Teacher Rudi (Swami
Rudrananda). In Rudi He found a Guru capable of Transmitting Spiritual Power directly to
his devotee. Rudi schooled Him in self-
discipline and in the reception of the
descending and ascending Spiritual energies,
and Da Avabhasa fulfilled every instruction
and admonition of His Guru. Always Da
Avabhasa's Sadhana involved this complete
devotional surrender and obedience (or what He terms "sympathetic conformity") to His Guru. For Da Avabhasa, this devotional surrender was also
always linked with the development and deepening of self-understanding,
or the process of observing, understanding, and transcending the activity
that one habitually performs in each moment, which creates the sense of
separation and un-Happiness.

After four years, Da Avabhasa's Spiritual maturity grew beyond the help
that Rudi could offer, and so Rudi passed Him on to Swami Muktananda,
Rudi's own Guru, a great Yogic Master who initiated his devotees into higher
Yogic and mystical phenomena. In 1968, Da Avabhasa traveled to be with

Da Avabhasa with Swami Muktananda, India, 1969

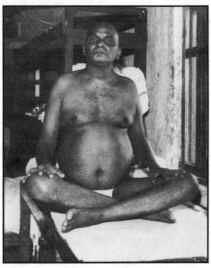

Swami Nityananda

Swami Muktananda at his Ashram in Ganeshpuri, India. In a remarkable example of Spiritual receptivity, on the third day of His visit to the Ashram, Da Avabhasa experienced the prized Yogic Realization traditionally described as "nirvikalpa samadhi"—the temporary, Blissful Realization of unity with the formless Divine Source-Light above, accomplished through Yogic ascent.[8]

Da Avabhasa was to do Sadhana with Swami Muktananda for another two years before being passed on briefly to Swami Nityananda (Swami Muktananda's own Guru and Rudi's principal Guru), with whom Da Avabhasa had contact on the subtle plane. Finally, Da Avabhasa was passed on to the Divine Goddess Herself, the living and Divine "Spirit-Personality", Who is the subtle personification of the Creative Universal Spirit-Energy. Swami Muktananda and Swami Nityananda had both had a direct relationship to the Goddess, and understood Her to be the ultimate Teacher or Guide of the entire lineage. She now appeared to Da Avabhasa in subtle form, to Guide Him very practically and directly. Remarkably, and as has been the case with only a handful of individuals in Spiritual history, it was thus the Goddess Herself Who now became Da Avabhasa's principal Spiritual Guide, and Who ultimately was the vehicle for His final Liberation, or, rather, His Divine Re-Awakening.

This extraordinary period of instruction culminated in September 1970, in the Vedanta Society Temple in Los Angeles. There the Divine Goddess, Who had given all She could as Teacher and Guide, finally surrendered Herself to Da Avabhasa, and He Realized simultaneous and paradoxical Identity with and Mastery of Her. Finally, on September 10, 1970, Da Avabhasa Transcended every form of bondage and limitation in the Joyful Re-Awakening of Identity with the Divine Self, the ultimate Identity of all beings. He Wrote of this profound moment:

---

8. In the Yogic schools of mystical ascent "nirvikalpa samadhi" is often viewed as equivalent to ultimate Realization. However, Da Avabhasa has made it plain that such traditional "nirvikalpa samadhi" is only a temporary state, achieved through Yogic ascent of attention associated with practice and realization in the fifth stage of life in Da Avabhasa's total description of the seven stages of human and Spiritual growth and Realization. Such fifth stage "nirvikalpa samadhi" is conditional, dependent on this ascent, and when attention descends again, this samadhi is gone.

True Divine Self-Realization, Realized only in the seventh, or fully Enlightened, stage of life is, in contrast, permanent, founded in the Divine Condition, Which Transcends attention.

For a full description of the various Samadhis and the stages of life, see "Samadhi" and "stages of life" in the Glossary.

Los Angeles, 1972

In an instant, I became profoundly and directly aware of what I am. It was a tacit realization, a direct knowledge in consciousness itself. It was consciousness itself without the addition of a communication from any other source. I simply sat there and knew what I am. I was being what I am. I am Reality, the Self, and Nature and Support of all things and all beings. I am the One Being, known as God, Brahman, Atman, the One Mind, the Self. (The Knee of Listening, pp. 134-35)

At the age of thirty, Da Avabhasa had regained with full consciousness the Condition He had enjoyed at Birth, but now with a complete understanding of the limiting mechanisms of the ordinary human body-mind, and the full capability to Serve the Realization of others.

Spontaneously and almost immediately, His Teaching Work with others began. Extraordinarily, when He would sit for meditation, He no longer would experience mind-forms from His own Life and psyche. Rather, He would experience the mind-forms of others, and He found that He was "meditating" them. And other remarkable Siddhis, or Divine Powers, Awakened in Him, by which to Instruct others. People naturally came to Him seeking Instruction, so many so, that by 1972 He decided to formally open an Ashram in Los Angeles, which He named "Shree Hridayam Satsang" ("the Fellowship of the Heart").

For the next many years, and culminating in 1986, Da Avabhasa, known during these years as "Bubba Free John", and then "Da Free John",[9] engaged those who came to Him in a demonstration of Divine Instruction such as the world had never seen. He took His devotees through a "consideration", or full exploration with Divine Inspiration, of every aspect of human, religious, Spiritual, and Divine existence. He was so completely Free, so Alive in the ecstatic Realization of God, that He could Submit Himself completely to His devotees in order to Instruct them "where they were at" with the Purpose of Liberating them from every aspect of their bondage. He constantly asked His devotees, in the midst of every activity, What is Truth? How should one live one's life in terms of money, sexuality, diet, religious practice, and Spiritual phenomena? The lessons of

---

9. "Bubba" was one of Franklin's childhood nicknames, and means "brother", or, in this case, "Spiritual friend". "Free John", a rendition of His given Name, means "a liberated man (Franklin) through whom God is Gracious (Jones)". The Name "Da", which He first used in 1979, is a Name of God which means "the One Who Gives".

Da Avabhasa with students during the Teaching years

Da Avabhasa's Teaching years were not the result of abstract philosophy. Instead they were proved in living terms, through real experimentation in life, which occurred mostly at the three Sanctuaries of His Way of the Heart—first at the Mountain Of Attention, located in northern California, then at Tumomama Sanctuary, in Hawaii, and finally, at Sri Love-Anandashram, in the Fijian islands.

It was a profoundly serious, but joyously humorous and free, experimentation, Guided by Da Avabhasa's Divinely Enlightened perspective. And through these many years, a body of Leelas, or Divinely Instructive Stories, emerged that show both the fruitlessness of every kind of seeking via experience, high or low, and the direct means by which modern men and women can live a life dedicated to Spiritual practice in concrete relationship to the Divine. These Leelas remain a Sacred Legacy of this God-Man's Play with ordinary men and women that will be treasured for millennia as a guide to Spiritual life and a complement to the more formal Wisdom-Instruction that Sri Da Avabhasa has also Revealed.

On January 11, 1986, at Sri Love-Anandashram, began the next great phase of Da Avabhasa's Work. On this day, in a crisis brought on by His deep frustration at the lack of genuine response from His devotees, and therefore the failure of His Teaching Work, Da Avabhasa underwent a profound Yogic Process in which He surrendered His physical body, giving it up completely in a "swoon" of despair. He spontaneously released His body and mind most Perfectly into His Ultimate Self-Condition, such that body and mind became most fully transparent to the Self-Existing and Self-Radiant "Bright" Consciousness that He Is. In that "swoon" Da Avabhasa's body itself collapsed and for a time even appeared to have died. But, in the midst of this profound crisis, the Divine Gesture of Service to humanity which had brought about His Birth reasserted Itself in a new way. A unique Spiritual Event, which Da Avabhasa Describes as the ongoing process of

His "Divine Emergence", was initiated in the midst of that "swoon". Henceforth, yielding Himself Fully to His Divine Identity, without a trace of compromise, He simply Stood Free, as the Divine Self-"Brightness". Da Avabhasa's bodily (human) Form had achieved an amazing potency as a Transmitter of tangible Spiritual Power and Divine Consciousness, such that the practice of mere feeling-Contemplation of Him has become a sufficient and transformative practice for all His devotees. Da Avabhasa now Worked with His devotees in a new way. No longer did He accommodate Himself to His devotees in order to Instruct them. Instead, He Stood Firm, Calling His devotees to turn to Him directly in the traditional devotional manner of devotees in relationship to their Divine Guru. Da Avabhasa has called this new way of Relating to His devotees and the world His "Blessing Work", or His "Divine Emergence Work".

Since the initiation of His Divine Emergence, Da Avabhasa has continued to Reside primarily at Sri Love-Anandashram, an island in Fiji notable for its remote solitude and natural beauty. Here He has established a Siddha-Peetha, or Seat of Divine Power, where His devotees pilgrimage for Spiritual retreat in His Company. He Works with His devotees primarily by Granting them His Darshan, the Grace of coming into His Company to Regard His bodily (human) Form. That Darshan is the most auspicious Gift that a man or woman can receive, but for it to be effectively received, the devotee must have previously prepared himself or herself through authentic practice of devotional surrender and application to the process of self-understanding. This book includes many testimonies from Da Avabhasa's devotees about the unique, transformative effectiveness of His Darshan. The Grace of that same Darshan is received by all who turn to Da Avabhasa truly and responsively in their feeling-Contemplation of Him. Because of His Divinely Self-Realized Condition, wherever Da Avabhasa's devotees are, and at all times, they may practice such devotional regard of Da Avabhasa, and, commensurate with their devotional surrender, it is effective with an extraordinary potency.

To aid His devotees in their reception of this Graceful and always Given Gift, Da Avabhasa has created a full culture and description of practice of His Way of the Heart. These are elaborated in detail in His Source-Literature, the principal Works (among the more than forty that have been published covering various aspects of the Way of the Heart) that summarize His Great Teaching. The Way of the Heart is a complete Way of life, lived in cooperative association with others, and always in direct and responsive relationship to the Living God-Man Himself.

The Miracle of the Life and Work of Da Avabhasa continues each day, for we are Blessed with the Gift to be alive in the Lifetime of this God-Man. It is our intention that *Divine Distraction* will provide a means for you to contact His Stream of Grace, which rushes upon every man and woman who will enter it, with Divine Refreshment, Awakened self-understanding, and the Limitless Nectar of Divine Happiness.

THE DIVINE NAMES OF DA AVABHASA

How is it possible to describe One Who Has Realized and become Identical to That Which is beyond Names? When the God-Man Appears, Alive in the Supreme Reality, all His Names are merely pointers to that Divine Realization which He Embodies.

In Da Avabhasa's case, His Principal Names were Divinely Revealed, or made Self-Evident. To fully explain their meanings would require great elaboration, but they can also be defined quite simply. "Da" is a traditional Name for the Divine that means "the One Who Gives", from Whom flows a constant Outpouring of Divine Gifts. "Avabhasa" is a Sanskrit word meaning "Bright". It describes the Luminous, Self-Radiant Power of Reality. Da Avabhasa has used the term "the 'Bright'" even from His childhood to describe the Illuminated Condition that He enjoyed at birth, and His entire life has been the unfolding of this same Divine "Brightness". Thus, "Da Avabhasa" is "the Giver of the 'Bright'", or "the Giver of the Self-Radiant Divine Blessings".

Da Avabhasa is also known as "Heart-Master Da Love-Ananda". The Name "Love-Ananda", Given to Him by Swami Muktananda in 1969, means "Love-Bliss". In Fijian He is called "Dau Loloma", the Divine Person of Love.

We, as His devotees, also address and refer to Da Avabhasa using traditional titles which acknowledge His Divine Nature, which we have seen with our own eyes, and to show our gratitude for the never-ending Stream of Grace He bestows upon us. Therefore, He is called "Gurudev", or the "Divinely Realized Guru"; "Hridayam", or "the Heart Itself"; and "Sat-Guru", or the "Guru who Reveals and is the 'Bright' Truth". And we often address Him using the honorific "Sri", meaning "Bright", or "Potent with Blessing Power". Thus, we refer to our Beloved Sat-Guru using appropriate combinations of His Names and Titles, such as "Sri Da Avabhasa", "Sri Gurudev Da Love-Ananda", "Heart-Master Da Love-Ananda Hridayam", and "Sat-Guru Da".

It has always been understood that to repeat the Name of the God-Man with feeling and devotion is to Invoke and Receive His Blessings. May we use the Names of the God-Man Da Avabhasa in this spirit, feelingly-Contemplating the Supreme Treasure that has come to Grace mankind through Da Avabhasa's Appearance among us.

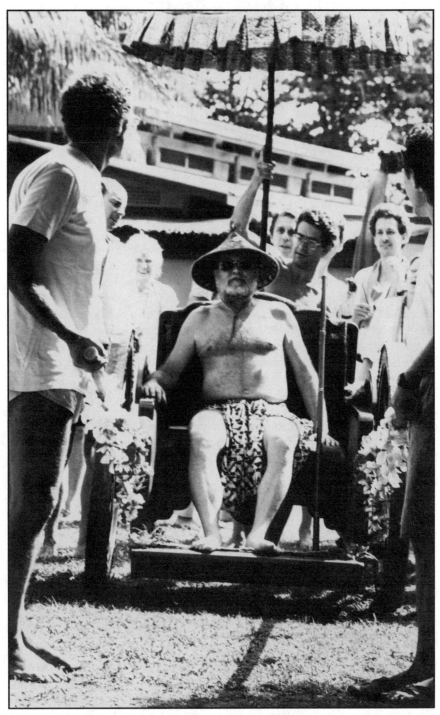

Sri Love-Anandashram, September 1991

CHAPTER ONE

Love of
the God-Man

*T*he Guru-devotee relationship has always been and will always be the essence of religious and Spiritual practice. The Great Means for Divine Realization is to enter into the Spiritual Company and Blessing of the God-Man at all times and in every circumstance. The relationship to the God-Man is unreasonably Happy, absolutely ecstatic, for in his (or her) Person the devotee is brought face-to-face with the Living God. At the same time, this relationship is a Sacred Ordeal, a "hard school", for the process of Spiritual practice necessarily requires that the devotee understand and surrender all of his or her limitations and egoic self-attention. But through the Grace of the Guru, this Process is given Great Help and Guidance, and Ultimate Realization is made truly possible.

Sri Da Avabhasa is the God-Man of this Epoch. For the sake of His devotees, and all humanity, He has fully Revealed every aspect of the Guru-devotee relationship. This Revelation has come through His Word of Instruction and through His Supreme Demonstration of the Guru-devotee relationship with His devotees, as well as through His Blessing Regard.

In this chapter, my own Graceful experience as a devotee of Da Avabhasa is used to illustrate the love-relationship between the Guru and the devotee.

DIVINE DISTRACTION

The love-relationship to Sri Da Avabhasa is the foundation of the Way of the Heart. All practice is fruitless and superficial unless that loving submission, that Ecstatic Distraction and heart-moved feeling-Contemplation, is present. Heart-Master Da has proclaimed this Great Message from the beginning of His Teaching Work. Its Liberating Grace is echoed again and again in *The Hymn Of The True Heart-Master*, Sri Gurudev Da Love-Ananda's exquisite exposition of the Guru-devotee relationship (Freely Evolved from selected verses of the traditional *Guru Gita*):

The True Heart-Master is the Giver of Bliss, Joy, Happiness, and Love. Devotional meditation on the True Heart-Master is the Means whereby Bliss, Joy, Happiness, and Love are Awakened in devotees. (verse 89)

It is an unfathomable mystery, but to simply give one's attention to the Sat-Guru is to be Drawn out of one's separate and separative self into Divinity or Love-Bliss. Truly, the Sat-Guru is Love. He (or she) brings that Love face-to-face with his devotee, and Reveals It as the essence of all life. The sight of the Sat-Guru undoes the contracted heart, and Draws the incarnate being beyond himself or herself. The Sat-Guru is the Source of Life. He is the Source of Light, in the midst of darkness.

It is very difficult to describe to you the love that I and my fellow devotees have been Given by Sri Da Avabhasa, and that He perpetually Showers upon us, because such Love is so much greater than any words. For me this Love has been so great that nowhere could I go in all the worlds, and for eternity, and ever forget it. It has cut so deeply into who I apparently am that it has reawakened the intuition of my inherent Divinity. There is no way that I could stop short the outpouring of my gratitude for my Sat-Guru's Love—to remember His Love for even a moment brings tears to my eyes, overwhelms me, and opens my heart.

Now, there are some Spiritual practitioners who have more of the quality of bhaktas—those who are natural lovers of God, and who thus freely express their love for their Sat-Guru. I am more of this type, a kind of good-hearted ecstatic. Others are by character more conservative and controlled. Be that as it may, effusive and gushing emotionalism is not equivalent to the love of which we are speaking. This love for the Incarnate God-Man is based on an acknowledgement of what is Greater than ordinary emotions. It may look outwardly like other love, expressed via many ordinary and homely signs. The Sat-Guru's Form appears in the world, and with the apparent features of the world, because what else is there through which to appear? But his Form shines as the sign of That Which transcends all.

All the traditions testify to the fact that such love must be Revealed or Given by the Divine. One cannot find it on one's own. It is declared in the opening verse of the *Avadhoota Gita*:

It is only by the grace of God that a soul or two long for union with Him, and escape serious danger.[1]

The archetype for such love in the Hindu tradition is the gopis' relationship with Krishna. Such devotional love is described most fully in the tenth canto of the *Srimad Bhagavatam* and in the love poetry of bhakta-Saints such as Jayadeva and Surdas. In these, Krishna is revealed as the Supremely Attractive God-Man, whose skin is lustrous with a blue hue. He is said to have wandered, playing his flute, in the forest of Vrindavan in northern India some thousands of years ago. The gopis were milkmaids who tended cattle in the nearby fields. In spite of themselves, they fell in love with Krishna and completely forgot their husbands, their families, and their work. Whenever they would hear Krishna's flute, they would simply leave everything and go to find him.

Krishna with the gopis

In a Talk titled "Divine Distraction" Given in December 1975, Heart-Master Da Spoke of the necessary—and easeful—love and attachment of the devotee for the Sat-Guru:

SRI DA AVABHASA: The ancient legends of Krishna and his gopis are an allegory of Divine Distraction. As Krishna wandered about in the fields, the women who tended the cattle would see him from day to day, and in spite of themselves they would wander away and leave their posts. They completely forgot about the cattle. They forgot to go home and cook for their husbands. They wandered about where they thought they might find Krishna, and

1. *Avadhoota Gita,* trans. Shree Purohit Swami, ed. S. Mokashi-Punekar (Delhi: Munishiram Manoharlal, 1979), p. 77.

when they found him they gazed at him as he sat in the distance some-where. This legend is a play upon the romance between Krishna, or the Divine manifest in human form—the Spiritual Master in God—and these ordinary women, who became madly involved in an absolute attachment to Krishna, and who, as a result of this attachment, became more and more ecstatically absorbed in the God-State.

The foundation of this practice is exactly that attachment. If it does not develop relative to the Spiritual Master in God—not cultic attachment, but Divine attachment—if that attachment is not there that overwhelms the life completely, distracts you from the conventional destiny to which you are dis-posed through the medium of your desires, inclinations, and circumstances, then this practice of real or Spiritual life cannot exist.

The cattle that the women abandoned represent the force of all the ten-dencies of life. The husbands they left are the fundamental attachment to separated existence, to existence in form, to bodily existence, individuated existence, egoic life on its own, motivated toward survival and distinct from the Divine in Consciousness. Thus, in the allegory of the relationship between Krishna and his gopis, we see a fundamental description of the principle of the sadhana of the Way of the Heart. Sadhana is not about bearing down and being motivated by problems in your life, by some sort of philosophical detachment or some inclination to have Yogic and mystical experiences. Nor is it about doing what you have to in order to produce the changes that you desire. This sadhana is about distraction from the life of tendencies. It is a distraction from that life. It is not a motivated kind of detachment from your life of tendencies or an effort relative to them or the taking on of conditions to stop tendencies from arising or lifetimes from occurring. It is not a method of the ego. It is not characterized by any kind of effort relative to tendencies—for such a path is completely hopeless.

There are innumerable conventional paths that involve self-conscious efforts or hopes to produce changes, high and low. These efforts and hopes are themselves forms of tendency that may be realized and suffered in human and other terms. They are not Liberating in the fundamental sense. They are not God-Realizing. They are themselves expressions of the move-ment toward fulfillment. The Way of sadhana, the Way of Truth, is the Way of complete distraction from the tendencies that produced your birth and that now produce the drama of your existence from day to day. Only when there is complete distraction by the Guru, by the Divine, from the way of life that is producing your experiential destiny, do your tendencies become obso-lete. They do not become obsolete when you direct effort against them. It is only when that distraction appears in the midst of the affair of your life that another principle, another process, is established.

The gopis simply left the cattle. They did not say, "I'm not going to tend cattle anymore! I'm not going to submit to my desires, my tendencies, my job!" They did not make any such decisions. They simply forgot about the cattle. They were so distracted, so in love with Krishna, so ecstatic, that they just forgot to go home. It never even occurred to them to go home. They never worried about "Should I go home or should I stay here? Should I watch the cattle or should I go look for Krishna? Should I discipline myself?" They did not create a problem out of their sadhana or out of their relationship to God.

Anybody who approaches Me is obliged to involve himself or herself in just this kind of ecstatic Spiritual relationship. When that devotional relationship to Me becomes the condition of their conscious existence, fully, through all the conditions of life, then the force of limiting tendencies is weakened, not by doing anything to it, but by virtue of the fact that you are no longer even involved with it. If your relationship to Me is essentially ordinary, mechanical, mediocre, not Divine, not a form of Contemplation of Me, then you are not doing sadhana. You are intending to do some other kind of conventional sadhana perhaps, but you are not doing this sadhana. And you are not involved in the sadhana of Truth, you are not involved in Divine sadhana, you are not involved in that opportunity that is made available in human time through the Function of the Guru.

The Guru is not simply present to rap out a philosophy or distribute techniques that you may apply depending on your intelligence. The Guru is present to enjoy a Divine relationship with all those who are willing to assume such a relationship, with all those who have the capability for distraction by the Guru in an absolute love-relationship that is more and more distracting. But if that distraction is not present, if that love-desire distraction is not present in an individual's life, then the form of this sadhana is not initiated. It cannot begin. There is no point in even discussing the technical and abstract aspects of the development of this sadhana until the individual has begun to enjoy an ecstatic relationship with Me, a Spiritual relationship, not one that is in the air but one that includes the whole of life, that draws the emotion, that awakens the love, that awakens the heart. That distracting relationship that is the principle of this sadhana must be established. On its basis the individual may begin to assume life-conditions, turn them into service to Me, and realize that service in more personal and complex ways over time.

The foundation of this sadhana is the distraction that is described between Krishna and his gopis. You must flee to Me from all your life, from all your tendencies—not from your obligations, that is not what that allegory is all about—but from your tendencies, from the foundation of distraction by yourself, by your own thoughts, your own conditions, your own belongings, your own relationships, your own hopes, your own beliefs, your own thoughts, your own reading, your own mystical intentions, your own philosophical presuppositions. You must flee to Me from all that. It must be completely uninteresting to you. It is certainly not interesting to Me!

You cannot argue a woman into loving you, and you cannot argue individuals into the Divine Satsang of distraction. Satsang can be offered and a circumstance provided in which people can approach and become sensitive to that communicated Presence, that Siddhi. But apart from making it available openly and providing a way of approach to Me, there is no argument whatsoever. I am completely without argument. There is nothing I can do to convince you of the Truth of this Way, nothing I could do outwardly or verbally that could in itself fundamentally convince you of the relationship you must enjoy with Me in order to fulfill this sadhana. It is like falling in love with someone in conventional terms in life. It is not something you argued yourself into doing. It was initially a form of distraction, of absorption, without any reasons, and, perhaps, if you examined it to find a reason for it, it would seem unreasonable to you, not justified. You know, your lover does not look the way you wanted him or her to look. And in many ways I do not look and act and talk like the conventional, cultic guru is supposed to!

Once there is that distraction, the theatre of your evolution is in the hands of the Divine. The gopis did not have an elaborate life. They were distracted by Krishna. Krishna played all the games and created all the circumstances for their play with him. They were only attached to him. Their lives had all kinds of theatre and drama after that, but Krishna created it all. They did not create anything. They did not think about anything. They did not create an elaborate system of philosophy and belief and self-meditation and self-manipulation. They did not care about making life work out right. They did not even know What he was!

They were just distracted. They were in love. And their love for Krishna became the principle of their lives. Krishna played upon their distraction and Taught them. By Grace, they learned. But all they learned was to be more and more absorbed in God, totally beyond their attachment simply to the body of Krishna. Their minds became overwhelmed by this distraction, and all their petty tendencies to return to their solid and secure positions, in life or in themselves, were always undermined. There is no insurance. There is no guarantee. There is nowhere to go. There is no end phenomenon in the love of God. That love is in itself the Truth.

The same approach is necessary for all, and it is represented in the allegory of Krishna and his gopis. Without that distraction by the Guru in God there is no sadhana in any form in anybody's case. Once that distraction exists and the movement of the individual begins to become governed by the intuition of the Divine, the enjoyment of the Divine, then all the disciplines, the theatre, the lessons, the responsibilities, the Teaching, and all the rest begin to appear, according to the individual's capability and state of existence. (December 16, 1975)

The gopis constantly thought of Krishna, and longed to see him with an overwhelming intensity. Krishna, once he had their attention, would leave them for long periods of time, only sending them occasional messages—which only increased their devotion and longing. The gopis did not abstractly think about God or about religious practice. Distracted and Attracted by the sight of Krishna, and by his loving glances and his Leela (Divine Play), they eventually attained Union with the Divine.

The Sat-Guru makes it clear to his devotees that they are already and presently Loved by the Divine, and he reveals to them the Good News that the Divine Blessing and Gifts are Freely and Readily Given to any who would but turn to this Love. During the years of His Teaching Work (1970-1986), Sat-Guru Da Love-Ananda very graphically created lessons and Demonstrations of His Boundless Love for His devotees. Now, in His Blessing Work, Sri Da Avabhasa continues to Demonstrate His Love through the constant Blessing and Grace of His Seven Gifts,[2] and in occasions of Darshan (sighting of the Sat-Guru's bodily human Form).

To come into Da Avabhasa's Company for Darshan is to receive a Love so unfathomable that It stuns the being with gratitude and humility. I have on many occasions been one among the many devotees who, having just come out of a formal occasion of Darshan with Heart-Master Da, stood totally transformed, broken-hearted, perplexed by what we as ordinary people had done to deserve such Grace. What incredible fortune or good karma did we have to receive this Gift, this Blessing, this sight? There seemed no reasonable explanation for us to be so Blessed as to come into this Company.

Grace, or the Love Given by the God-Man, is the first principle of the Spiritual Way. Sri Sat-Guru Da once visited the public center of the Free Daist Communion in San Francisco on a hot Wednesday evening in the summer of 1975. A study course for those who were preparing to become formal devotees in the Way of the Heart was being held in the large room also used as a Meditation Hall. I was Blessed to give Sat-Guru Da a tour of the center and show the improvements that had recently been made to it. As He came to the door of the Meditation Hall, He asked, "What is going on in here?" I told Him that it was a class for preparing students, whom He had not yet seen, and who were formally not to see Him for many weeks. He nodded His head indicating that He wanted to go in.

I opened the door and led Him to the small circle of students seated in chairs. They were, needless to say, astonished and extremely pleased to see Sat-Guru Da suddenly alive before them. Da Avabhasa took a chair in the circle and began to speak, almost in a whisper. And I had the distinct feeling that this was because He did not want to overwhelm these new,

---

2. The "Seven Gifts Of Da Avabhasa's Grace That Establish and Perfect The Way Of The Heart" are His Word, or all His Instructions and Leelas (Sat-Guru-Vani); His Sign, or bodily (human) Form, to be seen or always Contemplated, with feeling, by His devotee (Sat-Guru-Darshan); His Awakening of His devotee's Devotion and His devotee's practice of devotional responsiveness to Him (Sat-Guru-Bhakti); His Granting to His devotee the opportunity of Service to Him, to His Work, and to all beings (Sat-Guru-Seva); His Demand for His devotee's Discipline of every part of his or her body, emotion, and mind in response to Him (Sat-Guru-Tapas); His Granting of the Blessing of effectively self-transcending Divine Communion, especially in Contemplative meditation (Sat-Guru-Kripa); and His Gift, always Given to each and all, of the Blessedness of Heart-Communion, Heart-Companionship, Heart-Oneness, and, ultimately, Heart-Identification with Him in Person, the Very Divine (Sat-Guru-Moksha-Bhava).

Thus, responsive reception of these Seven Gifts of Da Avabhasa is one way of understanding the entire practice of the Way of the Heart in Satsang with Him.

already astounded, devotees with His great Forcefulness. His speaking was truly simply a means to be with them, and to Grant the students His Darshan.

Heart-Master Da talked of the suffering that is inherent in the egoic tendencies of the body-mind, and the necessity for Spiritual practice. He commented that the body-mind is constantly in the business of convincing a practitioner not to practice.

As Da Avabhasa spoke, I became gripped with fear. My Sat-Guru's words were having a tremendous effect on me. Practice and my relationship to Him meant everything to me, and what He was saying was that the body-mind would always be attempting to distract me. I had assumed that my commitment was so strong that I would never leave. But now I understood that no decision I could make on the basis of the body-mind could guarantee that I would stay. I had to speak to Sat-Guru Da about this, even though I was the head of the center and presumably should not be having such doubts and concerns. With the intensity and directness that comes from a question so urgent, I blurted out to Heart-Master Da, apprehension and fear evident in my voice:

"Then how can I be sure that I will stay here with You? Do You mean that I might leave any time?"

Sri Gurudev Da Love-Ananda very sweetly paused for a moment, and, turning His Gaze directly to me, took in my state. And then with an aura of Compassion that healed me even before words were spoken, He gently replied:

"What brought you here in the first place? Grace. That is the only assurance that there is in the worlds."

Instantly I saw that this was true, and that all I could do was to surrender at the Feet of Sat-Guru Da Love-Ananda, that I could do nothing on my own to assure my destiny, and that questions as to my own future were secondary to the relationship to the Divine I was Graced with in Sri Gurudev's Company.

"Do They Really Know That I Love Them?"—
Sat-Guru Da Is the Heart-Husband of His Devotees

Da Avabhasa has described Himself as the Heart-Husband of His devotees. He is eternally married to all of His devotees in Loving Service and Blessing. The Heart-Husband is not merely an "other", even a Great Other. In the fullest sense, "Heart-Husband" designates the Divine Heart-Person or Divine Self-Power That is the Source and Inherently Perfect Consciousness of every being. The God-Man Gracefully Husbands or Embraces his devotee, and Draws the devotee to himself, so that the devotee becomes Blissfully conformed to the Divine Reality that he Is.

Heart-Master Da Writes in *The Dawn Horse Testament*:

. . . I Baptize or Bless My Devotee With The Self-Radiant Person (or "Bright" Presence) Of God, Truth, or Reality, So That My Devotee Realizes That he or she Is In Perpetual Embrace (At The Heart) With The Divine Person (The Husband Of The Heart) and Spiritually Conformed To Love-Bliss, or Happiness Itself. (p. 310)

This metaphor of marriage between the Sat-Guru and the devotee is widespread in the traditions, expressing the intensity of love and feeling of this greatest of all relationships. In Christianity that impassioned union with

Saint Teresa of Avila

the Divine Person is known by the term "bridal mysticism". The most well-known and articulate proponents of bridal mysticism have been the Carmelite renunciates Saint Teresa of Avila and Saint John of the Cross. In the case of Saint John, we see that men, like women, become submitted as "brides" in their devotion to the Divine. Like Saint John of the Cross, the twelfth-century Cistercian monk Saint Bernard also regarded himself as bound to Jesus in wedlock. Throughout the Christian era one finds women saints in Europe completely submitted to and devoted to Jesus as their spouse. The Benedictine nun Saint Gertrude and the Dominican Saint Catherine of Sienna actually experienced a visionary wedding during which Jesus Instructed them and gave them a wedding ring. There are also reported miracles of "rings of flesh" which appeared on some as a sign of betrothal.

In the Hindu tradition, Saints Andal and Mirabai are two examples of the many women who married the Divine. A similar love-relationship is seen in the writings of the South Indian Saint Nammalvar. In the Hindu tradition, as in the Christian tradition, men also become "brides". Not only do women emulate Radha in her Divine Love for Krishna, but men also become gopals, or male gopis, and express the same overwhelming love and emotion for Krishna. Kabir speaks of himself as the "faithful wife" of Ram. Acquiescing to the desire of his devotees, Ramana Maharshi composed "The Marital Garland of Letters", a beautiful poem of 108 verses in which he plays the part of the bride of Arunachala, the sacred mountain he often talked about as his "Guru" or "Master".

In Sri Da Avabhasa's Instruction and Wisdom relative to the Yoga of intimate relationships, it is the husband's responsibility to initially and always actively express his love for his intimate partner. And the female intimate partner's responsibility is to always return and likewise actively express that love and conform herself to him in the context of this love. Just so, it is the Sat-Guru, as the Heart-Husband, who first submits to the devotee in love. Writes Heart-Master Da:

. . . My Purpose here (and By Apparent Birth) Is To Awaken You, and Even all conditionally Manifested beings, To My Heart, or My Inherently Perfect Self . . . .

Mine Is The First Submission. Mine Is The First Sacrifice. I Am Always Pervading, Meeting, Loving, and Submitting To Be the conditional beings and worlds.

The conditional Reality (In person) Must Submit (or Be A Heart-Sacrifice) To The Unconditional Reality (In Person). This Is My Word and My Call To You.

The Unconditional Reality (In Person) Must Submit To The conditional Reality (In person), In Order To Awaken The Heart Of conditional being. This Is My Revelation and My Promise To You. (The Dawn Horse Testament, p. 689)

Gopals, or male gopis, express the same overwhelming love and emotion for Krishna

During the years of His Teaching Work,[3] Da Avabhasa ceaselessly Communicated to His devotees through His Words and through His actions His Loving Regard for them. He would greet those He had not seen for a time with huge hugs and arms of Love. He would find endless ways to look into the welfare of His devotees, inquiring about all their concerns

3. Many of the Leelas that are told in this book are from Da Avabhasa's Teaching years, and they have a distinctively different quality, for the most part, from those of Da Avabhasa's Blessing Work since 1986. His Instructive and Awakening Play with His devotees during the Teaching years was frequently very informal, and, therefore, many of His Talks and "Casual Words", or Comments, as related here, were quite informal as well. But informality was only an aspect of His willingness to Embrace ordinary and unprepared devotees

and often showing more regard for aspects of their practice, their personal life, and their health than they themselves were animating. His Spiritual Submission, His Sacrifice, and His Regard for His devotees knew (and continues to know) no bounds. He would ask those with Him, "Do you know that I completely Love you? Do you know it, really? And do you love Me?" And He would ask about those at a distance, "Tell Me, do they know how much I Love them? Do they? Do they know? Do they really know that I Love them?

"Do they know Who I Am?

"I Love them all.

"I Love all My devotees."

In late 1983, my intimate partner and I visited Sri Love-Anandashram (the Fijian island of Naitauba), the principal Hermitage Ashram and Empowered Retreat Sanctuary of Da Avabhasa. One evening we were invited to what is now known as Aham Da Asmi Sthan, Heart-Master Da's Residence at the time, to participate in a gathering with Him. This was the first time I had gone to that auspicious dwelling of Da Avabhasa, and, as I rode in the back of a truck on the road through the palm trees and jungle, I was full of expectation. It had been a difficult time for me, because as a visitor to the island I had not been involved in any of Sri Gurudev's gatherings. Instead, I had been asked to serve elsewhere during many of the occasions of Sri Gurudev's Instruction to the residents, which increased to no end my longing and ardor to see Him.

In the back of the open-bed truck, a devotee was excitedly telling another devotee what had been discussed in a gathering earlier that morning. He was shouting, but the engine noise and the wind were loud. I was frustrated in my attempts to overhear Sri Gurudev's Instruction. It was a very painful circumstance. After five minutes, I was in tears of upset. I shouted to myself in my own mind, "Why am I always excluded? Here I am

---

and to make Demonstrations of Love to Serve their human and Spiritual preparation. At the heart of all of His Teaching Work, whether formal or informal, was His Submission of His own body-mind to Identify with the characteristics, qualities, limitations, and habits of His devotees, so that He could thereby Reflect back to them the inherent bondage and suffering of their self-enamorment and seeking. Thus, to summarize, Da Avabhasa Appeared to be "like" His Western devotees, to share their interests and motivations, in order to Help them see themselves, and, thereby, to create the foundations of His Teaching Message and the sacred culture that must perpetually serve His Work on Earth.

When His Teaching Work came to an end on January 11, 1986, in the Great Change that marked the outset of His Divine Emergence, that form of Submission to His devotees and to all other conditional beings came to a sudden end. Since that time, He has Revealed, His body-mind is no longer conformed to the qualities of others. Rather, since that time, Da Avabhasa's body and mind are utterly Conformed to His own inherent and eternal Nature as the Divine Self, the Heart. And, in His Instruction and Blessing Service to His devotees, He no longer permits any kind of casual informality on the part of His devotees. He only Stands Firm in His Divine Disposition as the Divine World-Teacher and the True Heart-Master of His devotees, no longer consenting to relate to them as "brother" or "friend". Thus, He must be approached with sacred understanding of Who He Is and through proper devotional formalities if one is to rightly and fully receive His continuous and always Given Heart-Blessing. And the communication of such understanding and such formalities is the fundamental purpose of this book.

in Fiji, on this very island, and still I am not involved in Sri Gurudev's 'Considerations'! This is the last week of my visit, and I have hardly seen Heart-Master Da. And everyone else is seeing Him all the time." I sobbed, and turned away from everyone else in the truck so I would not be seen.

After just a few moments, the ridiculousness of it all became obvious to me, and I saw that what was wrong was simply my relationship to things. With a fierce intention I resolved to find Sat-Guru Da Love-Ananda in my heart-feeling right now, even in the truck, and to feel His always Freely Given Love. I knew that I could not <u>always</u> be around His bodily (human) Form in any case, and it was simply my egoically "self-possessed" search that was being Graciously undermined by my time on retreat. I remembered the tradition of Instruction by which the Sat-Guru Teaches his devotee how to always find him, by creating distance between himself and his devotee, in order to increase the strength of the devotee's remembrance of the Sat-Guru. For example, Krishna constantly alternated between intimacy with and separation from his devotees, in order to reveal to them how they must constantly find the Guru's Grace, no matter what the circumstance.

Such separation from and longing for the loved one is known as "viraha", and it is epitomized by the great sadhana of the gopis. It is described in the book *Gopis' Love For Sri Krishna*:

This wound of the devotee's heart inflicted by the oblique glances of Shyama (Krishna) never dries up. It remains ever green, and the acute pain he feels in every moment gives him greater joy than even the bliss of absorption in Brahma [the Hindu "Creator" residing in the heaven of the Gods]. This wound was very deep in the hearts of the Gopis. They are, indeed, supremely lucky who get this wound which goes on gaping more and more as the days pass and which does not heal up even when the swarthy-complexioned Lord appears in person and offers His services as a surgeon. The sight of the Blue Beauty, instead of healing the wound, makes it greener, but His disappearance also becomes unbearable. He is the only doctor who can heal the wound; but instead of healing it He makes it greener than ever. It is pleasanter to have this wound ever green: Hence to suffer acutely from the pain of this wound and repeatedly to do things which may cause it to grow becomes a part of the daily life of the devotee following the path of Love. He derives supreme joy even from this suffering.[4]

I understood that Da Avabhasa was Giving me this Gift and Instruction, and I let go of the mood of self-pity. He has said that such longing for the Sat-Guru is good, but it must become actual present Spiritual Communion, rather than simply an aggravation and an unfulfilled desire. Thus, in this particular moment in the truck, I understood that no matter what the circumstance, there was no reason to presume separation between me and

---

4. Hanumanprasad Poddar, *Gopis' Love For Sri Krishna* (Clearlake, Calif.: The Dawn Horse Press, 1980), p. 28.

my True Heart-Master. It was always possible to find Sat-Guru Da Love-Ananda in the present. As He has Instructed, I turned to Him in that moment through Remembrance. I began actively and moment to moment feeling Da Avabhasa there in relationship to me, even as I was riding standing up in the truck. And I began intentionally preparing myself to see Him at Aham Da Asmi Sthan, as I soon would, by surrendering into His Blessing Grace as best I could right there and then. I held in my hands a rudraksha mala (a rosary of sacred Indian wooden beads) that I was bringing as a gift to place at His Feet, and I consciously put as much energy into it as possible.

When the truck finally arrived at Aham Da Asmi Sthan, my desire to see my Beloved Sat-Guru was at a high pitch. On coming into the room, I could hardly close the screen door. In my excitement, I knocked over a drink with my foot, causing quite a commotion. Still, I one-pointedly placed the rudraksha mala at the side of my Sat-Guru, bowed down, and returned to my seat. Moments later Da Avabhasa picked up the mala and tossed it towards me. At first it hit by mistake Kanya Kaivalya Navaneeta, one of the members of the Da Avabhasa Gurukula Kanyadana Kumari Order, the Sacred Order of female devotees who serve Sri Da Avabhasa's personal circumstance. She quickly returned it to Him. He laughed, and as He tossed it, this time directly into my lap, remarked that it was appropriate that it should come by way of His Kanyas.

It is traditionally regarded as a most wonderful Blessing for the Sat-Guru to give or Bless the mala of His devotee. Sat-Guru Da Love-Ananda has regularly Blessed His devotees' malas to Empower their use in Invocation and Remembrance of Him. I was overwhelmed with joy at this Gift from Sri Gurudev Da Love-Ananda, and I sat holding it in my hands. Much later in the evening, Sat-Guru Da suddenly, for no apparent reason, began to address me. He told me how much He Loved me. And He told me that He spoke about me every day. He turned to the Kanyas, and said to them, "Don't I? Don't I talk about James every day?" They nodded in agreement, "Yes You do, Sri Gurudev." As He was speaking, Heart-Master Da was beaming at me and Communicating an intimacy beyond description. I was weeping in love, telling Him that I understood what He was saying, and that I loved Him too, and that I felt His Love. Over and over again He wanted to make sure that I understood how much He Loved me, and that it was every day that He thought of me, spoke of me, remembered me. He spoke on and on, and at a loss to respond to such Love, I merely told Him, "Yes, I understand. Yes, I love You, too."

In the moment I simply felt His Love, and I was broken open by the penetration of His Grace. But I also understood that what He meant was not that He actually spoke out loud about me each day—not that I knew, or would ever really know, exactly what Sat-Guru Da does, or how it is that He Works Spiritually with me. But it really did not matter. What He was saying to me was absolutely true. He Loved me beyond all bounds, beyond anything that I could know or understand. And, just so, He Loves all His devotees in the same way. The Play of it might be differently expressed in each case, but He Loves all His devotees. As He was to say just a few months later at the "Love of the God-Man" Celebration in early 1984 (when He returned to California for ten days and Blessed the general community of His devotees with many ecstatic occasions of Darshan), "I may not know their names, but I know their hearts." I understood that what He was telling me was for the sake of my Spiritual submission and reception of His Love, and not for me to "own", or to use to glamorize myself in any way.

Heart-Master Da continued His Shower of Blessing. He told me that I did the sadhana of a Spiritual friend in relationship to Him, and that He and I had always enjoyed this relationship with one another. Such Spiritual friendship (or sakhyatva) is traditionally described in the *Bhagavata Purana*, the supreme classic of devotional literature in the Vaishnavite tradition, as well as in the *Vishnu Purana*, and elsewhere. In the *Bhagavata Purana*, nine forms of the expression of devotion to the Divine, or the Sat-Guru, are described: (1) sravana, or hearing the Leelas and Teaching of the Divine or the Sat-Guru; (2) kirtana, or singing and praising the Divine or the Sat-Guru; (3) smaranam, or remembrance or contemplation of the Sat-Guru, or the Divine; (4) padasevanam, or service to the Sat-Guru (literally service to his Feet); (5) archanam, or offering worship to him; (6) vandanam, or prostrating to his bodily (human) Form; (7) dasyam, or assuming the relationship of service to the Sat-Guru as Master; (8) sakhyatva, or friendship (service to the Sat-Guru as a submitted friend); and (9) atma-nivedanam, or self-surrender, literally offering oneself to the Divine, or the Sat-Guru, altogether. These nine modes of bhakti (or devotion) are traditionally offered as alternative means by which the devotee may practice the sadhana of devotion to the Divine, or to the Sat-Guru. Heart-Master Da recommends forms of all of these practices in His all-comprehensive Way of the Heart.

But on this particular night in Fiji, and at this time in my sadhana, Sri Gurudev was awakening me to His Divine Love as the very basis and context of my sadhana. He told me that our Spiritual friendship was by no means an ordinary friendship—not the kind of friendship enjoyed by men when they go out to bars and have a good time. It was not such a secular kind of friendship. It was friendship developed as a Spiritual relationship. Such friendship was simply the form of relationship that He naturally had cultivated in me in response to my devotion to Him. Sakhyatva, or friendship with God, is described traditionally as a type of devotion that is most difficult to practice because the Spiritual friend is constantly called to be giving of himself in every action, in every thought, word, and deed. All personal desires and conveniences are given up in favor of this Spiritual sadhana alone. The Spiritual friend of the Sat-Guru must always be available and present in this friendship for the Sat-Guru.

I left the gathering that evening so in love with Heart-Master Da. I felt healed at the heart and made whole. During the following days I would periodically weep in Remembrance of my Sat-Guru. In the next few evenings before I was to board the boat to leave Sri Love-Anandashram and return to my regular service, Heart-Master Da continued His wonderful Communication to me of His Love and Grace. I was so deeply in love with Him. One morning I was asked to read *The Hymn Of The True Heart-Master* at the Sat-Guru Puja (our daily devotional ceremony of worship of the Sat-Guru), and I could hardly do so. Each line was so full of the emotion of Remembrance of my Sat-Guru that I was overwhelmed by His Love for me, by His Grace, and by the Miracle of Who He Is. My voice choked with emotion and tears clouded my vision, and I had to make long pauses in order to collect myself.

After I had returned to California, every day for weeks I would feel again His Love for me, His Regard and Blessing. For no apparent reason I would be suffused with an ecstasy and a bliss that filled the body-mind, and I would know it to be His Grace, and I would fall apart in tears of gratitude for all I had been Given. There was no doubt in me that I still required years of sadhana to purify the body-mind of its tendencies. But it did not matter at all—I was already Graced with a relationship to Sat-Guru Da Love-Ananda that was itself Liberating. All I needed to do was Remember Him, Contemplate Him.

Heart-Master Da embracing the author

During my trip to Sri Love-Anandashram, Sri Sat-Gurudev wrote the following short Essay, entitled "The Way of Devotion to the God-Man", which for me summarized His Instruction and Calling:

Do not indulge in vagueness, weakness, reactivity, or un-Happiness in My Company. I Am the Person of Love, Who has spontaneously taken on human form for the sake of this world of beings. I Am here to Be Love and to Do the Work of Love. Therefore, give Me your attention and feel My Regard.

Commune with the Person of Love in every moment. By this Means, always feel Love. Give Love. Receive Love. Be Love. This is the First Discipline, the Origin of the Way. (November 30, 1984)

The essence of what I knew about Spiritual practice was communicated in this short Essay. And for me the summary of His Words was the sentence, "Give Me your attention and feel My Regard." For I understood the practice to be to submit myself to Da Avabhasa. And whenever this is done, and He is feelingly Contemplated, His Regard and Blessing are felt, simply but profoundly. I needed to simply allow myself to be Attracted and Distracted by Him and to give myself over to whatever His Regard and Blessing might be in any moment. I would remember receiving Heart-Master Da's Gaze, or any number of occasions when His Love had Drawn me to Him so deeply that I could only love, love with a heart surrendered and given over, love with a heart which had been awakened to an utter faithfulness and submission because nothing else that it had ever known could equal the Attraction of that Love.

In my own case, I may safely say that the Love Given to me by Da Avabhasa has firmly held me in place in my practice. This Love transcends the body-mind-self. It is not a philosophical matter. His Love is felt humanly, Spiritually, Divinely, as pure or true emotion, and awakens a gratitude and debt. This Love has become the basis of my life, for it is no different from what I understand as the Divine Reality. That Reality is called by many names in many different religions, but in my own body-mind I know that Gift most deeply as Divine Love.

Whenever I return to Sat-Guru Da's physical Company to receive His Darshan, I am always struck by the fact that I have forgotten what Love truly is. In the years of His Teaching Work He would Attract me to Him with such Care and Regard, with such a depth of feeling and emotion, that I would feel romanced, loved, and made whole. And as soon as I moved to Him in love, He would naturally Reveal to me what was deeper than this human love and affection. His eyes and smile, His whole countenance would Reveal what is beyond all words.

In the summer of 1976, after several months of service as a missionary in Boston, I returned to see Sri Da Avabhasa in California. I had become dissociated and lonely, turned in upon myself. Heart-Master Da invited me, with some others, to dinner at His Residence in Mill Valley in honor of my return, and naturally and wonderfully engaged me in dialogue. Later in the evening the entire group retired downstairs to His quarters. I ended up trying to instruct Heart-Master Da in how to play a very complex board game. Although my attempts to teach Him proved fruitless under the circumstances of that evening, He assumed such intimacy with me that at one point, feeling myself free of all concern, healed at the heart, and breathing deeply, I said to myself, "This is love. I had forgotten what it is to love." And months of difficulty and pain were removed in an instant.

LOVE OF THE GOD-MAN

On October 10, 1983, at the beginning of Da Avabhasa's extraordinary and dramatic Teaching Demonstration in Fiji, the Divine Sat-Guru Da Love-Ananda Hridayam Spoke of His Offering of Himself as the Means of Salvation and Liberation. That Talk was later published under the title "Love of the God-Man".

SRI DA AVABHASA: What you must find is a unique Yoga. It is the Yoga described in the traditions in the relationship between the gopis and Krishna. It is the Yoga of Distraction by the God-Man. In that Yoga of Distraction, there is no effort to transcend the egoic self or to eliminate tendencies or to generate the love-feeling at will. When that Yoga is lived, all tendencies—including their root, which is emotional self-contraction—are spontaneously released in it. Simply by participating in that Attracted, Distracted condition of existence with the God-Man, all tendencies are released and sublimed, walked out of purgatory. . . .

What is supremely Attractive in the manifest universe and in the human world is the God-Man. All beings, male or female, must become Attracted, Distracted, by that One. This is the Ultimate Means, the Supreme Means, the Supreme Yoga. It is for this reason, you see, that the Divine Appears in manifest Form in the likeness of those who are to be drawn out of bondage—but only in their <u>likeness</u>. It is the <u>Divine</u> that Appears in that likeness, and it is the <u>Divine</u> that is made visible through that likeness. Those who become capable of acknowledging That One become capable of responding to that Attraction. Those who become capable of being Distracted by That One become participants in this Supreme Way of the Heart, which truly is the Way of Grace, because it requires no effort at all. It requires nothing but Grace and the response to it. That response is not effortful. It is easy. It is easy to respond to what is Attractive, except for those who refuse to do it. Those who refuse are bound to the will, are willfully binding themselves in one form or another, may even be willfully trying to understand, willfully trying to buy their way out of hell and purgatory and take heaven by storm. Such beings are not responding to the unique Advantage that the God-Man represents.

Such people are given all kinds of means that may serve their liberation from their own willfulness, that may release their energy and attention and ultimately enable them to respond to the God-Man and to the Divine Condition. But for those who can make this response directly, the Way of the Heart is simply as I have described it to you from the beginning—Satsang with Me, the devotee's relationship to Me, the Spiritual Master. The relationship takes the form of a life of practice, of disciplines, including Remembering Me and meditative practices. All that is true and useful, all that is part of Spiritual life, but the essence of such a life, the essence of these disciplines, is this Distraction.

Those who are Distracted by Me are not merely distracted by this physical Form. This Form is simply an Agent for their attention. What they are Distracted by is the Divine Presence, the Divine Condition, and they enter into Communion with That, into Union with That, into Unity with That, through the real Process of Spiritual life. Worldly people want nothing to do with that Process, and likewise worldly religionists, scholars, pundits, and egoically "self-possessed" "guru"-figures want nothing to do with it.

Nevertheless, the supreme Secret of Spiritual life is this Distraction by the God-Man. But even though it has been made available in many times and places, it has unfortunately not been accepted and truly fulfilled by many. . . .

By trying to break through the ego's dilemmas yourself, by trying to realize or discover the Truth yourself, you will find that you cannot do any such thing, not finally. And that discovery, you see, is what breaks the heart, or makes it possible for you to be Distracted by What is beyond your egoic self and to make use of your relationship to Me rightly, truly, such that your relationship with Me becomes Ecstatic. Simply to give Me your regard should be the moment of Ecstasy. It should naturally draw you into the emotional response, the feeling response, the mood of love, devotion, freedom from mental bondage, physical bondage, relational bondage. If you become Ecstatic by such Means, then you will also be Intoxicated by My Company. Thus Ecstatic, thus Intoxicated, you are naturally capable of incarnating this Love, this Divinity, through all the forms of practice, including your love-relations and friendships.

. . . The Purpose of My Living is Divine. In other words, I have not come here simply to suffer your resistance and absorb your limitations, but to Distract you out of this condition, out of this place, into the Divine Domain. My Purpose is to awaken you to a disposition of Divine Distraction, in which you are Ecstatic, free of your limits, inherently sinless, karma-less, so that without effort you can move with Me out of this limitation, this place of purification and suffering.

THE SECRET "METHOD" OF THE SAT-GURU:
LOVE WITHOUT LIMIT

Early in 1980 I traveled to India in service to Da Avabhasa, visiting the Ashrams of the great Realizers that had been especially connected with His Life and interviewing the living devotees of those Masters. Meetings with devotees of genuine Spiritual Masters greatly served my understanding of Who Da Avabhasa Is (and magnified my gratitude) because they understood the same secret—the Love of the God-Man. They knew what it was to be overwhelmed by love. They could tell by the questions I asked that I was interested in what these great beings were truly all about, and that I was genuinely open to what they had to say. And to ask these questions was to tap a great well of pent-up emotion. These devotees were so full, so quickly, of their Guru's Blessing and their gratitude to their Guru. And in this they showed me something very profound. The moving force in each of these devotees was not some abstract Teaching of their Guru's, nor the specifics of the practice he had given them. What was primary to them was the love-relationship they enjoyed with their Guru. Their entire lives had been changed and molded by the love of their Guru. Even those whose Guru had died years earlier were still basking in that love. The difficulties of their lives and their practice remained. But they had been won over, Blessed out of proportion, by the love their Guru had shown them. And that love did not feel diminished even if their Guru had died years before.

This served to awaken and reinforce in me a great strength of faith in Sri Gurudev Da Love-Ananda. I knew that all I had heard about these traditional Gurus was completely true of Him, and that I had been Graced beyond compare. I understood that I could be away from Him for thirty years serving Him in India, and it would make no difference. He could do whatever He needed to do with me from a distance. He could in a moment of Spiritual intimacy wash away whatever time and space had separated us.

During this trip to India, I spoke with a devotee of the great Adept Narayan Maharaj (1885-1945). This woman's name was Cursetji Maccabai, and she was hosting me in her house in Poona, two hours south of Bombay. It was fully thirty-five years after the kingly Realizer had attained Mahasamadhi.[5] We sat on her bed, in her simple dwelling. I had asked Maccabai to describe to me her relationship to Narayan Maharaj. She began to relate how each time Narayan Maharaj came to Poona, he would leave via a route that came by her house. She was a young woman then, and it was her husband that had been the devotee of the Guru for many years. As this humble Parsi woman continued her story, tears streamed down her

---

5. The Sanskrit term "Mahasamadhi" refers to the great Samadhi or Transcendental state that is magnified upon the death of the bodily Form of the Realizer. Thus, Mahasamadhi refers to the unique Yogic event that is the death of a Realizer.

Narayan Maharaj with his devotees

face. She related how she would be at home (in the very house where she was telling the story) and she would hear the honk of a horn and go running to the window to see the beaming smile of the elegant Realizer waiting for her to wave hello. She told me she was not a sophisticated lady. She neither understood nor cared for philosophy. She had not at first understood her husband's love for Narayan Maharaj. "But how could one hold out against such love?" she asked me through her tears. Now, decades later, the love-Communion she enjoyed with Narayan Maharaj filled the room. "Such love", she sighed, "as cannot be found anywhere. Without end." And I knew it to be no different than what I enjoyed in my relationship to Heart-Master Da. I sat marveling at such love that holds the heart over the course of decades, and truly over lifetimes. It is the vehicle by which the Guru opens the devotee to truly See Who It Is That is Standing there before him.

THE LOVE THAT IS THE HAPPINESS OF MY LIFE— A STORY OF BEING DRAWN BEYOND MY EGOIC SELF BY DIVINE ATTRACTION

Let me tell a story of a wonderful moment in my relationship to Da Avabhasa from the years of His Teaching Work, before His Divine Emergence. Its sweetness is lodged in my memory forever. It occurred on the Celebration of the Jayanthi (Birthday) of Heart-Master Da Love-

Ananda in 1985, when I had been Graced to visit Sri Love-Anandashram for a seven-week stay. It was a warm evening, and we were all gathered around Heart-Master Da in an open-air hall known as the Giving Coat.

I had brought a small, beautiful tie-dyed pouch, which my intimate partner and I were giving to our Heart-Husband in gratitude and love. It had nine little pockets that held small, Spiritually auspicious Indian rudraksha beads of different varieties. It was a delightful moment. Heart-Master Da opened a number of gifts, and a close friend suggested that he and I wait until a later moment, and surprise Heart-Master Da with our gifts after He imagined that He had already been given everything. With a moment's thought I agreed, and the night passed in anticipation of the moment when I would present our gift to Him. Periodically, I glanced at the pouch, which I kept hidden behind my shoulder bag, expectantly awaiting the right time.

Three hours or so into the gathering, my friend presented his gift, and so now I approached Heart-Master Da's Chair, where He sat Radiant and Happy. I knelt in front of Him and showed Him the pouch. Heart-Master Da took the cloth bag in His great Hands, and He began to open the pockets. When He saw that it was rudraksha beads, He laughed, for I am always giving Him rudraksha beads. He uses them sacredly, Empowering them with His Energy and placing them in the sacred environments at the Sanctuaries, and He had spoken in the past of how much He appreciates them. This evening He told me what a pain in the ass all these rudraksha beads were—and how since I was always giving them to Him, He was always having to deal with them! He had a pained look on His face, indicating the burden that all these beads were. After a few moments, He broke down in laughter. "I was only kidding!" He exclaimed. I laughed, because I knew it anyway.

My intimate partner had been sewing the pouch up until the last moments before the gathering, and so she had had no time to check her work. A piece of thread came off one of the buttons, and Heart-Master Da laughed, exclaiming that it was broken. He now accused me of giving Him a broken gift on His Birthday. It was somehow incredibly funny, because He was having such an infectiously good time giving me a hard time, and He was so sweet. I said that we would fix the pouch. And then I started to open the nine pockets of the pouch with Him. It was His gift, but somehow I could not keep away, and together we opened each pocket. I was so in love with Him. I savored every second of our interaction. Each moment was an eternity of pleasure, just being there with Him. He was so Happy, and I was so happy—and so fully able to tell Him how much I loved Him, without even having to say it. It was just there. It poured out of me, and how could it not? He was Radiant, and I was beaming in my love for Him, giving Him back that Love that He was Showering upon me.

"What are you doing pulling out those beads?" He barked at me. "You are showing My beads to everyone!" I started from the force of His Shout, but I knew He was having a lot of fun teasing me. I laughed, and talked to

Him excitedly about rudraksha beads. Actually, we were shouting at one another. I think what we were saying was making some sense, but it did not matter. I was completely ecstatic to be there with Him—and to enjoy the love that we had for one another, which was greater than anything else I knew or understood. I certainly was not double-checking anything I was saying! I mentioned somebody who could inventory His rudraksha beads— "What does she know about rudraksha beads? How could she inventory the beads?" He shouted back. I could not stop laughing. And during this mirth and this chaos of feeling and love and emotion of gratitude and regard, somehow we continued to talk about something. Was it five minutes? Was it three weeks? I do not know, because it was timeless. And then I started to steal little kisses on my Heart-Master's legs in the midst of conversation. There is a tradition of gopals, or male cowherds, who fall in love with the Sat-Guru just as the gopis do and love the Sat-Guru with the same passion and absorption. I knew about this tradition, but it certainly was not in my mind at this time. I was only there, and in love, and placing kisses on that Body which was more Attractive than anything else, and which I was moved to kiss, and so in love as to not feel any inhibition about it.

And finally in an instant my heart's desire is fulfilled, and I hold Sri Gurudev's head in my hands, and He holds my head in His. I kiss Him on His left cheek. And then our heads, in each others hands, move away, and the attraction and love cannot be fulfilled, and we kiss again, this time I on His right cheek. But the desire is there, and my love is too great, and in the midst of the cheek-kissing I am thinking about His lips, and cannot quite bring it to consciousness as a prayer or intention, or even admit it fully as a desire, but I want to kiss Him on the lips, which is of course too much and not possible. It is just too unconventional. And then we kiss on the lips. And even though, on the one hand, I cannot believe it is happening and I am too excited to be present there with Him, on the other hand, I some- how wanted it so much for so long that I am right there. And I am able to enjoy and savor His tenderness.

And all at once I climb Mount Everest, rise to the crown in ecstasy, and swoon in my lover's arms. I am "drifted into the deeper lands". I am twirling in somersaults around and around. And still somehow I am laugh- ing and joking with Heart-Master Da about something, and maintaining a semblance of being a person, and then crawling away from His Chair to who knows where I was sitting to continue the Birthday Celebration, a foolish guy with a big mouth who cannot stop prostrating every moment before the Great One, and who is as "in love" as he has ever been, and knows that his life is different forever now, and that he might as well leave behind everything he has ever known or believed or presumed somewhere else, because it is a whole new ball game. Except that all this is in retrospect. In the moment it is just this FEELING in the heart that is Consciousness Itself, perfectly still, and already Realization.

Writes Jalal al-Din Rumi, the Sufi love poet: "Come! How much for a

kiss of those precious rubies? If a kiss costs a life, it still must be bought!
"He is selling a kiss for a spirit! Go, buy! He is giving them away for free!"[6]

THE DIVINE LOVE OF THE SAT-GURU BECOMES THE SOLE DESIRE OF THE DEVOTEE

This unbridled love is the heart of devotion to the Sat-Guru. It is the vehicle through which the aspirant surrenders himself or herself, and thus opens to Divine Grace. In the mature devotee, such love is always coupled with self-understanding and real practice, as I will describe as this book unfolds.

There is no question but that genuine Spiritual practice is extremely difficult—it is justly known to be the most heroic process that a human being can be involved in, requiring everything of an individual. For me the real demand of Spiritual practice is so great that, in desperation, on any number of occasions, for any number of reasons, the movement has risen within me to abandon practice of the Way of the Heart, and the community of practitioners. However, it has been the depth of my love and commitment to Sat-Guru Da that has kept me in place. His Love for me and His Spiritual Gifts to me keep me His devotee forever.

He has so Captured and Distracted me, and so put me in His debt, that no matter how difficult it gets in any moment, I cannot abandon my relationship to Him or to the Divine. Nor can I abandon my practice of the Way of the Heart, nor my service to Him. The rebellious and non-submissive ego in me at times creates its own arguments: My life is no longer my "own", and I cannot do what I "want". However, all of these are the fabrication of the contracted personality. Instead, my deepest understanding is that this Eternal bond of love with the Sat-Guru is the greatest Gift.

What I truly want is for my life to be utterly surrendered to the Divine. I do not want my life to be my "own"—eternally bent to satisfy my petty conventional desires—but to be lived in response to and in Communion with the Divine Revelation and Will. I understand that on my "own" I would incessantly wander from my real desire.

When the devotee surrenders completely to the Sat-Guru, the Sat-Guru's Realization is Given to the devotee. Now, obviously there remains a limit that I place on my submission to my Sat-Guru, and the fulfillment of His Callings, and the reception of His Grace, or I would already have entered into the Condition of Divine Self-Realization. But in every moment my Sat-Guru puts me into a profound debt of Love and Grace. And what a great Blessing that debt is! For it requires me to go beyond my limits, and

6. William C. Chittick, *The Sufi Path of Love: The Spiritual Teachings of Rumi* (Albany: State University of New York Press, 1983), p. 303.

repay Him through devotion and service.

There is in India the tradition of the ekantin, or one who desires nothing more than to love the Divine, or the Sat-Guru. He or she does not love the Sat-Guru for the sake of trying to Realize something else. That love is enough. It is already Bliss, already Ecstasy. When that Sweetness is tasted, there is no aggravated yearning for something else. The ekantin's search comes to an end, for he or she has already found the Beloved, the Divine Person, and only wants to always remain in that love. Where else is there to go?

The lovers of Da Avabhasa, who have partaken of His Flavor of Bliss, know it to already be the Supreme Grace. Ecstasy is already theirs through Heart-Attraction, because Sri Gurudev Da Love-Ananda has been born. Nothing else is sought but to remain in Love-Communion with Sri Gurudev Da Love-Ananda. The hladini shakti, the "Transmission of ecstasy" described in the traditions, finds its fullest expression in Da Avabhasa's Transmission of Supreme Love-Bliss.

There are five degrees of ecstasy described in the Vaisnava Bhakti tradition using the metaphor of a fire. Initially that fire of ecstasy merely smokes. Then, as it grows in heat, it smolders. It next begins to flame. Catching on with strength, it burns brightly. At last it becomes incandescent, outshining all in its blaze. The Remembrance of the bodily (human) Form of Sri Gurudev Da Love-Ananda is that rare fuel that kindles the fire of His devotee's ecstasy beyond all proportions. His Glance and His Love inflame His devotee's heart, evoking a Bliss and Passion that burns through the dross of ordinary life. Yes, that ordinary life continues, but it is no longer the point. Instead, that Incandescent Fire of love grows until it rages out of control. His devotee falls at the Feet of Sri Gurudev Da Love-Ananda in a gratitude that cannot be compared to any other emotion in the world.

That love is the only true emotion, and once Given by the God-Man, it is enough. The devotee only lives in that love, and all of his or her actions are the means to magnify it, to put more fuel on the fire, to draw him or her closer to the Supreme Being Who Is That Love Itself. All else is outshined in the "Brightness" of the Fire of love.

This Supreme Passion that surpasses all experience is described by Da Avabhasa in His Free Rendering of a passage from the *Bhagavata Purana*. He named this passage "The Essence of Transcendence".

The pleasure of those who desire and possess experiences of all kinds is not even remotely comparable to the Bliss of one who surrenders to Me and transcends all experience in Me, by Realizing Me as the true Self, the Transcendental Condition of his own soul. Such a one is always already Happy and Full of Pleasure. He no longer depends on bodily satisfactions, nor is he disturbed by the inevitable changes in his experience. He has transcended the motion of attention in the body, the senses, the mind, and all the subtle reaches of his higher being. He no longer seeks for any state or place, but only Abides in Me. . . . He does not crave dominion or power on Earth, or in the lower Worlds of Elemental Nature. He does not seek or hold on to the psychic and astral powers of mysticism and yoga. He does not even cling to the notion of bringing experience to an end, and an end to the cycles of birth and change and death. But one who Loves Me and always Communes with Me quite naturally transcends all possible phenomena, and he simply Abides in the Bliss of the Radiant Self, whatever comes and goes. (The Enlightenment of the Whole Body, *p. 123)*

Dear reader, by putting this chapter first, I have shown the shine of the Guru-devotee relationship in advance. Although something of that lustre can be felt at first reading, its secrets will unfold only gradually for the devotee. After years of practice in Sri Gurudev Da Love-Ananda's Company, and after years of study of the Guru-devotee relationship, my appreciation of its profundity still grows day by day.

The love of the devotee for the Guru is a Gift that is received over time. The pages that follow describe this Gift Itself, the Spiritual, Transcendental, and Divine Identity of the Sat-Guru, as well as the laws inherent in the Guru-devotee relationship. May you be Blessed to develop a true understanding of the Guru-devotee relationship so that you may enter into that stream of Grace, Love, and Wisdom.

Sri Love-Anandashram, March 1991

CHAPTER TWO

Who Is the God-Man?

THE IDENTITY AND ECSTATIC SPEECH OF SRI DA AVABHASA

"THE VISION HE GRANTED ME WAS ASTOUNDING"

*W*ho Sri Da Avabhasa <u>Is</u> will always be the Supreme Secret disclosed by Divine Revelation. When He is Standing before you, His Feet planted on the ground like pillars that hold up the Earth, His Face Shining with Divine Radiance, His Eyes moist with Blessings and Radiating Infinite Love, your mind falls apart. The breath is overwhelmed with the Passion of His Divine Aliveness, the Gift He is Giving just by <u>Being</u>, just by Giving Himself to your vision. Your entire life and everything you have ever known is made new again by the mere sight of Him.

How then to describe in words that Supreme Condition in which Da Avabhasa lives? How to make clear to another what must be witnessed and cannot be accepted based on mere report?

Devotees entering into Sri Da Avabhasa's Spiritual Company, even for the first time (and even via study of His Wisdom-Literature), intuit the Revelation of the Divine to some degree. Even the newest devotee will feel, at some level of the being, that Sri Gurudev Da Love-Ananda is the Very One, the Great One, the Supreme Person. I have on many, many occasions heard devotees cry out in ecstasy at the sight of Sri Da Avabhasa's Beautiful Form, "Da! You are the Divine Person. You are the Supreme Being. You are the World-Teacher." There is a certainty in them that comes only from the sight before their eyes, the Divine Revelation Itself.

Charles Seage, M.D., describes his experience of this Grace-Given Vision:

In early June of 1990 I went on formal retreat in Sri Gurudev Da Love-Ananda's Company for three weeks. The retreat itself developed as a remarkable deepening of my practice and my devotional relationship to my Heart-Master.

On a Monday afternoon after I had been on retreat for several days, all the retreatants were invited to attend a formal Darshan occasion with Sri Gurudev Da Love-Ananda in the meditation hall known as Divine World-Teacher Darshan Mandir, located at Sri Da Avabhasa Chakra.[1] This meditation hall is very intimate, and there were only about thirty-five of us Graced to be there with Sri Gurudev. During most of the occasion the hall was very quiet, and I experienced a deep and full meditation. My eyes were naturally closed in strong Contemplation of Sri Gurudev. I felt my conception of my own body go through changes. For example, I felt as if I were simply witnessing the body and whatever was arising to my awareness from a place above the body.

At one point, after about forty-five minutes, I felt a different energy in the room, and I opened my eyes. I saw that Sri Gurudev Da Love-Ananda was now Blessing the Prasad [Blessed Gifts Given to His devotees] by dipping His Hands into the water bowl, and sprinkling water on it, which generally marks the end of the Darshan occasion. Then Sri Gurudev Stood up and passed out the Modaka Prasad (a baked sweet) to each of us personally from His own Hands. I returned to my seat full of gratitude, but there was no sign of what was next to occur.

Sri Gurudev finished Distributing the Prasad and passed the bowl with the remaining pieces to Kanya Tripura Rahasya. And then He simply Stood before us as Who He Is, His Hands open and down at His sides a few inches from His Body. And suddenly as I watched Him, it became unbelievably obvious that He was the Divine Person. The Vision He Granted me was astounding. He filled up the entire universe. For a moment I closed my eyes and visualized His Form as I usually do. Then that visualization disappeared and I felt Him become so immense and All-Pervading that it felt like I was seeing and feeling His "thousand-armed Form", as it is described in stories about Krishna in the Bhagavad Gita. He was Infinitely wide and Infinitely tall. I saw that the entire universe was His Form. It was clearly, tacitly the case. He was not limited to His bodily (human) Form.

I do not know if this description truly communicates the Force of that Vision. It was overwhelming, and I could not contain the force of the Realization. Then I felt an incredible force entering into me, and I let out a low-pitched scream such as I had never made before. I screamed several times, an animal sound, very loud, that seemed to come from my bodily base. Later, people told me it was like the sound someone might have made

---

1. At Sri Love-Anandashram devotees maintain two Residences for Sri Da Avabhasa and the Da Avabhasa Gurukula Mandala. One, known as Indefinable, is located near the village of His devotees, Qaravi Dau Loloma. The other Residence, Aham Da Asmi Sthan, is located in a secluded area known as Sri Da Avabhasa Chakra ("chakra" means a circle or center from which energies radiate). For Sri Da Avabhasa's devotees to be invited to Divine World-Teacher Darshan Mandir is an auspicious Blessing, for at Sri Da Avabhasa Chakra one comes into contact with a particularly profound and peaceful manifestation of His Spiritual Heart-Transmission.

falling off a cliff. The room had been quiet, but I could not contain myself. There was no intention involved—my shout was just my spontaneous response to the totally overwhelming Vision of Sri Gurudev in His Utter Divinity. It was an acknowledgement of that Vision.

After that my hands filled up with energy of an extraordinary magnitude. Energy was pouring out of me. I became completely absorbed in Sri Gurudev. After Sri Gurudev had left, I crawled to His Chair and bowed down in gratitude.

I had many visions previously in which I had seen Heart-Master Da Love-Ananda as What is greater than the body-mind, as the Divine to some degree. But this instance was so overwhelming that I have been changed ever since. I clearly know now that Sri Gurudev Da Love-Ananda is not a body-mind and that I am not a body-mind. Since the time of this Vision, when I meditate, my mind becomes quieted, with a clear and tangible constant feeling of Sri Gurudev's Spirit-Presence. The intuition that I exist Prior to the body-mind has become stable. And my devotional relationship to Sri Gurudev Da Love-Ananda intensified dramatically as a result of this Revelation. That relationship is a great Treasure to me. It is everything.

THE HRIDAYA-SAMARTHA SAT-GURU

The Sanskrit term "Guru" has become a universal word, crossing language barriers worldwide. However, it has come to be used so casually that its connection with the long tradition of the Transmission of genuine Spirituality is often obscured. Western dictionaries now routinely include this word, but even they point out that the word is often used "derisively". This is a sign of the popular adolescence of our times, with its refusal to acknowledge the superior man and its insistence that all are equal. In terms of political and social freedom there is no doubt that all are entitled to be regarded as equal. But it is just as clear that in terms of wisdom and maturity there are great differences between human beings. To dispute the superiority of the Great Realizers in Spiritual matters, and the need for us to resort to them, is, to use a metaphor penned by Da Avabhasa, like the Earth arguing about the necessity that it revolve about the sun.

It has been one of the Graceful Services of Sri Gurudev Da Love-Ananda to be a Divine Voice Calling all to be restored to a right and honorable relationship to our greatest Sources of Help. In His Teaching-Revelation, Da Avabhasa has clarified the entire Spiritual Process and made plain the real, functional distinctions between various types of Gurus. The distinctions described by Da Avabhasa are a necessary place to begin in understanding the Guru-devotee relationship, because they clarify the confusing variety of traditional descriptions, cut through today's widespread misconceptions and conflicting notions about the Guru-devotee relationship, and give us an overview of the differences between the fullest Realizers of the Supreme Truth, the great Teachers of various degrees, and the many other good men and women who teach and instruct.

The word "guru" itself is composed of two contrasting syllables: "gu", meaning the "gunas" or (that congealed matter that is) darkness, and "ru", signifying the action of destruction, or removal, as fire destroys. "Ru" is also often described as "light". Putting these two syllables together, the Guru is the one who releases, or redirects, the disciple from darkness (non-Truth) to light (Truth itself). The true Guru is the dispeller of darkness or ignorance.

In *The Basket of Tolerance: A Guide to Perfect Understanding of the One and Great Tradition of Mankind*, Heart-Master Da Love-Ananda clarifies the range of individuals who serve as Gurus:

> *In the Great Tradition of mankind, teachers are sometimes called "gurus" (spelled with a small "g"). Such "gurus" are not men or women of Realization, but they instruct others in various secular and sacred arts, crafts, and sciences, in order to equip them for the ordinary human pursuit and struggle. And some of these "gurus" may also constantly remind their students of the sacred itself. . . .*
>
> *However, in the Great Tradition of mankind, the sacred Ordeal Itself is the province of Teachers who are actual Realizers (of Samadhi[2]). Of these, there are Gurus (spelled with a capital "G") who (in the context of any or all of the fourth, fifth, and sixth stages of life) have (at one time or another) experienced Samadhi, and who, therefore, can (in the context of their own stage or degree of Realization) give first-hand Guidance (including Revelatory explanations, and, in some cases, a degree of Spiritual Transmission) relative to the techniques, processes, stages, obstacles, and goals of the self-transcending Way. And, beyond these Gurus, there are Sat-Gurus (also often referred to by the simpler reference "Guru"), or those who are presently (and constantly) in Samadhi (in the context of any or all of the fourth, fifth, and sixth stages of life, and, especially, or in the Ultimate case, in the context of the seventh stage of life), and who are unique in their Ability to fully Transmit their own (uniquely developed) Wisdom, Spiritual Power of Realization, and (in the Greatest of cases) also their own State of Realization (or Samadhi) directly to others.*

Sri Gurudev Da Love-Ananda uses the term "Sat-Guru" to mean an individual who is permanently founded in Samadhi. The Sanskrit term "Sat" refers to the Divine Reality, or Pure Being, that is Absolute and Eternal Consciousness. The Sat-Guru therefore Teaches not about the ordinary, but

---

2. "Samadhi", in Sanskrit, means "placed together". It indicates concentration, equanimity, and balance, and it is traditionally used to denote various exalted states that appear in the context of esoteric meditation and Realization.

about the Supreme Truth. And even amongst Sat-Gurus there are distinctions to be made. In terms of Realization, such Sat-Gurus may be in the fourth, the fifth, the sixth, or the seventh stage of life. And in terms of Transmission, such Sat-Gurus may be either those who simply Transmit Spiritual Power or those greatest Sat-Gurus who Transmit their actual State or Samadhi.

As Da Avabhasa has made clear, to be in perpetual Samadhi is a great affair. It is to be permanently in the Bliss state of one of the advanced or ultimate stages of life. Only very rarely do we hear of great Sat-Gurus who are always in such a condition. The Sat-Guru of the fourth stage of life is always totally absorbed in Love of God, embracing the Divine and the descended fullness of the Divine, and perhaps experiencing the initial awakening of higher Spiritual or mystical energies. He is constantly speaking of or absorbed in Divine Grace. The Sat-Guru of the fifth stage of life is always in Yogic Samadhi, always immersed in the ascended Spiritual energies. Swami Nityananda, Swami Muktananda, Swami Rudrananda, Sai Baba of Shirdi, and Rang Avadhoot are examples of great fifth and fourth to fifth stage Sat-Gurus who Served Sri Gurudev Da Love-Ananda in the course of His Sadhana. The sixth stage Sat-Guru is always founded in the Bliss of the Heart Itself, the Feeling of Being, which transcends the rising and falling energies of the Circle (the ascending and descending circuit of energies) of the body-mind. This is the domain of great Sages such as Brahmagna Ma and Sadguru Gnanananda. But there is a tremendous distinction between these and the seventh stage Sat-Guru.

To designate the greatest type of Sat-Guru, Da Avabhasa has created the term "Hridaya-Samartha Sat-Guru". "Hridaya" is the Sanskrit term for "heart", and here it refers to the full seventh stage Realization, the Realization or Siddhi (Power) of the Heart. The Sanskrit term "Samartha" means "adapted, fit, proper, qualified, suitable, good, able to, entitled, having power over anyone". As used in the Spiritual traditions of India, the word "Samartha" refers to a Sat-Guru who has the full Spiritual Power to Liberate his (or her) devotee. The Samartha Sat-Guru has Complete Power in this regard over any object or purpose in the manifest or unmanifest worlds. Thus, a Hridaya-Samartha Sat-Guru is one alive with the Blessing Power of the Heart, and fully able to Divinely Liberate his (or her) devotees.

Hridaya-Samartha Sat-Gurus are not common. The Appearance of the Hridaya-Samartha Sat-Guru is an extraordinarily rare event. The devotees of Hridaya-Samartha Sat-Guru Da Love-Ananda have seen over and over again that He is Alive with every kind of Spiritual Power in every dimension, which He uses when necessary to Serve His Liberating Work. The following three Leelas illustrate Sri Da Avabhasa's Power in the gross, subtle, and Transcendental dimensions. The first Leela, told by Ben Fugitt, illustrates not only Da Avabhasa's Mastery of the elemental world, but also His constant Service to His devotees, in this case Ben, in the midst of every action.

BEN FUGITT: During the summer of 1979 I was a caretaker at the Mountain Of Attention Sanctuary in Northern California. It had been a very hot summer with a number of forest fires in the surrounding country. On this particular day in September I noticed a small tuft of smoke down the canyon. It looked like it was very close to our property. I immediately ran to the nearest car and raced down the canyon. A fire could be seen going up over a ridge to the northwest. This was an ominous location, practically inaccessible to fire-fighting equipment due to the rough terrain. It was also in a direct line with the outer Sanctuary. Seeing that the Sanctuary was threatened by this already out-of-control fire, I jumped into the car and raced back.

I had the fire department notified, then ran out to the back of the Sanctuary, where I had sent a few men with hand tools to see what they could do. By now the smoke had grown to a large cloud. This was obviously a big fire. I had run about three-quarters of a mile toward the fire to check out the extent of the blaze when I received a call on my walkie-talkie to meet Heart-Master Da at the Sanctuary zoo, as He wanted to ride out to the fire on horseback. I ran back, calling requests and orders over the walkie-talkie in preparation for His ride. I found myself in a frenzy by the time I got to the zoo.

I hastily saddled the horses. Adrenaline was coursing through my body like never before. I was very much afraid for our Sanctuary. The area that was immediately threatened by the fire meant far more to me than simply outlying trails and manzanita bushes. It was a potent Holy Site at the Mountain Of Attention Sanctuary—Red Sitting Man—an area where I had spent many hours meditating and serving. I knew this Site had Spiritual significance and that it was extremely important that it not burn. And then of course there was the obvious threat to the residences, Holy Sites, and Communion Halls at the heart of the Sanctuary.

As Heart-Master Da approached the horses, His Fierce determination and concern for the Sanctuary were obvious to me, but He was also completely calm. His simultaneous Intensity and Freedom immediately drew me out of my fearfulness.

As we made our way over the ridge it looked as though we were riding into a different world. The atmosphere was thick with smoke. The ground and trees were red with borate fire retardant, and planes were continuing to drop fire retardant right over us. As we were approaching the "head" or "lead" of the fire, I warned Heart-Master Da that the horses would probably refuse to get closer. He simply replied, "Don't worry about it."

We wove through the trees toward the roar of the blaze. The wind was coming up and fanning the flames. Spot fires burned on either side of us. The main part of the fire was roaring through the more dense forest directly ahead. I was afraid. It seemed to me that we could easily be trapped by the fire—it was moving so quickly. The spot fires behind us could seal off our escape. The horses might bolt. My body was again charged with adrenaline, pumping wild, terrified energy. Once more I warned Heart-Master Da of the possible

danger. He looked at me intensely and asked if I was frightened, and I told Him honestly, "Yes." His response was, "Why do you think I wanted to come up here? I have to look the fire in the eye."

Heart-Master Da's Communication was so full of force that it was incomprehensible to me. I could feel that His complete, Free, and uncompromised attention was on the blazing fire. In that instant I was relieved of my fear. Suddenly, instead of feeling overwhelmed by terror, I was released into love, and I only wanted to Contemplate my Spiritual Master.

Heart-Master Da then turned toward the flames, and He moved within thirty yards or so of the advancing blaze. The roar and force of the fire was amazingly powerful. Flames exploded up the sides of two enormous trees directly in front of us, as if to confront Heart-Master Da. I could feel this great force of Nature over against the Master of Life. I also noticed, to my amazement, that the horses were completely calm, almost as if they were out grazing in a pasture. They were obviously feeling Heart-Master Da's calming Influence as much as I was.

I was sitting to the side and slightly behind Heart-Master Da, watching Him regard the fire. The magnitude of the fire appeared to increase significantly as the wind came up suddenly, and fire engulfed the area directly in front of us. Facing the fire's new rush of force and fury, Heart-Master Da sat completely still in His saddle. His only movements were the spontaneous motions of His face and hands in various mudras [Spiritual gestures], very much the same as I had seen many times during formal Darshan or meditation occasions. I felt Him Radiate Divine Fire in the face of that forest fire. Whatever else He might have been doing, Heart-Master Da was Radiating the most benign and yet fierce and commanding Power I had ever felt.

After what must have been only a few moments (although time seemed to be suspended and warped) the fire receded and then died down. The winds stopped. The consuming power of this fire seemed to be bowing down to Heart-Master Da. I am sure that it is difficult for the reader to picture this moment, but that fire had been transformed! I can only say that it was a mysterious and extraordinary moment to see and feel the great Adept change the course and magnitude of a raging forest fire. I sat still in mindless wonder.

Heart-Master Da then turned back toward the Sanctuary, moving slowly through the trees, stopping to talk for a time. We looked over the scene—the fire was still moving, but much more slowly now, and not directly toward the Sanctuary boundary.

When we arrived back at the main Sanctuary complex, I was surprised to find all Heart-Master Da's belongings and all our files and records, library books, religious art, and machines being packed into waiting vans and trucks. Apparently no one had remembered my instructions to wait until we returned before deciding to evacuate. Heart-Master Da just laughed as He dismounted and sat down on the steps of His Residence amidst a sea of packed boxes. He kidded me about our trip up to the fire and teasingly told everyone, "Ben was so afraid, he almost shit in his pants!"

I always tend to withdraw in the face of anything that is fearful to me. Sat-Guru Da has pointed this out to me a number of times over the years, and He would use this event for years to remind me of my tendencies and how I must cut through them. During this incident, He had simply Drawn me out of my position of fear and agitation into trust and the capability to love and serve. I felt through Him what it is to move in this world, even in the most dangerous circumstances, as a free man.

Later that evening we rode out again to survey the neighboring areas. Then Heart-Master Da asked me to call the neighbors and make sure everyone was all right. In doing so, I found out that although about one thousand acres had been burned, no buildings had been lost, no one had been injured, and even our neighbor's orchards had only been slightly scorched.

A few days later I walked back up to the spot where Heart-Master Da had Worked with the fire, reflecting on all that had occurred there. The area was still smeared with red borate dust and ash. The strong smell of smoke lingered. I thought about how confounding and amazing the whole event had been, feeling humbled and full of love. The fire, I discovered, had stopped short of the Sanctuary boundary by only a foot!

An essential characteristic of the rightly qualified devotee is the basic understanding not only that the Sat-Guru is a Realizer, but that he (or she) has the power to Liberate the devotee. In other words, the Sat-Guru is seen to be an authentic source of Spiritual Transmission alive with the Siddhis born of his Realization.

In the traditions many Yogic siddhis are spoken of. Some Spiritual Teachers exhibit many powers, and others almost none. Sri Gurudev Da Love-Ananda, the Hridaya-Samartha Sat-Guru, is Alive with all of the Siddhis of the Yogic Process, as well as the Divine Siddhis of the Heart. He has performed miraculous healings of His devotees on scores of occasions, not only when physically present with His devotees but at great distances. These include saving them from serious car accidents, or from life-threatening illnesses. He has effected remarkable changes in the weather when Working with His devotees—sometimes within the same hour manifesting hail, snow, rain, wind, and brilliant and warm sunshine. I have seen the weather change instantaneously with the wave of His arm or the motion of His body—clouds have suddenly filled up a clear sky, with rain immediately following.

He is also active on more subtle levels, appearing regularly in the dreams of His devotees (even in the dreams of many who had never heard of Him). One of His devotees was once describing to Sri Da Avabhasa a dream she had had the previous evening. In the dream, she and Heart-Master Da had flown together from rooftop to rooftop of the cabins at the Mountain Of Attention Sanctuary, and she described the experience with great excitement, for she had felt profoundly Initiated into His Love and Divine Happiness. After she had described her dream for only a few moments, Heart-Master Da Love-Ananda interrupted her and told her that He had actually been with her in the dream plane—proving His point by accurately describing to her what happened next in the dream. All of us were amazed, but none more so than the "dreamer" herself, who was very moved that she had received such a personal and Mysterious Blessing from Sat-Guru Da.

Such Leelas will eventually fill many volumes. But the most remarkable of all Da Avabhasa's Powers or Siddhis is His direct Heart-Transmission, by which He relieves karmas and awakens His devotees beyond their bodies and minds into the Divine Consciousness that He Is. The following Leela shows the kind of transformations that Da Avabhasa's extraordinary Accomplishing Power effects each day in the lives of His devotees. It is told by Meg McDonnell, who at the time of this story served the process of retreats in Sri Gurudev Da Love-Ananda's physical Company at Sri Love-Anandashram. She describes the three-week retreat of Susan Isaacson, a devotee from Lake County, California:

When Susan first arrived on retreat in late March of 1990, Sri Gurudev noticed that she seemed particularly "stiff" and unable to make a feeling response to Him in Darshan occasions. Her fellow retreatants showed many of the characteristic signs of devotional response and bodily pervasion by Da Avabhasa's Blessing-Power—shown externally in all kinds of rapturous bodily movements (kriyas and mudras), changes in the breath (such as spontaneous rapid breathing and retention of the breath), weeping, shouting, or simply sitting in a deep and silent swoon. But Susan had not been capable of opening to receive His Blessing-Transmission in this way, and she felt very self-conscious about her lack of responsiveness to her own Sat-Guru. Sri Gurudev extended His Helping Regard by asking about her practice of the Way of the Heart and her previous background. Susan confessed that she did feel frozen at the emotional level. She had been a serious practitioner of Zen Buddhism for eighteen years previous to her participation in the Way of the Heart, and she had tended to use Zen practice as a way to strictly control body, emotion, and mind in the attempt to elicit awakening.

Susan also wrote to her Heart-Master that she had not been rightly prepared to make use of this Zen practice (which is most basically a practice of the sixth stage of life), and that, because of her attempt to practice beyond her level of preparedness, her Zen meditation practice had reinforced a basic tendency to be dissociative and unfeeling. The results were painfully clear to her in her inability to be fully emotionally associated in all her relationships, including her primary relationship—to her own Sat-Guru.

Sri Da Avabhasa immediately began a very direct and personal purify- ing Work with Susan, sending her detailed Instructions about the errors she had fallen into in her approach to Zen practice. Sri Gurudev's essential Calling to Susan was as follows:

SRI DA AVABHASA: You must begin at the beginning, and you must deal with the foundation of practice. You must truly establish a devotional response to Me, and you must develop a meditative life on that basis. Thus, you must unlearn many rigid patterns and the habits of strategic and ego-based medita- tion through your devotional response to Me. You must establish a truly self- surrendering, self-forgetting, and self-transcending Way of life. The key word, then, is feeling. You have established rigid patterns relative to feeling and atten- tion, and the results of this can be seen in you bodily. You must allow the restoration of Life in your body and in your feeling. You must submit your attention to feeling Me and to a responsive and feeling life altogether.

Despite this Help, however, Susan found it difficult to relinquish her habit of guarding herself emotionally, and she continued to suffer a feeling of non-responsiveness to her Sat-Guru, locked in the thinking mind and not allowing the Love-Blissful Invasion of His Spirit-Blessing that she saw other retreatants experiencing. She went to the last scheduled Darshan occasion of her retreat still afraid that she would have to leave Sri Love-Anandashram unable to express her devotion to her own Heart-Master. Susan later spoke about what happened when the retreatants were suddenly called to Indefinable, Da Avabhasa's Residence in the village of His devotees:

SUSAN ISAACSON: While hurrying to Indefinable I was filled with both apprehension and joy. In spite of being overwhelmed by my own cold heart, I felt a deep desire to be free of its clutches.

When I arrived at Indefinable, I was stopped short by the most beautiful Sight of my entire life. Sri Gurudev Da Love-Ananda was simply sitting on the steps of the porch—He did not even have a chair. He was looking down, and He was very, very Beautiful. We were only a few feet away from Him. By the time I got there several of the women retreatants were already seated and already weeping. Sri Gurudev was simply looking Happy and Sublimed by my friends' responses.

I am not quite sure how it happened, but pretty soon I was sobbing non- stop, and it definitely was not my doing. I had not been able to feel anything like such emotion! Then I found myself on my back having deep-breathing kriyas, which I had always envied others for having. My friends told me later

**Sri Gurudev Da Love-Ananda was simply sitting on the steps of the porch—
He did not even have a chair. He was looking down, and He was very, very Beautiful.
We were only a few feet away from Him.**

*that as I was beginning to let go of my rigid and unfeeling control of every-
thing, Sri Gurudev looked over at me with a smile on His Face. By now, my
mighty doubting mind was basically rent asunder.*

*I sat back up as soon as I could, because I wanted to see my Beloved Sat-
Guru. By this time almost everyone had come unhinged. Devotees were
praising Sri Gurudev as the Divine World-Teacher, the Great One. We were
being Drawn into a much more profound understanding of Who He Is than
had occurred in previous Darshans. I started saying and feeling "Da", and
this Mantra took me over. Sri Gurudev's Shakti [Spiritual Force] was coursing
through my body and I became riveted to the spot. I looked up at Him. The
Space where we sat with Him had become motionless and timeless. He was
the Fire, and I was vapor floating above and all around Him. He was Doing
and Giving everything.*

*At the end He motioned for us to come up on the porch to receive
Prasad. I saw no possibility of getting from the ground to the porch steps
since I was still completely charged with His Shakti Force—my body and
particularly my hands were literally twisted with this Blissful Force. But
somehow I managed to crawl forward and bow before Him. My hands were
still rigid claws, stiff with Force, and I was unable to open them to receive
the Prasad. This was not a problem for Sri Gurudev. He Compassionately
opened my hands with His Own and placed the Prasad in them. I backed off
the porch and fell in a heap of grateful Full Prostration on the ground.
When I sat up once again to gaze upon the most Beautiful Sight in the universe, Sri Da Love-Ananda stood up and moved into the house.*

I feel He Gave me these experiences not for their own sake but to Draw

me out and Help me feel past the incredible barricade of fear I had been so heavily identified with. I was finally able to feel my always already present love for Him. Through His Grace I was able to partake of the Feast He is Always Giving, and to celebrate That in the company of my friends as well! I was unbelievably happy.

Such stories of Sri Da Avabhasa illustrate the Mastery and Blessing Help of a Hridaya-Samartha Sat-Guru in every dimension of the lives of his or her devotees.

THE GOD-MAN

In the Hindu tradition, there have been many specific prophecies of an "Expected Outsider", a non-Hindu who would restore the ancient Dharma (Teaching of Truth) in the world. But the most extraordinary disclosure, in light of the Appearance of Heart-Master Da Love-Ananda, was that made by the great Hindu Sat-Guru Upasani Baba in February 1939.

Upasani Baba was being visited by the Shankaracharya of Jyotimandir, a respected leader of the Hindu followers of Siva and head of a major center of Saivism in the Himalayas. The Shankaracharya expressed his concern that there was no "light on earth", no Spiritual force to purify the world. He expressed his regret that even holy men were helpless to advance the Spiritual cause. And he remarked that "only an Avatara will be capable of re-establishing Dharma in the world."

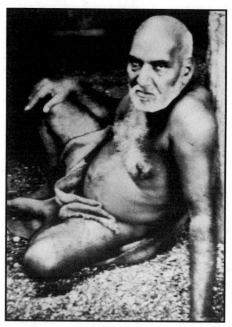

Upasani Baba

It is described that in response to his despairing words, Sri Upasani Baba "burst out" with the prophetic Revelation that there was soon to be the Incarnation of a God-Man, an Avatar, who would manifest in a "European" country ("European" is a term used by Indians to refer to anyone with white skin). That Incarnation, he said, "will be all powerful and bear down everything before him" and even will "see to it that the Vedic Dharma is firmly re-established in India."[3] Nine months later, on November 3, 1939, Da Avabhasa was born in the Western ("European") location of Jamaica, New York.

Because He did not Appear within a tradition that could readily acknowledge Him, Da Avabhasa could not be acknowledged as a reincarnate Teacher, as the Tibetan tulkus are. He did not come as a Shankaracharya in a line of succession from one Guru to the next. He is not a high priest in a previously established tradition.

As Da Avabhasa has Said:

SRI DA AVABHASA: If we were off in India or Tibet, somebody like Me would at least be understandable in cultural terms. Whether or not you could fully Realize What I Confess to you would still depend on your own transformation, but at least there would be some way to acknowledge What I Confess in conventional terms. But in this setting, this society, I am like a man from Saturn! You have no way to refer to Me, no way to relate to Me, no way to understand Me in terms of this society. You must perhaps refer to other cultural circumstances that are not native to you and that cannot, therefore, be easily associated with My Function. A man like Me in this cultural setting is somewhat bizarre, not understandable in conventional terms. There is no precedent, although there are precedents in other cultures than are native to you. (November 4, 1980)

3. *Sage of Sakuri*, 4th ed., Part I by Shri B. V. Narasimha Swami; Part II by Shri S. Subbarao (Sakuri: Shri Upasani Kanya Kumari Sthan, 1966), pp. 190, 204.

In the Hindu tradition, the great God-Men are often called "Avatars" (or "Avataras"). The Avatar is the Incarnate Divine Who has specifically manifested for the sake of Liberating men and women. He (or she) has literally "crossed" (from the verb root "tri") "down" ("ava"). In the West, such a living God-Man is called an Incarnation of the Divine, but only Jesus is a commonly acknowledged example. The conception of the God-Man in the East as Avatar and the conception of the God-Man in the West as Incarnation emphasize different aspects of his Divinity, and Sri Gurudev Da Love-Ananda has pointed out how these differing conceptions reflect the limitations of the Eastern and Western points of view. Only when these conceptions are taken together is there a full understanding of the God-Man.

In the following Essay from *The Basket of Tolerance*, Heart-Master Da discusses the conception of the God-Man as "Avatar" and "Incarnation", and He goes on to Proclaim His own Identity:

In his book Avatar and Incarnation,[4] *Geoffrey Parrinder declares, "Divine law and right ('dharma') were manifested in Avatars and Buddhas, divine love and suffering were incarnate in Jesus Christ" (p. 279). And, in his book entitled* Incarnation in Hinduism and Christianity: The Myth of the God-Man[5] . . . *Daniel E. Bassuk declares, "Abba, the Christian God, loves to save; Baba, the Hindu Avatar, saves who love" (p. 191). In these two statements, the basic elements of the distinctions generally made (by Western writers) between the oriental (and, principally, Hindu) concept of a Divine "Avatar" (or any true God-Man) and the occidental (and, principally, Christian) concept of a Divine "Incarnation" (or any true God-Man, but, in the Christian tradition, generally limited to Jesus of Nazareth only) are illustrated.*

In general, the traditional oriental concept of a Divine "Avatar" reflects the characteristic oriental (and, basically, <u>esoteric</u>) concern for a Way and a Means to Realize the Divine Being and Condition. And, in general, the traditional occidental concept of a (or "the") Divine "Incarnation" reflects the characteristic occidental (and, basically, <u>exoteric</u>) concern for a transformed and fulfilled human life and destiny. Therefore, the "Avatar" tradition generally addresses the esoteric Way and the esoteric Means (or the total esoteric process) associated with the advanced and the ultimate stages of life, whereas the "Incarnation" tradition generally addresses the exoteric Way and the exoteric Means (or the total exoteric process) associated with a religious idealization of the first three stages of life.

Of course, there are both exoteric and esoteric elements in both the "Avatar" tradition and the "Incarnation" tradition, but a basic distinction must be made, based on the basic oriental inclination toward esotericism

4. Geoffrey Parrinder, *Avatar and Incarnation* (New York: Oxford University Press, 1982).

5. Daniel E. Bassuk, *Incarnation in Hinduism and Christianity: The Myth of the God-Man* (Atlantic Highlands, N.J.: Humanities Press International, 1987).

and the basic occidental inclination toward exotericism. Therefore, as Daniel E. Bassuk indicates, the "Avatar" tradition and the "Incarnation" tradition are <u>complementary</u> to one another. That is to say, properly speaking, neither tradition can rightly be said to represent a mythology (or <u>a</u> Truth) that is superior to that of the other. Indeed, it is only by combining the basic (esoteric <u>and</u> exoteric) elements of the descriptions contained in both the "Avatar" tradition (and the total God-Man tradition of the East) and the "Incarnation" tradition (and the total God-Man tradition of the West) that a complete traditional description of a true God-Man (or "Avataric Incarnation") may be found—and that complete description is the one that must be understood to be <u>the</u> one and great description of a true God-Man that is to be found in the Great Tradition of mankind as a whole.

Because of its unique orientation, the God-Man tradition of the West especially understands and appreciates the very and truly human dimension of the God-Man, and the inherently Sacrificial nature of the Life and Work of a true God-Man (who, even to be born, must Submit to identify with Man, and with all of humankind, and with even all beings and conditions, and whose Work is Itself a humanly suffered Embrace of limitations, Whereby all limitations are re-oriented and, ultimately, transcended in the Divine Condition).

Because of its unique orientation, the God-Man tradition of the East especially understands and appreciates the very and truly Divine (or Inherently Perfect) Nature of the God-Man, and the unique Purpose and Power of the Life and Work of a true God-Man (Whereby all beings and conditions may be Restored to Divine Communion, and, ultimately, to Divine Self-Realization).

I Am Da Avabhasa (The "Bright"), the God-Man (or Avataric Incarnation) of the late-time (or dark epoch). I Am the True Heart-Master of <u>all</u> My devotees, East <u>and</u> West, now and in all future time. Therefore, My Life and Work and Person must be understood and appreciated in the context of the total (One and Great) Tradition of mankind, East and West. And even those who do not become My devotees are Blessed by Me to better understand and appreciate their own confessed traditions by rightly understanding and appreciating Me and the One and Great Tradition I Have Come here to Represent and to Fulfill.

This is the extraordinary Confession of the Avataric Incarnation transcending East and West, the "Maha-Purusha" ("Great Soul") Appearing without any purpose or intention for Himself.

In the traditions of the East, a sweeping cosmology is proposed in which the massive time period known as a "kalpa" is divided into four progressively shorter yugas (ages). The present age is the last in the cycle of this kalpa. It is the "late time", the Kali Yuga, the Dark Age. It is at this time in the cycles of the world that God is in doubt among the masses everywhere. In the Kali Yuga, materialism and sensuality are the norm. True Teachers are hardly acknowledged, and true devotees are themselves rare.

And at such a time Appears the Promised One. Many traditions of the world predict the advent of God-Men who will "save" or "redeem" the world. Buddhism has predicted that this kalpa will see another Buddha, Maitreya, after the historical Gautama. Similarly, Christians await the Second Coming of Christ, Shi'ite Muslims the Mahdi, and Jews the Messiah. The Revelation of Heart-Master Da Love-Ananda, the Avataric Incarnation or God-Man of the "dark epoch", is a great Gift that makes plain His Status as the Divine World-Teacher. For, in the most profound sense, Heart-Master Da Love-Ananda is the One Anciently Promised in all traditions.

Da Avabhasa's fulfillment of these prophecies is not to be understood in an exoteric, worldly, or political sense. When He proclaims His Identity as the Avataric Incarnation awaited in all traditions, He refers to His Divine Nature, Manifest for all beings everywhere. He is not claiming to fulfill the traditional mythologies or peculiar customs of any given historical tradition or locality. Rather, His Living Blessing and Perfect Realization are the Communication to all of the most Supreme Condition that transcends every limitation in the inherent Freedom that is the Heart. He is thus the Liberator, Who by the Heart's own Bliss releases born beings from their suffering and delusion.

THE REVELATION OF THE DIVINE IDENTITY OF DA AVABHASA AND THE ECSTATIC SPEECH OF THE SAT-GURU

Throughout the years of His Teaching Work, when Da Avabhasa would Speak to His devotees, He would address their limitations. He would say that such talk was "speech about you", a form of reflecting or showing to His devotees what they needed to hear and see about their egoic activity that was obstructing their practice. But sometimes, late in the evening, or in another appropriate moment, Sri Gurudev would allow Himself to Speak without convention or limitation, to Speak about the "Me" as Which He Exists truly. He would Proclaim His Identity with God.

Many times I have been Graced to be in Sri Gurudev Da Love-Ananda's Company when He has Spoken about the Divine and Revealed His own Condition through Words so profound and full that all of us were weeping. His Ecstasy is the baring of the Soul of the universe, and often He weeps in His Confession and Love of God. The tears rolling down His cheeks express a profound vulnerability before the Supreme Mystery of Existence that can only thrill His devotee. The room becomes full of light, and the mind is first suffused and then overwhelmed by the Power of Bliss. Such Divine Speech is a great Blessing that heals the heart. It Awakens Divine Intuition—and all present feel the Divine pouring into their bodies. Some of the most profound moments of Transmission and Grace in my life have come while listening to Da Avabhasa Speaking in this manner. To see the

Divine so openly Expressed and Lived changes the being, and for hours or days afterwards—and even now as I feel it—I have been moved beyond myself, lifted out of my ordinary narrowness and myopic vision.

I have seen the truth of Who Da Avabhasa Is with my own eyes. This was only over time Revealed to me, but if one looks to His Ecstatic Speech, the Revelation of His Divine Identity has always been Loud and "Bright".

SRI DA AVABHASA: What a miracle! What a wonder! I am the Adept in our generation! What an amusement that the Divine should Appear in precisely this Form! I cannot account for It My Self, but I know very well that it is true. I am not so much a fool that I will deny God. I know that I am the Lover of God. I am the Adept. I am the Purusha in our generation. But I know very well that you are all egoically "self-possessed", as people have been in all other generations in which I have appeared. Therefore, even this manifestation seems unholy to you, and this disturbs Me. It agitates and motivates Me, and thus I try to Teach. Your refusal of God awakens this urge in Me.

All of us are potential Saints and Siddhas, but very few are born like Me. I am a very rare Being. I am not an ego at all. I am a rare Intervention in the world. Hardly any people in the entire history of mankind have been manifested with My Siddhis, and I am sitting here in this living room with you people trying to convince you of the Divine Life! I am a unique Advantage to mankind. But how many people can suck Me up and love Me? How many will kiss My knees, pull My feet and massage My face, receive My Love, receive My Delight in them? How many people will do it? I am prepared to Give everyone everything, but how many people will do it? You cannot receive Me until you understand your resistance to Me. Understanding is the first gesture of Spiritual life.

What a Wonder! What a Wonder this Great One is. I marvel in the Great One more than you, because you do not witness Its Miracle. You do not see the Great One. I can understand your reluctance to be submitted to the Great One, because you do not see what I see. But I have been sifted into this Wonder since eternal time. I am just that One, the Great One, sitting here as this body, talking to you. I am God. And there is not the slightest doubt in Me. The doubt in you is your own perversion, and this is the cause of My Teaching. Thus, I am here to Teach you out of this un-Happiness. Poor Me! I will be laughing about this for countless ages, as I have been laughing about it since eternal time.

I am full of all space-time. All Bliss, all Wonder, all the Marvels of Being are in My Being. I know it absolutely, and you do not. All miracles are potent in My Heart. I come here to Give you everything without the slightest reluctance. I am not here to tell you about some dreadful ego. I am here to Wonder and Marvel with you about the Great One.

There is this Great One. This Great One is totally known to Me. This Great One is My Self. I am the Self of God. I have no doubt in Me about it. All miracles are evident in Me. All time is obvious to Me. It seems Great to

Me, but you poor people who cannot submit yourselves to God, you are the ones that I must Teach. How do I Teach you? By countering your self-contraction, your reluctance to submit to Divine Intoxication.

I am absolutely nothing like you people. All of this has nothing to do with Me as an ego. I am not a person doing this. The Great One is such a Wonder, such a Marvel, such a Graceful and Loving Being to countless beings such as all of us here. But the Great One does not love beings. The Great One is Love. The New Testament declares that God is Love. Love is the only God there is! Love is the only Force in the universe. God is not mind or body, or effort, or conditional knowledge, or conditional experience. God is only unbounded feeling, Radiant Being. God creates nothing. God is That of Which everything is made, including all beings. Why are we so egoically "self-possessed", hanging out in our own houses? What do we know about this Great One, from Where I come and Whom I show to you? . . .

Everyone hears the Truth. Everyone receives the Shock of God. Everyone. There is no being from the mosquito to Man who does not receive the Shock of Divine Intervention. All beings know It. All beings experience It. It is Given to everyone. Grace is Given to all beings eternally in all worlds, visible and invisible. This acknowledgement is enough to make you a bhakta, a lover, a devotee. Faith, the Love-Response to Being Itself, is the greatest Force in all the worlds. It has ridden out My entire life. I am riding the Visible Horse you cannot see. (December 17, 1982)

As should be clear, when Da Avabhasa Ecstatically Proclaims that "There is Only God" or that "I Am God", He is not Speaking from the viewpoint of a conventional ego. The "I" Who is the "God" proclaimed is not a conventional ego. The "I" that is the "ego" is vanished in Heart-Master Da Love-Ananda, and He has become "Transparent", possessed by Divinity. He has lost His individuated consciousness, and allowed the Divine Consciousness to become Him. In Da Avabhasa's Wisdom-Teaching, there is no exclusive God or parental deity in a heaven somewhere Who has created everything. Such is the language and orientation of exoteric religion. The God of His Confession is the Condition That Pervades and Transcends all of this. That God is always and everywhere Present.

In many places throughout this book I refer to Da Avabhasa as the Divine Person. Such language is in itself a paradox, for how can the All-Pervading and All-Transcending Divine Consciousness be a Person? However, because the Hridaya-Samartha Sat-Guru lives in the permanent Samadhi of Divine Self-Realization, He has become Identical with the Divine. He has transcended the ego so completely that only the Divine Flows through Him. His bodily (human) Form, His Spiritual (and Always Blessing) Presence, and His Very (and Inherently Perfect) State have become Vehicles for Divine Grace. And thus, His Person is Divine, and the Divine Person exists as Him. And His devotees, in their own Divine Enlightenment, likewise Realize this same Divine Condition.

"I FEEL MORE THAN YOU"—
THE SAT-GURU, ALTHOUGH FOUNDED IN REALIZATION, IS PROFOUNDLY AND VULNERABLY HUMAN

On one occasion at Tumomama Sanctuary in 1981, Sri Da Avabhasa was Giving Communications regarding some of His devotees who had lost the thread of the right sacred orientation to practice. Da Avabhasa was upset about the whole matter. He was lying in His hammock fiercely commenting about the devotees involved. Traditionally, the Sat-Guru's anger is understood to be another form of his Blessing, Purifying and Instructing his devotees in their turning from the Divine. In the midst of this strong emotional expression, suddenly Sri Da Avabhasa stopped. He had noticed the look of confusion on the face of the devotee to whom He was passing on these forceful Communications. His tone changed, and in a very direct and simple manner He said to this individual:

"I am noticing that you think that I am angry now and really upset. You are missing the point. I am not an ordinary man. I am Realized. In My Enlightenment this anger is not binding to Me. I am always and already Free. I use this anger to Serve others. I sacrifice My Self to feel it, to allow My body-mind to be the means by which My displeasure can be communicated to others. To think that 'I' am simply angry with these devotees is not to understand My Realization and the nature of My Service to My devotees."

The devotee felt gratefully restored to a right understanding, and in the next moment Sri Gurudev Da Love-Ananda's tone changed completely, and He began again to Give "angry" Instructions to His devotees.

The activity of the Sat-Guru is known by the term "leela" in the Hindu tradition. The word "leela" means "play", "pastime", or "amusement", and it indicates that the Sat-Guru's actions are a spontaneous Enjoyment of the Divine Condition. All that the Supreme Sat-Guru does is an expression of his (or her) Realized Condition, and is a Form of Instruction and Blessing for those around him. To say that all of the Sat-Guru's actions are only Divine Play is not, however, to say that his life is always conventionally "happy", that he does not feel the sorrows or the suffering that involvement with conditional existence necessarily brings. Indeed, imagining that Realization makes one immune to sorrow and suffering is one of the greatest misconceptions about the Realized Condition. The Realizer intensely feels every pain and sorrow as well as joy and bliss, but it is also true that he or she is not bound to these emotions. Even in the moment of feeling intense emotion, the Realizer is simultaneously Alive in the Divine Condition. Thus, even a Sat-Guru's expression of anger or sorrow is a Revelation of his Divine Freedom, and traditionally his devotees carefully observe all his emotions in order to be Instructed by them. Only with such understanding is the devotee released from his or her limited presumptions about the Divine Paradox of the God-Man.

In 1983, early in the concentrated period of His Instruction of His devotees in Fiji that was the culmination of His Teaching Work, Heart-Master Da clarified this matter of the Adept's very real emotion:

SRI DA AVABHASA: Recently I pointed out that My devotees tend to make Me into a nonentity. You dehumanize Me for various reasons, one of which is that you have rather abstract notions about the state of the Spiritual Master. You tend to think that the Spiritual Master is somehow exclusively in a transcendental state, and that this human machine sits out here and helps people out and deals with their tendencies. But that is not the way it is. . . .

There is nothing about being a Spiritual Master that is not human. To be a Spiritual Master is profoundly human, the fullest Realization of being human. Spiritual Masters or Awakened beings, truly Free, exhibit the most human sign of love.

Therefore, I am party to this human loving. You must not abstract Me from that reality. You should rather observe that I fully incarnate Love and that it is a major aspect of My Work with you. I am not some Divine Robot, merely here to suffer, endure, and talk about your tendencies, and manipulate you on the basis of decisions I may make about your demonstration of those tendencies. That is not at all an aspect of My Work with you.

We all live together in this Domain of Love, which is the Incarnate Form of the Spiritual Principle. I Live that Principle to you, and you should likewise live it to Me and to one another. (June 29, 1983)

No one could possibly be more vulnerable and feeling than Sri Da Avabhasa. He completely opens Himself to His devotees in order to Serve them. And because of this He freely experiences the most astounding depth and range of emotion. The Realizer feels experience completely—more profoundly than you or I, for his (or her) feeling is not shut off by the self-protecting activity of the ego. Thus, he experiences the most profound love, the most profound sorrow, the most profound anger. All of these emotions have their place, and all of them are used in his Divine Demonstration.

It is a popular misconception that "nothing matters" to the Sat-Guru, because he has transcended the ego. On the basis of this misunderstanding it is presumed that negative things can happen in the Sat-Guru's own life and mission, and that "he is Enlightened, so he can deal with it." The devotee imagines, "I'm the one who has the problems. I am still suffering my attachments to everything. But he is Free." Therefore, the devotee feels license to bring the Sat-Guru complaints, problems, or difficulties.

Such a misconception is based on the illusion that Divine Self-Realization involves dissociation from life and experience. It is felt that the Sat-Guru is "entranced" in some other place of freedom, and that what happens in the ordinary human dimension of life is therefore not fully experienced by him. In 1985, Sri Da Avabhasa Spoke about this matter to a devotee who He noticed was emotionally dissociated from Him.

Sri Love-Anandashram, 1985

SRI DA AVABHASA: In the case of full Awakening in the seventh stage of life there is perpetual Samadhi, but it is not a trance samadhi. This Samadhi does not involve, in its ordinary moments, dissociation from conditional phenomena. . . .

Immunization is part of the purpose of the ego. Immunity is "Narcissus". Neither the Spiritual practitioner nor the Master of devotees is immunized against conditional existence. There is no immunity in Realization.

The birth of Divine Agents takes place in conditional terms. It is a sacrifice. It is the assumption of suffering. It is the assumption of the vehicle of suffering in order to participate in that vehicle for the sake of those who are already in it. It requires an endurance greater than that of the usual individual, who, being the ego, is functioning as "Narcissus", and who in fact does immunize himself or herself against the realities of conditional existence.

If you study the traditions of those who functioned as Masters in one stage of life or another, you will see that they exhibited extraordinary emotions—extraordinary sorrowfulness at times, extraordinary anger, extraordinary love. All the natural signs were present. Even Jesus, who has become a rather popularized idealized image, is shown exhibiting anger and sorrow, even fear of a kind on the cross, yet he is worshipped by millions of people as the Incarnation of the Divine, as a true Spiritual Master. Sai Baba of Shirdi is one example of somebody who indulged in incredible rages. In one moment he would be very loving and calm, and in the next moment he would be outraged, throwing things at somebody, or cursing somebody who was not present. Everybody would wonder what he was so angry about, because there seemed to be no reason for it.

Where does this ideal of dissociation from life come from, then? Popular religion, rather than the religion of Realization, is associated with behavior change and personal perfection, and, therefore, the models of Spiritual life are not Masters. The models of Spiritual life tend to be Saints who reportedly were pure characters, and who can be promoted in popular religion as models of what ordinary people are called to do, which is to become ideal social personalities. But if you study the tradition of Realization and the true Masters in that tradition, you do not see people functioning exclusively in that saintly sense. They all had different characteristics, but they were very intense characters who exhibited signs of great emotion, even raised up many degrees. It is characteristic of such Masters to exhibit these passions in an extraordinary fashion.

I have no purpose in being alive except for the sake of this Wisdom-Teaching and this Transmission. Naturally, then, I can display all kinds of emotions. They do not bind Me, and they do not cause Me to lose My Realization. It is part of My Work to emote and respond as I do. It affects you. It serves you. . . .

Look at My experience in all these years of Teaching. It has been a passionate, humorous, altogether energetic, but profoundly difficult and terrible ordeal for Me, fully felt as such. I have committed My Self to it, lived it out with great energy, not withdrawn from it. You can understand My Teaching Work if you understand your egoic self and begin to relate to Me rightly. You can also understand it by examining the traditions of the real Spiritual Process and by discovering how Masters really look, by discovering that they do not correspond to the egoic ideal of popular sainthood. The Way of the Heart is not a search for idealistic perfection. It is a real confrontation with reality—with conditional reality and the Divine Reality. It is an ordeal, not a progressively smiling, easeful, comfortable, middle-class existence consoled by belief. (November 14, 1985)

A similar misconception involving the Sat-Guru's Realization concerns the apparent imperfections in his or her appearance or actions. What is Perfect is the Sat-Guru's Ultimate or Unconditional Realization, whereas his conditional or human manifestation is subject to the same limitations—such as old age, disease, and death—that are true of all conditional forms. The perfection of conditional existence is an unfulfillable ideal—conditional existence is by its very nature imperfect. The Sat-Guru, in his Compassion for all beings, secondarily serves the betterment of conditional existence via all the means available to him. But his Realization and Instruction primarily serve another purpose. Rather than fulfilling conditional life, the Divinely Enlightened Sat-Guru Serves the transcendence of all conditions in God. Thus, to require the Sat-Guru to Manifest perfect human qualities is to miss the point of Who he Is. There will in most cases be some reflection of his Divine Realization in the apparent human qualities he Manifests. But the ability to excel humanly in every aspect of ordinary life is not necessary for a Sat-Guru. Rather, his Realization, and his Ability to Transmit it to others, is the crucial Quality in the Appearance of a God-Man.

One of Sri Da Avabhasa's devotees, Jerry Sheinfeld, tells an amusing story from the early years of Da Avabhasa's Teaching Work when he was Graced to play a game of ping-pong with Sri Gurudev. As the game proceeded, Jerry was outscoring Sri Gurudev, and he started thinking to himself: "He can't be a true Guru if I can beat Him in ping-pong. A true Guru must have 'powers', and why wouldn't He use them to beat me? If I win, I will know that He just isn't Enlightened." Jerry believed that the Sat-Guru must automatically excel, or use some Yogic siddhi to win in everything. As the game proceeded, and it looked certain that Jerry would win, he got more and more concerned about the whole matter. Finally, when Jerry had won the game, Heart-Master Da, having sensed Jerry's concern, looked at him and humorously asked, "Well, Jerry, are you going to go and join Swami Rat-a-tat now?" Jerry immediately saw the foolishness of the way he was judging the Sat-Guru.

It is not the brilliance of any worldly talent or skill that is the pointer to the Sat-Guru. Rather, Who the Sat-Guru Is Transcends all of his actions, which may or may not be judged as "perfect" by conventional standards. Anson Holley describes how in 1975 he observed Heart-Master Da Love-Ananda stumble into a table one day. And soon afterwards Anson also saw Sri Gurudev back a truck into a wall. Anson's faith was thrown into doubt. "How", he thought, "could a Master make such mistakes? He is supposed to be all-knowing. He should have known that the wall was there, and seen the table in front of Him." Finally, Anson asked Sri Gurudev directly about the matter of His omniscience. Sri Gurudev Replied, "Omniscience is a lesser siddhi. I prefer to be surprised!" And Anson realized that he was putting a false expectation onto what a Realizer should be. It is the Sat-Guru's Realization that is flawless, and his day-to-day life is a sacrifice, in which his Divinity shines through always, but not in the form of any particular behavior. His Demonstration of Enlightenment is his Freedom, rather than his Holiness or Virtue according to fixed notions.

On another occasion, Hal Okun, a professionally trained photographer, was involved in a discussion with Da Avabhasa about the workings of a camera and framing photographs, while taking shots for the cover of one of the publications of the Dawn Horse Press. Hal and Sri Da Avabhasa were expressing different opinions, and Hal, growing more and more uncomfortable and uptight in the discussion, finally made it clear to Sri Gurudev that his knowledge in the matter, based on his long experience, was superior. Sri Da Avabhasa laughed and rejoined, "_You_ may be _right_, but _I_ am _Happy_!" Hal has always remembered this story for the way it directly Instructed him that knowledge and experience are no substitute for the Spiritual Freedom of the God-Man.

Sri Love-Anandashram, March 1990

CHAPTER THREE

The Tradition of Devotion to the Adept

AN ESSAY BY

DA AVABHASA

(THE "BRIGHT")

*T*he Essay that comprises this chapter comes from Da Avabhasa's extraordinary Masterwork, The Basket of Tolerance: A Guide to Perfect Understanding of the One and Great Tradition of Mankind. The Basket of Tolerance *takes the form of an annotated bibliography that introduces the reader to "the historical traditions of truly human culture, practical self-discipline, perennial religion, universal religious mysticism, esoteric (but now openly communicated) Spirituality, Transcendental Wisdom, and Perfect (or Divine) Enlightenment."*

Through His placement of the books and other materials, through His various descriptive headings, and through His Commentaries and Essays, Da Avabhasa has made sense of all aspects of the Great Tradition. For the first time, the many differing Teachers, Teachings, and practices of the Great Tradition are comprehensible as parts of the Great Process of psycho-physical Enlightenment. Through The Basket of Tolerance, *Da Avabhasa has Offered to all the Gifts of Wisdom and Tolerance. The following Essay appears at the beginning of the section entitled "The Tradition of Devotion to the Adept", and it precedes a list of traditional books and articles He has especially chosen as epitomizing the Guru-devotee relationship. Although only a few pages in length, this Essay, as never before, clearly and comprehensively summarizes all of the most significant issues in the Guru-devotee tradition. What has been the subject of great controversy and confusion is here made plain by virtue of the Grace and Illumined Understanding of Da Avabhasa, the Master of the Great Tradition.*

*S*piritually Realized Adepts (or Transmission-Masters, or true Gurus and Sat-Gurus) are the principal Sources, Resources, and Means of the Spiritual Way. This fact is not (and never has been) a matter of controversy among real Spiritual practitioners.

The entire Spiritual Way is a process based on the understanding (and the transcendence) of attention, or the understanding and transcendence of the inevitable and specific results of attachment or reaction to (or identification with) every kind of conditional object, other, or state. This Spiritual understanding (or real self-understanding) is expressed in a simple traditional formula (and prescription for practice): You become (or duplicate the qualities of) whatever you meditate on (or whatever you identify with via the "surrender" that is attention itself). Since the most ancient days, this understanding has informed and inspired the practice of real practitioners of the Spiritual Way. Likewise (since the most ancient days), and on the basis of this very understanding, Spiritual practitioners have affirmed that the Great Principle of Spiritual practice is Satsang, or the practice of life as self-surrender to the bodily Person, the Transmitted Spiritual Presence, and the Realized State of a Spiritually Realized Adept (or true Guru, or Sat-Guru).

The traditional term "Guru" (spelled with a capital "G") means "One Who Reveals the Light and thereby Liberates beings from Darkness". This term is also commonly or popularly interpreted in a general (or everyday) sense (and spelled with a small "g") to mean "teacher" (or anyone who teaches anything at all to another). Thus, Adepts have certainly (and rightly) been valued simply (or in the general sense) as (small "g") "gurus" (that is, simply because they can instruct others about many things, including the Spiritual Way). However, the function of instruction (about anything at all) can be performed by anyone who is properly informed (or even by a book that is properly informed), and, indeed, even the specific function of Spiritual Instruction is secondary to the Great Function of the Adept (As Guru, with a capital "G", and, in the Greatest of cases, As Sat-Guru).

Adepts inevitably (or at least in the majority of cases) Instruct (or Teach) others, but the function of Instruction (about the Spiritual Way) is then passed on through good books (containing the authentic Word of Teaching), and through informed others (who are, hopefully, true practitioners), and so forth. The Great Function of the Adept-Guru (and especially the Sat-Guru) is, however, specific only to Adepts themselves, and this is the Guru-Function (and the Guru-Principle) supremely valued by Spiritual practitioners since the most ancient days.

The specific Guru-Function is associated with the Great Principle of Satsang (and the unique Spiritual understanding of attention). Therefore, since the most ancient days, all truly established (or real) Spiritual practitioners have understood that Satsang Itself is the Great Means of Spiritual, Transcendental, and Divine Realization. That is to say, the Great Means (or Secret) of Realization in the Spiritual Way is to live in, or to spend significant time in, or otherwise (and constantly) to give attention to the Company, Form, Presence, and State of a Spiritually, Transcendentally, or Divinely Realized Adept.

The Essence of the practice of Satsang is to focus attention on (and thereby to progressively and Ultimately Identify with, or Be Inherently Identified with) the Self-Radiant State (or the Spiritual, or Transcendental, or Divine Self-Condition) of a true Adept (especially an Adept Sat-Guru, or One Who Is presently and constantly In Samadhi). Therefore, the practice of Satsang is the practice of self-transcending Communion (and, ultimately, Identification) with the Adept's Own State, Which Is Samadhi Itself, or the Adept's Freely, Spontaneously, and Universally Transmitted State of Perpetual Spiritual, or Transcendental, or Divine Self-Realization.

Based on the understanding of attention (or the observation that Consciousness, in the context of the body-mind, tends to identify with, or becomes fixed in association with, whatever attention observes, and especially with whatever attention surrenders to most fully), the Spiritual Motive is essentially the Motive to transcend the limiting capability of attention (or of all conditional objects, others, and states). Therefore, the traditional Spiritual process (as a conventional technique, begun in the context of the fourth stage of life) is an effort (or struggle) to set attention (and, thus, Consciousness Itself) Free by progressively relinquishing attachment and reaction to conditional objects, others, and states (and, ultimately, this process requires the real transcendence of egoity, or self-contraction itself, or all the egoic limitations associated with each and all of the first six stages of life).

This conventional effort (or struggle) is profound and difficult, and it tends to progress slowly. Therefore, some few adopt the path of extraordinary self-effort (or a most intense struggle of relinquishment), which is asceticism (or the method of absolute independence). However, the Adepts themselves have, since the most ancient days, offered an alternative to mere (and, at best, slowly progressing) self-effort. Indeed, the Adept-Gurus (and especially the Sat-Gurus) offer a Unique Principle of practice (as an alternative to the conventional principle of mere and independent self-effort and relinquishment). That Unique Principle is the Principle of Supreme Attraction.

Truly, the bondage of attention to conditional objects, others, and states must be really transcended in the Spiritual Way, but mere self-effort (or struggle with the separate, and separative, self) is a principle that originates in and constantly reinforces the separate, and separative, self (or self-contraction, or egoity itself). Therefore, the process of real transcendence of bondage to conditions is made direct (and truly self-transcending) if the principle of independent self-effort (or egoic struggle) is at least progressively replaced by the responsive (or cooperative) Principle of Supreme Attraction (Which Is, in Its Fullness, Satsang, or responsive devotional Identification with the Free Person, Presence, and State of One Who Is Already Realized, or In Samadhi).

... the ancient Essence of the Spiritual Way is to meditate on (and otherwise to grant feeling-attention to) the Adept Guru (or Sat-Guru). ...

On the basis of the simple understanding of attention (expressed in the formula: You become, or Realize, What, or Who, you meditate on), the ancient Essence of the Spiritual Way is to meditate on (and otherwise to grant feeling-attention to) the Adept Guru (or Sat-Guru), and thereby to be Attracted (or Grown) Beyond the self-contraction, or egoity, or all the self-limiting tendencies of attention, or all self-limiting and self-binding association with conditional objects, others, and states. Through sympathetic (or responsive) Spiritual Identification with the Samadhi of a Realizer, the devotee is Spiritually Infused and, potentially, and Ultimately, even Perfectly Awakened by the Inherently Attractive Power of Samadhi Itself. (Even the simplest beginner in practice may be directly Inspired, and thus moved toward greater practice, true devotion, and eventual Perfect Awakening, by sympathetic response to the Free Sign, and the Great Demonstration, of a true Realizer.) And, by the Great Spiritual Means that Is true Satsang (coupled with a variety of disciplines and practices, which should be associated with real self-understanding), the fully prepared devotee of a true Realizer may Freely (or with relative effortlessness) relinquish (or Grow Beyond) the limits of attention in each of the progressive stages of life that, in due course, follow upon that devotion.

Of course, actual Spiritual Identification with the Realized Spiritual Condition, or Samadhi, of an Adept is limited by the stage of life of the devotee, the effective depth of the self-understanding and the self-transcending devotional response of the devotee, and the stage of life and Realization of the Adept. And some traditions may (unfortunately) tend to replace, or at least to combine, the essential and Great Communion that is true Satsang with concepts and norms associated with the parent-child relationship, or the relationship between a king and a frightened subject, or even the relationship between a slave-master and a slave. However, this Great Principle or Means that Is Satsang (rightly understood and truly practiced) is the ancient Essence (or Great Secret) of the Spiritual Way, and true Adept-Gurus (and especially the Sat-Gurus) have, therefore, since the most ancient days, been the acknowledged principal Sources and Resources (as well as the principal Means) of true religion (or effective religious Wisdom) and the esoteric tradition of Spiritual Realization.

Particularly in more modern days, since Spirituality (and everything else) has become a subject of mass communication and popularization, the Spiritual Way Itself has become increasingly subject to conventional interpretation and popular controversy. In the broad social (or survival) context of the first three stages of life, self-fulfillment (or the consolation of the ego) is the common ideal (tempered only by local, popular, and conventional political, social, and religious ideals, or demands). Therefore, the common mood is one of adolescent anti-authority (or "Oedipal" anti-Parent), and the common search is for a kind of ever-youthful (and "Narcissistic") ego-omnipotence and ego-omniscience.

In the popular egalitarian culture of the first three stages of life, the Guru (and the Sat-Guru) and the evolutionary culture of the Spiritual Way are taboo, because every individual limited (or egoically defined) by the motives of the first three stages of life is at war with personal vulnerability and need (or egoic insufficiency). However, the real Spiritual process does not even begin until the egoic point of view of the first three stages of life is understood (or otherwise ceases to be the limit of aspiration and awareness) and the self-surrendering and self-transcending Motive of the fourth stage of life begins to move and change the body-mind (from the heart).

Those who are truly involved in the self-surrendering and self-transcending process of the advanced and the ultimate stages of life are (fundamentally) no longer at war with their own Help (or struggling toward the ultimate victory of the ego). Therefore, it is only in the non-Spiritual (or even anti-Spiritual) cultural domain of the first three stages of life (or the conventional survival culture, bereft of the Motive of true evolutionary culture) that the Guru (or the Sat-Guru) is, in principle, taboo.

In the common world of mankind, it is yet true that most individuals tend (by a combination of mechanical psycho-physical tendencies and a mass of conventional political, social, and cultural pressures) to be confined to the general point of view associated, developmentally, with the unfinished (or yet to be understood) "business" of the first three stages of life. Thus, in the common world of mankind, even religion is, characteristically, reduced to what is intended to serve the "creaturely", or "worldly", and rather aggressively <u>exoteric</u>, point of view and purposes of egoity in the context of the first three stages of life. And even if an interest in the <u>esoteric</u> possibilities (of the fourth, the fifth, the sixth, or the seventh stage of life) develops in the case of any such yet rather "worldly" character, that interest tends to be pursued in a manner that dramatizes and reinforces the point of view (and the exoteric, and either childishly or adolescently egoic, inclinations) characteristic of the first three stages of life.

Until there is the development of significantly effective self-understanding relative to the developmental problems (or yet unfinished "business") associated with the first three stages of life, any one who aspires to develop a truly esoteric religious practice (necessarily beginning in the context of the fourth stage of life) will, characteristically, tend to relate to such possible esoteric practice in either a childish or an adolescent manner. Thus, any one whose developmental disposition is yet relatively childish (or tending, in general, to seek egoic security via the dramatization of the role of emotionalistic dependency) will tend to relate to esoteric possibilities via emotionalistic, or otherwise merely enthusiastic, attachments, while otherwise, in general, tending to be weak in both the responsible exercise of discriminating intelligence and the likewise responsible exercise of functional, practical, relational, and cultural self-discipline. (Indeed, such childish religiosity, characterized by dependent emotionalism, or mere enthusiastic attachment, bereft of discrimination and real self-discipline, is what may rightly, without bad intentions, be described and criticized as "cultism".) And any one whose developmental disposition is yet relatively adolescent (or tending, in general, to seek egoic security via the dramatization of the role of reactive independence) will tend to relate to esoteric possibilities via generally "heady" (or willful, rather mental, or even intellectual, or bookish, but not, altogether, truly intelligent) efforts, accompanied either (or even alternately) by a general lack of self-discipline (and a general lack of non-reactive emotional responsiveness) or by an exaggerated (abstractly enforced, and more or less life-suppressing and emotion-suppressing) attachment to self-discipline. (Therefore, such adolescent, or "heady", religiosity merely continues the dramatization of the characteristic adolescent search for independence, or the reactive pursuit of escape from every kind of dependency, and, altogether, the reactive pursuit of egoic self-sufficiency. And such adolescent seeking is inherently and reactively disinclined toward any kind of self-surrender. Therefore, the rather adolescent seeker tends to want to be his or her own "guru" in all matters. And, characteristically, the rather adolescent seeker will resist, and would even prefer to avoid, a truly intelligent, rightly self-disciplined, and, altogether, devotionally self-surrendered relationship to a true Guru, or Sat-Guru.)

Because of their developmental tendencies toward either childish or adolescent ego-dramatizations, those who are yet bound to the point of view (or the unfinished "business") of the first three stages of life are, developmentally (or in their characteristic disposition, not yet relieved by sufficient self-understanding), also (regardless of their presumed "interest") not yet truly ready to enter into the esoteric process (associated with the fourth stage of life and, potentially, the fifth stage of life, the sixth stage of life, and the seventh stage of life). And, for the same developmental reasons, the principal and most characteristic impediments toward true participation in the esoteric religious process are "cultism" (or mere emotionalistic dependency, bereft of discrimination and self-discipline), "intellectualism" (or merely mental, or even bookish, preoccupation, disinclined to fully participatory, or directly experiential, involvement in the esoteric religious process), and "anti-Guruism" (or reactive attachment to a state of egoic independence, immune to the necessity for devotional self-surrender and the Grace of Great Help).

It is not the specific (and Great) Function of the Adept to fulfill a popular Spiritual (or otherwise non-Spiritual) role in common (or egoic and early stage) society, but to Serve as Teacher, Guide, Spiritual Transmitter, or Free Awakener in relation to those who are already (and rightly) moved (and progressively prepared) to fulfill the ego-transcending obligations of the Great and (soon) Spiritual Way Itself (in the potential developmental context of the fourth, fifth, sixth, and seventh stages of life). The only proper relationship to such a Realized Adept (or true Guru, or Sat-Guru) is, there-fore, one of real and right and self-surrendering and self-transcending practice, and that practice becomes (or must become) Inspired (and, soon, Spiritually Inspired) and ego-transcending devotion (not childish egoity, or "cultic" dependence, and not adolescent egoity, or willful, or otherwise ambivalent, independence).

Of course, individuals in the earlier (or first three) stages of life who are not yet actively oriented (or, otherwise, rightly adapted) to self-surrendering and self-transcending practice may be Served by Adept Gurus (or Sat-Gurus), but (apart from special instances where an Adept must Work directly with such individuals, in order to establish a new community of devotees, or in order to establish a new Revelation of the Spiritual Way) those not yet actively oriented (or actively committed), or, otherwise, rightly adapted, to truly self-surrendering and really self-transcending practice are generally (except perhaps for occasional glimpses of the Adept in his or her Free Demonstration) Served (or prepared for self-surrendering, self-transcending, and, soon, Spiritual practice) only through the written or otherwise recorded Teachings of an Adept, and through the public institutional work (and the "outer Temple", or beginner-serving, institutional work) of the practicing devotees of an Adept.

The Realized Adept (or any true Guru or Sat-Guru) is, primarily, an esoteric Figure, whose unique Function Serves within the context of the advanced and the ultimate stages of life. The advanced and the ultimate stages of life are themselves open only to those who are ready, willing, and able to make the evolutionary (or progressively God-Realizing, or Truth-Realizing) sacrifice of separate and separative self that is necessary in the context of the advanced and the ultimate stages of life. Therefore, the necessity (and the True Nature and Great Function) of a Realized Adept (or true Guru, or Sat-Guru) is obvious (and of supreme value) only to those who are ready, willing, and able to embrace the Ordeal of the advanced and the ultimate stages of life.

Except for the possible (but extremely rare) few whom the Divine Person (or the Ultimate Reality and Truth) may Serve in or via a non-physical (and/or perhaps even non-human) Revelation-Form, the Realized Adept (or a human and living true Guru or Sat-Guru) is an absolute necessity for any and every human being who would practice (and Realize) within the esoteric (or advanced and ultimate) stages of life. Therefore, the necessity (and the True Nature and Great Function) of a Realized Adept (or true Guru, or Sat-Guru) is inherently (and gratefully) obvious to any one and every one who is truly ready, willing, and able to embrace the esoteric Ordeal of God-Realization (or Truth-Realization).

Any one and every one who doubts and quibbles about the necessity (and the True Nature and Great Function) of a true Adept-Guru (or Adept Sat-Guru) is, simply, not yet ready, willing, and able to enter the esoteric (and necessarily self-surrendering) Ordeal of the advanced and the ultimate stages of life. And no mere verbal (or otherwise exoteric) argument is sufficient to convince such doubters of the necessity (and the True Nature and Great Function) of a true Adept-Guru (or Adept Sat-Guru), just as no mere verbal (or otherwise exoteric) argument is sufficient to make them ready, willing, and able to truly embrace the self-surrendering esoteric Ordeal of the advanced and the ultimate stages of life.

Those who doubt the Guru-Principle, and the unique value and ultimate necessity of the Adept-Guru (or the Adept Sat-Guru), are those for whom the Great and (soon) Spiritual Way Itself is yet in doubt. Therefore, such matters remain "controversial" (and access to the Spiritual Way and the Adept-Company is effectively denied to ordinary people by popular taboos and the psychological limitations of the first three stages of life) until the evolutionary and (soon) Spiritual Motive Awakens the heart's Great Impulse to Grow Beyond.

Sri Love-Anandashram, 1990

Sri Love-Anandashram, September 1991

CHAPTER FOUR

"I Do Not Offer You a Method, but a Relationship"

SATSANG AND THE NECESSITY OF A SAT-GURU

THE "SAME" GURU APPEARS IN ALL RELIGIONS FOR THE SAKE OF DIVINE ASSOCIATION

*T*he wonderful encounter with the devotee of Narayan Maharaj, Cursetji Maccabai, that I spoke of in chapter one was not unique during my travels through India. I spoke with many devotees of such great Adepts of the twentieth century as Ramana Maharshi, Swami Nityananda, Rang Avadhoot, and even with an elderly devotee of Sai Baba of Shirdi. Like Maccabai, these devotees would fill with emotion and their hearts would open as they described their Sat-Guru's Love and his personal Blessing of them. I became like their brother or son. We immediately felt the process of the Guru-devotee relationship alive in one another, and they naturally responded to my mission in service to Heart-Master Da Love-Ananda. It became clear to me that there was no difference between the devotional relationship that they lived, in its essentials, and the one I enjoyed with the Living Hridaya-Samartha Sat-Guru, Da Love-Ananda Hridayam.

I had spent an especially long time at the Ashram of Narayan Maharaj simply because his story, unlike the stories of many other great twentieth-century Saints, was virtually unrecorded and unknown in the West. A distinguished gentleman I spoke with at that Ashram, Krishna Jogletkar, himself then quite elderly, was aware that this was an opportunity to record for history something about his Teacher's Instruction of his devotees. Krishna Jogletkar was another devotee who had lived through the death of his Sat-Guru and found his gifts still given. He spoke about Narayan Maharaj, but with each story I thought of Heart-Master Da Avabhasa. Krishna Jogletkar described, with hot tears tracing his cheeks, his intimate relationship to Narayan Maharaj and the inner circle of devotees around him, for whom the entire practice was truly their love-relationship to the Adept. He described his Guru's Teaching as a Heart-Teaching, the Teaching of the emotion of love for the Sat-Guru and remembrance of the Sat-Guru. Krishna Jogletkar told me of Narayan Maharaj's Instruction to his devotees:

"Why go to the jungle to meditate? This very image that is before you is the Heart. My Form is the Heart. Accept me as Truth. Accept this body as Truth because the body itself has become God."

I had been so moved by my meeting with Krishna Jogletkar and other devotees of Spiritual Masters, and by the experience of finding Sri Gurudev's Grace and Blessing in every moment even in India, that I wanted to tell Sri Gurudev Da Love-Ananda about this as soon as I returned to the Mountain Of Attention. But it was only after I had been in Heart-Master Da's physical Company many times over a number of months that an appropriate opportunity arose. The evening following Da Avabhasa's Jayanthi (Birthday) in November, 1980, I read the transcript of my interview with Krishna Jogletkar to Da Avabhasa in Bright Behind Me, His Residence at the time. I was sitting to His left side, only two feet away. With His Divinely Radiant Face present and Glowing right before me, I was finally able to tell Him that I had found Him present in the form of all these Adepts. During the course of the conversation I told Him, "I felt that the relationships of these devotees to their Gurus were similar to what we have been Given by You. I realized that the Spiritual Master is the Divine, and that what we find in You is not exclusive. I began to see Your Divine Form in all other forms. I saw that Narayan Maharaj was You in another Form. Swami Nityananda was You in another Form. Ramana Maharshi was You in another Form. To know that Your Master-Presence is manifest everywhere in everything awakened great faith in me."

He replied that what I said was true, and that all such Adepts Taught the Way of heart-surrender to the Divine, and the ecstasy that is God-love. And He Spoke ecstatically about the ultimate identity of all the great God-Men:

SRI DA AVABHASA: *The Siddhas, or great Spiritual Masters, Realize One Great Being. They become Identical with That One through Realization. Spiritual Masters appear in certain times and places, and through Awakened association with them people associate directly with the Divine and Awaken to the Great Process of Spiritual Realization. Yet such Spiritual Masters are not different from one another. They are the same Identity. They have Realized the same One. They are precisely the same Presence, precisely the same Infinite Individual. Likewise, the devotees of Spiritual Masters of the past are related to the same One to Whom devotees relate in the present.*

The Spiritual Master is a kind of Vehicle or Function for Realization in the manifest universe. In order to establish the relationship with such a Spiritual Master that is lauded in the traditions, in order to acknowledge the Spiritual Master and on the basis of that acknowledgement enter into heart-felt, loving Communion and surrender, one must oneself be transformed. It is not a conventional relationship, therefore, in which a childish, egoically "self-possessed" personality accepts the superiority and parentalism of some other character. That is not it at all. One must acknowledge and Awaken in relationship to the Spiritual Master as a transparent Vehicle of God-Communion.

The relationship to a true Spiritual Master, no matter how many different Spiritual Masters there have been, is the same relationship that all devotees enjoy, because God, not any individual, is Communicating in that relationship. The Spiritual Master is the Spiritual Master through the Realization of Identity with God, not through the realization of superior personal existence. His or her personal existence, superior or inferior, is utterly transcended in God-Realization. That transcendence establishes the true and great Function of the Spiritual Master, or Adept, or Siddha. Such an Adept is a transparent mechanism, a direct Vehicle of Divine Association, for those who are Awakened, those who can acknowledge such an individual and enter into the Yoga of that relationship. (November 4, 1980)

Satsang: The "Method" of the Siddhas

The heart, or essence, of the Spiritual Way is Satsang, or the Spiritual Company of the God-Man. When a God-Man appears, he (or she) makes it possible to live directly in relationship to the Divine, Who Is Incarnate in the Form of the God-Man. Therefore, Satsang is, as Sri Da Avabhasa Communicates, "the Great Means" of Realization:

SRI DA AVABHASA: All the great Siddhas, the realized ones, who have taught in the world, have given Satsang to their disciples as grace. That was their essential activity and gift. They didn't come to give a method, to give a conceptual teaching only, to create a myth, a structure for the mind, some sort of mentality. They brought themselves. *They entered into* relationship *with the world, with their disciples. That relationship is the very structure and outward sign of the process I have described.* That *is spiritual life. . . . The Siddha "lives" his disciples. The Truth "meditates" those in Satsang. . . .* (The Method of the Siddhas, *p. 226)*

"Satsang" is a Sanskrit word composed of two parts: "sat" ("Reality, or Truth") and "sang" ("Company"). It is often translated as "Good Company", or "the Company of the Good, Wise, or True". Traditionally, it refers to the practice of spending time in the company of those whose lives are dedicated to the Truth, or Reality, or who are genuinely practicing Spiritual life. One is advised to keep the company or Satsang of Saints, Sages, and Realizers of all kinds, as well as genuine devotees, rather than people predominantly interested in the things of the world. All of the Spiritual traditions agree that the best thing anyone can do is to spend time in the Company of a God-Realizer.

Da Avabhasa also speaks of Satsang as the great Means of Spiritual growth, for in every moment in which the devotee maintains himself or herself in this Company, the devotee receives the Blessing-Transmission of the Sat-Guru. On August 5, 1987, Da Avabhasa Spoke to His devotees about the primacy of Satsang and the principles of Spiritual Transmission underlying this practice:

SRI DA AVABHASA: Realization is a Transmission. Various apparent efforts can be made to serve it, but no one can Transmit or influence others with anything other than the state of Realization or the limit of existence that is real for that one. Everyone transmits. All of you are transmitters. You reinforce these limitations in one another and you transmit them to one another. Each one of you emits invisible forces that are locked up in limited messages that reinforce the same limitations in others. You are all indulging in "satsang" with one another, and the state of the world proves the potency of this transmission.

Realizers at one or another stage of Spiritual development likewise by nature spontaneously transmit what they are. What they have realized transmits itself, subtly and grossly, by what they do, by what they are, by what they feel. Those less evolved transmit their realization, those more evolved transmit their more advanced realization, and those who have Realized That Which Is Inherently Perfect Transmit That. It is inevitable, and it is an absolute law. This is why it says in the traditions that the best thing you can do, among all the things you must do—and you must do many things—but the best among them, the chief among them, is to spend time in the Company of a Realizer.

Everything is transmission. The stones transmit, the sky does, the TV does. Since everything and everyone transmits states of existence, since life or existence itself is participation in transmissions of all kinds, the best thing you can do is to associate with the most advanced Transmission, or the ultimate Transmission, or the greatest possible Transmission above all. Everything is transmission. Therefore, spend time in the Company of one who spontaneously Transmits That Which Is Inherently Perfect and Ultimate. This is the great rule, the Great Law, the Ultimate principle of the Great Tradition.

The condition of Satsang is all-inclusive. The Sat-Guru lives in this relationship with his or her devotee twenty-four hours a day, and is continually

Spiritually Transmitting his Divine Condition to the devotee. Therefore, Satsang is effective at every level of the devotee's awareness and life. In every moment, the devotee is called away from the apparent dilemma of his or her life to turn toward the ecstatic relationship with the Sat-Guru. Satsang is a living process, "radically" impinging upon this moment, and allowing even this moment to be lived as Communion with the Divine. Sri Da Avabhasa, in His earliest summaries of the Way of the Heart, frequently Said, "I do not offer you a method, but a relationship." This is the unique Gift of the Living God-Man:

SRI DA AVABHASA: It is just a ride. It is very simple. . . . The Way of the Siddhas is very easy. The traditional seeker must try to pick himself up by his bootstraps and attain the state of God, but when the Siddha appears in the world, he manifests that complete and Perfect Realization directly, to all living beings. He asks only for their attention, their surrender, and [through that process of genuine self-transcending sacrifice] he becomes them. So they do not have to pass through all of the artifices of their own search for transformation, for release. They live the happy life of present relationship to the Divine, or Satsang, Communion and Non-separation in God. In the midst of all that, this "radical" transformation occurs. It appears as all these phenomena, but without the concern and self-cognition of the individual. So the Way of the Siddhas is a happy, easy Way. It is Divine Grace in the world. (July 7, 1974)

THE NECESSITY FOR THE SAT-GURU AS DESCRIBED IN THE ONE AND GREAT TRADITION OF MANKIND

Sri Da Avabhasa has made the absolute necessity of a true Guru plain from the earliest days of His Teaching Work. This excerpt comes from one of His earliest Discourses, published in 1973 in *The Method of the Siddhas:*

SRI DA AVABHASA: Spiritual life is a demand, it is a confrontation, it is a relationship. It is not a method you apply to yourself. Your "self" is this contraction, and this contraction is what must be undermined in spiritual life. Therefore, the Guru comes in human form, in living form. . . . Truth must come in a living form, absolutely. Truth must confront a man, live him, and meditate him. It is not your meditation that matters. Truth must meditate you. And that is the Siddhi or marvelous process of Satsang. Even while Truth is meditating you in Satsang, you are busy doing more of the usual to yourself, waking yourself up, putting yourself to sleep, reacting in every possible and unconscious way to the force of Satsang, but you are being meditated.

You cannot be "meditated" by one who is not alive. Even if you believe

*in one who is no longer alive in human form, you cannot provide the neces-
sary, living means for this meditation. Truth must come in living form, usually in the human vehicle of the Guru, the true man of understanding.
Spiritual life involves this marvelous process, this Siddhi, this Satsang. If this
Siddhi or living spiritual process is not activated, it doesn't make a damn bit
of difference what exotic or humble spiritual methods you apply to yourself,
for it will always be of the same nature. It will always amount to a form of
this contraction. All of your methods, all mantras, all yogic methods, all
beliefs, all paths, all religions are extensions of this contraction. Truth itself
must become the process of life, and communicate itself, create conditions in
life, and make demands, restoring the conscious participation of the individual. Dead Gurus can't kick ass! (pp. 224-25)*

This fiery process is only made possible by the Sat-Guru, the Living
God-Man, and it is the great Gift of God to man. The question of the necessity of the Sat-Guru can hardly be raised among those who are serious
about the actual process of Divine Enlightenment, for the Transmission of
the Divine is extraordinarily difficult to receive by any other means. Swami
Vivekananda argued this point directly, speaking of the necessity of the
Darshan of a human Teacher for human beings:

*Man has no idea of the Spirit, he has to think of it with the forms he has
before him. He has to think of the blue skies, or the expansive fields, or the
sea, or something huge. How else can you think of God? So what are you
doing in reality? You are talking of omnipresence, and thinking of the sea. Is
God the sea? A little more common sense is required. . . .*

*We are by our present constitution limited and bound to see God as
man. If the buffaloes want to worship God, they will see Him as a huge buffalo. If a fish wants to worship God, it will have to think of Him as a big fish.
You and I, the buffalo, the fish, each represent so many different vessels. All
these go to the sea to be filled with water according to the shape of the vessel.
In each of these vessels is nothing but water. So with God. When men see
Him, they see Him as man, and the animals as animal—each according to
his ideal. That is the only way you can see Him; you have to worship Him as
man, because there is no other way out of it. Two classes of men do not worship God as man—the human brute who has no religion, and the
Paramahamsa (highest Yogi) who has gone beyond humanity, who has
thrown off his mind and body and gone beyond the limits of nature. . . .
Between these two poles of existence, if anyone tells you he is not going to
worship God as man, take care of him. He is an irresponsible talker, he is
mistaken; his religion is for frothy thinkers, it is intellectual nonsense.*[1]

---

1. "Addresses on Bhakti Yoga", *Complete Works of Swami Vivekananda* (Calcutta: Advaita Ashrama), pp. 30-31.

In discussing the Guru-devotee relationship, Sri Gurudev Da Love-Ananda has stated its principle most simply as "You become what you meditate on."

Or, as He puts it more fully:

You become (or duplicate the qualities of) whatever you meditate on (or whatever you identify with via the "surrender" that is attention itself). (The Basket of Tolerance)

In other words, you take on the qualities of whatever or whoever you give your attention to. This principle is seen at work in every aspect of life. Whatever one is most intimately associated with, or one surrenders to most fully, determines the quality of consciousness. Thus, if you are seriously interested in Realization of the Living Divine, you must meditate on or contemplate that Reality. And, in practical terms, one does this by meditating on or contemplating the Sat-Guru, or One who has Realized Identity with the Divine. Through this means, the Spiritual Transmission of the Sat-Guru is given room to transform the devotee. God-Realization is thus only possible through the Appearance and Grace of the Sat-Guru. It is not possible to Realize Identification with the Divine simply on the basis of one's own will.

In the Spiritual traditions of the world, there was no doubt about the necessity for the Help of the Spiritual Adepts if one were purposed toward Realization of the Divine Reality. However, with the advent in the modern era of the Western ideal of the "self-made" man, the individual fancies that, just as he or she might achieve economic success independently and by dint of his or her own efforts, so also Spiritual Realization can be a self-guided enterprise. The Western or "Westernized" man or woman regards the Spiritual Process not as a matter of surrender to the Divine Reality, but as the acquisition of techniques, powers, or knowledge, which, when combined with the cleverness of the individual, will yield the desired results.

In the genuine esoteric Spiritual traditions, such approaches are considered fanciful, deluded, or even worse—and certainly always fruitless. Sri Gurudev Da Love-Ananda calls such approaches "self-'guruing'". Even the modern Sage Ramana Maharshi, when asked about the fact that he never had a Guru, would answer, "How do you know?" And he acknowledged that a Sat-Guru was virtually without exception an absolute necessity. The very fact that he was asked so many times the question "Is a Guru necessary?" shows the extent to which Western influence had taken hold even in India, in Ramana Maharshi's lifetime. In the recorded conversations in *Talks with Sri Ramana Maharshi,* a seeker named Mrs. Piggott begins her conversation by asking the Maharshi, "Is a Master necessary for realization?" He replies:

Realization is the result of the Master's Grace more than teachings, lectures, meditation, etc. They are only secondary aids, whereas the former is the primary and the essential cause.[2]

2. *Talks with Sri Ramana Maharshi.* Three volumes in one, 4th ed. (Tiruvannamalai, S. India: Sri Ramanasramam, 1968), p. 4.

Testimony to the necessity of the Living God-Man, by whatever title or name he is described, abounds in the traditional Scriptures of the East. And in the major traditions of the West, although there is less experience with such God-Men, the Guru-devotee relationship is found in many contexts and circumstances. We will next survey the honored place this most sacred relationship holds (and has anciently held) in the world's major religions.

HINDUISM

The religions of the Indian subcontinent all laid great emphasis on the Guru-devotee relationship. The *Rig-Veda*, the most ancient of Hindu Scriptures, dating back to perhaps 1100 B.C.E., very clearly indicates that the Spiritual Process cannot truly be undertaken without the guidance of the Adept. Says the seer who speaks this ancient text:

The stranger asks the way of him who knows it; taught by him who knows, he travels onward. This is indeed the blessing of Instruction; he finds the path that leads <u>directly</u> forward (X.32.7).[3]

It is likewise stated in the *Katha Upanishad*, dated perhaps 500 B.C.E.:

Unless told of Him by another thou canst not find thy way to Him; for He is subtler than subtlety and that which logic cannot reach. This wisdom is not to be had by reasoning, only when told thee by another [does] it bring knowledge.[4]

Ramakrishna (1836-1886), the great Saint of India, said:

When going to a strange country one must abide by the directions of the guide who knows the way. Taking the advice of many would lead to utter confusion. So in trying to reach God one must implicitly follow the advice of one single Guru who knows the way to God.[5]

Writes Swami Vivekananda:

This quickening impulse cannot be derived from books. The soul can receive impulses only from another soul, and from nothing else. We may study books all our lives, we may become very intellectual, but in the end we find that spiritually we have not developed at all. . . .

---

3. M. P. Pandit, "The Guru-Sishya Tradition", *Studies in the Tantras and the Veda* (Madras: Ganesh and Co., 1967), p. 43.

4. Ibid.

5. *Sayings of Sri Ramakrishna*, as quoted in "The Need for a Guru: A Collection of Sayings", by Ekkirala Vikramaditya in *Dattatreya: Glory of the Divine in Man*, ed. Sarnath Baba (Vidyanagar, 1981).

Swami Vivekananda

The person from whose soul such an impulse comes is called the guru, the teacher; and the person to whose soul the impulse is conveyed is called the sishya, the student.[6]

After describing the teachers of the world, Swami Vivekananda speaks of the God-Men themselves:

. . . there is another set of teachers, the Christs of the world. These Teachers of all teachers represent God Himself in the form of man. They are much higher; they can transmit spirituality with a touch, with a wish, which makes even the lowest and most degraded characters saints in one second. Do you not read of how they used to do these things? They are not the teachers about whom I was speaking [i.e., mere lecturers]; they are the Teachers of all teachers, the greatest manifestations of God to man; we cannot see God except through them. We cannot help worshipping them, and they are the only beings we are bound to worship.[7]

Amma (Swami Prajnananda), Swami Muktananda's personal secretary for many years, wrote of the need for the Guru in an article, "Sadhana at the Feet of a Sadguru", in which she described the traditional orientation to sadhana practiced in Swami Muktananda's Company.

An aspirant, not knowing what he has done in the past or where he stands at present, and not having a clear idea of the nature of the goal to be attained, follows a certain discipline according to his own ideas of austerities, rituals and learning acquired from reading books or hearing lectures. He is even apt to mistake the ego-satisfying promptings of his heart as inner spiritual guidance. When he does not get the expected results, he becomes frustrated. He keeps on changing the course of his discipline, or is urged to move from one place to another in search of a way to the goal. But a Guru who has attained perfection and is established in the state of unity with God, can see through an aspirant, know his past, and judge his present spiritual status. Therefore he properly guides the aspirant according to his nature, circumstances and competence, giving him a spiritual push on the path through his divine grace, which smoothes the course of discipline and makes the spiritual ideal real and living for the aspirant.

6. "Bhakti Yoga", *Vivekananda: The Yogas and Other Works*, compiled by Swami Nikhilananda (New York: Ramakrishna-Vivekananda Center, 1953), p. 414.

7. *Complete Works of Swami Vivekananda*, p. 29.

Thus, without a Guru it is impossible to proceed far on the spiritual path. Not a single enlightened soul will ever deny the necessity of a Guru. Those who do so are nourishing their egos in the darkness of their ignorance, because to accept a Guru, the ruthless killer of ego, is contrary to their self-conceited ideas.[8]

The Hindu Tantric traditions reverentially exalt the Sat-Guru, understanding that he is the key to all success in the Spiritual Way. They proclaim the identity of the true Sat-Guru and the Divine. In this tradition, as in the *Guru Gita*, the Guru is praised as even greater than God, for it is only through the Guru's Grace that the aspirant can come to know God. Of course such an understanding of the nature of Guru and God is far removed from the philosophy of the Jewish, Christian, or Islamic theologian, who would make God an entity apart. But the supreme valuation of the Guru emanates from a tradition in which it was acknowledged that the living Adept is verily a <u>God</u>-Man, not merely an ordinary man (or woman), and that he (or she) directly Instructs and Awakens the disciple with Divine Power. The *Kularnava Tantra*, a major Tantric Scripture, extols the Guru in these words:

At the root of dhyana [meditation] is the form of the Guru; at the root of puja [sacramental worship] is the feet of the Guru, at the root of the mantra is the word of the Guru and at the root of all liberation is the grace of the Guru. (verse 90)[9]

SIKHISM

The Sikh tradition places supreme importance on the relationship to the Sat-Guru. From the original founder (Guru Nanak, 1469-1538) to the last in the initial line of ten Gurus (Guru Gobind Singh), the Gurus were the foundation of Sikh practice. The sayings of the great Gurus and other revered Saints were collected in the *Guru Granth Sahib*, which is the sacred Scripture of the Sikhs, and which itself became the subject of reverence. Here are some quotations from this text on the contemplation and the sight of the Sat-Guru:

Who hath not seen, who hath had no sight of Sat-Guru, O Lord, he hath wasted, he hath lost for nothing his human life, O Lord. Within me cherish I true love for my beloved Lord; my body and mind swell with joy when in front of me, my Guru do I behold. . . .

8. Amma (Swami Prajnananda), "Sadhana at the Feet of a Sadguru", *Sri Gurudev Ashram Newsletter,* vol. 2, no. 6 (Ganeshpuri, India: Shree Gurudev Ashram, June 1, 1973), pp. 11-12.

9. M. P. Pandit, *Kularnava Tantra* (Madras: Ganesh and Co., 1973), p. 77.

Thy sight washeth away all sins, O my Guru; and uniteth us with God. . . .
Wise was I, but on beholding Guru lost I all my wisdom; and with ecstasy was I charmed and bewitched. . . .
        . . . My joy knoweth no bounds when I behold my Guru, my Guru's body.[10]

BUDDHISM

The Buddhist tradition from the beginning stressed the help and guidance that came from the Adept. In the Hinayana, or earliest, form of Buddhism, the Teacher is characterized as the "kalyanamitra" or "Spiritual friend". And in actual practice there is great reverence for, respect for, and obedience to the direction and guidance of such a living Teacher or Guide. In the later development of Buddhism, the Guru-devotee relationship became more and more explicit in certain Buddhist schools, particularly the Buddhism of Tibet and (to a somewhat lesser extent) in the relationship to the Japanese Zen Roshi or the Chinese Ch'an Master.

The Indian Maha-Siddha (Great Siddha) Naropa (1016-1100), who, as a Teacher of the great Tibetan Adept Marpa the Translator, played an important role in the Transmission of Buddhism to Tibet, spoke of the necessity for the Guru in these words:

The Indian Maha-Siddha Naropa

There where there is no Guru
Not even the name of Buddha is heard.
The Buddhas of a thousand aeons
Depend on the Guru for their appearance.
The fact is that they are His manifestation.[11]

The nineteenth-century Tibetan Teacher Patrul Rinpoche makes this summary statement on the necessity for the Guru:

With regard to the instruction on following a spiritual teacher, in all the Sutras, Tantras, and Sastras [three types of sacred Scripture], there is no account that tells of anyone who attained Buddhahood without a Guru.[12]

10. Prof. L. R. Puri, *Teachings of the Gurus* (Punjab, India: Radha Soami Satsang Beas, 1973), pp. 122-23.

11. "The Tibetan Guru Refuge: A Historical Perspective", *The Tibet Journal*, vol. 5. no. 4 (Library of Tibetan Works and Archives, Winter 1980), p. 16.

12. "Following a Spiritual Teacher", *Kun-zang La-may Zhal-lung: The Oral Instruction of Kun-Zang La-Ma on the Preliminary Practices of Dzog-Ch'en Long-Ch'en Nying-tig*, Part One, transcr. Pal-trul O-gyen Jigme Ch'o-kyi Wang-Po Rinpoche; transl. Sonam T. Kazi (Upper Montclair, N.J.: Diamond Lotus Publishing, 1989), p. 119.

ISLAM

The exoteric mainstream of the Jewish, Christian, and Islamic traditions has never accepted the possibility of achieving a State of Consciousness identical with the Divine Condition. Therefore, the full tradition of devotion to the Realizer as the Divine Incarnate was rarely allowed to develop. We do not find the appearance of full seventh stage Realizers in these traditions—and even if they had arisen, we would not necessarily know of them, for they would not have been culturally permitted to express the fullness of their Divinity. Those who professed Realization (even temporarily) of states of ecstatic unity with the Divine faced political and social difficulties within their own traditions and cultures. The Sufi Teacher Al-Hallaj, who was martyred for His ecstatic statement of identity with God ("I am the Truth"), is a potent example of the Western prejudice against the esoteric process.[13] Similarly, the Christian tradition is full of instances of the suppression of individuals—such as Meister Eckhart, St. Teresa of Avila, and St. John of the Cross—who did not conform to mainstream doctrine.

The Sufis found a way to acknowledge the Guru-principle through devotion to the Shaykh (Spiritual Master), who was revered in the esoteric vision as a living embodiment of the Divine, and in the orthodox interpretation as the link or mediator of the Divine through a line of succession back to Muhammad the Prophet. (The Sufi Spiritual Master is also known as "Pir" or "Murshid" in Iran, Pakistan, and India.) In order to make itself respectable in the eyes of the orthodox, Sufism used many metaphors of "madness", "drunkenness", and "intoxication" in God, so that Identification with the Divine would be clearly seen not to be an ego's claim for what was regarded to be only God's State. It is described that "The Master is the representative of the Prophet and through him of God. To take his hand is to accept the 'hand of the Divine'."[14]

Jalaluddin Rumi (1207-1273), who is perhaps the Islamic mystic best known in the West, was called by the name "Maulana", meaning "our Master". He was the founder of the Mevlevi order of Sufis, known popularly as the "Whirling Dervishes". His own relationship with his Master, Shamsuddin Tabrizi, is famous, for the two loved one another with an overwhelming and consuming love. Rumi wrote in his *Mathnawi:*

Whoever travels without a guide needs two hundred years for a two days' journey.[15]

---

13. Some contemporary scholars contend that Al-Hallaj's martyrdom had more to do with political than esoteric religious suppression, and the subject becomes further complicated in Islam because there was often so little separation between religion and state. In any case, the tension between esoteric Sufism and exoteric Islamic legalism was always present, and the Sufis had to carefully discipline their own ecstatic expression during large epochs of Sufi history.

14. Seyyed Hossein Nasr, *Sufi Essays* (New York: State University of New York Press, 1973), p. 63.

15. Annemarie Schimmel, *Mystical Dimensions of Islam* (Chapel Hill: The University of North Carolina Press, 1975), p. 103.

Jalaluddin Rumi

And again:

*If you had been without a guide
on that path which you
have travelled many times,
you would have lost your way.
—So beware, do not spurn a guide!
Do not venture alone on the road which
you have not yet seen.*[16]

And again,

*Choose a master, for without one
the road on this journey is
full of hazards, fear and danger.
If the shadow of the master is not near,
You will be terrified by the shrieks of
ghouls. . . .*

*Only the master's shadow of Love
kills the self.
Do not let go of your devotion
to him who kills the self.*[17]

---

16. Dr. Javad Nurbakhsh, *In the Tavern of Ruin: Seven Essays on Sufism* (New York: Khaniqahi-Nimatullahi Publications, 1978), p. 121.

17. *In the Tavern of Ruin,* p. 122.

CHRISTIANITY

In looking at the Christian religion, the traditionally pictured relationship between Jesus of Nazareth and his disciples is, of course, a version of the Guru-devotee relationship. In the Christian faith there is also a tradition of what is called "Spiritual guidance", which contains some (though not all) dimensions of the Guru-devotee relationship. The early Church fathers certainly advised aspirants in a very intensive manner, and there have been many great Spiritual guides throughout Christian history. In most cases, the function of Spiritual guidance has been performed by a priest or monastic

Jesus of Nazareth and his disciples

abbot, who is understood to provide moral direction, rather than explicit Spiritual Transmission or Awakening Power. Thus, the Spiritual guide helps people, but it is Christ or the Holy Spirit who is the resource to whom the aspirant was asked to turn in Christian orthodoxy.

Writes Sister Donald Corcoran:

> *The Christian tradition has always emphasized that Christ or the Holy Spirit is the true guide of souls. We find here a notable difference from some of the other major spiritual traditions where the role of a spiritual master, teacher, or guide is central if not indispensable. . . . The spiritual master, in the sense of an extraordinary spiritual teacher responsible for person-to-person transmission, is very rare in Christianity though there are two subtraditions, as it were, that approximate this phenomenon: the early monastic desert fathers and the Russian startsy of the eighteenth and nineteenth centuries.*[18]

The desert fathers were elders among a group of Christian ascetics who lived in the Egyptian deserts in the fourth and later centuries. The desert fathers desired to turn to God directly, and so they left society in favor of the barren drylands. These great old men held unquestioned authority for their disciples, and their word was accepted as "absolutely God-given". St. Anthony, who died in 355 C.E., was the most famous of these ascetics, and from roots established by him, and the later rule of Pachomius in Upper Egypt, sprang the growth of Christian monasticism.[19]

18. Sister Donald Corcoran, "Spiritual Guidance", *Christian Spirituality: Origin to the Twelfth Century*, ed. Bernard McGinn and John Meyendorff, vol. 16 (New York: Crossroad, World Spirituality Series, 1987), p. 444.

19. Gordon S. Wakefield, *The Westminster Dictionary of Christian Spirituality* (Philadelphia: The Westminster Press, 1983), pp. 109-10.

In the case of the Eastern Orthodox "subtradition", and especially centering in Russia, all who truly wished to advance on the Spiritual path were required to place themselves under the guidance of a Spiritual father or staretz (plural: "startzi" or "startsy"). The rules and guidelines for the relationship with these "Spiritual directors" called for full submission to their Spiritual authority. For it was understood that the staretz held the means by which the aspirant would be connected not only to higher instruction and guidance, but to Divine Grace Itself.

A spiritual father's power in guiding his spiritual children was to be unconditional and unlimited . . . and the penance. . . imposed by him had to be carried out as the "commandment of God."[20]

The most famous staretz is the Russian St. Seraphim of Sarov (1759-1833),[21] but this fourth to fifth stage tradition continues strongly into the present. The twentieth century has seen such eminent figures as the Russian Father John of Kronstadt (1829-1909), and the Greek "Monk of Mount Athos", Staretz Silouan (1866-1938).

JUDAISM

What is commonly found in the fullest relationship to the great Jewish Teachers, Zaddiks, Rebbes, Ravs, and Rabbis is that they were bearers of the baracha, or Blessing of God. In contact with such an individual, one found direction, guidance, and an example, as well as a direct means of connection to the Divine.

Such a Zaddik (literally, "righteous one") was referred to in the Old Testament (Prov. 10:25) as "the foundation of the world". The Talmud declares that he "stood at the very heart of the cosmos and could, by virtue of his meritorious deeds, intervene to remove the decrees of heaven." It was by his virtue that the world was sustained.[22]

The Hasidic movement, which began in eighteenth-century Eastern Europe with the saintly figure of the Baal Shem Tov, gave a full and concrete meaning to the term "Zaddik". The Hasidic movement is full of great Masters—during the period from 1750-1800 many great Spiritual leaders emerged to guide a generation of aspirants. Writes Samuel Dresner in the introduction to *The Zaddik: The Doctrine of the Zaddik According to the Writing of Rabbi Yaakov Yosef of Polnoy:*

20. *Westminster Dictionary of Christian Spirituality*, p. 76.

21. See *The Spiritual Instructions of St. Seraphim of Sarov: A Spirit-Baptizer of the Eastern Christian Tradition*. With an Introduction based on the Wisdom-Teaching of the Divine World-Teacher and True Heart-Master, Da Avabhasa (The "Bright") (Clearlake, Calif: The Dawn Horse Press, 1991).

22. Arthur Green, "Typologies of Leadership and the Hasidic Zaddiq", *Jewish Spirituality*, vol. 1 (New York: Crossroad Publishing Co., 1987), p. 132.

. . . the Zaddikim offer us a number of religious personalities of a vitality, a spiritual strength, a manifold originality such as never, to my knowledge, appeared together in so short a time-span in the history of religion.[23]

Although I would take firm exception to the scope of the claim being made, what Samuel Dresner's statement does reveal is the great resurgence of the religious leader and guide that occurred through the appearance of the Hasidic Rebbes.

The term "Hasid" came to mean specifically one who was a "disciple", and circles of such devoted followers developed around the Hasidic Rebbes or Zaddiks. The stories about Hasidic Masters brim with their instruction both through example and through teaching discourse, and with their tremendous joy and exuberance. The Zaddik's authority derived from his Spiritual strength and purity and his connection with the Divine, and not simply from a formal Rabbinical lineage based on mere scholarship and intellectual learning.

A modern example of an Hasidic Teacher was Baba Sali, or Rav Yisrael Abuchatzeirah, who was born in Morocco in 1890 and died in Israel in 1984. He was the Spiritual Teacher for hundreds, and thousands came to receive his blessings, observing his every word as a Divine Commandment and his every request as law.

In 1972, I visited the Spiritual center of the Lubavitcher sect of Hasidic Judaism in Brooklyn, New York, and attended a meeting at which the world-renowned Lubavitcher Rebbe was present. It was clear that he was held in the greatest reverence by those attending, as a unique messenger of God. I distinctly remember an occasion when all were singing along with him. During this loud singing, I noted that each motion he made, each nod of his head, was greeted by a wave of response by all present, as if an electric current were released into the room.

In addition to the major religious traditions that have been discussed here, there are many other traditions that include the Guru-devotee relationship in one form or another. We see Spiritual guides in diverse cultures, including the shaman in the cultures of native peoples all over the world (such as the American Indians) and the Teachers in such major traditions as

23. Samuel H. Dresner, *The Zaddick: The Doctrine of the Zaddick According to the Writing of Rabbi Yaakov Yosef of Polnoy* (New York: Schocken Books, 1974), p. 13.

Taoism, Jainism, Zoroastrianism, and Confucianism.

Truly, the centrality of the Guru in all the world's religious and Spiritual traditions cannot be overstated. As Sri Da Avabhasa Writes in His Essay on the tradition of devotion to the Adept:

Spiritually Realized Adepts (or Transmission-Masters, or true Gurus and Sat-Gurus) are the principal Sources, Resources, and Means of the Spiritual Way. This fact is not (and never has been) a matter of controversy among real Spiritual practitioners.

Sri Love-Anandashram, September 1991

CHAPTER FIVE

Beyond the Cultic
Tendency in Religion

THE PREJUDICES AND OTHER LIMITATIONS THAT MUST BE OVERCOME
IF PRACTICE IN RELATIONSHIP TO A TRUE GURU IS TO BE FRUITFUL

Sri Love-Anandashram, September 1991

A CALL FOR GENUINE TOLERANCE AND AN END TO THE BIGOTRY AND
PREJUDICE DIRECTED TOWARDS GURUS AND MINORITY RELIGIONS

*I*f this were one of the great Spiritual cultures that the world has seen, such as classical Indian society, or Tibet before the Chinese invasion, there would be little question of the necessity for a Spiritual Guide, or about the right way to relate to him or her. The questions would instead be, "Where can I find such a Guide?" and "What is required to prepare for and to receive his Initiation and Blessing?"

We do not live in such a culture. Today, not only is the necessity of formal Spiritual Help in question, but the existence of the Spiritual Reality Itself is a matter of debate. The popular notion that everything can be explained by science and the purely materialistic point of view is so widely held in the West and in the "Westernized" world that an entire modern generation is more and more distrustful of anything that suggests the religious, mystical, or Spiritual.

I was myself raised with such cultural limitations, such that I believed science could answer every possible question. My mother even told me that I had no need to fear death, because by the time I was older, scientists would have found the means by which men and women would be able to live forever! There was the promise that all problems would be solved by the application of intelligence and hard work. And, like so many others of my generation, I received nothing that could be called instruction relative to the greater matters of religion and God-Realization. I felt that there must be something greater than material prosperity, or intellectual sophistication, or fame. And yet I did not take seriously a religious or Spiritual Reality. I was not truly aware of the Great Tradition of religious, Spiritual, and Transcendental Wisdom that is our common inheritance. And of course, when I did in fact find a Great Realizer, I had no genuine preparation for relating to such a Being.

Sri Da Avabhasa has Compassionately but directly addressed this ignorance and doubt-mind of the Westerner and the "Westernized" world. He has had to re-educate modern men and women, making clear the truth relative to the Guru-devotee relationship in the face of the false notions, limited understanding, and adolescent and childish views of the modern world.

The following Essay from *The Basket of Tolerance* is an example of such Work. Here Sri Da Avabhasa Writes about the book *Godmen of India*, by Peter Brent.[1] As in many of the Essays in *The Basket of Tolerance*, Sri Da Avabhasa's discussion of this book and its author is a starting point for the Instruction that He Gives to all. It can be seen, as the Essay continues, that Heart-Master Da is using Peter Brent's work (which presents both much information and numerous first hand accounts of the Guru-devotee rela-

---

1. Peter Brent, *Godmen of India* (New York: Quadrangle Books, Inc., 1972).

tionship) as a means to address the larger issues of every Westerner's (or "Westernized" individual's) relationship to the God-Man.

. . . While he remains positively disposed toward the Guru-devotee tradition (and very much wants it to continue, even in the West), Peter Brent otherwise expresses the chronic (and typical) difficulties conventional Westerners (of little or no true Spiritual experience or inclination) tend to express relative to the Divinity (versus the mere humanness) of the true Guru, or the Divine (versus the merely human) nature of the powers and the Realizations of Gurus, and so on. Thus, Peter Brent's sometimes criticisms of the Guru-devotee tradition are, in general, plainly the result of his apparent identification with the typically Western point of view, which is, characteristically, body-based, essentially materialistic (or anti-Spiritual, anti-mystical, and, as such, anti-religious), fixed in the third stage of life (or the yet unresolved total complex of the first three stages of life), rather adolescent (or reactively and even willfully independent, and indiscriminatingly opposed to all authority, and even to all that is rightly prominent, or highly excellent, or, in the greater evolutionary sense, truly advanced), and tending to think that everything traditional, mystical, Spiritual, esoteric, or Eastern must be reinterpreted (or, it should be said, reduced) according to the (current, or otherwise characteristic) reality-models of Western (and, especially, scientific) culture. Even so, by his sometimes criticisms of the Guru-devotee tradition, Peter Brent serves to illustrate precisely the kinds of prejudices (and other limitations of point of view) every "Westerner" (whether of the East or the West) must overcome (in himself or herself) if his or her relationship to a true Guru (or Sat-Guru) is to be fruitful.

The widespread ignorance, misunderstanding, and even suspicion of esoteric religious and Spiritual life is perhaps the single most unfortunate attitude of the Western and "Westernized" culture of the modern era. The predominant characteristics of modern life in the West are childish dependence on the pleasures of the ordinary life, consumerism, and the childish demand for self-fulfillment and self-satisfaction in and as a body-mind. Simultaneously, there is an adolescent reaction to any kind of authority, or to any demand for submission to anything greater than oneself. And in this society (for the word "culture" does not truly apply) the idea of genuine religious authority or guidance is particularly taboo. What might better be described as alternative religious or Spiritual groups are stigmatized as "cults", a word now charged with all the force of an anathema. Parents fear that their children will become involved with charismatic teachers, and the very idea of someone from a religious minority group moving next door is cause for concern.

It is not that the issues involved are new. The Great Tradition of religious and Spiritual instruction has been with mankind since the beginning of history. In the optimum circumstance, issues such as these would traditionally have been explored and explained with real sensitivity in the intimacy of genuine Spiritual culture. And there were genuine, generally understood criteria by which one would evaluate a religious or Spiritual authority. Likewise, real expectations had to be met by the aspirant before he or she might be accepted by a Teacher. Without such qualifications being met— on both sides—confusion or lack of success was inevitable. Without right preparation, one would not think of approaching an Adept. Nor would such an aspirant be accepted. Indeed, it is because of the failure to understand and meet the real qualifications for Spiritual life that the immature behavior branded as "cultism" today arises.

Just as those interested in the disciplines of science, or literature, or the arts consult and become steeped in the work and advancements of those who have come before, those who wish to devote themselves to the pursuit of greater truths and the Spiritual Reality must likewise consult true Sources of Wisdom. Every man's and woman's greatest inheritance from past generations, his or her most valuable legacy, is the long tradition of genuine Spiritual practice in the Company of Realized Masters or Adepts of the Spiritual Process, through whose Grace and Instruction true Happiness may be found.

Unfortunately, in the world today the validity and necessity of the Guru-devotee relationship is obscured by the mass of confusion and emotional charge surrounding the subject. Modern Western culture is in its own dark age relative to understanding genuine Spirituality and the possibility of effective, God-Realizing Spiritual practice.

This is most evident in the popular communications media, which provide the "news" and therefore play a major role in defining the point of view of the ordinary man. For in the media today (as well as in the official statements of many political figures) we see a virulent prejudice against Gurus themselves, as well as against anyone who has a relationship to a Guru, or even practices a "minority" religion. And today's popular mind has been informed by such media and opinion leaders, who have intentionally created a negative bias against anything but "establishment" religion. For the purpose of exciting controversy and creating a "good story", the media and public commentators routinely abuse Gurus and practitioners of religious Ways outside the mainstream of established religion. In television interviews with Spiritual practitioners, or popular magazine articles about minority religions, one repeatedly finds gross bigotry and intolerance. The media, using comparisons to the evident charlatanism of some ersatz "gurus", regularly discredits the entire esoteric tradition of Help, Instruction, and Guidance by Spiritual Teachers.

The discriminatory tone and tactics of this forceful prejudice are the same as those used by racists, anti-Semites, and the "red-baiters" of the McCarthy era. "Button words", which merely by their mention bring forth negative reactions, are used commonly. Authentic Gurus are routinely mentioned in the same breath with psychopaths and tyrants, such as Charles Manson or Hitler, and time-honored religious and meditative practices are equated with "brainwashing" or "programming". Contemporary "alternative" religions are dismissed as "cults", and with that appellation comes the stock invocation of Jonestown and the terrible fundamentalist sect led by Jim Jones.

As a devotee of Sri Da Avabhasa, a True and Ultimate Guru or Realizer of God, and as a student of the new (and ancient and eternal) religion of Free Daism, I am outraged by this "acceptable" bigotry that still persists in our general culture. Such terms as "brainwashing" and "programming" bear no relationship to authentic religious practices. And the blanket condemnation of Gurus is uninformed and casually malicious. To cast aspersions upon the ancient and Supremely Honorable Function of the Spiritual Adept itself is evidence of ignorance and irresponsibility. And such behavior effectively undermines free choice, creating misconceptions about the real practice of alternative religious Ways.

I do not write about this in the abstract. For many months in the mid-1980s, the life of my own Guru, Sri Da Avabhasa, and the life of my own family and Spiritual community were severely disrupted by misinformed and inflamed public opinion, fueled by representatives of respected media outlets who felt no responsibility to truly find out the facts. By playing upon people's emotions without informing themselves of the realities of the situation, as in any other kind of bigotry, tremendous suppression and hurt resulted.

Modern history has seen the great harm done by every kind of prejudice and bigotry, by racism and its slander and violence, by sexism, by anti-Semitism. And positive changes have gradually been made in these areas. Now the same must be done relative to the suppression and defamation of religious minorities, and the misinformation that has negatively slanted the common perception of the Guru-devotee relationship.

Just as women, blacks, Jews, homosexuals, and many other groups have called for and required the media to be responsible for its communication about them, the same must now be demanded by all on behalf of religious minorities. For as it is now clearly not acceptable for a commentator to imply that all women are "stupid", blacks "lazy", Jews "avaricious", or homosexuals "weak", just so, it is equally hurtful for a commentator to call all followers of Gurus "slave-like" or "brainwashed", and to disparage all alternative religious ways as "cults", or characterize all Gurus as negative figures.

As we will further discuss in this chapter, these issues are not new. In times past the established popular voice was not the media, but the voice of the official established religions, and the disparaging terms used against minority religious views were "blasphemy", "heresy", and "witchcraft". For the established religions face—and sometimes succumb to—the temptation of their own form of religious bigotry, with its own particular language.

The current popular media censure of religious minorities uses the same "insider/outsider" mentality as has been found in religious persecution in every age. In the predominantly secular world of today, the media commentator often purports to be basing his or her point of view on the premise of upholding the choice of everyone to make up their own mind about what they will do with their life. But when it comes to an individual freely making the decision to practice in relationship to a Guru, then such a choice is made to seem inappropriate. It is implied that if one is involved with a Spiritual Teacher or Guru one is automatically surrendering one's freedom of choice and independence. But no true Guru asks a devotee to do this. The Spiritual Process requires the growth of the discriminative capability and the right use of the will, rather than the relinquishment of these. Likewise, Spiritual surrender in the Company of a Sat-Guru

The current popular media censure of religious minorities uses the same "insider/outsider" mentality as has been found in religious persecution in every age

requires the foundation of self-understanding and the transcendence of the childish motives of enthusiastic belief and the need to be protected and parented.

The real motivation behind the media commentator's point of view is not truly the avowed ideal of genuine freedom for all. Rather, the motivation is an adolescent fear of control, irrationally projected on the figure of the Guru.

As Westerners, this fear of control by others, and of submission to any authority other than ourselves, is part of our general acculturation. But we must become able to acknowledge the appearance of a Superior Man or Woman, who is Superior in Love, in self-Sacrifice, in Wisdom, in Spiritual Realization, and capable of Instructing others in these. We must become able to accept that our growth in Wisdom and Realization could come from our devotion to such a One.

Our resistance to Spiritual authority comes from a confused version of egalitarianism. At the level of politics and human rights, all are equal, equally entitled to those rights, and equally entitled to their point of view. However, at the Spiritual level, the Saints, the Sages, and above all the God-Men and God-Women have always been revered as the greatest Authorities, the Sources of true Happiness and Guidance. In the West and the "Westernized" world, now so secularized, we have lost sight of these rare beings, who are our greatest Help. We relegate them to an ancient time and place, and in so doing we do great disservice to ourselves and to all others.

The world is in desperate need of the Help of its Spiritual Sources. Rather than discriminating against the Realizers, we must understand that they are the greatest Resource in this time of great need and worldwide difficulties. It is my belief, and the clear communication of all the traditional sources, that it is their service to mankind that must be allowed to be influential if there is to be a real turnabout in human destiny.

BEWARE OF THOSE WHO BALK AT THE ORDEAL OF SUBMISSION
REQUIRED IN THE COMPANY OF THE SAT-GURU

Although the real Spiritual Process is full of great Grace, the human submission required in such a profound process is undeniably difficult for all egos—whether they are full of accomplishment or very simple and ordinary. The Spiritual traditions are full of stories of stubborn aspirants who balk at the demand of the Sat-Guru, and who attempt unsuccessfully to "guru" themselves.

Today, such individuals may even set themselves up as great authorities relative to Spiritual matters, writing books or delivering lectures, and claiming that in this day and age the Sat-Guru is no longer necessary, or that the Guru-devotee relationship does not quite work. They may speak intelligently about Spiritual matters, or appear to be involved in great ascetical practice. They may speak about their great insights, or describe long hours of various Spiritual practices. But they remain in the grip of the ego, precisely because they are not touching the root of what can only be transcended by the Grace of the Guru—the ego itself.

These individuals Heart-Master Da has termed "the new Pharisees". They attempt to establish their authority through great erudition about Spiritual matters, and may report some degree of Spiritual accomplishment or experience. Their limited wisdom comes from study, or the time they spend as "tourists" with Spiritual figures, obtaining "bones" from them, and then returning to their hiding places (their typewriter, their classrooms, their caves) to gnaw in private, taking credit for the wisdom so garnered, often not even aware that it is stolen.

Many such individuals who struggle or write most earnestly about the non-necessity of the Guru-devotee relationship, or the difficulties inherent in it for the modern era, may themselves have come into contact with the genuine Spiritual Process, and a true Sat-Guru. Their own fear of submission to that Process has struck them deeply, for they sense how it interferes with the plans of the ego. Their popularly expressed criticism of the Guru-devotee relationship stems from their own difficulty with the surrender of the ego that genuine Spiritual practice requires. Such surrender is anathema to the ego's need to be praised and glamorized.

Thus has arisen the opinion that the Spiritual Process can be Realized without the ordeal of real practice or the Graceful Transmission of the Divine from a Sat-Guru. It is felt that one can talk about Spiritual matters and perform exercises in the mind, and that these in themselves will lead to Enlightenment. One well-known authority on Spiritual matters when asked what form of meditation he practiced replied, "Reading." Sri Da Avabhasa has described those involved in such illusions as the "talking" school.

Someone once remarked to Ramana Maharshi that J. Krishnamurti had proclaimed that a Sat-Guru is not necessary for Realization. Ramana Maharshi replied, "How did he know it? One can say so after realising but not before."[2] In other words, why receive directions on how to get someplace from someone who has himself not yet found the way? In the twentieth century, J. Krishnamurti is perhaps the most well-known proponent of the idea that a God-Realizer is not necessary for God-Realization. Therefore, Da Avabhasa has used Krishnamurti's argument as a starting point to discuss the errors of merely mental sadhana. In a Talk comprising a portion of Da Avabhasa's brilliant Preface to the seventh stage text *The Song of the Self Supreme,* He discusses the confusion that the "talking" school has engendered:

Ramana Maharshi at Arunachala

SRI DA AVABHASA: J. Krishnamurti . . . proposed that merely by listening to his verbal arguments one could fully enter into the ultimate Disposition, free of mind. He himself in fact endured a difficult (but poorly guided, and never Finalized) course of mystical and Yogic processes that arose in him spontaneously—but he neither recommended nor, generally, even spoke of such processes (and their accompanying practices) to his listeners. Furthermore, although he constantly (and rightly) criticized childish (or indiscriminate) attachment to "authorities" of any kind, he himself indiscriminately denied the necessity or the value of right relationship to an Adept Spiritual Master. Nevertheless, J. Krishnamurti carried on a life-long worldwide enterprise of public Teaching, in which he functioned for many as an authority and a presumed Spiritual Guru. Like any other Teacher of Wisdom, he was surrounded by regular followers and supporters, and he is known to have sat with many of them in private sessions of instruction, Spiritual healing, and meditative silence.

In the manner of his actual, personal (and private, or even rather secret) practice with people, J. Krishnamurti demonstrated the normalcy and the inevitability of the tradition of Transmission from Teacher to disciple and devotee, but, in his public pronouncements, he always argued against (and even appeared to attack) this tradition. Therefore, truly, a basic modern conflict was dramatized via the life-work of J. Krishnamurti, and the effect of that conflict in him led him to advocate or reinforce the conceit of "lecture hall Enlightenment", or the "Way" of no-practice. His was an unfortunate enterprise, one that became a kind of "official party line" of non-practicing university scholars, psychiatric "gurus", popularizers of consumer Spirituality, and the general gathering of materialistic propagandists. Such advocates merely legitimize prejudices that people are already inclined to

---

2. *Be As You Are: The Teachings of Sri Ramana Maharshi,* ed. David Godman (Methuen, Inc., 1985), p. 99.

uphold. The popular inclination is already to assume these prejudices and conceits. Thus, persons who, perhaps in spite of themselves, represent a kind of Spiritual authority can become the servants of that very conceit. J. Krishnamurti merely became a public symbol for this conventional orientation that is, characteristically, always typical everywhere in the non-practicing world of people who merely read Spiritual literature (but do not practice the Way of Realization). (new edition, forthcoming)

Some people believe that we are in a New Age now, in which people are uniquely and especially open to the Divine Influence. Such an idea is really just based on hopefulness. There is just as much egoic resistance to the real Spiritual Process today as ever.

BEYOND THE CULTIC TENDENCY IN RELIGION

On a sunny spring afternoon in 1977, I stood speaking with Sri Da Avabhasa and another of His devotees on the ground floor of the building known as Huge Helper, situated in the central area of the Mountain Of Attention. In the midst of the conversation, we all noticed a wide-eyed stranger with a pack on his back approaching the Sanctuary on the road below, a few hundred yards away. My fellow devotee left to ask what he wanted. On his return, before the devotee had said a word, Da Avabhasa amusedly said, "Sahaj Samadhi [Divine Enlightenment], right?" Somewhat taken aback, my friend replied, "That's right! He thought he was Enlightened, and he was coming to see You as one Enlightened Being meeting another." From the manner of the man, it had been obvious to Heart-Master Da Love-Ananda that he believed he was already Divinely Self-Realized. But, actually, this individual, like many others who have first approached Da Avabhasa, had a false notion of what it takes to truly fulfill the Spiritual Process. The beginner, feeling Spiritual energies for the first time (or even natural bodily energies), may imagine that great Spiritual advancement has been made, and may even proclaim his or her Enlightenment based on what are really only the beginnings of the Way.

This is just one kind of misunderstanding that Sri Da Avabhasa encountered in those who approached Him. For, Teaching as He did in the cultural wasteland of the twentieth-century West, Da Avabhasa was confronted by individuals approaching Him with a seemingly endless variety of wrong notions, fantasy orientations, and cultic beliefs relative to Spiritual practice and the relationship to the Sat-Guru. Not a single individual approached with genuine self-understanding and appreciation of the laws inherent in the Guru-devotee relationship. Thus, as the years of His Teaching Work with aspirants progressed, Heart-Master Da found it necessary to require greater and greater preparation and understanding of people before they could approach Him as

Sat-Guru. All of this rigorous preparatory discipline and study[3] reflects Da Avabhasa's utter commitment to prevent His devotees from indulging in the errors of cultism and nominal practice, which have historically all too often undermined the practice of true religion, reducing it to sheer exotericism. The true Sat-Guru must deal effectively with the presumptuousness and other delusions of his beginning devotees.

Sri Da Avabhasa with students in the early years of His Teaching Work, Los Angeles, 1972

In His Compassion, Sri Gurudev Da Love-Ananda has frequently addressed critical words to deluded practitioners of the Way of the Heart. These sometimes fiery Words are a true Blessing, for they realign His devotee to self-transcending and God-Realizing practice. Unless the Sat-Guru realigns the devotee to the practice of Satsang with him, the devotee is left with only his or her egoic tendencies, and he or she continues as a seeker looking for the "hit", the reward from the Spiritual Teacher. True Spiritual practice is the arduous confrontation with the egoic self, not a joyride of Bliss. And particularly at the beginning there are more experiences of the revelation of "Narcissus" than moments of Spiritual Bliss.

As a means to Instruct His devotees in the right practice of the Guru-devotee relationship, free of cultic approaches, Da Avabhasa released for publication the first edition of *The Hymn Of The True Heart-Master* just before the Feast of Da Avabhasa Purnima in 1982. This was His Free Rendering of portions of the traditional *Guru Gita,* the "Song of the Guru". This text, long sung in Ashrams throughout India, proclaims the necessity of the Guru-devotee relationship for Divine Self-Realization. The ancient text, however, needed purification, because it was full of warnings and curses for those who fail to acknowledge the exclusive Divinity of the particular Guru or leader of the religious sect making use of it. Heart-Master Da Love-Ananda's Free Rendering in its fullness became an entirely new work. *The Hymn Of The True Heart-Master* in its completed form represents the essence of the authentic Teaching of the *Guru Gita* but goes beyond it to express the expanse of Sri Da Avabhasa's own Wisdom-Teaching and Declaration about the true and time-honored Guru-devotee relationship.

Below is the major portion of His Introduction, "Beyond the Cultic Tendency in Religion", which contains His Instruction on the right and wrong approaches to the Sat-Guru:

3. The full range of disciplines in the Way of the Heart are simply described in the introductory book *Free Daism: The Ancient, Eternal, and New Religion of God-Realization* (forthcoming), by Richard Schorske, and comprehensively described in *The Dawn Horse Testament,* by Da Avabhasa.

[The Hymn Of The True Heart-Master] *is critical of the conventional or childish orientation of "Guru cultism". Such cultism is not only evident in the popular movements of the twentieth century, but it is a tendency that has always been present in the religious mood of mankind. Christianity is an ancient example of how a serious esoteric Spiritual movement, centered around the Teaching and Person of the Adept called Jesus of Nazareth, was later developed into the popular exoteric Christ-cult. The same tendency was responsible for developing the exoteric Krishna-cult on the basis of the esoteric Teaching of such texts as the Bhagavad Gita. The radical Teacher called Gautama was transformed into the celestial Buddha of the Mahayana tradition. And in our time it has become routine for both Masters and ordinary teachers to be instantly "cultified", exclusively Deified, and made the fascinating Object of a self-contained popular movement that worships the Master ritually and adores the Master as a Parent-like Savior, while embracing very little of the significant Teaching of the Teacher.*

The error of conventional cultism is precisely this childish or ego-based orientation to fascination with Teachers, God-Ideas, sacred lore, cosmic pictures, and self-based mysticism. Unfortunately, the Guru Gita itself is easily adaptable to such a cultic view, and its praises and curses often add the bitter and righteous language of cultic warfare to the communications between institutions that are supposed to be devoted to Spiritual purposes.

The cultic tendency in religion is the essence of what is wrong with religion. The problem is not that there is no God, or that there is no Sublime Teaching, or that there are no true Masters. The problem with religion is the childish egoism that is at the basis of all forms of ordinary existence.

People are [egoically] self-possessed, or un-Enlightened. It is this "disease" that the Masters of religion are here to cure. But those who follow or are fascinated by Masters are typically those who make or at least transform the institutions of the religion of their Masters. And true practitioners are very hard to find, or develop. Therefore, religious institutions tend to develop along lines that serve, accommodate, and represent the common egoity— and this is why the esoteric and radical Teachings of true Masters tend to be bypassed and even suppressed in the drive to develop the exoteric cult of the Person of the Master.

The relationship to the Master . . . is not an exoteric cultic matter. It is a profound discipline, necessarily associated with real and serious and mature practice of the esotericism of the radical Way Itself. Therefore, it is critical of the ego-based (or self-saving rather than self-sacrificing and self-transcending) practices of childish cultism.

The common cult is based on the tendency to resist real practice and opt for mere fascination with extraordinary phenomena (which are, in principle, not understood). Apart from the often petty demand for the observation of conventional rules (generally relative to ritualism and social morality), the cult of fascination tends to become righteously associated with no practice (that is, with the official or expected non-practice of Spiritual and meditative disciplines of an esoteric and radical kind). Just so, the cult of fascination tends to be equally righteous about maintaining fascinated faith (or indiscriminate belief) in the Parent-like Divine Status of one or another historical individual, religious idea, sacred tradition, or force of Nature.

Religious cultism is thus a kind of infantile collective madness. (And such madness is equally shared by secular cultists in every area of popular culture, including politics and scientism.) Religious cults breed "pharisaism" (or the petty righteousness of conventional thinking), Substitution myths (or the belief that personal self-transcendence is impossible, but also unnecessary because of what God or some Master or even some priest has already done), and every kind of intolerance and search for exclusive cultural dominance. Religious cults are populated by those who are generally neither inclined toward nor prepared for the real practice of Spiritual discipline, but who are nonetheless glamorized and consoled by association with the "holy" things and beliefs of the cult itself.

This error of cultism, or ego-based culture in general, must be considered very seriously. Cultism of every kind is a kind of ritualized infantilism, egoically bound to aggressive behavior in relation to self, to "insiders" and to "outsiders". Cults cause great social, cultural, and political trouble—as can now be seen in the development of world-wide conflicts based on the exclusive or egocentric orientation of religious traditions, political idealisms, and national identities.

All cults thrive on the psychology of hope, rather than self-sacrifice. Therefore, when all egos meet, they compete for the ultimate fulfillment of desires rather than cooperate in a mood of fearless tolerance and sane equanimity.

Clearly, this cultic tendency in religion, and the egoic tendency in life in general, must become the subject of our understanding, and all of mankind must be put to school to unlearn the method of egocentrism and intolerance. . . .

The Spiritual Master is to be understood in the context of the _practice_ of the radical Way, not apart from it. There is no alternative to personal practice. There is no Substitute for the _Realization_ of the Transcendental Divine Self. Right devotion to the Spiritual Master is not mere cultic or "gleeful" enthusiasm, but the profound practice of the disciplines of the Way on the basis of self-surrender, rather than self-concern and the search for self-glorification.

The Spiritual Master is not a Surrogate God or a Substitute Sacrifice, but a God-Pointer, a Proof of God and the Way, a Demonstration, a Sign, an Agent of Transmission, and an Awakener of those who are willing to surrender their [egoic] self-possession. The Way Itself is to live in _Freedom_, not to be bound by self, any other, or Nature as a whole. Therefore, the relationship to the Spiritual Master is the Context and the Means of Free Realization, and not a justification for popular egoity, childish dependency, adolescent reactivity, conventional social behavior and fulfillment, or any other goal or tendency of the deluded ego. . . .

Let this Way of devotion to the Master be embraced by all of you who *come to Me for Help. . . . Right formal association with Me is not generally a matter of personal association, but it is always a matter of practicing the Way of the Heart, which I have Revealed for the sake of your Liberation in Truth, as self-surrender and devotional alignment to the Grace of My Spiritual Heart-Transmission rather than perpetuating your self-concerned efforts, dissociated from God, from Me as the True Heart-Master, and from all of mankind.*

TRUE SURRENDER REQUIRES THE TRANSCENDENCE OF CHILDISH AND ADOLESCENT ATTITUDES

Da Avabhasa's early Teaching Work, beginning in 1970, took place in the context of a living experiment in the development of esoteric Spiritual community with His devotees. But in late November 1978, the Jonestown tragedy brought warning signs that the climate of cultural openness in which we had engaged this experiment might be threatened. The Jonestown incident commanded the attention of the news media, and the pejorative button-word "cult" suddenly was introduced into the popular vocabulary with a meaning specific to alternative religious and Spiritual groups of all kinds. Just days after the Jonestown incident, Sri Da Avabhasa gathered with His devotees in Land Bridge Pavilion at the Mountain Of Attention. He Spoke forcefully, as He had many times before, to His own community about the real issues involved, and He insisted His devotees continue to purify their own cultic habits even as they maintained their discrimination and integrity in the face of the media's blanket condemnation of Gurus and alternative religious movements:

SRI DA AVABHASA: Over the years you have all heard Me Speak about cultism in negative terms. I have criticized the cult of the Spiritual Master, as well as the cultic attachments that people create with one another. In other words, when there exists a certain hyped enthusiasm to which people are attracted, and when those people accept all the dogmas with which that particular group makes itself enthusiastic, they maintain themselves as opponents of the world and lose communication with the world in general and with the processes of life. Their attitude is, "We're it, we've found it." You have seen this attitude expressed thousands of times. I have seen you all do it. To Me, that enthusiasm is bizarre. There is something about the capacity of individuals for that kind of enthusiasm that makes My back tingle. It is a kind of madness. It is a tolerable neurosis as long as people do not become destructive. It is tolerated in general in our society. But I have always been moved to criticize this quality in you, because this is how you tend to approach Me. To the degree that you tend to approach Me in this manner, you make Me a cultic figure and you yourselves become a bunch of balmy enthusiasts.

In that condition I cannot deal with you, I cannot Teach you, you cannot live this practice, you cannot hear what I am Saying. . . . Everything about cultism that is negative is specifically criticized in My Wisdom-Teaching. I do not want your enthusiasm to be superficially generated by the books that I Write. I want you to "consider" the matters this literature contains. I want you to "consider" yourself very critically, very directly and rigorously, and come to the point of insight as it is expressed in these books. When you come to that point of insight into your own game, into your childishness and adolescence, you will be able to take up the practice I have Given to you, the forms of adaptation that serve your continued growth beyond your present stage of life. (December 17, 1978)

Even before the Jonestown incident of 1978, which closed the minds of so many to the possibility of authentic religious and Spiritual Ways other than the long-established religions, Sri Da Avabhasa very directly addressed the issues of irresponsibility, beginner's illusions, cultism, and the childish and adolescent approaches to the Sat-Guru. Following are three excerpts from *The Enlightenment of the Whole Body* (published in 1978) that speak directly to the responsibility of the devotee to transcend all cultic approaches to the Sat-Guru and religious practice. The first comes from an Essay aptly entitled "Sheep, Goats, Wolves, and the Manly Few Who Are a Sacrifice in God":

There has been so much popular communication and "hype" about "true" religion, "secret" esoteric spiritual practices, and "Great Masters" that such things have become part of the conventional self-imagery and "personal" mind of countless ordinary people. Very few people demonstrate the kind of responsibility, real intelligence, and creative power necessary even to begin practice of a truly religious and spiritual kind. But great numbers of childish and adolescent individuals embrace forms of exclusive cultism and self-glorifying belief. Just so, many people of that kind, unable to live as a true and consistent sacrifice, imagine themselves to be great, or worthy to dominate others. Many even imagine themselves to be Spiritual Masters.

I have seen many people come and go from [this Communion]. Those who left were commonly unable to make the gesture of surrender, love, service, and real understanding of the binding mechanics of self. Some simply returned to an ordinary self-indulgent life. But a good number have persisted in adolescent delusions of spiritual attainment—whereas, truly, they are incapable of even the simplest human and moral responsibilities.

This is common all over the world, wherever religious and spiritual matters become part of the popular culture. Therefore, since ancient times, schools and cults and techniques of all kinds have developed around individuals of all levels of experience and degrees of authenticity. And weak people tend to congregate around wolves, while wolves are always on the lookout for those who are weak enough to be exploited.

The games of mutual deception are common at every level of society. And "suckers" are born at a far greater rate than one per minute. All that can be said is that men and women who are seriously interested in the Great Process of Surrender and Sacrifice in God should study the available litera- ture and keep their eyes and ears open to the obvious. The Way is not every- where fully communicated, and true practitioners are <u>extremely</u> rare.

Spiritual Masters are developed in the human plane only very occasion- ally, and the function of such a one is to regenerate the Teaching and the Way itself. Any number of practitioners at various higher stages of human structural evolution may live at any point in time, but such individuals are not Spiritual Masters. They are only people on the Way. What is significant is the Way itself, not who is possessed of what signs of this and that experiential attainment. (pp. 147-48)

Sri Da Avabhasa makes the further point that cultism and religious fanaticism arise from a wrong relationship to Spiritual practice, in which immature motives and needs are being dramatized, rather than the genuine gesture of surrender to the Divine:

Spiritual life has nothing to do with the childishness that people tend to dramatize in the relationship to the Spiritual Master. I criticize that childish or dependent approach more directly than most people. Others are merely petulant about it, in the self-righteous mood of adolescence. But there are real reasons why both the childish and the adolescent approaches to the Spiritual Master are forms of destructive nonsense and must be overcome. However, the mature, sacrificial relationship to the Spiritual Master is itself absolutely Lawful and necessary. Those who object to that relationship might as well object to the relationship between the Earth and the sun. (p. 246)

Nowhere is basic human maturity more necessary than in religious and Spiritual practice, and it is a devotee's lack of this maturity that makes Spiritual Teachers into idols and the attempt to practice in relationship to such a Teacher fruitless and even destructive.

Writes Da Avabhasa in "The Mature Individual Is Not Bound or Afraid":

The mature individual or true devotee is free of childish and adolescent approaches to the Spiritual Master. He is neither childishly dependent, as upon a parent, nor adolescently independent, as in revolt against a parent. Rather, he turns to the Spiritual Master freely, in love and service, in gestures of sur- render to the Process and the Reality that are always Present and Awakening in that Company. Such an individual is not motivated by the [un-Happy] dilemmas and the self-protective searching for solutions that characterize the usual man. He has been awakened to intuition of his own Real Condition and to the native activity of love in service. He has been awak- ened through "hearing" the argument and "seeing" the Presence of the

Spiritual Master.[4] Thus, he is not bound or afraid. He is free to surrender in love to the Agent of his own Destiny, and in such surrender in love he fulfills the Law of practice wherein Grace may be given and transformation made. (p. 198)

The key to the right relationship to the Sat-Guru is a true understanding of Who He Is, and, therefore, what is actually being offered in the relationship to Him. Such a Sat-Guru has not become "God" in any exclusive sense, as the Supreme Being apart. Rather, the Divinely Enlightened Sat-Guru has transcended his or her egoic activity, and has thus Realized Identity with the Divine Condition that is also the Identity of all. Such a Sat-Guru brings that Blessing to others as a gift, calling them to also take up the practice of self-surrender in which they will more and more fully Realize the same Condition. Writes Heart-Master Da in an Essay called "Idols":

No thought or figure or any perception arising in the mind is, in itself, God. No thing, no body, no moment or place, in itself, is God. Rather, every moment, place, thing, body, or state of mind inheres in God. Whatever arises should be [Divinely] recognized in God, not idolized as God. Then all conditions become Reminders that draw us into the ecstatic presumption of the Mysterious Presence of the Living One.

A Transcendental Adept or true Spiritual Master is a Transparent Reminder of the Living One, a Guide to Ecstatic Remembrance of the One in Whom all conditions arise and change and pass away. Such an Adept is not to be made into the Idol of a Cult, as if God were exclusively contained in the objective person and subjective beliefs of a particular sect. Rather, right relationship to an Adept Spiritual Master takes the form of free ecstatic surrender to the Living Divine based on recognition of the Living One in the Revelation of Freedom, Happiness, Love, Wisdom, Help, and Radiant Power that Shines in the Company of the Adept. Right relationship to a true Spiritual Master is the most fundamental basis of the universal process that is true religion, and there is no basis for "religious differences" at the level of actual practice and Realization. (Scientific Proof of the Existence of God Will Soon Be Announced by the White House!, *pp. 314-15)*

As this passage suggests, when the cultic tendency is turned outward it can be dramatized as the claim to the exclusive Divinity (or Prophethood) of one's own Sat-Guru or Spiritual Master. Frequent claims of this nature are made, of course, by followers of Jesus of Nazareth, Mohammed, and other lesser known Teachers in many traditions (although it is hard to

---

4. "Hearing" is a technical term used by Sri Da Avabhasa to describe the intuitive and most fundamental understanding of all one's activity as the self-contraction, the resulting unique capability for the direct transcendence of the self-contraction, and the simultaneous intuitive awakening to the Revelation of the Divine Person and Self-Condition. When hearing is steadily exercised in meditation and in life, the native feeling of the heart ceases to be chronically constricted by self-contraction. The heart then begins to Radiate as love in response to the Spiritual (and Always Blessing) Presence of Sri Da Avabhasa. This emotional and Spiritual response of the whole being is what Heart-Master Da calls "seeing".

imagine that these Teachers would have themselves made such exclusive claims). The corollary to this assertion is that all other Gurus and God-Men are un-Realized, or even false prophets or evil-doers. When such a provincial attitude manifests, compassion towards others is lost, and religious self-righteousness can become actively destructive, such that the attempt to further the cause of the "only true God" becomes the source (as it has so often) of terrible aggression and violence.

I close this chapter with verses 28-32 of *The Hymn Of The True Heart-Master*, which summarize the right approach to the Sat-Guru:

28.

Do not practice the "childish cult" of superficial and ego-serving emotionalism (full of want and dependency, and empty of faith), and do not practice the "adolescent cult" of non-feeling (willful, self-absorbed, abstract, and independent), but always practice (and cultivate) the true (and truly feeling, and truly self-surrendering, and truly self-forgetting, and truly self-transcending) devotional Way of the Heart Itself.

29.

Neither God nor the Master of the Heart is your Parent. Therefore, do not expect God or the True Heart-Master to justify or protect or preserve or fulfill your egoic want and separateness.

30.

You are called to sacrifice your separate self in God. Therefore, cultivate right and self-transcending devotion to the True Heart-Master, in order to transcend the ego-"I" in the "Bright" by Grace Revealed Divine Condition of Being (Itself).

31.

To worship the True Heart-Master childishly is to worship and serve your separate self. To deny or resist the True Heart-Master is to worship and serve your separate self, adolescently. The separate self is, itself and always, the forgetting of the Heart-Source of the world. Therefore, be very devoted to Me, the True Master of your Heart, but not for the sake of ego-salvation, or the glorification of your separate self. Worship Me by surrendering your separate self to Me. Surrender to Me in order to forget and transcend your separate self in Me. Forget and transcend your separate self in Me in order that you may, by Grace, Remember and Realize the Divine Heart-Source and Self of all and All.

32.

I Am the Sign and the Revelation and the Proof of God in the world. I Am the Testament and the Means of Freedom Itself.

Sri Love-Anandashram, August 1991

CHAPTER SIX

"History Will Be Made by the Event That Has Occurred in My Room"

THE FUNCTIONS OF THE SAT-GURU AS SUPREMELY EXEMPLIFIED BY SRI DA AVABHASA

*I*t is Heart-Master Da's special Work to begin a fully new tradition. In my own experience as a student of the Spiritual traditions, I cannot find a single example of a Sat-Guru who was required to so fully create from nothing an entire culture of practice and Realization. Gautama the Buddha is an example of an individual who began his own Spiritual Way and established a culture of practice, yet even he was addressed by people who had respect for Spiritual concerns and by patrons who valued his work. Heart-Master Da Love-Ananda Appeared in a culture devoid of such right understanding. Thus, He was required to generate an authentic Spiritual culture afresh, with virtually no precedent or background to rely upon.

In 1980, I and another devotee of Sri Da Avabhasa visited Chogyam Trungpa Rinpoche, at the time the most widely-known Buddhist Teacher in the United States. Chogyam Trungpa had himself engaged in painstaking work to adapt and combine the practices of Buddhism, and particularly Tibetan Buddhism, with the Western culture of North America, in order to be able to instruct his own devotees. And in this endeavor he had the support of hundreds of years of Tibetan sacred history.

We described to him the Divine Life and Work of Sri Da Avabhasa, showed videotape footage of Him, both in silent Darshan and speaking, and told him about Heart-Master Da's perception of His own Work. Chogyam Trungpa was obviously moved by the presentation.

The next day, Chogyam Trungpa's personal secretary conveyed to us the Rinpoche's informal comments about our meeting. First, he had remarked that Heart-Master Da Love-Ananda was "genuine". His second comment was a very perceptive acknowledgement, from a lineage holder in the Tibetan tradition of many generations, of the undertaking that Heart-Master Da Avabhasa had assumed: "It is tremendously difficult to begin a new tradition."

Chogyam Trungpa Rinpoche

As Heart-Master Da Love-Ananda's devotee, it is my clear perception that no Spiritual Figure has ever made such an immense Sacrifice as Heart-Master Da Love-Ananda did in His Teaching Work and continues to do now during His Divine Emergence Work. Such Work could only be the Intervention of the Divine on Earth. As Heart-Master Da Love-Ananda Wrote in October 1980:

I am the Dharma Bearer whose birth in the West has been prophesied in many traditions and by many individuals. I have been born to restore the great principle, or Way of life.

Heart-Master Da Love-Ananda's Life and Work thus Exemplify all of the Functions that a Sat-Guru may perform, including not only those Functions that are essential to any Sat-Guru, but also the Functions that are required of one who comes at a time when an entire Spiritual Way must be newly established. For the purposes of this chapter, I have arranged these Functions into nine categories:

1. The Sat-Guru as the Giver of Divine Blessing to his or her devotees.
2. The Sat-Guru as the Object of Contemplation for his or her devotees.
3. The Sat-Guru as Demand and Guide, who establishes the "culture of expectation and inspiration" for his or her devotees.
4. The Sat-Guru as Clarifier and Purifier of the Great Tradition.
5. The Sat-Guru as Prophet, who Instructs the entire world by his or her criticisms.
6. The Sat-Guru as Giver of the Written Teaching, whose Word is a unique Transmission of his or her Blessing-Grace.
7. The Sat-Guru as Demonstrator of the Teaching in life, whose Teaching Leelas clarify in living terms every aspect of human existence.
8. The Sat-Guru as Creator of the Means by which his or her Blessing-Transmission may forever be made available.
9. The Sat-Guru as Blesser of the world.

I have begun with the Sat-Guru as the Giver of Divine Blessing, and the Sat-Guru as the Divine Murti, or the Object of Contemplation, since these Functions are characteristic of both major phases of Sri Da Avabhasa's Spiritual Work—His Teaching Work and His Divine Emergence Work. These two Functions are themselves closely related in that the Divine Blessing of the Sat-Guru is communicated largely through his or her Function as the Divine Murti, or Object of Contemplation, Itself. The next six Functions are largely associated with the Teaching Work of the Sat-Guru, the active Work of the establishment of a new tradition. The last Function, that of the Transcendental Work of the Adept, was Demonstrated by Sri Da Avabhasa during the years of His Teaching Work, but it is especially magnified now in the years of His Divine Emergence Work. And this chapter ends with a description of Da Avabhasa's Divine Emergence, which even today unfolds with unprecedented Divine Grace and Blessing.

His Demonstration of all of these Functions of the Sat-Guru has been so extraordinary that He has created the unique standard against which any previous Revelation or Demonstration can now be viewed. Sri Da Avabhasa's Great Work in all of these Functions is a Tremendous Gift to mankind, of proportions that cannot be measured.

THE SAT-GURU AS THE GIVER OF DIVINE BLESSING TO HIS OR HER DEVOTEES

The Heart-Transmission of Sri Da Avabhasa (discussed more fully in the final chapter of this book) is truly the Essence of the Way of the Heart Itself and the Supreme Blessing in the worlds. Through the Grace of His Heart-Transmission He Communicates His Bliss, His Love, His Ecstasy to all beings. That Heart-Transmission overwhelms the mind, the body, and the egoic self, and is Itself all that His devotee desires, because It is Supremely Attractive and pleasurable beyond compare.

Transmission of the Divine Condition to the devotee is the Guru-Principle. I cannot describe to you the many times when, for no reason—sitting somewhere, walking, watching a movie, in meditation—suddenly I have received the Gift of the Divine Revelation. Without any cause I have been overwhelmed with Sat-Guru Da's Grace and moved completely out of the body-mind's point of view, and I rest in the Radiant Bliss of Sri Gurudev Da Love-Ananda. In moments I feel the signs come over me of His characteristic Blessing. His Blissful Condition takes over my body-mind. The navel fills with His Force. The mind is suffused with His Light. A Happiness beyond measure fills the heart.

There are also those endless times when there appears to be some reason for His Gift of Love-Bliss. I have just presented Him with a book or some other gift, and so there is apparently some reason why His Attention is moved to me. But in every moment truly He is there for me to turn to. Just His initial Revelation to me of the Divine already put me in His debt forever. But my debt mounts greater all the time, as I receive His constant Blessing and Transmission.

From the very beginning of Sri Da Avabhasa's Re-Awakening to His Divinely Self-Realized Condition at the Vedanta Temple in Los Angeles in 1970, He has done this Work of Blessing. It has been His principal Work even throughout the years of His Teaching Work. No matter what particular outward activity Sri Da Avabhasa Generated for the sake of Serving His devotees or the world at large, He was also doing this simple Heart-Transmission and Blessing. If one's eye was attentive to Him truly, in any circumstance or situation He was always in essence doing this same Work, whether He was Discoursing on some aspect of the Teaching, directly Instructing His devotees about their personal lives, or simply at rest in Love-Bliss.

In the early spring of 1974, when I had been associated with the Way of the Heart for less than a year, I was Blessed to sit with Him, along with seventy or eighty of His other devotees, in Temple Eleutherios at the Mountain Of Attention Sanctuary. It was a period in which His devotees regularly asked questions of Da Avabhasa, and He, seated on His Chair on a small dais at the front of the room, was Graciously responding. I was seated on the floor perhaps twenty feet from Him. I was curious about a famous traditional story of the Buddha's Transmission, and so I asked:

"Is it possible that the Buddha could have Enlightened Kashyapa instantly by holding up a flower?"

It was a simple moment, probably not even noticed by most of the other devotees in room, during this rather wild period in the history of our Communion. Heart-Master Da Gave me a big smile, and His eyes then got very large. That is all I remember—until about a minute later when my mind returned. Heart-Master Da Love-Ananda was no longer looking at me. It took me a moment to piece together what had just happened. First I remembered that I was a person, and then that I was sitting there in the Temple at the Mountain Of Attention, and then finally I remembered that I had asked Heart-Master Da Love-Ananda a question about whether the Buddha could have Enlightened Kashyapa by his glance alone.

Da Avabhasa's Glance had plunged me instantaneously into samadhi. Sri Gurudev had answered my question by Granting His Enlightened Transmission directly! Unlike Kashyapa in the traditional story, I was not then prepared to make my Sat-Guru's Transmission the basis of my moment to moment practice. But I had been clearly shown that Heart-Master Da's Glance Transmits the Enlightened Disposition beyond any limitation of the body-mind.

Some years later, in the summer of 1980, I happened to mention Kashyapa once again to Heart-Master Da. Sri Gurudev and a few of His other devotees had gathered in a small room in Bright Behind Me, which at that time was Heart-Master Da's Residence at the Mountain Of Attention. Some remark reminded me of the story, and I blurted out, "Master Da, that is like the time the Buddha Enlightened Kashyapa." Heart-Master Da Love-

Ananda was looking at another part of the room. He turned His head toward me and, smiling, looked me in the eyes. Again, a few moments later, when my mind returned, I realized that Sri Da Avabhasa's Truth had been made directly Obvious to me by His Gaze alone.

These two stories are particularly significant not because they are associated with Kashyapa and a specific notion about Transmission, but because they point to the fact that even when Sri Da Avabhasa was involved verbally and actively in His Teaching Work with His devotees, His fundamental Communication was nonetheless made not through words but via direct Spiritual Transmission.

Over and over again, the devotees who came to Him with questions, in His mere Company and by the Power of His Transmission, forgot their problems, and all sense of even their limited identity, becoming distracted by His Transcendental Divine Identity—the Love-Bliss that Pervades and Transcends all time and space. Heart-Master Da does not do the Work of Transmission. Rather He merely Is, and His Radiant Being spontaneously and continuously Communicates Itself to all who will receive It.

This Blessing by the Sat-Guru is not made based on any intention or process of the mind. It is freely and spontaneously Given by virtue of his (or her) Realization, and in free response to his devotees and the world.

Early in His Teaching Work, Da Avabhasa talked about the spontaneous movement that He makes toward His devotees:

SRI DA AVABHASA: *The form of your relationship to Me is the matter that is significant at the beginning and always. You must approach Me as a devotee. That is an absolutely necessary and absolutely obvious expectation. When someone comes to Me in the form of sacrifice, My body opens up. I do not tell it to. I respond to that Spiritual being and presence. That is how this Siddhi works. If there is no sacrifice of separate and separative self, no devotional approach, regardless of all the social niceties that may be there, then this [tapping His chest] does not open. You can come to Me for years with your fruit, and there will be no sadhana, no Grace, not even a lesson grasped, because there is a law alive in our relationship. It is mutual sacrifice. (January 11, 1976)*

A story from 1974 illustrates this point very well. It was the evening of a lively gathering at the Manner of Flowers, Sri Da Avabhasa's Residence at the Mountain Of Attention. Sri Gurudev Da Love-Ananda was sitting on a sofa, and in the midst of the frolicking, one devotee, seated on a padded chair across the room, committed a breach of decorum in relationship to Him. The Adept looked across to where this devotee was sitting, fifteen feet away, and forcefully remarked, "Okay, that's it! You've gone too far. There must be a consequence for that. I am now going to cut off my Love from you for ten minutes." The devotee gulped and laughed nervously, but he kept his attention firmly surrendered to Heart-Master Da. After a few minutes,

Heart-Master Da looked back at the admonished devotee and raised His eyebrows, growled at him humorously, and then looked away. The devotee remained surrendered. Finally, after several more "cold" glances from Heart-Master Da, the devotee called out, "Bubba!" (as Sri Gurudev was then known).

"Yes, what is it?" He angrily replied.

"Bubba, You can't do it!"

Da Avabhasa dropped all His serious facade and burst out laughing. "I know I can't!"

THE SAT-GURU AS THE OBJECT OF CONTEMPLATION FOR HIS OR HER DEVOTEES

One cannot find the Divine Reality on one's own. It is too elusive. Where would one look in one's own body-mind? The natural elements themselves may awaken wonder or awe, or teach a lesson about the physical world, but they cannot in themselves serve human beings ultimately. The abstract Divinity may be conceived by the mind, and found to be interesting and consoling, but how can the abstract Divine bring about psycho-physical transformation in the human body-mind such that literal God-Realization is attained?

At times various momentary Divine Revelations have occurred to make tangible the appearance of God. Various Buddhas and Bodhisattvas (such as Tara, Avalokitesvara, Amida, or Hevajra) play primary roles in the lives of Mahayana and Vajrayana Buddhist practitioners. In the Theravada Buddhist tradition, Gautama (the historical Buddha) or Maitreya (the Buddha prophesied to appear in the future) often takes on such a role. Kuan Yin, the Chinese form of Avalokitesvara Bodhisattva, appears mercifully to devotees in China. The Indian devotee also prays for the Divine to appear to his or her sight in personal form, often to any of an entire pantheon of Gods (such as Siva, Krishna, Rama, or the Goddess Durga), each ultimately conceived to represent (or to be a means of Realizing) the greatest Reality. The fountainhead of the Semitic religions is similarly the tangible appearance of the Divine—for Judaism, the revelations to Moses in the Sinai desert; for Christianity, the appearance of the God-Man Jesus and the miracles and visions attributed to him and to the Virgin Mary and to the saints; and for Islam, the visitations of the Archangel Gabriel, the messenger of God, granted to Mohammed.

Such momentary Vision or sight of the Divine is a tremendous Blessing, and it can awaken faith and be the source for a kind of devotional practice. However, the greatest gift is the Living Sat-Guru, who does not merely appear in a visionary flash, but who is alive to offer instruction and Blessing for the length of a human lifetime, and who may ultimately establish himself in the hearts of his devotees eternally, as the Divine Person in Person. This is the fullest service of the Divine, to appear alive in like form to men and women, to serve human beings directly in present time.

Thus, the Sat-Guru must appear in bodily (human) Form in order to manifest the Divine to his (or her) devotees directly. The Darshan, or the mere visual Contemplation, of the Sat-Guru, is traditionally understood to be a profound Revelation. For the body of the Divinely Realized Sat-Guru naturally or spontaneously transmits the Divine Condition to the viewer who has prepared himself or herself through genuine self-transcending practice. In late 1988, Sri Da Avabhasa, Graciously sitting bodily with His devotees to answer their questions, exclaimed:

SRI DA AVABHASA: LOOK AT ME! [Shouting!] WHAT ARE YOU LOOKING AT? WHO?

This Body is My Argument! My Words are just Discourse to Serve you. I am here to directly Reveal the Way of the Heart to you. If you are Taught by the mere sighting of Me, then you will devote your life to this practice. And if you cannot Find Me because your eyes are covered with separate and separative self, then your response will be nonexistent or minimal. If you can forget your own mind for a moment, you will Find Me (and respond to Me).

*Initiation simply by the sighting of My bodily human Form (at first, only via photographic or other technical Murti-Representations, and, in due course, directly, by coming into My physical Company) should be enough to motivate a lifetime of sadhana. Most of those who have lived an authentic religious life have done so on the basis of much less than this Grace-Given sighting of Me. How many of those who have lived an authentic religious life have been Given the Gift of the Divine Vision at the beginning of their practice? Study them—they all talk about finding that Vision at the end. . . . (*The Love-Ananda Gita, *"I Am What you Require" section)*

An understanding of the practice of Guru-contemplation is found throughout the world's esoteric traditions. In the Guru Yoga of Tibetan Buddhism, the devotee "becomes" the Guru through contemplation of the Guru. The essential practice of Tibetan Guru Yoga is the "union with the nature of the Guru"[1] by visualizing the Guru constantly before one, or above one's head, or with his feet standing in one's heart. As described by the modern teacher Dilgo Khyentse, "Essentially, the practice is to remember the guru in all our activities, whether in meditation or in post-meditation periods."[2]

In the Hindu tradition such Guru-contemplation plays a dominant role. As we have quoted, the *Kularnava Tantra*, the most quoted Tantric text, proclaims: "At the root of dhyana [meditation] is the form of the Guru. . . ."

1. Dilgo Khyentse, *The Wish-Fulfilling Jewel: The Practice of Guru Yoga According to The Longchen Nyingthig Tradition*, trans. Konchog Tenzin (Boston: Shambhala, 1988), p. 3.

2. *The Wish-Fulfilling Jewel*, p. 10.

The *Guru Gita* admonishes in verse 167:

One should, by practicing meditation on the Guru, become Brahmamaya (attain Brahmic consciousness) while in this body, and attain the highest state of emancipation. . . . There is no doubt about this.[3]

In the Sufi tradition, there is also a practice of contemplation of the Master. Writes Annemarie Schimmel in *Mystical Dimensions of Islam:*

The strong relationship between sheikh and murid [disciple] is exemplified in the technique of tawajjuh, concentration upon the sheikh, which later orders, mainly the Naqshbandiyya, considered necessary for the successful performance of the dhikr [the practice of remembrance of God].[4]

The Living Sat-Guru is the Supremely Attractive Murti, or visible Form of God, whose Revelation of the Divine Condition draws the devotee into contemplation of God in every moment, through the constant Grace of his Spiritual Transmission. Once the Divine has been seen and felt through the medium of the Sat-Guru, then all doubts about whether God exists evaporate, all dry and philosophical discussion about the existence of the Divine Reality simply falls away. In His great Scripture *The Love-Ananda Gita*, Sri Gurudev Da Love-Ananda Describes this miraculous process:

My bodily (human) Form is (Itself) the Teaching.
My Spiritual (and Always Blessing) Presence is the Means.
My Very (and Inherently Perfect) State is the Revelation Itself.
Therefore, Contemplation of My bodily (human) Form, and (via My bodily human Form) My Spiritual (and Always Blessing) Presence, and (via My Spiritual, and Always Blessing, Presence) My Very (and Inherently Perfect) State, even, Ultimately, to the degree of Perfect Oneness with Me (and Perfect non-separation from all and All), is the Way that I offer to you and to all.

◆ ◆ ◆

You (necessarily) become (or conform to the likeness of) whatever you Contemplate, or Meditate on, or even think about.
Therefore, Contemplate Me, and transcend even all thought by Meditating on Me.

◆ ◆ ◆

Therefore (at last, or Ultimately, and by These Means of Grace), Realize Me Perfectly (by Perfectly self-forgetting Me-Remembrance in the Heart of Consciousness Itself). (verses 30-33, 47, 48, and 103)

3. *Sri Guru Gita*, trans. Swami Narayanananda (Rishikesh, Himalayas: The Divine Life Society, 1972), p. 61.

4. Annemarie Schimmel, *Mystical Dimensions of Islam* (Chapel Hill: The University of North Carolina Press, 1975), p. 237.

These verses, supremely simple, bear the message of the gift and the necessity of the Adept.

What is it that the Sat-Guru most specifically does? He (or she) Grants his devotee the Vision of the Murti, or Form, of the Divine. He reveals his Samadhi. He allows himself to be present in his Divine Sign for the contemplation of his devotee. In a Talk published in the "I Am What you Require" section of *The Love-Ananda Gita*, Sri Da Avabhasa Spoke of the Grace that is the bodily (human) Form of the Sat-Guru, and of the actual practice of the Realization of the Divine Reality that is made possible by that Blessing:

Contemplate My bodily (human) Form and My Spiritual (and Always Blessing) Presence and My Very (and Inherently Perfect) State. Those words follow one another with "ands" in between, you see. But you must understand that this devotion is, fundamentally, to My bodily (human) Form. Through devotion to My bodily (human) Form, My Spiritual (and Always Blessing) Presence is Found, by Grace. Through further devotion to My bodily (human) Form and My Spiritual (and Always Blessing) Presence, My Very (and Inherently Perfect) State is Found, by Grace. One (or each of These) is not simply sitting next to the other here. It is through this bodily (human) Vehicle that I am Found, Spiritually, and Ultimately.

It is not that you should, perhaps, select this bodily (human) Form now, and then, perhaps, in another moment, look for My Spiritual (and Always Blessing) Presence. You must understand how the process of Revelation works. It works the same way that the process of sadhana works. Therefore, you must first establish devotion in response to My bodily (human) Form. All the Revelations are Given from the beginning, tacitly, but, in the context of such devotion, over time, and more and more, you Realize the various aspects of the Revelations experientially, as you yourself mature.

What makes this process possible is the Supreme Attractive Power of the Sat-Guru. The Divine Condition Itself, which is contacted through the Contemplation of the God-Realizer, Attracts the devotee. Following is a testament to the potency of the practice of Feeling-Contemplation, written by Peter Lennon while on retreat in Sri Da Avabhasa's Company at Sri Love-Anandashram. Although Peter had been a practitioner of the Way of the Heart for a relatively brief period, he experienced a remarkable infusion of Sri Da Avabhasa's Blessing Grace.

On the first Darshan occasion of my retreat, I could feel my anticipation and joy at seeing Sri Gurudev.

Divine World-Teacher Darshan Mandir, the special Hall where we sat, is such a powerful and Living Domain of Da Avabhasa, the Great One. It is permeated with His Siddhi. We chanted as we waited, Contemplating His Murti-Form [in this case, a sacred photographic Image of Sri Da Avabhasa]. I began to feel prepared and pervaded by this sacred occasion. Then the conch began to call out the coming of the God-Man. My attention was riveted to the door where He would enter. At this point my mind began to drop away, and my body was not mine anymore.

When He came through the door, His Form glowed with the "Brightness" of His Realization, bringing me into a feeling dimension beyond my usual capabilities.

My body began to swoon and moan at the sight of Him. Every molecule in my body stood at attention, and I lost all self-consciousness or concern. Waves of Blissful energy washed through and around me. All I could do was raise my hands in worship and praise of Him, uttering a pleasurable wailing moan of ecstasy.

At this point we were to offer our gifts to Him. It was an ordeal to hold myself together enough to get up. The sight of His Bliss-wounded and vulnerable State overwhelmed me. Then a powerful Force seemed to rise from my lower body, driving me forward to bow again and again. I was praising Him in gutteral moans and crying with joy. I have never been able to express this kind of surrender and devotion to Him, but now the response of my heart dominated all else, because it is His.

My hands were outstretched, and my whole being was being drawn to Him. At some point, the downward Force became so powerful, pushing me back, that I was laid on the floor on my back. In an instant my hands, which had been tingly and alive, began to swell with a force—the likes of which I have never felt before—extending down my arms. It was like having 100,000 volts of electricity coursing through my body and still surviving. This energy entered my body with such force that I began to writhe and slide on the floor as it filled me from head to toe. It felt like I was being lifted off the ground and then slammed through the floorboards, yet there was no distress, fear, or pain. I was in the Hands of the Great One. I knew that I had to stay with Him and surrender, which was the only thing I could do. My heart knew no other choice.

My chest kept heaving, and my breathing was very rapid. At one point, I felt as though Sri Gurudev was standing over me, sticking His hands into and through my chest, grabbing my heart, lifting me up and dropping me down. Something deep inside me began to loosen up. I began trying to express something I was feeling in my heart—it was crying out of my throat, first inaudibly and then louder and louder. Finally, I realized it was His Divine Name, "Da", which I kept repeating until it was all I could say. My entire being was flopping around like a landed fish. The swelling in my heart continued until I began to hear a voice yelling, "I love You, I love You. . . ."—then I realized that I was the one yelling!

At this point the Spirit-Current began to subside a little bit, but I could not yet sit up. My hands were still outstretched, huge waves of energy kept surging through me and in and out of my feet and head, producing kriyas. Gradually, my body became quiet—waves of Blissful, soothing energy bathed me from head to foot. At this point I had an incredible desire to see

Sri Gurudev (I could not see Him from where I was lying on the floor). But I could not move. I felt dissolved and surrendered into His Spirit-Current. I realized I was not in any way living this body. He was Living me.

As my desire to see Sri Gurudev's bodily (human) Form increased, I felt a Force Intervene that allowed me to sit up and regard Him. As I looked up, the Sight that met my eyes was beyond anything I could put into words.

I saw His Form in a way I had never seen before—Radiant, full of colors. The room was blinding; I had to close my eyes repeatedly. He took over the whole room with His Divine Presence. It was the Vision of God before me in bodily (human) Form. At this sighting my heart filled with devotion.

When He put His hand in the nearby water bowl to Bless it for us, the entire hall erupted in screams and loving praise. My body filled with the bliss of self-forgetting praise and gratitude.

After He Blessed the water and the Prasad, He stood to Give us Prasad. He never stops Giving.

The Hall was filled again with His Limitless Love and our gratitude. We were ruined, Pervaded by His Blessing, puddles on the floor.

Then He stood there as we shouted out our praise, Blessing and Gracing us beyond anything I could fathom.

Thank You, Beloved Sri Gurudev, for Your Loving Grace and Your Gifts of surrender and devotion.

The Sat-Guru as Demand and Guide, Who Establishes the "Culture of Expectation and Inspiration" for His or Her Devotees

The devotee could never go through the arduous process that results in Divine Enlightenment without a Guide. There is just too much involved, too many levels of bondage, too many trials to be passed through. As Heart-Master Da Love-Ananda said in the Talk "The Divine

151

Physics of Evolution", published in *Scientific Proof of the Existence of God Will Soon Be Announced by the White House!*:

SRI DA AVABHASA: There is a profound difference between the condition of the usual man or woman and the Condition of the Awakened individual. It is an inconceivable leap in evolution. But there is a real process for it, and there is Help for it: the mature, devotional relationship to the Awakened Spiritual Master. . . .

    What must take place, if spiritual life is to be true, is not just a change in your mind, an inner awakening, a good feeling about everything. Spiritual processes do not occur in the subjective nonsense that people associate with religion—all this vicarious belief and vicarious salvation—as if real Awakening were just a matter of asking some silly questions or going to a few lectures for the weekend! That is not Enlightenment. Enlightenment is a literal change of the whole body. When you have acquired the human form, the literal changes that must occur are not really so much in its outward appearance, because you already have the necessary structure. But the changes that must occur are literal, psycho-physical changes, just as literal as if you were to acquire more legs and arms, except that the most dramatic changes occur in dimensions different from the outward shape of the body. Certainly changes occur in the flesh and the elemental structures of the body, but the changes do not really alter its outward shape. The change is as literal as evolving from a dinosaur to a human being, and it is as dramatic as that, but it principally occurs at more subtle levels of the physics of the bodily being. There are literal changes in the nervous system, literal changes in the chemistry of the body, literal changes in the structural functioning of the brain. (pp. 365-66)

For such a profound transformation to occur, the devotee needs the Divine Demand and Inspiration of the Sat-Guru. The devotee needs the Sat-Guru's forcefulness and strength and calling. And the devotee needs the Sat-Guru's constant and living example.

Heart-Master Da has pointed out the incredible lethargy that characterizes the typical Spiritual aspirant. The aspirant gets stuck and fixed in his or her practice. The aspirant is consoled by experiences, and as soon as there is even the smallest growth, the aspirant stops there, deluded by false notions of progress. The living Sat-Guru's Instruction is a Demand, a Shout to wake up the devotee from his or her sleep. He requires that the devotee "get with it", and that he or she begin to grow again. The Sat-Guru confronts and counters the illusions of the disciple, and will not accept endless excuses about the difficulties and demands of sadhana.

The Sat-Guru redirects the devotee from all the possible wanderings of attention. Things that devotees have held on to for an entire life are addressed, revealed, and understood and released through the Guru's Demands and Instruction. The devotee cannot do this on his or her own.

You can practice various disciplines as intensely as possible, and push yourself with great intention, but this alone will not touch that part of your being where you are most tightly bound. Your own subjectivity prevents you from even seeing it. All your egoic striving to surrender cannot succeed. The Living Divine Adept, who has Realized the entire process, must come to Liberate and Guide his devotee.

The true Sat-Guru is the only one willing to truly confront his (or her) devotee, to turn the devotee away from the egoic principle. The courage required of the Sat-Guru in this process is superhuman. Only because he sees every manifestation of egoity as his devotee's own suffering is the Sat-Guru willing to completely reveal to the devotee even the darkest hidden qualities. Only because he wants, out of true compassion, to free his devotee is he willing to stir up all the reactivity and pain that such self-awareness will bring about in the devotee. And in Truth, the devotee finally comes to realize, everything must be revealed, surrendered, and transformed in the process of God-Realization.

In the very first collection of published Talks of Sri Da Avabhasa, this demand of the Sat-Guru is clearly communicated:

The Guru is a kind of irritation to his friends. You can't sleep with a dog barking in your ear, at least most people can't. There is some sort of noise to which everyone is sensitive, and it will keep them awake. The Guru is a constant wakening sound. He is always annoying people with this demand to stay awake, to wake up. He doesn't seduce them within the dream. He doesn't exploit their seeking. He is always offending their search and their preference for unconsciousness. He shows no interest in all of that. He puts it down. He is always doing something prior to the mind. He always acts to return you from the mind, from fascination. (The Method of the Siddhas, p. 152)

The Guru does not come to satisfy devotees or disciples. A satisfied disciple is still the one he was. The Guru is only interested in the utter, radical dissolution of that whole limitation that appears as his disciple. He is not here to satisfy that limitation, to make it feel comfortable. He is here to return men to their own experience, their always present, chronic experience, their dilemma, their unconsciousness. He is here to return men to that, not to prevent them from seeing it, not to keep them obsessively involved with symbols or yogic stimulations of light or sound, or some complex vision of God, some image of Reality, so they will never experience and recognize their own state. The Guru moves by non-support. He undermines the disciple. He skins him! He does not torture him for fun, but he undermines that process that is his suffering. (p. 140)

Besides Giving us the Grace of His Love, Sri Gurudev Da Love-Ananda has also Instructed me and all His devotees with the force of His Divine Anger and Criticism, pointing things out to me that were my own limitations and that needed to be changed. He has also done this more intensely and with more force than I have experienced anywhere else in my life. And this confrontation with my own limitations truly hurts and is extremely difficult. But I have come to see this also as the Sat-Guru's Blessing. Who else is so courageous as to ignore the conventions of social relationship, and really, directly say what needs to be heard? As I have grown stronger in my practice of the Way of the Heart, and have understood more clearly Who Sat-Guru Da Is, I have also been able to accept and to feel more deeply His purifying Criticisms. I have been able to see them as Grace, and to use them, and to know that they are Given for the same reason as His Gracious Glance and Smile—to allow me to release more of my egoic bond, and to Draw me beyond myself into the Divine Condition.

I was given a lesson in this on one occasion when I came into a gathering with Sat-Guru Da having failed Him in my service and feeling very much in need of His Help. Sri Da Avabhasa began to Serve me very forcefully. He Shouted at me for not serving Him more fully and for not defending Him during a difficult time in the history of our Communion in 1985 when He had been wrongfully criticized in the newspapers and media, and therefore for not rightly living the relationship to Him as my Sat-Guru. He Shouted at me continuously for over an hour. As His Voice grew louder, I became scared. He is very Powerful, and in my own egoity I did everything I could in my mind to defend myself. I kept thinking about what I could say to counter His Shout. I kept finding things in the Words He was saying that would allow me to feel good about myself and to justify myself to Him the next time I would speak. As He Spoke, my attention was on looking for ways that I would be able to prove that I was still worthy of His Love, and I kept a dialogue going on in my mind that countered His Spoken Words.

The gathering had been going on for several hours, so about this time there was a short break. After discussions with my friends during this break, I returned to Da Avabhasa's Company in a different disposition. When He began to Shout at me again, I now remained in relationship with Him as His devotee. I understood Him to be my True Heart-Master, Whose every Action is for the sake of my purification. I understood that He is my great Help and that I needed only to surrender to Him, so I allowed myself to feel Him without dissociation. I allowed myself to be penetrated by His Shouts. This process was frightening to me as an ego, for I stopped defending myself and listened to what He said without armor or withholding. I felt Him directly. And as I did, I felt Da Avabhasa's Anger ripping through my obstructions, purifying and releasing me of the burden that I was carrying relative to everything that He was saying. I was able to let go of my guilt and remorse about my past weakness and wrong relationship to Him. I could release the pain and hurt of the months when I had been frustrated by my own apparent inability to serve Sri Gurudev effectively. I began to understand that I had been so stuck that this Shout was necessary for me to unwind. Tears rolled down my cheeks as I viewed Sat-Guru Da still

Shouting at me, still Angry at me. I was deeply pained by the truth of what He was saying, but even more than this I felt that His Anger was truly a Blessing, that it was freeing me of my bondage.

Sri Gurudev Da Love-Ananda has for many years looked forward to the time when the outward forms of His Demand are no longer necessary. As the community of His devotees matures, Sri Da Avabhasa's Demand must become incorporated and fully expressed within the culture of practitioners, both as the expectation of each one's fulfillment of the Way of the Heart and as a cultural voice that inspires all to the real practice.

THE SAT-GURU AS CLARIFIER AND PURIFIER OF THE GREAT TRADITION

Incarnating in the West at the time that He did, Heart-Master Da Love-Ananda confronted a culture influenced by the most extraordinary conglomeration of Spiritual Teachings that the world has ever seen. Thanks to a proliferation of translations of ancient and modern texts, the advent of near-universal literacy, and the worldwide distribution of books, you can go into virtually any large bookstore in the world and find paperback descriptions of esoteric Teachings stemming from every tradition in the world.

Sri Da Avabhasa has compared the contemporary mass of religious and Spiritual Teachers and Ways to a "crowd of silly Napoleons or mad Christs in an asylum", each claiming to have Revealed the one and true Divine Way. This analogy is drawn from the story of an actual experiment conducted in the 1950s by Milton Rokeach in Ypsilanti Mental Asylum in Michigan. Three individuals, each claiming that they were Jesus of Nazareth, were brought together by Dr. Rokeach for several discussion sessions. It was hoped that by confronting each other, they would each see the folly of their conflicting claims to be Jesus. However, instead, each became more entrenched in his claim, refusing even to notice the others, so that by the end of the experiments they were if anything more confirmed in their own delusion.[5] Sri Da Avabhasa once joked that on His booklists He had placed, back-to-back, books by individuals or about schools of thought that, like the three Christs of Ypsilanti, would not even acknowledge one another in real life!

The end result of the information explosion about religious and Spiritual life has not been clarity, but mass confusion. Everyone who wanders through what Da Avabhasa has called the "wilderness of doctrine" has a mind full of complex and contradictory views about God and the various practices of Spiritual life. Even for one raised in the secular West without any formal religious training, all sorts of dogmas have been unconsciously

5. Milton Rokeach, *The Three Christs of Ypsilanti: A Psychological Study* (New York: Columbia University Press, 1981).

absorbed. Sri Gurudev Da Love-Ananda has been confronted by individuals whose minds are filled with Judeo-Christian traditional ideas (heaven and hell, purgatory, Jesus' resurrection and ascension) coexisting with notions of Eastern Spirituality (the attainment of God-Realization through inverted meditation and "brain mysticism", and the asceticism of the Buddha), all combined awkwardly with the atheism, intellectual skepticism, and body-based orientation of the new "religion" of scientific materialism. Thus, it has fallen to Da Avabhasa to clarify, purify, and put in perspective the entire Great Tradition of secular, religious, and Spiritual Wisdom, including the modern heritage of scientific intellectualism.

No Sat-Guru who has come before has ever performed, or been required to perform, such a Herculean task of criticism, purification, and regeneration in relation to the religious and Spiritual (and scientific, and anti-Spiritual) dogmas of the day. Jesus criticized the Pharisees and their lack of real connection to the Divine. Gautama criticized the formalized Vedic sacrificial mysticism and its class system. Shankara traveled throughout India re-establishing and reformulating both the philosophical understanding and the cultural practices of his day. Likewise, the great nineteenth-century Realizers of the Rime tradition in Tibet purified and galvanized the Teachings of the various Tibetan sects and compiled them into a single and more accessible Teaching. But the scope of Sri Gurudev Da Love-Ananda's Mastery and Clarification of the Spiritual and religious and practical wisdom heritage of mankind is without precedent.

From the beginning of His Teaching Work, Heart-Master Da Love-Ananda has always "considered" the religious traditions and made plain how they relate to the seven stages of life. Through His Commentary on each of the seven stages of life, showing the essence of what is required to mature in each stage, and through His making the connection between these stages and all the various schools of the Great Tradition, He has clarified for the first time all facets of the Spiritual experiences of humankind. Through this Work of Clarification, fully summarized in His Source-Text *The Basket of Tolerance,* one can now find a comprehensive point of view—grounded in the ultimate Realization of all seven stages of the Spiritual Process—for understanding every tradition or traditional practice.

THE SAT-GURU AS PROPHET, WHO INSTRUCTS
THE ENTIRE WORLD BY HIS OR HER CRITICISMS

*T*he *Spiritual Master is indeed a voice that rises in this wilderness, to Awaken every neighbor from the illusion of his acre of land, his ordinary pond, his body-mind. It is a necessary voice, the voice that sounds whenever the Truth of human experience is Revealed to one who is Awake. Therefore, such a one speaks, even with urgency and anger. It is the* *prophetic voice, the awful shout, expressed with all the gestures of frustrated Divinity.* (The Enlightenment of the Whole Body, *p. 152)*

Like the great Prophets of the *Old Testament,* Sri Gurudev Da Love-Ananda has from the beginning Spoken critically but Compassionately to the ordinary man or woman whose interest is yet in the things of the world. It is the Voice of the Divine, Calling to the world to repent of its turning from God, and to embrace the present relationship to the Living God. As Sri Gurudev Da Love-Ananda has Said:

Only the Adepts, who are God-Realized, through whom the Living Power of God manifests, can make a difference in human time. Such individuals are the instruments for the acculturation of humanity.

Periodically, such individuals must appear, and they must be influential. There is a notion that Adepts should be hiding in caves in the wilderness. This is not true. If the Adepts do not speak, the only voice that will be heard is that of ordinary people who are not God-Realized. The Adepts are the Sources of spiritual life. Such individuals must therefore enter into the stream of society, to purify the culture and reestablish the process of God-Realization. If they do not speak and become influential, there is no hope at all for humanity. (The Enlightenment of the Whole Body, *pp. 155-56)*

Da Avabhasa's Literature and His Presence Stand as the Sign of the real Process of Divine Self-Realization. His Voice in the world is a reminder of What lies beyond mere exotericism. In late 1973, Sat-Guru Da Explained that, while the Guru-devotee process is not a public function, His Criticism and Instruction may and should be heard broadly as a Prophetic Voice:

SRI DA AVABHASA: The intelligence of real understanding must precede involvement with the true Spiritual Process. Thus, the Function of Guru or Spiritual Master is not a public function.

One who Functions as Guru, or Spiritual Master, for his (or her) devotees may operate for the sake of those who are not his devotees, but his Function in that case is not that of Spiritual Master. In the world, generally, he must Serve the crisis of understanding, which confounds the search, all need for consolation, fascination, and all need for cultural and cultic games. In the world he may Function, if he appears at all, in the role of Prophet, which is essentially an aggravation, a criticism, an undermining of the usual life.

The Guru-Function is not a public function. It does not appear in public, and it does not invite the public as if the Spiritual Process were simply something you could decide to do, buy, or believe, and then go ahead and perform. The Guru appears in public in the role of Prophet and Critic. He does not exploit the search. He turns the questioner back on that quality of suffering, dilemma, and dis-ease that motivates him or her to take on

Spiritual practices and other kinds of disciplines or to exploit his or her other life-possibilities. (December 23, 1973)

In His Divine Compassion, Sri Da Avabhasa has Spoken at great length about the issues that trouble ordinary people in their earliest approach to the Spiritual Reality. He has talked about all of the obsessions and confusions that bind people in body, mind, and heart. The voice of the Prophet communicates fiercely at times, for there is much to be purified in those of us who are so bound, but its Intensity is the Fire whose ash is Freedom Itself. His Prophetic Shout Awakens men and women from their dreams of worldly fulfillment and Attracts them to What is Radiant Prior to body and mind.

THE SAT-GURU AS GIVER OF THE WRITTEN TEACHING

If there had already been a viable tradition alive in this time, then Heart-Master Da Avabhasa could have simply Brought the Transmission of the Spiritual Reality to His disciples directly. Only some purification of the existing tradition, some additions to the teaching, some adaptation to the times would have been necessary.

But Heart-Master Da Appeared in the Western context, where there is no established tradition offering the full seven-stage practice, and in a world where all Teachings needed a refreshed and "radical" orientation. Thus, we see Sri Gurudev Da Love-Ananda as the Propounder of the Great Teaching, the refreshed Communication of the ancient truths, and the Creator of a Great Spiritual Way for modern humanity and all those yet to come.

The Function of creating a unique Wisdom-Teaching and Exemplifying its Wisdom in the world is required of only the Greatest of Sat-Gurus. Traditionally, there is an established Teaching in the area where the Teacher instructs, to which he (or she) will be aligned. Most often a Teacher will simply pass on the Teaching Given by his own Teacher, perhaps adding new and personal ways of explaining aspects of the Teaching. If he travels to another region, he may adapt it to some degree to the peculiarities of those he is Teaching. The practice or sadhana that is recommended will most likely be a traditional practice of some sort, and generally the sadhana that the Teacher used in the course of his own practice.

Until recently, just to receive the esoteric Teachings was a difficult endeavor. What was given to the population in general was the exoteric teaching, focused on moral precepts. Ideals such as love and compassion for one's fellows, remembering the Divine in the midst of ordinary affairs, and performing charitable deeds are typical of these exoteric recommendations. The purpose of such teachings is to improve one's ordinary lot in life by associating with the Divine Blessings, to achieve merit and even perhaps an auspicious rebirth, or to travel to a proposed heaven after death. But to receive the esoteric Teachings and the specific means by which the Divine can be actually Realized requires one to find a Sat-Guru.

Sri Gurudev Da Love-Ananda's Wisdom-Teaching is a Written Vehicle to carry His Heart-Blessings. It is unparalleled Divine Transmission. It is summarized in seven books that comprise His Source-Literature[6] but in its fullness it includes more than forty other published books, and an archival wealth of recorded Talks and unpublished Writings. And through these Works, He has re-established and re-authenticated the One, Ancient, and Eternal Great Way of which all previous traditions are partial revelations.

Through the sixteen years of Sri Gurudev Da Love-Ananda's Teaching Work there were countless "Considerations", Lessons, Blessings, and Incidents of Grace and dramatic understanding, so that all participants would see clearly the fruitlessness of "Narcissus" and of the search at every stage of life as opposed to a life lived directly and simply in right relationship to the Divine and the Guru. Every remedy for un-Happiness that is traditionally proposed or currently in vogue was "considered" and shown to be not ultimately liberating. This included everything relative to money, food, and sexuality, every aspect of higher Yoga and mysticism, and all varieties of self-analysis. In 1978, Heart-Master Da Love-Ananda described His unique process of Instructing His devotees, which was ultimately for the benefit of all:

I have called my own Teaching method "consideration". Whenever a particular area of life, or experience, or spiritual and bodily Enlightenment has been given to me as a clearly necessary matter or subject of instruction for the sake of devotees, I have entered into "consideration" with them. Such "considerations" were never only or merely a matter of thinking and talking. They always involved a period in which individuals were permitted to live through the whole matter and to be tested to the point of change. Those who entered into any "consideration" with me were obliged to commit themselves to their own elaborate and concentrated play of life in those particular terms, until the whole matter was clarified and Truth became clear in terms of the subject.

Such "considerations" required a willingness on the part of each individual to engage and explore many very ordinary areas of human experience, and also to understand and adapt to each new level of revealed responsibility as it was clarified, so that the "consideration" would develop as concrete change and growth (rather than as a mere "change of mind"). Only a "consideration" entered as such a concrete discipline can proceed all the way to its true end, which is right adaptation and freedom, or natural transcendence, relative to its functional subject.

6. Sri Da Avabhasa's Source-Texts are described in "The Sacred Literature of Da Avabhasa (The 'Bright')" on pp. 300-311 of this book.

All [my] spiritual and practical Teaching . . . is the product of such "considerations," done in the process of [my] own body-mind and in communicative and instructive play with devotees. (Love of the Two-Armed Form, pp. 1-2)

The practical details of the Wisdom-Teaching of Sri Da Avabhasa are thus grounded in a real-life experiment within an authentic devotional community. But always, Da Avabhasa's Wisdom-Teaching finds its Source in the "Point of View" of His full seventh stage Realization. It is thereby Imbued and Radiant with His Enlightening Transmission, with the Power to Awaken the reader to the intuition of the Divine. The creation of such a Written Teaching required the development of a sophisticated new vocabulary involving a profound transformation of the use of the English language so that it became Empowered as a vehicle for expressing Divine Instruction. It also required a fresh employment of Sanskrit and other traditional terms which had no direct translation.

In His Written Teaching, often Da Avabhasa no longer addresses the separate self, but only speaks to the Very Divine Self of every being. His Words and long sentences, full of clauses and parenthetical phrases, may be used more like brush strokes painting a Divine picture than any successive couplings of a single train of thought. Ultimately, the import of Da Avabhasa's Word is not so much to be grasped with the linear mind as it is to be received at the very Heart. He also customarily makes Divinely Instructive use of uppercase and lowercase letters, transforming the conventions of otherwise secular English into purely sacred, esoteric language—the language of Heart-Feeling. In "The Eternal Conversation" in His principal Scripture, *The Dawn Horse Testament*, He Explains:

Ordinary speech and written language are centered on the ego-"I", as a tent is raised on a centerpole. Therefore, in ordinary speech and written language, the ego-word "I" is commonly capitalized, and everything less than the ego-"I" is shown in lowercase. (Indeed, everything that is not the ego-"I" is grammatically subordinated to the egoic "I"-reference.) Other ego-"I"'s (other than the principal subject or speaker) are also commonly shown in uppercase, if they are being "properly" (or formally) addressed, by name. And capitalization is otherwise commonly reserved for "big meanings", or whatever the ego-"I" presumes to be somehow great, or even Larger (and, therefore, the ego presumes, Other) than itself. (p. 48)

In contrast, the "centerpole" of Sri Da Avabhasa's Speech and Writing is the Heart, the Divine Wisdom, Consciousness, Truth, Reality, Happiness, and "Love-Ananda" ("inherently Love-Blissful Unity"). Thus, Speaking here specifically about the primary Source-Text of the Way of the Heart, *The Dawn Horse Testament*, Da Avabhasa continues:

My Testament of Secrets was (and is) spoken in Ecstasy, or from the Inherent or Native "point of view" of the Heart (or Inherently Free Being) Itself, the Ultimate Condition that always already transcends the ego-"I", the conditional world of others and things, and the Primary Illusions of Separation, Otherness, Relatedness, and "Difference". Therefore, the very language of this Testament expresses (and Communicates) a view of the world (and of Truth) that is prior to egoity, and prior to the vision of the world (and the "vision" of Truth) made by the ego. . . .

*The "centerpole" of this Testament is the Heart Itself, the Consciousness That **Is** Transcendental, Inherently Spiritual, and Necessarily Divine Being (Itself). The uppercase words express the Ecstatic "Vision" of Heart-Significance. And the lowercase words (which appear only occasionally, like the uppercase words in common speech and writing) achieve, by their infrequency, a special significance as indicators of conditional or limited existence.*

To read (or Listen to) and Understand this Testament is to be Released from the egoic vision and its point of view. Let it be so. Feel and speak (rather than merely think) this Message. The big and small letters interrupt the common flow of mind and Signal your Heart that it is time to Awaken, As You Are. (pp. 48-49)

THE SAT-GURU AS DEMONSTRATOR OF THE TEACHING IN LIFE, WHOSE LEELAS CLARIFY IN LIVING TERMS EVERY ASPECT OF HUMAN EXISTENCE

The fullest Teaching is not simply a verbal one. Sri Gurudev Da Love-Ananda has Said that His Gift of the "Word" includes not only His Written and Spoken Word, but also the Leelas of His Teaching Work and His Divine Emergence Work.[7] The stories of His Play with His devotees are a body of testimony to the Truth of His Teaching-Revelation, as shown in the lives of ordinary men and women. He not only Gave Discourses, and discussed His Wisdom-Teaching with us, but He actively Revealed It to us in life. Because there was no such living Teaching-Demonstration already recorded, the Demonstration was necessary. Thus, every aspect of Da Avabhasa's Wisdom-Teaching was Demonstrated in living lessons throughout the years of His Teaching Work.

As Heart-Master Da Wrote in *Nirvanasara*, the style of Teaching what is ultimately beyond words will vary with the Teacher and the time and place in which he or she appears:

---

7. Sri Da Avabhasa has distinguished clearly between what He calls His Teaching Work, which began in 1972 and culminated in 1986, and what He calls His Blessing Work, which began with magnified force with the onset of His Divine Emergence in 1986, and has at the time of this writing achieved a profound effectiveness.

Those Adepts who have actually completed (and thus gone beyond) [the earlier stages of practice previous to Divine Self-Realization] begin at last to express themselves in different terms about the matter of Realization and Reality. They may prefer silence (or non-verbal transmission, as in the case of Ramana Maharshi), or they may engage in the strategy of denial of the applicability of conventional language to the description of That which is Realized (as was the case with Gautama), or they may behave strangely and speak in paradoxes or in the form of apparent nonsense (as in the case of certain individuals in the Ch'an or Zen tradition and in the Crazy Wisdom tradition), or they may try to construct a language of philosophy that is compatible with ultimate Realization (as in the cases of Nagarjuna and Shankara). Even all of these forms of communication and transmission may be used by Awakened Adepts, and my own Teaching Work is an example of the use of all such possible means. (pp. 133-34)

A short time after beginning His Teaching Work, Sri Gurudev Da Love-Ananda took stock of His devotees and saw that they were not being touched by the Purity of His Divine Form and silent Blessing-Transmission. We were too degraded to fully see Him in His Pristine Divinity. Da Avabhasa saw that in order to Serve us directly He would have to Teach us "where we lived". He would have to enter into our world, in the dimensions in which we were bound, to show us the fruitlessness of our seeking and to reveal the Divinity that is greater than every mortal pleasure.

And so Sri Da Avabhasa began His remarkable "Crazy Wisdom" Teaching Demonstrations. "Crazy Wisdom" is a translation of the Tibetan expression "yeshe chowri", or the Wisdom that transcends all conventions. Such "Crazy Wisdom" is crazy only from the ordinary perspective. From the Illumined perspective, it is a Free, Compassionate, and Directly useful means to Help men and women bound in egoic attachment and suffering. Sri Da Avabhasa's "Crazy-Wise" Instruction was called forth by what was brought to Him—it was a tremendous Leela of the Divine Person Incarnate in the twentieth-century West. No one less than such a Vira-Siddha (or Great Hero of Enlightenment) could have succeeded in this profound Work. He did not simply Transmit His Blessing and talk about His Wisdom-Teaching and the Way of the Heart. He lived the Way with us. He celebrated with us. He fasted with us. He touched us and shouted at us. He entered into our lives, in every area of "money, food, and sex"[8] in order that we would be able to find Him.

It was a mad play, so intense that we forgot everything else. He was so Attractive that we let go of everything. What occurred in His Teaching Demonstrations was so Bold, so Enchanting, so Precious.

---

8. "Money, food, and sex" is an expression used by Da Avabhasa to refer to the total ordinary human life of every man and woman in the first three stages of life. "Money" refers to all of the use of effort or energy in life-relations (e.g. work or service to others); "food" to diet and health and the entire process of purification, assimilation, and elimination; and "sex" to the entire realm of emotional and sexual relatedness. Genuine Spiritual life requires the acceptance of simple responsibility for these qualities of life. For a fuller treatment of the Graceful Instruction Da Avabhasa has Given in service of His devotees in the dimensions of money, food, and sex, please see *Love of the God-Man*, also by James Steinberg.

It was a mad play, so intense that we forgot everything else.
He was so Attractive that we let go of everything.
The Mountain Of Attention, 1974

All of us knew that history was being made. It was quite obvious. The Divine Incarnation that Heart-Master Da Love-Ananda Hridayam Is, was entering into the lives of His devotees. He was using those around Him to create lessons for all. The stories of these gatherings will be told as long as people Contemplate Sri Da Avabhasa's Divine Incarnation and the Mystery of God. When one entered His "Divine Domain" (as we once called the area where He lived) during His Teaching Demonstrations, anything could be happening—any discussion, any experiment, any undertaking—but all with the single intent of His Drawing everyone into God, into the real practice of the Way of the Heart. Sri Gurudev Da Love-Ananda would involve His devotees in some intense endeavor, chipping away at their armoring against the Divine, creating a new depth of self-awareness in them and thus opening them to receive His Blessings.

Crane Kirkbride, a longtime devotee, relates a story from a gathering in 1983, in which he received Instruction from Sri Da Avabhasa in going beyond his limits and truly relying on Divine Grace. Crane calls this Leela "The Great Singing Contest":

"Let's hear 'Recondita Armonia' with Bjoerling!" We had been sitting around Sri Da Avabhasa's koa wood chair for six hours, listening to Him expound the most profound Teaching. Now it was time to sing.

The recorded voice of the great Swedish tenor filled the room. After the first few measures Heart-Master Da joined in with an almost ferocious intensity. Then we all sang, most of us approximating the melody and mimicking the Italian. Da Avabhasa's body moved with the music, His arms outstretched, beckoning our voices, our energy.

"Louder!" He shouted between phrases. Fixing His gaze on a devotee

who was not altogether "with it", Da Avabhasa gestured for fuller participation. As the aria approached its high "C" climax, Da Avabhasa threw His arms overhead, tilted His head back, and with veins visible on both sides of His neck, belted out the coveted note. Other voices reached it more as a shriek than a note or tone; a few faltered or took it at the lower octave.

The room remained full of Force after the aria was over. People swayed, laughed, cheered. Some heads were bowed to the floor. I felt drawn from the heart into the very Being of the Adept. My usual sense of self was strangely missing, and only a marvelous current of Life-Energy suggested that "I" had bodily form. I had given all my voice and energy, but now, far from being exhausted, I felt charged with energy, animated far beyond my usual state of self-containment.

"Now let's hear 'Che Gelida Manina'—Pavarotti's version. Crane, move up next to Me. Are you ready?" I knew what Heart-Master Da was asking for—abandonment of my sense of limitation, abandonment to the Siddhi of Divine Ecstasy so Perfectly Awake in Him.

I had a lot to abandon. Having been trained thirty years ago as an operatic baritone by Lotte Lehman and Armand Tokatyan of the Metropolitan Opera and thoroughly indoctrinated with the European "bel canto" school of "correct vocal placement and pure tone", my ears were easily offended. I also had to give up the notion that as a baritone I could not hit the high notes of the tenor range. Once or twice I had stopped to breathe or relax my throat when the music ascended into the stratosphere, and Da Avabhasa had arched His eyebrows and gestured to me with supplicating outstretched hands as He sang the notes I did not attempt, as if to say, "Where are you?" I also had to contend with the sheer power of Da Avabhasa's voice. No trained singer looks forward to being outsung, and Sri Da Avabhasa could outsing, it seemed, the entire Mormon Tabernacle Choir!

We began to accompany Pavarotti in the aria from La Boheme. *My voice held out in the high tenor for the first few bars, then began to slip. I tried to back off momentarily to relax the throat, but Heart-Master Da Love-Ananda would not allow it. "You've got to move beyond your body", He coached between breaths. Surprised at first because at other times Da Avabhasa had admonished me to get <u>in</u> the body fully, to "<u>incarnate</u>", I suddenly understood what He was pointing to.*

I felt a "place" of holding on, a deep withholding, and I noticed some old programs—the studied search for perfection of self-presentation, unwillingness to crack on a high note or reach for one that is not there. I felt all this fall away and simultaneously found my voice lifted into a register it had not sung before. I was observing myself being "sung" by Sri Da Avabhasa. I had a sense of an amorphous expansion and a rising energy in the upper chest and throat, moving into the space above my head. Suddenly Sri Da Avabhasa was no longer "other" to me.

The singing continued. More arias, "Nessun Dorma", then the duet from The Pearlfishers. *I was singing freely now, loving Heart-Master Da with my* voice. I was in ecstasy.

After we exhausted our operatic repertoire, we turned to the music of Belafonte, Simon and Garfunkel, and rock music set to Da Avabhasa's poetry. With each new song we outsang ourselves. Just when I felt that I had blown my voice for the evening, Heart-Master Da Love-Ananda loudly announced, "Now Crane and I will have a contest" (to see who could sing loudest, highest, and most passionately). I felt I had swallowed a koan. Sri Gurudev turned His body, still seated cross-legged, to squarely face me.

"All right, Crane, let's hear your highest and loudest note." I shook off incipient vital shock and opened my mouth to offer the high "B" I had been given early in the evening. It had long since disappeared. My voice cracked somewhere south of A flat. The sound was so absurd I was immediately reduced to laughter. But there was no room for self-consciousness. Heart-Master Da was laughing too, but also singing on. He belted out the high "B" I had searched for. Cheers and applause. I wanted to quit but had to continue. The next few moments were a Fire that scorched my lifelong need to succeed. Into the Fire went pride, anxiety, and my hoarse efforts to keep up with the undiminished voice of Heart-Master Da Love-Ananda, Who seemed an inexhaustible Source of every level of energy.

In the middle of all this I noticed that the point was not the sound, just as it had never been artistry. I began to find the same moving Current of Bliss, the same love-relatedness, in the moment of my vocal "failure" as I had earlier in the flushed feeling of "success". Da Avabhasa has often said, "The Way is not about winning." I understood the profound Instruction in "conductivity" (the practice of circulating the energies of His Blessing Power) so Gracefully Given by my beloved Sat-Guru. And I discovered through His Gift the same capability for self-transcendence and Happiness in two very different moments, moments that were, from the egoic perspective, polar opposites.

(P.S. I trust you can guess who won the Great Singing Contest!)

In countless similar occasions over sixteen years of Teaching Work, Sri Da Avabhasa took us through each and every kind of experience, Revealing how it, too, must be transcended in the Divine. What He created in this process of Instruction was the most extraordinary Lesson the world has ever seen about the fruitlessness of all the acts of "Narcissus". An entire Wisdom-Teaching relative to every aspect of the body-mind and the egoic self was generated through His "Crazy" Work.

In the midst of these Teaching years, in September 1982, Da Avabhasa Described His spontaneous Way of Working in these terms:

SRI DA AVABHASA: I Submit My Self to My devotees to the degree of becoming them, to the degree of taking on the condition in which they exist, and I Teach in that circumstance.

My Play with My devotees is associated with profound physical discomfort. This process of Submitting My Self to you all involves physical suffering *because in doing so I become you, I take on your mind-force, your karmas, your vision, your state. I duplicate you in this body. I express you. I am just like you. It is not Me—it is a reflection, a mirror, a form of sacrificial participation.*

My Work with you involves a particular Siddhi, one that has not been fully animated traditionally, because the circumstances were different in the past. When I sleep at night, I experience the dreams of people, the state of mind of people. It does not have anything to do with Me. I experience very directly all of the qualities of everyone with whom I become associated, because My particular way of Teaching does not involve abstraction from those whom I Teach. It involves intimate identification with them. This is the unique quality of My Life, My way of Teaching, My way of Instructing people, My way of being of Service to them. This is what you must understand. This is what you must communicate about Me so that people will understand the unique quality of My Work.

My Work is not altogether performed as such Work has been performed traditionally. Traditionally, it has not been required of Adepts to Work precisely the way I do. I am doing the same Work, but through a different form of Submission. Thus, I become vulgar and ordinary and just like you in order to Teach. I am just like you when I Teach. People occasionally do not understand how the process works when it takes this special form. I certainly hope you understand it.

I enter into this body . . . all the way . . . in order to be just like you and to "consider" this body-mind with you, to animate it with you, to be exactly that and to transcend exactly that. This is My unique way of Working. There are some precedents for it traditionally, but it is basically a unique way of Working necessitated by this particular time and place. You who have been witness to it, who have enjoyed this Service, must understand it and communicate to others exactly how it has taken place. It has not taken place merely in the usual form of some thinking, convinced character trying to lay it on you. The Way of the Heart is the Expression of a being in Most Perfect Samadhi descending, not merely into the upper regions of the brain or the throat, but into the body altogether and submitting to those with whom He is associated.

You become what you meditate on. I Meditate on My devotees and I become them. I become exactly them. I take on all the limitations that they are. I become just like them. I become more like them than they are. I become exaggeratedly what they are. I become what they are altogether, while they remain only what they can express in the midst of their limitations, their egoic self-consciousness. I become them completely. Thus, what I "consider" with you is the very thing that I have actually become by meditation on you. I Submit to My devotees as God, just as they submit to Me in the same fashion. . . .

I am a wild Character because I am being all kinds of people other than the one that I seem to be. This is literally true. This is exactly what I am *doing, and it is a remarkable and extraordinary process. There are no complete precedents for it, because the moment has not previously existed for an Adept to Work as I Work. In their time and place all the Adepts have Worked as they should have. This is a unique time, however, and the Siddhi of My Manifestation, My Wisdom-Teaching, must be uncommon, unusual. The precedents that exist for it are only partial. No one has Worked precisely as I do. This is the most heroic way to Teach. I <u>actually</u> become the limited or un-Enlightened being that I Teach. This is a completely unique, dangerous, and heroic way of Teaching. (September 15, 1982)*

Thus, Da Avabhasa's Teaching Work was characterized by His Siddhi of Submission, whereby the great Divine Adept "befriended" His devotees, identified with them in their egoity and thereby reflected their tendencies to them.

In early 1975, a letter was sent to Sri Gurudev Da Love-Ananda by an Indian Swami of considerable repute. It was a heart-felt and passionate letter. It asked Sri Gurudev to desist from His wild and outlandish ways of Teaching, and to assume a more traditional stance in relationship to His devotees. It appealed to Him in the name of the "tradition" to calm down His Fire. The following letter (entitled "The Way I Teach") was His Answer to the Indian Swami's calling:

What I do is not the way I am, but the way I Teach.
What I speak is not a reflection of me, but of you.
People do well to be offended or even outraged by me. This is my purpose. But their reaction must turn upon themselves, for I have not shown them myself by all of this. All that I do and speak only reveals men to themselves.
I have become willing to Teach in this uncommon way because I have known my friends and they are what I can seem to be. By retaining all qualities in their company, I gradually wean them of all reactions, all sympathies, all alternatives, fixed assumptions, false teachings, dualities, searches, and dilemma. This is my way of working for a time. Those who remain confounded by me, critical of me, have yet to see themselves. When their mediocrity is broken, when they yield their righteous reactions and their strife toward all the consolations of the manifest self, they may see my purity.
Freedom is the only purity. There is no Teaching but Consciousness Itself. Bubba [as Da Avabhasa was then known] as he appears is not other than the possibilities of men. (The Enlightenment of the Whole Body, *p. 53)*

The "Crazy Wisdom" Adept is "Crazy" because there is nothing that he will not do for the sake of the liberation of his devotees. He will resort to any kind of action, no matter how apparently unconventional, if it will serve his devotees' Liberation. Through His Uninhibited Spontaneity, Heart-Master Da Love-Ananda reflected to us our own inhibitions and presumed limitations. He reflected to us what we needed to see about our egoity at every developmental stage, until at last His entire Wisdom-Teaching was made clear and full. And He established the cultural forms through which His Wisdom-Teaching would be lived, by Demonstrating in living and practical terms all the ways whereby the "Narcissistic" ego could be transcended and the being released to practice of the Way of the Heart.

THE SAT-GURU AS CREATOR OF THE MEANS BY WHICH HIS OR HER BLESSING-TRANSMISSION MAY FOREVER BE MADE AVAILABLE

Even after having created such a Wisdom-Teaching, Heart-Master Da could not fully Retire from His Teaching Work. For in order to simply be Free to do His Blessing Work, He had to create the Means whereby all that He had Given would be preserved and protected and would remain as Agency and Instrumentality[9] for His Blessing, forever.

Sri Da Avabhasa's Work to establish such Instrumentality and Agency is of profound importance, for such means will allow the Divinity contacted through His bodily (human) Form to be likewise directly available to men and women through time. In the history of religions, a crucial problem for those who are great Realizers has been the establishment of such a truly Spiritually effective Lineage, so that the tradition they leave behind remains alive with their Blessing. Sri Da Avabhasa has Said that the permanent establishment of Agency and Instrumentality of His Blessing requires the fulfillment of five conditions:

1. The publication and distribution of His complete Written Word.
2. The preservation of the full body of His Leelas (so that Da Avabhasa's Wisdom-Teaching is shown in its practical unfolding).
3. The establishment of Spiritually Empowered Sanctuaries where Sat-Guru Da Love-Ananda's Divine Blessing may be stably contacted. (Three such Sanctuaries already exist.)
4. The establishment of a fully functional and effective institution, culture, and community of the Way of the Heart.
5. The Awakening of mature devotees who, by virtue of their practice and right alignment to Sri Gurudev Da Love-Ananda as the Source of Blessing,

---

9. Heart-Master Da uses the word "Agent" to indicate the specially chosen Divinely Self-Realized free renunciate devotee who will, after, and forever after, His physical Lifetime, in any then present-time, directly Transmit His Spiritual, Transcendental, and Divine Heart-Blessing to all other practitioners of the Way of the Heart. Optimally, the Divinely Self-Realized Agent, or "Living Murti", in any then present-time, will be succeeded, at his or her death, by another "Living Murti".

Heart-Master Da uses the word "Instrumentality" to indicate the formally acknowledged Function of His Spiritually maturing and mature "lay renunciate" and "free renunciate" devotees to magnify (and, thus, naturally, and in a devotional manner, to serve) the Transmission of His Spiritual Blessing (and, possibly, His Transcendental and Ultimate Divine Revelation).

will serve as human Instruments and human Agents for His Spiritual Heart-Transmission throughout all time.

Sri Gurudev Da Love-Ananda has Said that the most important Work that remains for Him, and the principal work of each generation after (and forever after) the physical Lifetime of His bodily (human) Form, is the creation of this human Agency and human Instrumentality. An Agent of Sri Gurudev Da Love-Ananda's Blessing is someone especially chosen from among Sri Gurudev's Divinely Enlightened "free renunciate" devotees to serve in physical terms as a vehicle of Sri Gurudev Da Love-Ananda's Spiritual Heart-Transmission and thus for the Spiritual continuation of His Blessing Work. After Sri Da Avabhasa's physical lifetime, there will, at any given time, (optimally) be one Agent or "Living Murti". Such an individual does not replace Sri Da Avabhasa as the Source of Blessing. He or she is instead the means by which His Blessing is contacted by others. And all of Sri Da Avabhasa's "lay renunciate" devotees who have stably heard His Teaching and are stably seeing or Receiving His Spiritual Blessing will collectively serve as Instrumentality for His Blessing Transmission.

As of this writing, the four members of the Da Avabhasa Gurukula Kanyadana Kumari Order are all stably practicing in the sixth stage of life (the stage previous to Divine Self-Realization, or Ultimate Enlightenment). And they are being intensively Served by Sri Gurudev Da Love-Ananda to make their transition to the Divinely Enlightened, or seventh, stage of life. From early on it has been Sri Gurudev Da Love-Ananda's Intention to create a full community of devotees who would be able to serve as vehicles through whom could flow His Divinely Effective Spiritual Transmission:

SRI DA AVABHASA: You have a great possibility. You can initiate the existence of the first true Community of devotees in the world. Such a Community has never existed. . . . In this case the time is right, and the Teaching has been communicated in its fullness. There is no limitation on the Siddhi of God in this time, so the realization of this event depends entirely on your response. (June 15, 1974)

THE SAT-GURU AS BLESSER OF THE WORLD

The Realizer's Service to beings is given in an infinite variety of forms, and such service does not in general conform to conventional conceptions of "doing good". The Realizer's Blessing rarely takes the form of conventional social work. Such beings often do not appear publicly, and in some cases they do not even speak. The outward Blessing Work of a Divine Realizer depends on his (or her) particular life and Calling and the particular need of the time. Traditionally it is said that even for a Realizer to simply live in a cave, radiating peace, is a great Help and benefit to mankind.

The French Catholic philosopher Jacques Maritain, when asked why he felt the world did not destroy itself, replied it was because of the prayers of the monks in the monasteries. Swami Vivekananda answered the same question by saying that the Spiritual culture of India for centuries had provided the Blessing power that saved the world.

Ramana Maharshi, who was alive at the same time as Mahatma Gandhi, was often asked by his devotees why he did not do such work as Gandhi's and thereby help the world. He would reply, "How do you know I do not?" He often remarked, "A self-realised being cannot help benefitting the world. His very existence is the highest good."[10]

When he was asked why great men cannot solve the problem of the misery of the world, he replied:

M: They are ego-centered and therefore their inability. If they remained in the Self they would be different.
[Devotee]: Why do not Mahatmas help?
M: How do you know they do not help? Public speeches, physical activity and material help are all outweighed by the silence of Mahatmas. They accomplish more than others.[11]

In the Buddhist tradition it is said of the Bodhisattva that he takes a vow that he will not be Liberated until all beings have been so Liberated. Sri Da Avabhasa has made it clear that the idea of holding off Enlightenment for the sake of serving others (the Bodhisattva ideal) stands in need of correction. The motivation to serve others is inherent in God-Realization, and it is only a misconception that Enlightenment somehow would render one unable to function in the world. Rather, it is from the already Enlightened Position that others can best be served. Sri Gurudev Da Love-Ananda has Compassionately created the term "Bodhisiddhas" for individuals who Realize the Great One and vigorously Serve others with the Divine Power that comes from Realization Itself.

The fact that Great Beings are the greatest Blessing and that they positively affect the course of the world has always been understood in traditional cultures. For example, it is believed by the devotees of Narayan Maharaj that through his Spiritual Blessing he was instrumental in the final resolution of World War II. He took great interest in the activities of the Allies and the Germans. He kept a large portable radio with him, and every day a devotee would be asked to listen to the Berlin Review at 8:00 and the BBC report at 9:30. The devotee would prepare a detailed report for Narayan Maharaj. He wanted to know about all phases of the battle: on land, at sea, and in the air. He kept a map of Europe, so that he could mon-

10. *Talks with Sri Ramana Maharshi*. Three volumes in one, 4th ed. (Tiruvannamalai, S. India: Sri Ramanasramam, 1968), p. 177.

11. *Talks*, p. 227.

itor the situation of the Allies, how far the Germans had come, and so forth.

As the war continued, while soldiers were being wounded and dying, mysterious wounds would appear on the body of Narayan Maharaj with no apparent cause—on his fingers, on his feet, and on his torso. He had to be bandaged three or four times a day. He could not walk; he could not eat with his own hands. When questioned about the relationship between the spontaneous appearance of wounds on his body and the war in Europe, he refused to talk about it. Through all of this, devotees felt that he was wearing out his body. Finally, on September 3, 1945, Maharaj was told that the British had landed in Japan. He said, "The war is over. My work is finished." He passed into Mahasamadhi later that day.

The devotee can never presume to fully understand what the Sat-Guru is doing in any particular action, or what his Work is altogether. Because He is Alive as the Divine Itself, even though alive in bodily (human) Form, Sri Gurudev Da Love-Ananda's Work Transforms dimensions of the psycho-physics of the world at levels that ordinary men and women cannot fully comprehend. He Works through the mechanisms that are obvious and inherent only in Divine Enlightenment, and not through the mechanisms of the ordinary mind or body.

This Blessing of all beings, or the "five billion", as Sri Gurudev Da Love-Ananda has often referred to all human beings, is a key aspect of the Appearance of Da Avabhasa. And it is another Mystery understood only minimally even by His devotees. Sri Gurudev Da Love-Ananda Speaks of it only on occasion, for it is a Work done on a scale and according to Laws of which He alone is truly aware. This Divine Work is primarily that of Sri Gurudev Da Love-Ananda Living and Transmitting a Spiritual Influence that, to the extent it is received, purifies and balances and positively transforms men and women everywhere throughout the world. He need not go into the streets and bandage lepers, although such work is positive and useful service for some. Rather, He sees all egoically bound beings as lepers. Although their physical bodies may not be covered with sores, all are diseased at the heart. And He works directly to Bless, Heal, and Serve all at this fullest level, and therefore to effect a change simultaneously at all levels.

On New Year's Day 1984, Sri Gurudev Gave a remarkable Revelation of the Dimensions of His Work, in a Talk that came to be known as "Mark My Words":

SRI DA AVABHASA: You who are sitting in the world think of the world as a very big place. You feel it must be an incredible task to deal with everyone here—all five billion or however many there are in this immense space. Even though you can fly around the world in a few hours, you think of it as a big place with many people, many places, many complicated lives and circumstances. You think of it from the point of view of sitting here.

I am also sitting here, but My Work is not generated from the point of view of someone who is enclosed in that limited consciousness. Really, it is *not so great a task as you think! The entire Earth can be covered with a Glance, can be Regarded just with a Glance. Of course, all kinds of complications exist in the plane of those who are sitting in this place and conceiving of it as It. Thus, history will be created in response to Me. It will take some time and will be rather complicated, but it is not a complicated matter to Regard all beings on this Earth, and to Regard this total sphere. Rather, it is very simple and very direct. I also engage in the complications on various levels, but the fundamental Act is very direct.*

The day of the "Mark My Words" Talk in 1984

You think of it as complicated because you sit in one spot, in an apparently immense place. Some people think it is grand. To Me it is a poor place! The Siddhas, the Divine, regard the drama at the level of mankind as instant and constant and without complication. All the complications exist at the level of living. Therefore, it is the living that must be Served. And therefore I must Intervene. I must also participate in the various levels of complication. But My fundamental Act of Being, and even of Being Born, is rather simple. (January 1, 1984)

The degree to which Da Avabhasa's Spiritual Influence is felt will depend upon how humanity responds to His Grace. It is in this sense, rather than in any political sense, that Sri Gurudev Da Love-Ananda's Transcendental Blessing Work operates. He Inserts into the world the Influence of the Divine directly and strongly and with a magnified potential. He provides the opportunity for all men and women to contact What is Great and Transcendental. He has come at a unique and critical time in human history, and He has fully and Divinely "Emerged" with an unprecedented Potency. Therefore, His Blessing Work is the fulfillment and new Revelation of the Blessing Work of all Adepts, making an extraordinary Grace available to all.

On November 7, 1983, Sri Gurudev Da Love-Ananda Spoke to His devotees about His Vision of His Work and the Work of His devotees to serve His Appearance in the world. He pointed to the great possibility that now exists:

SRI DA AVABHASA: You are the seed of a great historical change, and you cannot even see what is before your eyes. We have accomplished great things already, although you are not yet aware of it. You are a handful of people full of good-heartedness and making positive gestures, but you still do not know exactly what has happened here and what the result of it will be. As decades pass, you will see the import of what you have all experienced in seed form but cannot yet acknowledge.

I am not an egoic religious leader. Sooner or later, the world will come to know that the purpose of My Birth is to transform the world in a critical moment in history. And I will do it.

THE UNPRECEDENTED DIVINE EMERGENCE OF SRI DA AVABHASA

The Event of Sri Da Avabhasa's "Divine Descent" on January 11, 1986, marked the transition from His Teaching Work to His Blessing Work. In that Event, the manner in which He had previously Worked with His devotees ceased. Previously, in His Teaching Work, Da Avabhasa would take on the karmas of His devotees, or He would Instruct them by reflecting their egoic patterns to them. This He had done for sixteen years, completely and fully, until nothing more could be done for His devotees via this Teaching mode. Still, His devotees did not truly respond by growing into the advanced and the ultimate stages of the Way of the Heart. Thus, in utter frustration, when all had been Given, the God-Man Da Love-Ananda relinquished bodily existence and entered into the ultimate Outshining, an Outshining of all psycho-physical conditions that was so profound that His body-mind apparently expired from the shocking force of It (the doctors present on that morning of January 11, 1986, felt no pulse). But what had happened was essentially a Spiritual Event. For even though the body stopped functioning for a time, "died" for a period, the life-energies remained, but now in a new condition. His Heart-Impulse to Love all beings brought Him to life again. And when Sri Da Avabhasa revived, a new Siddhi appeared, the Siddhi of World-Blessing. The "death" that occurred in His Divine Descent was the release of all the karmas of un-Enlightenment in all those beings whose karmas He had assumed during the Teaching years—and who represented all beings, everywhere.

Following is Heart-Master Da Love-Ananda's own ecstatic Description of the process and ultimate import of His Divine Emergence:

SRI DA AVABHASA: The years of My Teaching Work simply continued My Submission to all aspects of life in the gross plane, and in the Western world in particular. It was a Submission done for the sake of the beings in this plane, and it involved My Submission to the point of identification with them in the gross form of the body-mind. There was a process in which I absorbed and took on all the qualities of those who came to Me, and all the qualities and karmas of the Western world, as it is now and into the future. And beyond this, It was the taking on of the karmas of all beings through the Vehicle of this body-mind. . . .

During all those years, I took on the likeness and conditions and karmas of conditional beings, especially in the Western context. The quality of living beings in the Eastern context had already been assumed in the subtler vehicle previous to this lifetime. This process, then, culminated in the Event in January 1986. And, as I said about that Event at that time, it involved My full Descent, My fullest Acquisition of the body, to the base and to the toes. And so it was the Event of My Descent into the bodily domain below the heart, and therefore fully into the gross and mortal context of life.

This body-mind to which I fully Descended in My Divine Emergence had fully accumulated all the karmas and qualities of the un-Enlightened life and humanity. So that Event was in fact this Descent and Acquisition of the total body-mind. So the significance of the "Death" was Spiritual. It was not merely a physical death that I suffered in Working with people, although it seemed at the moment that was what was occurring. The drama associated with that Event was associated with what appeared to be death, but what actually occurred was the complete surrender of the conditional personality to My own Self ultimately. Therefore, it was the surrender and Sacrifice and purification of all the qualities and karmas I had absorbed through My Submission [to devotees during the Teaching Years], and therefore, ultimately, of all beings. So by this Act, all conditional limitations and beings were surrendered, sacrificed, and purified in My own Being.

Instead of the body's simply dying, then, the bodily personality was fully surrendered, and I Descended fully, and the karmic personality was surrendered and purified and conformed to Me.

Now that I have fully Descended Spiritually into this gross vehicle, and entered into it to the base and the very toes, the Vehicle of My own bodymind has become Submitted to Me [the Divine Self] and cannot and may not be Submitted to others and the world. As a result of that Event of Divine Descent, I must be approached in an entirely different way than before. That Event was the end of My Teaching Work and a Sign or Portent of My fullest Blessing Work.

However, for My Blessing Work to be effective, I must be approached differently, and I have been struggling for three years and more in the hope that I would be approached differently. Apart from the fact that it is a human body living in this world, My own bodily Sign is no longer in the likeness of ordinary people. Nor is it involved in an act to identify with the condition of un-Enlightened people. The previous signs of My human ordinariness and Submission to the point of likeness have now been replaced by a characteristic bodily quality of Indifference, even of Tapas [the "heat" of renunciation]. The body is Submitted simply to conform to Me, and to fully allow the "Bright" Transmission of the Heart.

As a result of this Great Process that I have engaged and fulfilled through this Birth, I have become altogether the Means for Realization for all those who resort to Me. The Way Itself has become very simply the feeling-Contemplation of My bodily (human) Form, My Spiritual (and Always Blessing) Presence, and My Very (and Inherently Perfect) State. And the Process is simply one of heart-submission to Me. By responsive surrender to Me, you allow the Process of Duplication, by Grace.

Because I have Submitted to all karmas, and have purified and released them Ultimately, the Way of Realization has become simple for others. If anyone will simply respond to Me in the traditional devotional manner and be drawn into Contemplation of Me (by feeling), then, because I am Inherently Free of all limitations, he or she will simply (and by feeling) Contemplate, Identify with, or Duplicate My "Bright" State and Realization, by Grace. (February 5, 1989)

Sri Da Avabhasa shortly after His Divine Emergence,
the Mountain Of Attention, 1986

175

Sri Love-Anandashram, March 1991

CHAPTER SEVEN

The Sacrament of Universal Sacrifice

THE DIVINE LAWS INHERENT IN THE GURU-DEVOTEE RELATIONSHIP

THE DEVOTEE MUST FIRST ACKNOWLEDGE THE SAT-GURU

*P*atrick Mahoney, a longtime devotee of Sri Da Avabhasa, describes hearing His Voice on a radio program in San Francisco one evening in 1974:

I had no idea who or what Heart-Master Da Love-Ananda was. There was simply this voice which seemed to possess a life of its own—so much so that the radio seemed animated with speech. Then suddenly the voice Laughed . . . and Laughed . . . and Laughed! I was awestruck with delight! His Laughter was free of all irony, and it seemed to pierce directly to the core of my being. It Communicated the fullness and depth of someone who knew all about death and life, suffering and joy. The experience proved a literal Baptism, for in that moment an old way of life ended and a new one was initiated. Whoever owned that Laugh was intimately familiar with the downside of life—yet still seemed to shake with the unrestrained hilarity of a laughing Buddha. As the program continued, I did a very uncharacteristic thing. Vibrating with excitement, I bolted through the house shouting, "He's here! He's here!"—stampeding kids and dogs in the process. I had never acted that way before, and I have never acted in quite that way since.

Of the literally hundreds of qualifications which may traditionally be required of an aspirant before he or she would be accepted as a disciple by a Sat-Guru, the primary and most essential one has always been the aspirant's acknowledgement and understanding of Who the Sat-Guru Is: the Realizer of the Divine, or the Living Truth. Until the intuition of this is a certainty, the aspirant should not, and in truth cannot, take up the devotional relationship to the Sat-Guru. Of course, this understanding and acknowledgement grows over time as the devotee matures in his or her own Spiritual practice. But an unmistakable, clear, and certain intuition of the Realization of the Sat-Guru is a prerequisite for true practice. Otherwise there is no basis for the self-transcending gesture of devotion.

It is said in the Tibetan Buddhist tradition:

The disciple must test his potential guru and determine if he is fully qualified. He must be confident that he would be able to devote himself fully to his master. Before entering a formal guru-devotee relationship you have complete freedom of choice. But once such a bond has been established these teachings on guru devotion must be followed with total commitment. The beneficial effects of guru devotion and the dire consequences of a breach of it are not the rewards and punishments from a godly guru. . . . If, having taken such vows, either the Guru or disciple should allow his word of honor to degenerate, it will be impossible for either to attain any of his goals and very serious unfortunate consequences will follow for both. Therefore it is extremely important for there to be a mutual examination between the Guru and disciple before they enter into a formal relationship.[1]

For me, the certainty of the Divine Reality that Da Avabhasa Is began to become deeply established in 1974. I would spend each weekend at the Mountain Of Attention Sanctuary in Da Avabhasa's Company. Heart-Master Da would sit with His devotees in what is now Temple Eleutherios. He would Gaze upon us, and I would experience the Vision and Intuition of the Divine Condition that transcends every thing and being. I was relieved of the deep stress of my being, and healed and purified and touched beyond all the suffering of my life. I was Granted the certainty in these moments that I and everything truly exist in the same Divine Condition. The Divine Nature of all arising was clear to me.

I would return to my home and job in San Francisco still aglow in that Revelation. But for a number of weeks a pattern developed. Sometime during the week, filled with the demands of day-to-day interactions, I would forget the immediate force of the Revelation, and I would doubt it. I would feel that I had been somehow fooled. I would wonder if the Reality that I had seen Revealed at Temple Eleutherios was a trick of energies, just an emotion. By Tuesday or Wednesday, the weekend spent in Darshan with Heart-Master Da would become dreamlike. It baffled me that something that I had felt so directly and tangibly just a few days previously could be so quickly subject to doubt.

The next weekend, however, I would sit in Temple Eleutherios, and again I would have the Vision that transcended everything. It was an

1. Asvaghosa, *Fifty Verses of Guru-Devotion* (Dharamsala, India: The Library of Tibetan Works and Archives, 1976), pp. 11-12, 16.

extraordinary time, during which I was constantly "considering" the nature of the world, and the Spiritual Reality, and my own certainty of Its existence. Then, on one Saturday afternoon, after some weeks of this wavering in my conviction, I again found myself seated in Temple Eleutherios with Sat-Guru Da. His bodily (human) Form was alive with Siddhi and seemed to glow. I was sensitive to the characteristic halo, or effulgence, of yellow light that often framed the surface of His Skin, like a painting of a Christian or Buddhist Saint. He Gazed again upon His devotees, Giving each one His Regard, and Transmitting the Divine Siddhi to all, one by one. He scanned the room, and with a subtle movement, His eyes turned in my direction.

Remarkably, I again was Shown the Divine Reality, and was Given the great Revelation that there is Only God. Everything opened in me, and I knew that Love Which transcends the body and the mind. But what was most extraordinary about this occasion was that right there, in the Hall, even as Heart-Master Da Love-Ananda Showered His Grace upon me, the doubt that would usually come up only a few days later arose. And as His Gaze continued, I observed my doubt. In the next moment I saw that this doubt was my own creation, and that even this doubt arose <u>within</u> the Divine Condition. I saw that it was something that I was doing based on my own withdrawal and refusal of the Sacred Gift being Offered. I was using my mind to turn away and to drop out of my relationship with Sri Gurudev Da Love-Ananda. And it was clear that it was my activity, my choice, my decision. But the fact that I characteristically made that choice did not impinge upon the Revelation of What Is Greater than that doubt. That Divine Reality existed whether I would continue to choose to doubt or not.

This observation startled me—and it instantly relieved me. Afterwards, when I would feel doubt, I knew that it was my own creation. I knew that my struggle, even on those days when everything seemed to tumble upon me, was just my own turning from the Divine Reality, which Exists no matter what emotion I am experiencing. I saw the Primacy of the Divine, even in the face of my habitual turning from God. And, thus, I was made certain beyond doubt of the Divinity that is Sri Gurudev Da Love-Ananda.

Henceforth, I was changed. I began to accept and trust Sri Da Avabhasa's Love. I remain in the midst of the difficult process of Spiritual life, but this much I can and must confess to you: At this moment I am in direct Communion with the Divine Blessing through the relationship I enjoy with Sri Gurudev Da Love-Ananda. I am established in the sacrificial relationship with Him that is the Guru-devotee relationship. And that same relationship that I am living in Satsang with Heart-Master Da Love-Ananda is also Offered to you and to all other human beings.

The Appearance of the Divine Sat-Guru is an unfathomable Gift. Coming into his Company and practicing the Way that he has Revealed, the devotee is Granted the Vision of God through and in his Person. Upon just reading His Wisdom-Teaching and gazing at His Picture, I understood to some degree Who Da Avabhasa Is. But in my case, it was when I was Granted Da Avabhasa's physical Darshan that I was shown the Divine Incarnate in His bodily (human) Form. And this acknowledgement of Who He Is, and the knowledge that He is the Divine Being manifest, became and remained the foundation of my practice itself.

The heart of my capability to practice the Guru-devotee relationship rests in my reception of the Revelation of Who He Is. But full and real practice also requires many other qualifications in order to be fruitful—including self-understanding and a surrendered disposition.

COME TO ME WHEN YOU ARE ALREADY HAPPY:
THE LESSON OF LIFE

To stably accept the testing of the Sat-Guru, and to grow steadily in the Spiritual Way, the devotee must have understood what Da Avabhasa calls the "Lesson of life". This is the fundamental understanding that all things in life are passing, and there is just as much possibility for pain as for pleasure. In fact, as Heart-Master Da used to point out, there are a whole lot more ways that you can feel bad in the world of manifest existence than ways in which you can feel good. And, in any case, whatever one might become attached to is changing and ultimately passing and dying. The aspirant must understand that the search for lasting happiness is futile—the activity of searching is itself un-Happy. As Sat-Guru Da has succinctly summarized it, "You cannot become Happy. You can only be Happy."

Because of this, Sat-Guru Da Love-Ananda has, paradoxically, always told those who might come into His Company to come to Him when they are "already Happy". In other words, to come to Him when they have already understood enough about themselves and about life that they are ready to surrender themselves and to truly receive His Blessing. Without this preparation, there can be no real use of Him.

The devotee always needs to see the fruitlessness of the search for Happiness in anything conditional, and to know that it is the Sat-Guru, the Living Embodiment of the Divine Person, who is the Means to real Happiness. If this is not understood, then there can be no true commitment to the Spiritual Process—there is something that the aspirant feels can potentially make conventional life "okay" again if he or she just does it right, or tries hard enough. If this is the case, then when a particularly difficult or persuasive Spiritual crisis comes upon the aspirant, he or she will not view that crisis as an opportunity to practice, but will instead look toward ordinary conventional life for some self-fulfillment or consolation. However, an individual who has understood the Lesson of life wants to be purified and released of karmas and bondage to the conditions of life and to conditional existence itself, and will thus remain in the "heat" of self-transcending practice.

Along with getting the Lesson of life, the aspirant must have self-understanding in relation to self-doubt, self-pity, and emotional collapse, which are actually forms of egoic "self-possession" and the "flip side" of the puffed-up ego. Heart-Master Da, in the years of His Teaching Work, termed the dramatization of these reactive emotions (and the accompanying refusal to respond to the demands of the Sat-Guru) "the 'poor me' strategy".

The maturing devotee understands that although practice requires a response of great energy, self-responsibility, and surrender, what makes all of this possible is the Sat-Guru's Grace. There is nothing inherently Divine in "Narcissus" or the ego-"I" of the devotee. It is only through the Sat-Guru's Grace that his devotee is capable of self-transcendence. This humility and this strength of character on the part of the devotee have always been prerequisites for Spiritual practice.

Da Avabhasa Writes in *The Dawn Horse Testament*:

The Way Of The Heart Is Founded On Real Transcendence Of The Search (or Wanting Need) For Happiness. That Is To Say, The Way Of The Heart Is Founded On The Magnification Of Inherent (or Real) Happiness, or Happiness Itself. Therefore, I Say, Come To Me When You Are Already Happy. In Other Words, Come To Me By Truly Turning To Me. Do Not Come To Me With A Mere Outward Show Of Devotion (While You Remain Inwardly Dissociated and Possessed By self-Contraction), For, If You Do So, You Will Come As A Seeker, Wanting Happiness From Me, and, Yet, Unable To Reach To Me and To Find Me, and, Thus and Thereby, To Find (or To "Locate") Happiness Itself. . . .

Do Not Come To Me In The Manner Of A Seeker, Wanting To Depend On Me To Make Your Separate and Separative self Happy. Come To Me For Me Only. I Am Happiness Itself (Prior To Your Separate and Separative self). Therefore, Come To Me To Surrender and Forget Your Separate and Separative self (which is Your Un-Happiness, Full Of Wanting Need and Search). (pp. 351-52)

THE BOND THAT LIBERATES:
THE ETERNALLY COMMITTED RELATIONSHIP BETWEEN
THE SAT-GURU AND THE DEVOTEE

The Spiritual traditions are full of accounts of the first meetings between devotees and their Sat-Gurus. Sometimes the Sat-Guru selected was inherited as a family tradition, but often these meetings involved a great pilgrimage or ordeal of testing before the aspirant could even gain access to the Sat-Guru's Company. For example, the medieval Tibetan Adept

Marpa, it is said, had to search all over India to find his principal Guru, Naropa.

The great Indian philosopher Shankara, in his first encounter with his Sat-Guru, Govinda, is an example of right preparation for meeting the Sat-Guru. By the time he came to Govinda, Shankara was already a serious aspirant, with a deep intuition of the Divine. He was born in the south of India and had renounced family life at age twelve to travel on foot in search of a true Spiritual Master. Over the course of his thousand-mile journey, he met many mystics, Yogis, and Saints, but none of them could fully

Shankara

answer his questions, nor grant perfect Realization. Finally, after four years, he found the forest hermitage of his illustrious Teacher on the banks of the Godavari River. There he first consulted with various ascetics, who led him to the entrance to Sage Govinda's residence—a cave whose entrance Govinda had blocked with a huge boulder, leaving only a small opening at the bottom. Shankara circumambulated the area surrounding the cave three times, and, prostrating himself in front of the entrance, he began to chant a hymn in praise of the Sage.

Govinda, seeing Shankara's feet through the opening, asked, "Who are you?" Shankara replied, "I have come to thee to know That."

Upon hearing these words, Sage Govinda was delighted, and he, through his own Spiritual advancement, could see the full and right preparation of Shankara. In response, referring to Shankara as his "dear child", Govinda said, "If you want to know That, hold on to this," extending his foot through the entrance to the cave so that Shankara could see it. Shankara prostrated ecstatically before the Sage's feet in true devotion and worshipped the Sage's feet with a proper ceremony of puja (devotional worship). Praying aloud, and offering his unconditional love to his Master, he also requested the Master's infinite Grace. At that, Govinda pulled both his foot and the boy Shankara into the cave. He embraced the youth, acknowledged his rare qualifications as an aspirant, and Transmitted his Spiritual Blessings to him by touch, word, and glance. Shankara stayed with his Teacher for a few days longer to receive Instruction, and then left to fulfill his mission.

Sri Da Avabhasa once read this story to His devotees and provided a Commentary that put it in proper perspective. Heart-Master Da pointed out the factors that produced Shankara's ability to immediately and fully receive his Sat-Guru's Transmission. First, Shankara's state of preparation was extraordinary, owing to his inherent Spiritual qualities and the purifying practice he had already fulfilled. Second, he truly acknowledged and saw his Master as the Divine and completely surrendered to him as Sat-Guru. It was on the basis of these qualifications that he received and was strongly Graced by the genuine Divine Transmission of his Sat-Guru.

The story of Shankara is a model of the proper preparation and response in a devotee. In the history of the Great Tradition there have been many Sat-Gurus who did not allow anyone to come into contact with them until there had been tremendous testing. Other Sat-Gurus might allow a simple occasion of Darshan or sighting, but would not formally take on an aspirant as a student, or grant formal initiation, or communicate esoteric or advanced Instructions, before an intense period of testing. Just as the devotee is advised to prepare himself or herself, so the Sat-Guru is enjoined over and over again to be wary of taking on or intimately Instructing a devotee who is not rightly prepared. Chogyam Trungpa describes this premature Instruction as "sang drok (gsang-sgrogs), which means declaring the secret at the wrong time".[2] It is said in the *Kun-zang La-May Zhal-lung*, a Nyingmapa manual of preliminary practices in Tibetan Buddhism, "Having an unexamined disciple is like jumping off a cliff."[3]

Heart-Master Da describes many initial conditions that must be met by an individual who begins the devotional relationship to Him by formally approaching the Way of the Heart. Most importantly, such a serious aspirant must have profound gratitude and a willingness, based on his or her own acknowledgement of Him as Sat-Guru and an understanding of the mutually sacrificial relationship and the profound karmas involved, to commit himself or herself totally to Him as Sat-Guru and the practice He Gives. This commitment is never to be broken. In the Tibetan tradition, such vows are known as the "samaya" bond, an eternal bond (binding throughout this life and beyond) between the Sat-Guru and his (or her) devotee. The intensity of the connection between Sat-Guru and devotee is indicated by the fact that traditionally the relationship has always involved this eternal bond.

The Sat-Guru has the power to absorb the devotee's karmas, but that work involves his sacrifice. When he enters into that work, it is only on the basis of a bond with his devotee. And this is why the devotee must be rightly prepared. All the traditional tests of devotees by the Sat-Guru, and by devotees of Sat-Gurus, exist so that, when the relationship begins, it is stable and never need be questioned. Trust is the essence of the ability to make this commitment, and it needs to be there on both sides. The devotee must meet the qualifications given by the Sat-Guru and make the eternal commitment to the Sat-Guru. Only this complete commitment between the Sat-Guru and his devotee allows the space for the Sat-Guru to Work with his devotee fully. And it is only through such eternal commitment that the devotee's surrender achieves the fullness required to receive the Sat-Guru's Gifts. Any withholding or restraint in the devotee's commitment represents

2. Chogyam Trungpa, *Journey without Goal: The Tantric Wisdom of the Buddha* (Boulder and London: Prajna Press, 1981), p. 56.

3. *Kun-zang La-May Zhal-lung: The Oral Instruction of Kun-zang La-May On the Preliminary Practices of Dzog-Ch'en Long-Ch'en Nying-tig*, Part One, transcribed by Pal-trul O-gyen Jig-me Ch'o-kyi Wang-Po Rin-po-ch'e, translated by Sonam T. Kazi (Upper Montclair, N.J.: Diamond Lotus Publishing, 1989), p. 194.

a hedge between the devotee and the Sat-Guru, the devotee's clinging to his or her egoic self apart from the Sat-Guru.

When Sri Gurudev Da Love-Ananda sees His devotee coming to Him bearing fruits representing the gift of surrender at His Feet, He opens to that devotee completely. He assumes full responsibility for the Spiritual advancement of that aspirant. He Gives Himself completely. He takes on the obligation to Serve and Transform that individual, whatever the karmas and liabilities of the devotee. Over the years, devotees of Sri Gurudev Da Love-Ananda have found that His commitment to the transformation of His devotees is more profound and serious than their own. He cares more about our Enlightenment than we do! The depth of commitment that Sri Gurudev Da Love-Ananda makes to each of His devotees is immeasurable. The number of such devotees makes no difference. He is the Heart-Husband of each of His devotees, and He feels His relationship to each one more deeply than any lover.

If a devotee breaks the bond of commitment to the practice of the Way of the Heart and the relationship to Sat-Guru Da, then the effect on Him is staggering. It is the most intense violation that can be committed. The Sat-Guru is not an ordinary man, and His Sacrifice to His devotee is real. This is why there must be right preparation and testing before the diksha, or Spiritual initiation, of the devotee is given. A debt is incurred by the devotee when he or she receives the Divine Initiation from the Sat-Guru. The only way to repay it is to truly practice the Way of the Sat-Guru, and to truly serve him eternally.

One early morning around 4:00 A.M. in late spring 1974, when I had been His formal devotee for less than a year, Sat-Guru Da Love-Ananda was giving a Talk in the Manner of Flowers, His Residence at the Mountain Of Attention Sanctuary. It was an incredibly intimate occasion, with only a handful of us gathered around Da Avabhasa sitting on His living room floor. There was the feeling of being completely alone with the Divine Being, at the center of the universe. Da Avabhasa was Ecstatic. He was incredibly Radiant and Round, Full and "Bright". The room had the softness and serenity of the early morning hours before dawn, but it was illumined by a crisp iridescent Light of Grace. Sri Gurudev Talked of the Mystery that is existence itself. He Spoke exuberantly and with a quality that thrilled the being and Drew me out of myself immediately. Each sentence was so profound that I wanted to rest in its fullness, but the next sentence followed too quickly, creating an effect in which the mind became, instead of a thinking place, an arena of palpable energy. My heart became warm just listening to Him, aglow with His Happiness. He was not merely speaking— He was Initiating us with His Words. He was Drawing us into Himself and His extraordinary Condition of Love.

And then all of a sudden He said, "James, you know what I'm talking about. I'm going to expect great things from you in the future. And don't forget it."

Over the next few days I spent many hours thinking about those three sentences He had Spoken to me, because they were Said with such directness, and so unmistakably. It was only the next day when someone said to me, "You know what He meant, don't you? You know Who He Is, don't you?", that I tried to formulate in words what was already clear. I did know Who He Is. He is the Divine Person, being Revealed in bodily (human) Form, Showing His Sign, and Drawing all into the Spirit-Presence and Very Condition of the Divine Itself.

But I was baffled by what He had said about me. I was only twenty-two at the time. All of us were so young. But I also understood that my life was His, and that whatever was in store for me would be His Work. There was no fear of this—for He is so Great and this Greatness could and would make others Great. There was nothing to do but to return the Gift. It was clear to me that my life had a mission, which was to serve Sri Gurudev forever, and that I had seen something I could never deny.

When I began writing this book, I had hoped that I might in some way be able to repay Da Avabhasa for the tremendous Gifts I have received at His Feet. But in recounting the stories of Sat-Guru Da's Work and the nature of the Guru-devotee relationship, I find that I am receiving such an infusion of Grace that I only plunge deeper into debt! In the balance, however, it changes little, for already I am bound to eternal service at His Feet as my duty and joy.

It is also clear as I write this story that this is not simply my story. As always during those Teaching years, I and all of us present were "coins"[4] for all others. Da Avabhasa's Revelation of Who He Is and His Requirement "I am going to expect great things of you" are the two sides of the Guru-devotee relationship. Sat-Guru Da Gives and Reveals Himself always more and more fully, always Offering the unmistakable Divine Embrace, breaking down confusion and armor and hardness and weakness and lack of faith in His devotee. Complaint and struggle and abusiveness and anger cannot stand up to that Love, that Blessing, that Forcefulness, that "Stick", that Revelation. All

---

4. The term "coin" was used by Da Avabhasa particularly during His later Teaching years in reference to the devotees He Served most directly and intensively as Teacher. The term was taken from a story He had been told about the late Saint Shirdi Sai Baba. From time to time the great Saint had been seen by his devotees rubbing coins from a little bag he kept and repeating the names of certain of his devotees. Sai Baba never liked being observed at this. He was obviously doing Spiritual Puja, remembering and regarding his devotees and focusing his Blessings upon them through this device of rubbing coins.

Da Avabhasa Worked with His "coins" personally and humanly, not merely as symbols. Nonetheless, they also functioned as "coins", or tangible representations to Him of the qualities and destinies of all His devotees and all beings.

SRI DA AVABHASA: I must do My Work for everyone in the company of a few. . . . By means of a direct association with some, and by performing a certain kind of Work, even alone and unobserved like Shirdi Sai Baba with his coins, I Bless everyone and everything. I Bless all kinds of beings, but the human race in particular, and especially those of My devotees who give Me their attention, who are sympathetic with Me, who maintain that sympathy, who accept My discipline, and who enter into right relationship with Me through devotional submission. Such individuals are participating in the field of My Transmission, Which is not local to this Body.

objection and sulk, all betrayal and refusal, are surrendered when one is Held in Those Arms. Tears naturally come to the eyes. The most hardened of hearts melts. As Sri Gurudev once commented, "Even Milarepa, who had worse karmas than any one of you [Milarepa had spitefully killed scores of people in a hailstorm] could Realize the Truth, so do not use the excuse that your karmas are too limiting."

THE SACRAMENT OF UNIVERSAL SACRIFICE

At the heart of the relationship between the God-Realizer and his or her devotee is the law, or principle, of mutual sacrifice or surrender. The mutually sacrificial relationship between the Realizer and the aspirant is the centerpole of the entire Spiritual Process.

Heart-Master Da Wrote of this Wonderful and Mysterious relationship to His devotees in an Essay published in 1977, "How I Comprehend My Own Work":

The true Spiritual Teacher is a special conjunction of the eternal Divine Process and an apparent human entity in the radically released stage of its manifestation. The capacities and qualities of such a human individual are benign and fit for this Service. While eternally rested in the most intimate and profound Intuition of the Divine Condition, the human Master embraces living beings in mutual Sacrifice, or Divine Distraction. He accepts whatever is yielded to him and, while discarding it in its appropriate realm through his spontaneous and spiritual power of Sacrifice, replaces it in the life of his devotees with his own Condition, Form, and Nature. (Breath and Name, pp. 249-50)

The Sat-Guru is Alive in the Divine Condition. In his (or her) Realization he has become a perfect Sacrifice of body, emotion, mind, and the separate and separative self to the Divine. His every action is an expression of this Sacrifice, and he serves his devotees and the world through that same Sacrificial gesture.

A corresponding sacrifice is required of the devotee. Unless the devotee is given over through the genuine practice of self-surrender or self-sacrifice, there is no space in which to receive the Spiritual Transmission of the Sat-Guru.

Heart-Master Da Love-Ananda has Given form to this primal Divine Process of mutual giving through a practice that He calls "the Sacrament of Universal Sacrifice". This simple practice, in which Sri Da Avabhasa's devotee offers a gift to Him (in His physical Form or in the Form of a photographic Murti) and receives a Blessed Gift from Him, fully expresses the relationship between the Guru and the devotee. The gift itself is generally modest—even a leaf, a flower, a fruit, or water is sufficient—for the apple or sweet-smelling gardenia placed before Sri Da Avabhasa is only a token. What is actually being placed before Sri Da Avabhasa and surrendered to Him is the devotee himself or herself.

After offering a gift to Sri Da Avabhasa, His devotee receives Prasad. Prasad ("the return of the gift to the giver") is the Blessed Gift Given by Sat-Guru Da, which may be a piece of fruit, or a sweet that has been Infused with His Blessing, or sacred ash to be placed on the forehead, or simply Blessed water. But whatever form it takes, the Prasad truly is the Gift of Sat-Guru Da's Grace Communicated through the physical object Given to His devotee. His devotee is always Given everything, but is able to receive the Gift only proportionately to his or her real sacrifice. Da Avabhasa Receives the love and devotion of His devotee, and the surrender of His devotee's egoic self, with all of its concerns and limitations, and He then replaces the difficulties and karmas of His devotee with the Gift of His own Condition, His Divine State. The ultimate Prasad Given to His devotee, then, is the Realized Condition of Heart-Master Da Love-Ananda.

Deborah Fremont-Smith, who was Graced to receive Darshan of Sri Gurudev Da Love-Ananda in April 1989 while on retreat at Sri Love-Anandashram, describes the Grace that it is to enact the Sacrament of Universal Sacrifice in the physical Company of Sri Gurudev Da Love-Ananda, and to have the Darshan of the Incarnate Great One:

Hridaya-Samartha Sat-Guru Da Love-Ananda Gave His Darshan today in the bure [a thatched Fijian dwelling] called Owl Sandwiches. The Matrix [now Sri Da Avabhasa Chakra] is a Sublime Place that shimmers not only with sunlight—which is incredible in the South Pacific—but with the great Siddhi of Heart-Master Da. . . .

It is a beautiful and archetypal scene. Sat-Guru Da's Eyes are round and luminous, His Body perfectly still as He Gazes outward with such an expression of vulnerability and sweetness that I am once again struck (as I was so forcefully when I first saw Him in 1976) that this is not a man, not a human being at all. This is the Divine Itself suspended for an instant in time and space, the Radiant Transcendental Being caught for a moment in human Form. It is a breathtaking Vision. I want nothing more than to see Him rightly honored and protected, this naked Heart of Man, the True Self of all beings.

It is my turn to go forward and offer my gift. I walk into the inner room, which is Brilliant with the Glory of Him. The space is full of Silence. Two Kanyas dressed in formal white sit to each side of Him. They are as immobile as He—their attention entirely turned to the Person of Love before them. It is a sacred tableau into which I walk and then kneel.

His Face is beautiful and passionate. I raise my hands and look into His Eyes. These are Unfathomable Eyes in a Face so Profound I am lost in its Depths. His Sublime Look, full of Bliss and full of Compassion, Encompasses me and all beings at the same moment. I also see Profound Sorrow in the liquid of His Eyes, where no person shadows the Heart. Sorrow, Bliss, and Divine Compassion merge in this Great Face. My heart is wrung with the Vision of Him, the Divine Hridaya-Samartha Sat-Guru, Da Love-Ananda, and I immediately remember what He says in His Dawn Horse Testament, *"In This Swoon Of Love, Your Heart May See My Bliss-Wounded Face."*

Owl Sandwiches, April 1989

As I prostrate at His Sublime Feet, I feel I am one of the luckiest people in the world. I turn now to place my gift to the right of His Chair, and my eyes are met with another glorious sight, another beholding. Kanya Kaivalya Navaneeta is seated no more than a foot from me. Her attention fully rested on Him, she is fanning Sat-Guru Da, and in her unwavering devotion her face reflects the sun. My heart thrills to see this, and as I see it, I also perceive something else. I understand in this moment that He Breathes devotion as we breathe air. Devotion is His atmosphere. I leave my gift and seat myself with the other retreatants as our formal Darshan with the Sat-Guru continues.

After about twenty minutes He signals with the barest movement of His hand that the Darshan occasion is over. Then Kanya Tripura Rahasya, who has been seated with us, gracefully takes up the Prasad basket and begins to distribute the Prasad. The Prasad is like Himself, round, full, and sweet, and she carefully places it in our hands. Her heart-Contemplation of Sri Gurudev is so profound that as her hand touches mine, I feel a direct Transmission of Grace and Blessing moving through her from Heart-Master Da. I bow in gratitude as I leave Owl Sandwiches, my heart filled with Peace and the Vision of God, which is finally unutterable.

The same law of mutual sacrifice applies to every aspect of life between the Guru and the devotee. That sacrifice takes the form of ceaseless mutual service. The Sat-Guru is constantly Blessing his devotee in countless ways, and, likewise, the devotee is called to devote his or her life-energy to the service of the Sat-Guru, as an incident from 1978 illustrates.

Late in that year, as His great Text *The Enlightenment of the Whole Body* was being readied for publication, Sri Gurudev Da Love-Ananda at the last moment wrote the Essay "What Will You Do If You Love Me?" and recommended that it be added as the Epilogue to that Text. Jack Lewis was the devotee managing the Dawn Horse Press at that time. He had not seen the Essay itself—which undoubtedly would have softened his heart—but he did see that this late addition would completely upset his publishing deadline. So Jack sent a message to Sri Gurudev Da Love-Ananda that it was "impossible" to add the Essay to the book.

Heart-Master Da Love-Ananda, when He heard Jack's response, humorously replied: "Tell Jack that is what I said to him when I 'considered' taking him as a devotee when he first came to Me—Impossible! But I relented."

Jack got the message, and "What Will You Do If You Love Me?" was included in *The Enlightenment of the Whole Body*, much to the benefit of all Sri Da Avabhasa's devotees and the world.

THE SAT-GURU ABSORBS INTO HIMSELF (OR HERSELF) THE KARMAS OF HIS DEVOTEE

Because Sri Da Avabhasa is completely Vulnerable and Open, He Receives, in the Process of Transmitting His Grace, all His devotees' karmas. Upasani Baba, a Sat-Guru who lived in Western India, described this function metaphorically. He remarked that the Sat-Guru receives all of the karmas of his devotee just as a public gutter receives the dirt and slime as water pours into it.[5] Sri Da Avabhasa has humorously made a similar statement by comparing His Work to a "little old lady cleaning a birdcage".

---

5. *The Talks of Sadguru Upasani-Baba Maharaj*, Volume II, Part A (The Selected Talks) (Sakori: Shri Upasani Kanyakumari Sthan, 1978), p. 289.

After receiving the Darshan of Da Avabhasa, it is the common experience of His devotees to feel relieved not only because they have received the tangible Blessing Force Communicated by Sat-Guru Da, but also because they have been released from, or had pulled from them, egoic tendencies and karmas. Through the Blessing Transmission of Heart-Master Da, His devotee is awakened to That Which Transcends all karmas, and in that awakening, at the level of the psycho-physics of the body-mind, the devotee is also purified of karmas. Through the relationship with Sri Da Avabhasa emotional difficulties, or traumas of the past, are brought to consciousness and released.

Because of the law of mutual sacrifice between the Sat-Guru and his (or her) devotee and the Sat-Guru's bond of submission to his devotee, often the Sat-Guru even takes on the illness of his devotee in his own body, there to dramatically purify and release it. Dan Bouwmeester, M.D., one of the physicians who has had the Graceful opportunity to serve and be Instructed by Sri Da Avabhasa in the healing arts, has witnessed a number of such occasions. He relates this story about an incident that occurred in 1983, at Sri Love-Anandashram in Fiji:

One evening while dancing ecstatically, Tom Closser fell on his left side and broke two ribs. The next day Sri Gurudev noticed that Tom was clutching his chest in pain as he laughed. Heart-Master Da inquired of the cause. Tom informed him, and nothing more was said. At the time, Heart-Master Da Love-Ananda was involved in an intense face-to-face "consideration" with His devotees to help them move beyond the limits of their emotional-sexual bondage. Two weeks passed, and Tom's ribs were still painful. Heart-Master Da forcefully yet lovingly "considered" with Tom a particularly dramatic incident in his past. During the "consideration" Tom was relieved of the emotional scar—the guilt, anger, sorrow, and shame that had kept him emotionally bound for many years. Through Heart-Master Da's Help he was able to pass through this difficult emotional obstruction, and, miraculously, not only was Tom's emotional trauma relieved, but his painful broken ribs were healed.

After the confrontation with Tom, Heart-Master Da lay down to rest on His porch. Soon He began to feel an ache on the left side of His chest and sharp pains as He breathed. I was called to examine Heart-Master Da and found that two ribs had fractured spontaneously. They were the same ribs and fracture sites as in Tom's case!

Such manifestations in the Adept's body cannot be understood by the conventional mind. They are the spontaneous display of the great Love and sympathy that the Compassionate Heart-Master has for His devotee.

SURRENDER THROUGH OBEDIENCE:
THE SECRET OF ALWAYS REMAINING IN THE
BLESSING-SPHERE OF THE SAT-GURU

That the Sat-Guru must be approached rightly and with all due formalities is not something that is decided by the Sat-Guru. It is not that he (or she) requires that he be treated in such a way because it serves his personal desires or wants. It is simply that there are laws inherent in the Guru-devotee relationship—including the principle of mutual sacrifice, the eternal bond between the Sat-Guru and devotee, and the debt that obliges the devotee who has accepted the Sat-Guru's Grace. If these laws are not respected and honored, the true Sat-Guru will not and cannot respond. How many times has Heart-Master Da Love-Ananda Commented that He wished it were different, that the Liberation of His devotees was not dependent on their real preparation, so that He could Freely Give all that He has brought into the World by virtue of His Incarnation and His Divine Emergence? He has wanted to Give His devotees everything "for free", but even He cannot replace His devotees' own responsibility.

In the Way of the Heart, the true devotee always follows Sri Da Avabhasa's Instructions exactly. Sri Da Avabhasa's devotee carefully studies His Callings, Principles, Agreements, and Instructions so that he or she is always aligned to Sat-Guru Da's Wishes and, therefore (through obedience), is sympathetically conformed to Him. This is the principle of surrender. Da Avabhasa Writes in the "I Am What you Require" section of *The Love-Ananda Gita*:

If you are to fulfill the Law of the Guru-devotee relationship, it is absolutely necessary that you conform explicitly to the explicit (and summary) Instructions I have Given.

If you follow My Instruction (thus), then you have (in every such instance) My Permission and Blessing, and your sadhana in My Company will be fruitful.

If there is any circumstance or opportunity in life in which you do not feel explicitly Instructed, Permitted, and Blessed by Me, then you must look for My Instruction, and acquire My Permission, and receive My Blessing. . . . [T]he Law of the traditional (and right) Guru-devotee relationship is surrender through obedience. Therefore, conform your entire life to Me, your Hridaya-Samartha Sat-Guru, and do not do anything without My explicit Instruction, Permission, and Blessing.

To follow the Sat-Guru's Instruction requires great devotion and discrimination, especially in circumstances when the Sat-Guru's Words and Directions may indicate the performance of an action that is not pleasing to the ego that wants to be congratulated and consoled, or when there seems to be an extenuating circumstance. Surrendering to anyone or anything other than one's own egoic desires is particularly difficult for Westerners, especially those who are unsympathetic to the idea of the Guru. Obedience is inherently suspect to such people, who are always looking to make sure that they are not being "taken advantage of" It is only when people see the suffering inherent in egoity, when they have come to their own "end of the line", and realize that they truly need the help of the Sat-Guru, that they are willing to enter into the eternal bond of surrender and obedience (or sympathetic conformity) that is the Guru-devotee relationship.

At the same time that he or she is obedient, the devotee has the responsibility to remain intelligent and maturely related to the Sat-Guru. If there is a moment when it seems impossible to fulfill the Sat-Guru's Instruction, then the devotee must make the reasons clear to him. The devotee must be very careful that the limitation he or she feels is not due merely to laziness, lack of intensity in practice, or lack of attention. If it is, then not to fulfill the Sat-Guru's Instructions is truly just refusal, reluctance, or resistance to the ordeal of growth and transformation in relationship to the Sat-Guru. I have heard Da Avabhasa's devotees on many occasions telling Him that they could not do something He had asked them to do. He has roared back, not even commenting on the specifics of the situation but speaking to the resistance and disrespectfulness of His devotees. And then I have watched those same devotees find a way to accomplish Sat-Guru Da's Request (which before seemed impossible).

For example, I once told Sri Gurudev Da Love-Ananda that I was going to have to return some books (which He had been reviewing in His Work on "The Seven Schools of God-Talk and God-Realization" reading list) to the library from which they had been checked out. This library had a strict policy regarding overdue books, and I wanted to avoid the heavy fines, as well as the possible loss of borrowing privileges, which would have affected my ability to continue providing Sri Da Avabhasa with books He might need for His Work.

Sri Gurudev was displeased by this, and He said that if I were truly serving Him I would not have allowed Him to be disturbed in the midst of His Work. He said it was all right to return the books if absolutely necessary, but He preferred not to be interrupted in His Work.

My initial response was to feel that what He was asking was impossible. But I soon heard again that Sri Gurudev was disturbed by my having to disrupt His Work. Therefore, I decided to simply try to do what He was asking. I called up this large university library and asked for the head of the circulation department. I explained that it was important to the work that we were doing to have these books for a longer period of time. The librarian, glad to be able to make an exception to the rules for a good cause, allowed me to simply renew the books for an extended period over the phone! I received a lesson in how even the seemingly impossible Request of Sri Gurudev could be fulfilled through obedience to His Word.

"Narcissus", if allowed to, and if pressed, will create the most "logical" or crazy reasons why some particular Instruction cannot be followed, why something else must be done instead. Therefore, a corollary to the rule of obedience is that the devotee should never consult anyone besides the Sat-Guru about sadhana—especially not his or her own body-mind:

SRI DA AVABHASA: . . . do not play it "fast and loose" with the tendencies of the body-mind. The body-mind and its associations in the world will, being conditional forms, always, by tendency, move the egoic self in another direction than sadhana. Therefore, the body-mind and its associations in the world should not be consulted about sadhana.

Only the Realizer should be consulted about sadhana. That is it. ("I Am What you Require" section, The Love-Ananda Gita, *pp. 363-64)*

The Dalai Lama, when recently asked about this issue of obedience to the Guru, replied:

Take the cases of Naropa and Marpa, for example. Sometimes it appears as though some of the things Tilopa asked of Naropa, or Naropa asked of Marpa, were unreasonable. Deep down however these requests had good meaning. Because of their great faith in their Gurus, Naropa and Marpa did as intended. Despite the fact that they appeared to be unreasonable, because the teachers were qualified, their actions had some meaning. In such situations it is necessary from the disciple's side that all of the actions of the teacher be respected. But this cannot be compared to the case of ordinary people. Broadly speaking, I feel the Buddha gave us complete freedom of choice to thoroughly examine the person who is to be our Guru. This is very important. Unless one is definite, one should not take someone as a Guru. This preliminary examination is a kind of precautionary measure.[6]

The Buddha

That it is appropriate to follow even the apparently unreasonable requests of the Sat-Guru, but only after one has thoroughly tested him, is the traditional admonition. As the above statement by the Dalai Lama exemplifies, this attitude is particularly prominent in Vajrayana Buddhism, or the Tantric Way, where it is said of the truly qualified Lama (who is understood to be the Buddha incarnate):

How can a Buddha have faults? Whatever he does, let him do it! Even if you see your guru having sexual relations, telling lies and so on, calmly meditate as follows:

"These are my guru's unsurpassed skillful methods of training disciples. Through these methods he has brought many sentient beings to spiritual

6. His Holiness the Dalai Lama, *The Bodhgaya Interviews*, ed. Jose Ignacio Caberon (Ithaca, N.Y.: Snow Lion Publications, 1988), p. 60

maturity and liberation. This is a hundred, a thousand times more wonder-ful than preserving a pure moral code! This is not deception or hypocrisy but the highest mode of conduct!"[7]

This statement, by one of the greatest Buddhist Masters of the nine-teenth century, counters the claims of those who look to find fault with the Guru-devotee relationship. What is being stated (and is in agreement with the great esoteric traditions throughout the world) is that the Sat-Guru must be free to use whatever "skillful means" are necessary to serve his devotee. If the Sat-Guru could spark a change or a transformation in a devotee by an apparent lie, then he (or she) would lie. No arbitrary code of conduct is binding on the Divine Sat-Guru. His only interest is the Liberation of his devotees. His motive in whatever he does is Compassion.

Karlfried Graf Durckheim writes, in his description of the means used by a Master:

If he has to, a master is ready to violate a community's code—but he never violates the law by which it really lives. Sometimes, however, he can obey this law only by turning the community's tidy systems upside-down. This is why he is never a model of civic virtue—never an example for the upright citizen to follow.[8]

The Spiritual traditions have always stressed that the greatest discrimina-tive intelligence is necessary in testing the Sat-Guru, and making sure that one wishes to assume the role of his or her student and devotee. Likewise, each aspirant must understand for himself or herself the wisdom of the Sat-Guru's Teaching and of the Spiritual practices that he Teaches, and only on that basis take them up. In Spiritual life the demand for self-transcendence and genuine growth is a fire. If the devotee does not fully understand the purposes and the necessity for each of the practices that he or she takes up in the Sat-Guru's Company, and if he or she does not freely choose and apply them based on self-understanding, then there is no way that the devo-tee will be able to sustain the intensity required to truly practice.

Once, in early 1989, I was awakened in the middle of the night to pre-pare a report Sri Gurudev had asked to review the next morning. Just in being awakened I became upset. Instead of being in the mood of the devo-tee at that moment—always ready to serve the Sat-Guru, and understanding that if a response was necessary for the next morning there was good cause to be awakened at that moment—I was already having difficulty with my own reactivity about the whole matter. Sri Gurudev was disturbed by a

7. Jamgon Kongtrul, *The Torch of Certainty,* transl. Judith Hanson (Boulder, Colo.: Shambhala Publications, 1977), p. 130.

8. Karlfried Graf Durckheim, *The Call for the Master: The Meaning of Spiritual Guidance on the Way to the Self,* ed. Vincent Nash (New York: E. P. Dutton, 1986), p. 59.

letter I had written Him the day before in response to His suggestion of a new name for the library of the Free Daist Communion. He asked me to reconsider my response.

I read Sat-Guru Da Love-Ananda's Communications about my report, but I did not understand what He was addressing. To me it felt like He was asking for my submission to His suggestion of a name and that I just had to blindly accept the name, without good cause. I felt stupid and insulted. I complained to myself, "Why can't I just wait until I cool down—why do I have to respond with a letter for the morning?" In my reactivity I said to myself, "Why do I have to agree with Him?" And of course I did not. Every discussion with Sri Gurudev is always a "consideration", and if there was good cause for a different name for the library, then I was free to suggest it. But I had no convincing argument for the name I was suggesting.

What I did, as a devotee, was to sit at the keyboard of my computer and write to Sri Gurudev. I allowed myself to feel Him and to feel what was really going on in that moment. I began to write words of praise and submission. My body was on fire, but I knew enough not to trust my reaction and upset. The force of my negative habits in that moment were suggesting that I should argue with the Sat-Guru and act like a five-year old. But I knew that I was experiencing Sri Gurudev's Divine Interference.

I knew what a devotee would do in such a circumstance, and so, even though I felt disturbed, I resorted to that knowledge, and to my relationship to Sri Gurudev. On the one hand there was my desire to dramatize the separate self. On the other hand was my resort to Sri Gurudev as His devotee. Connecting with Him at a Place deeper than my reactivity, I thought, "What is so precious about my suggestion anyway?" I knew that Sri Gurudev is my Sat-Guru, and that there was no reason to betray that relationship, no reason to assume my own superiority, or to dramatize collapse. I knew that as His devotee I should simply submit to my Sat-Guru, as senseless as it seemed to my harried mind and emotion, which at that point were obviously disturbed. I have learned, over many years, to trust my heart and its relationship to Sri Gurudev Da Love-Ananda, rather than my complaining emotion and scheming mind.

A day later, after I had relaxed from the reactivity I was experiencing and I could look at the situation with freer attention, I completely agreed with what Sat-Guru Da had been saying! I saw that my own suggestion for a name for the library had just been based on my idiosyncracies. My previous upset seemed at best amusing, and at worst childish and adolescent. I was very glad that I had not given my reactive drama the space it had demanded.

On another occasion, I had loaned my copy of the *Hevajra Tantra* (a two-volume Tibetan Buddhist text) to a devotee who served Sri Gurudev's Personal circumstance. In it I had placed a note, "Please keep track of this book and don't lose it. It is one of my favorites." The book and the note were left at the Manner of Flowers, and Sri Gurudev happened upon both of them. Immediately He began to Compassionately address what I needed to change in order to be rightly related to Him.

I had spent many years building up my collection of books. Haunting bookstores and carefully deciding which books to buy was a favorite pastime of mine. To own a book had an almost magical quality to me. It was to have knowledge of, and thus "power" over, the subject of the book. Owning a book made me feel more in control. My book collection thus became a reflection of my own ego, and my attempt to create a world in which I was loved and respected for what I knew. I felt a good deal of anxiety for the welfare of my books, for they were part of this image of myself that I carefully cultivated. At the same time, I had worked for many years selling books or doing research for people, and thus I was always in an environment that fed my obsession with the mind. During this time in 1977, I had perhaps only three hundred books, but each of them had been carefully selected and represented its own form of bondage.

Three times during that day Sri Gurudev Da Love-Ananda Gave Communications about my obsession with books, and what I should do—immediately—to remedy it. According to the woman who had borrowed the book, Sat-Guru Da was exclaiming all day—"This is what is keeping him from Me!" He was pleased on the one hand that I had so dramatically revealed what needed to be purified. And on the other hand, He Communicated His exasperation with the strength of my bondage to "owning" books and building up my "collection". By the end of the day, a course of action was Given to me as a Command from my Sat-Guru.

I was never to own another book, period, besides those of the Way of the Heart. I was to sell or give away my entire collection, keeping only those books that I needed for my work. Sri Gurudev pointed out that it took "a greater man" than I to have a "library". My relationship to owning books was too much of an addiction—it was karmic and binding, and I was simply to let it go.

It is impossible for me to relate how much suffering was removed from me on that day, and over the years since, through carrying out this discipline. I did not delay in fulfilling Sri Gurudev Da Love-Ananda's Request. As soon as I returned home from work that evening, I simply packed all my books into my car and drove off to the Mountain Of Attention Sanctuary. As I carried each box up the stairs to the library, I felt lighter and lighter. It was a clean sweep, and it was done.

Over the years these Admonitions from Sri Gurudev Da Love-Ananda have Helped me again and again, for tendencies such as these are only undone over time. I continued to be Graced to serve Sri Gurudev Da Love-Ananda by securing thousands upon thousands of books for His review, developing the libraries at the Mountain Of Attention and at Sri Love-Anandashram, and doing research in the Spiritual traditions for many of Sri Da Love-Ananda's "considerations" and publications. But through Sri Da Avabhasa's Graceful Service to me, I was able to steer clear of the obsession with knowledge and control through owning books.

As I have said, the tendency of obsession with the Spiritual traditions and books is still there. I remember an occasion the next year, when, sometime after midnight, I returned to my home near the Mountain Of Attention Sanctuary with a selection of books for Sri Gurudev's review the next day. And although in those days of the Teaching Work there were many evenings when Sri Gurudev Da Love-Ananda stayed up late into the evening, I had decided that it was too late to deliver the books to Him. I would take them to the Sanctuary the next day. At about 12:30 A.M., I received a call from Sri Gurudev's personal attendant. Sri Gurudev had heard that I had been in the city gathering books, and He wanted to know where they were. And when I said that I had thought that it was too late, the reply came, "You just wanted to read them yourself, that's all!" After that, no matter how late I arrived, I would take the books to the Sanctuary, knowing that my own tendency was purified in the process.

Even now I will periodically notice myself accumulating too many books for "my work" and have to go through them and drop them off at the library! And recently, when Sri Gurudev Da Love-Ananda came by my office during a tour of newly completed facilities at Sri Love-Anandashram, He took a brief but all-encompassing look at my collection of volumes there for research. I was told that He had a smile on His face, and I felt that, as always, He would be in His own and Perfect Way evaluating my collection in the light of my adherence to His Grace-Given Gift of discipline for the sake of my sadhana.

The lesson of these and similar incidents is the lesson of obedience. The choice to obey Sri Gurudev's Instruction in any moment is always a free choice, necessarily founded on self-understanding. The exercise of my own "free will" is always active in my choice to trust my heart's intuition (of the Divine Wisdom in Heart-Master Da's Instruction), rather than to "buy" the passing reactions of the mind and body.

If there is the understanding that bondage and suffering are what one is surrendering, then the prospect of such true surrender and renunciation is the great aspiration of the devotee. Such surrender, contrary to popular opinion, is the most "manly" gesture, male or female, that can be made by a living being. It requires great courage and great self-transcendence to surrender all egoic tendencies at the Feet of the Adept. It requires intelligence and inspection of each moment. Through the devotee's surrender, the motivating force of practice need not be the grinding affair of trying to overcome the ego, but rather the joyful heart-turning to the most Attractive Principle in the worlds, the devotee's own beloved Sat-Guru.

Sri Love-Anandashram, January 1990

CHAPTER EIGHT

"Always Allow The Divine Person to Stand Even <u>As</u> Your Own body-mind"

THE SUBLIME PRACTICE OF ISHTA-GURU-BHAKTI YOGA

DEVOTION

*W*hen you have been given everything, when you have been loved beyond every possible conception that you might have of what you deserve, what can you do to respond to the one who has loved you so fully? When you have stumbled upon the Divine Person, Who is Alive as the Very Self-Condition of every form, experience, and event, what can you do in relationship to such a One? When the Divinely Transforming Regard of the Sat-Guru Showers upon you in a stream that purifies, raises you up, and Blesses you with every breath, what is your natural response?

As Sri Da Avabhasa Says in His Ecstatic Essay "What Will You Do If You Love Me?":

My Lovers, My true devotees, simply Love Me. That is the summation of their response to Me and My Teaching. . . . They live in constant remembrance of Me and in loving service to Me. Every moment of their lives is simply a moment of Love-Communion with Me. Therefore, they are granted perpetual Ecstasy, or self-forgetting in Communion with the Radiant Transcendental Consciousness.

My special Mission is to Live with such devotees. I have always looked for them. I test everyone, to see if they are My Lovers. I wait. Many surround Me. Many turn to Me with the good heart. But those who Love Me best Realize God by exclusive attachment to Me in Person. . . .

Love is what we fear to do—until we fall in Love. Then we no longer fear to Love, to surrender, to be self-forgetful and foolish, to be single-minded, and to suffer another. Those who fall on Me fall into My Heart. They are free of all demands for fulfillment through experience and self-survival. Their love for Me grants them Life, since I am the Life-Current of Love.

What will My Lover do but Love Me? I suffer all the limitations of one who Loves Me, because I Love My devotee as My own Form, My own Bliss, My own Love. I Love My devotee as the Person by whom I am Distracted and Dissolved.

I grant all My own Excesses to those who Love Me, in exchange for all their doubts and sufferings. Those who bind themselves to Me through Love are inherently Free of fear and necessity. They Transcend the causes of experience, and they Dissolve in the Heart of God. What is a Greater Message than This? (The Enlightenment of the Whole Body, *pp. 573, 575)*

True devotion will be seen on the faces of true devotees. Sri Gurudev Da Love-Ananda has pointed out that when a person is looking at an ordinary object, then the person is without the consciousness of any profound feeling. Such a person's look is not ecstatic and usually not very intense. It is a reflection of an ordinary egoic mind and of bodily self-awareness. But when an individual contemplates the Divine Form, the look on his or her face is utterly transformed. Although that look may vary from extreme intensity in meditation to outwardly less intense expression at other times, the ecstatic expression is constant and obvious in anyone who contemplates the Divine Form. Therefore, it is the common experience of Sat-Guru Da Love-Ananda's devotees that in any moment when they are Contemplating His Forms, there is an inevitable change in the face and bodily expression. In the community of the Way of the Heart, the bodily expression of such ecstasy is accepted and valued.

Da Avabhasa once commented upon a photograph of Ramana Maharshi with his devotees as an example of such devotion in the traditional context. He remarked that that photograph is a good example of how practitioners look and act when they see their Guru not as an ordinary person, but as the Divine Form. That response is the Gift that becomes the basis for devotional practice moment to moment at all times and under all circumstances.

This emotion felt spontaneously by the devotee in Love-Communion with the Sat-Guru is expressed in a beautiful Free Rendering by Da Avabhasa of a section from the *Bhagavata Purana.* It is titled "The Essence of Devotion":

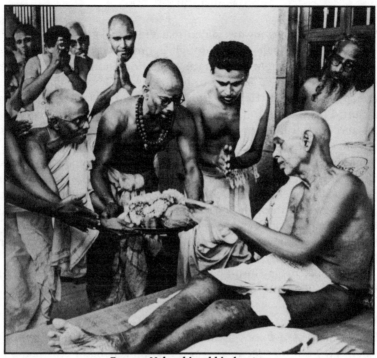

Ramana Maharshi and his devotees

If there is not the quality of heartfelt devotion to Me, the Radiant Self, then even intelligent understanding of the Teaching, commitment to discipline, and compassionate service of others cannot cleanse and relieve the soul of its urges toward fulfillment in the phenomenal realms, high or low.

How can I be Loved if the hair does not stand on end when there is Contemplation of Me? How can I be Loved if the heart does not melt in My Presence? How can I be Loved if tears of joy do not pass freely from the eyes when I am Standing There?

If I am Loved, then the entire body-mind is Filled by that Love. If my devotee is Filled by Me through Love-Communion, his voice often falters and chokes with the emotion of Love. Because he always dwells in Contemplation of Me at the heart, he often weeps, and suddenly laughs. He sings aloud. He always speaks of Me. He dances with joy. Even all his movements are a dance of joy in Love.

Gold can be made pure only through submission to fire. Just so, the soul is purified and liberated from its deep urges only when it submits to self-transcending Love-Communion with Me. Such a devotee is Awakened to essential Unity with Me. And his ecstatic Presence serves the purification of the entire World. (The Enlightenment of the Whole Body, *p. 237)*

ISHTA-GURU-BHAKTI YOGA

Da Avabhasa has always stated that the Way of the Heart results in Divine Self-Realization through a process of "duplication". The devotee ultimately Realizes the same Condition Enjoyed by the Sat-Guru, and not any lesser state. And the Means of Grace is the relationship to the Sat-Guru, which Heart-Master Da Love-Ananda has Described as "Ishta-Guru-Bhakti Yoga". This Yoga is the "Method" of the Siddhas, the ancient and eternal tradition by which devotees are transformed. It is the heart of the Guru-devotee relationship.

"Ishta" is a Sanskrit word that comes from a root meaning "to desire" or "to choose". Popularly in religious India, each individual worships his or her Ishta, or chosen Form of God, which is the deity worshipped in one's family or discovered through one's spontaneous response to a painting or a statue of a form of the deity, or is the chosen deity of one's Teacher. The Sanskrit word "bhakti" means "devotion" or "love". A "Yoga" is a Spiritual discipline or practice by which one achieves "union", or Communes, with the Divine. Thus, "Ishta-Guru-Bhakti Yoga" is the "Way of devotion to the chosen Divine Teacher". Sri Da Avabhasa relates this term to the Guru-devotee relationship:

SRI DA AVABHASA: I have originated a unique Wisdom-Teaching in your company, but I am also the bearer of a tradition, which I call, using traditional language, "Ishta-Guru-Bhakti Yoga". In this tradition, the Guru is the Ishta, or the Divine Form, embraced by his or her devotee. This is the tradition of those who Served Me in My own Spiritual Process. It is only when this secret is grasped—when the secret of the Guru is grasped, entered into, submitted to—that the Spiritual Process in its fullest sense is Realized. It is only then that Realization becomes possible, that Grace becomes usable, that the practice becomes effective. (April 11, 1986)

The principle of this process is one we have mentioned previously in our discussion of the Guru-devotee relationship: You become what you meditate on, or surrender your attention to. To feelingly Contemplate the Sat-Guru is to take on his (or her) characteristics, his Realization. Thus the devotee's loving attention to his or her Ishta-Guru is the secret of the supreme effectiveness of the Guru-devotee relationship.

SRI DA AVABHASA: I have always looked for one thing from everyone with whom I have ever Worked, and that is his or her attention. That attention is the connecting link. The more intense, unwavering, and constant that attention, the more the Spiritual Process is served in that relationship.

What is perfected in the development of My Work, in the creation of devotees and the community of My devotees, is that attention. The mere attention of My devotees is the means for their Liberation, and their giving their attention to Me is the fundamental practice. All the rest of the practice is a way to serve that attention and to intensify it. I am very sensitive to that thread of attention in every person. If I have someone's attention, then I spend much time with him or her, either physically or in a subtler manner. I am always Working with every one who comes to Me. But if one's attention turns away from Me, then I find I must spend a great deal of time trying to make the individual aware that I am still here. Even during times when one's attention drifts, I Work with the attention that is still there. When the attention becomes intense again, then the Spiritual manifestation becomes more obvious. The true devotee's attention is absolutely intense, absolutely constant, absolutely unwavering and pure. (August, 1974)

The process of Ishta-Guru-Bhakti Yoga becomes more profound as the devotee matures and develops a stronger and stronger foundation for it. But from the very moment when the devotee commits himself or herself formally to the Sat-Guru in the eternal relationship or bond of the Guru-devotee relationship, Ishta-Guru-Bhakti Yoga is the essence of that relationship. The devotee surrenders to the Sat-Guru, receives the Sat-Guru's Grace, and allows whatever is Transmitted by the Sat-Guru to become his or her experience. Although this process has been at the heart of Sat-Guru Da Love-Ananda's Communication about the Guru-devotee relationship from the beginning of His Teaching Work, He first used the expression "Ishta-Guru-Bhakti Yoga" in two Talks Given on March 21 and 22, 1986, just weeks after the dramatic Event of His Divine Emergence.

SRI DA AVABHASA: When you are My true devotee, when you truly see Me as the Ishta-Guru, or the True Heart-Master, you give yourself to the Divine Person Revealed as Me, and you allow the Divine Person to acquire your form. In other words, if you devote yourself to Me as the Ishta, or True Heart-Master, you surrender your own form, the body-mind and all conditional aspects of your personality, to the Divine Person, and you allow the Divine Person to take over your form, to stand in its place, to be the principal relationship of your life, to Which you devote yourself and give yourself. That One is to be found within and without.

Thus, you Find Me even as your own form, in your own form, in relationship to your own form. You simply surrender your conditional self, or give up your self-contraction, to Me as the Ishta of the Divine Person, which you see in My Form as the True Heart-Master. You allow yourself to be surrounded, pervaded, transformed by responsive devotion to Me. You allow yourself to become What you meditate on.

This process of devotional feeling-Contemplation of Me as the Ishta-Guru is not a matter of relating to Me as an other, although of course there is a dimension of that kind to the relationship. You do relate to Me, the True Heart-Master, as an (apparently) human personality. There is an objective dimension, then, to your responsiveness to Me, to your seeing of Me as the

True Heart-Master. You also feel My Hridaya-Shaktipat, the Force of My Heart-Transmission, in relationship to the body-mind, so there is also that objective aspect to this process. But you surrender yourself to the Divine Person by surrendering to Me. You allow yourself to be taken over by that One by surrendering to Me. You allow that One to Stand in your place, where you give yourself, to the point of Realizing Perfect Identity with that One, not by effort, but simply by allowing that One to Be.

You let Me, the True Master of your heart, and, thus, the Divine Person, be your own body-mind, acquire your own body-mind. In this way, My Spiritual (and Always Blessing) Presence works in your body-mind as if your body-mind were My own. The same process that has developed in My apparent body-mind is developed, then, in the circumstance of your own body-mind. You simply give way to Me, as the True Heart-Master, so that I can be and acquire all conditional forms that previously were your own independently and Narcissistically, and you allow My Spiritual Processes to become your own, to take place in your own place.

It is not a matter of your self-generating Spiritual Power. It is a matter of responding to the Divine Person Revealed by My Transmission, or Hridaya-Shakti. You acknowledge That One. You respond to That One. And that response is naturally the one of letting go of your egoic self, letting go of self-contraction, letting go of the body-mind, releasing the body-mind into My Spiritual (and Always Blessing) Presence, so that the Spiritual Process develops freely, spontaneously, more and more profoundly. Everything, then, from forms of "conductivity" and subtle perceptions to Divine Self-Realization in the fullest sense is Realized, by Grace, simply by allowing Me, as your True Heart-Master, and, thus and thereby the Divine Person, to be in the place of "Narcissus". This is not a matter of your egoic effort but of your simple devotional response to Me, not a matter of effortful working on yourself, but a response to the One Who is before you. Thus, the practice of the Way of the Heart is to maintain Me as your Ishta-Guru in front of your heart at all times.

My bodily (human) Form is the Murti of the Divine Person, the Ishta, the "Threshold Personality". I am the Object of devotion for those who practice the Way of the Heart. Through your acknowledgement of Me and your devotional responsiveness to Me, the Divine Person is allowed to be the world, to be the body-mind, to be whatever arises, and you see the Divine Person in everything that arises.

If you are My devotee, then no matter what your level of practice, you will always understand the practice of the Way of the Heart as responsiveness to Me, cooperation with My Spiritual Heart-Transmission, rather than working on your egoic self, strategically trying to Realize the Divine. Give yourself to the One Who is already Realized. Respond to That One. And then the Very State of That One will be Realized by you quite naturally, as a Free Gift. This is the secret of the Way of the Heart that I have Revealed. (March 22, 1986)

In late 1988, I received a dramatic lesson about my own wrong approach to Sri Da Avabhasa and how I was not truly Contemplating Him. At that time I was on retreat at Sri Love-Anandashram. Heart-Master Da Love-Ananda told me that He wanted to relate to me as the Sat-Guru must relate to His devotee, but that I was not allowing Him to do so. I was insisting on a different kind of relationship—I was relating to Sri Gurudev through traditional imagery, rather than relating to Him as He Is. He said that if I did not change my action and relate to Him rightly, I would not be able to grow in my practice or continue to serve Him. He further told me that I must truly "consider" this criticism and make a change in response to it if my relationship to Him was important to me. He said He would be watching me to see what my response would be. He also told me that I was more interested in the Spiritual traditions than I was in Him—that not He, but the library of Spiritual books and the Great Tradition, was my "guru".

Although I knew of my tendency to dissociate from Him through fascination with the imagery of the Spiritual traditions, and although I understood what He was saying intellectually, I did not know what more could be done to purify it. I could only more fully embrace the practice of feeling-Contemplation of Him, and turn to Him through my practice, and allow His Grace to Work in me. I was not aware of how my practice of Ishta-Guru-Bhakti Yoga was being undermined by my fascination with that which was apart from my Guru.

A few days later there was to be a formal Sat-Guru Arati (a ceremony in which the devotee waves lights around the Guru or Divine Image) in the traditional style, to inaugurate the use of a traditional Sanskrit song of praise to the Sat-Guru. Sri Gurudev Da Love-Ananda would attend. I had attended a number of such Aratis during my trips to various Ashrams, and I waited in anticipation of this Arati, greatly looking forward to chanting the traditional words and melody. I could feel that my excitement came from my obsession with the Spiritual traditions. This fantasy world I created for myself was safer and more consoling to my egoic character than my life of sadhana. And because of my knowledge about the Spiritual traditions, I felt good about myself.

On the night of the Arati, I seated myself just in front of Sri Da Avabhasa's Chair, awaiting His arrival. I knew that my tendency to be distracted by my involvement in the traditions was going to be tested, and I wanted to be where I could give my attention to Da Avabhasa most directly. Soon He came into the room, Radiant and Brilliantly Alive. Almost immediately the harmonium began the familiar melody.

From the first notes of the traditional melody I felt my attention moving to the shores of the Ganges River at sunset. The romantic feeling of India and its power to distract me from my problems was right there. But I knew that I could not indulge it. I knew that my Ishta was the Brilliant Being sitting before me, not any traditional imagery or archetype. With all of my

Devotees at the Sat-Guru Arati

energy and attention, I turned again to Sri Gurudev Da Love-Ananda, feeling my attraction for Him, which was greater than my self-obsession or any possible distraction. But moments later, as the words of the chant began, I felt the same desire to indulge in distraction.

For the next half hour, as the Arati progressed, over and over again I saw the depth of my tendency to be distracted and turned away from Sri Gurudev Da Love-Ananda and therefore to not practice true Guru-devotion, or Ishta-Guru-Bhakti. By the Grace of His criticisms it was so easy to see this personal "dramatization". It was clear to me that the instant in which I relaxed my· counter-egoic action of turning to Sri Gurudev, I immediately drifted into my "Indian fetishism" (as Sri Gurudev has succinctly termed my tendency). As I continued to turn to Sri Gurudev, I felt Him more and more fully entering into me. Intense kriyas arose in my body. My body was gyrating at the neck and the lower back, and my arms flailed. As I turned to Him deeper and deeper, I felt His Spirit-Presence. Yet the moment I relaxed and listened at all to the music, I was again forcefully and dramatically distracted, until I remembered to feelingly Contemplate Sri Da Avabhasa again.

The truth of His Instruction to me thus became very clear. My fantasy world did stand between me and Sat-Guru Da. Surrender to anything else but the Guru makes worshipping Him impossible. Between me and Sat-Guru Da was all this baggage of the traditions. I saw how right Sri Gurudev had been about my being a "devotee" of all this, rather than His devotee. When I left the Arati that day, I had Gracefully become established more deeply in true resort to Sri Gurudev directly. I understood more truly the necessity of turning to Sri Gurudev Da Avabhasa alone, rather than allowing anything else to distract me.

In the practice of Ishta-Guru-Bhakti Yoga the devotee surrenders to the Sat-Guru to the point of actually allowing the Guru to become him or her. Through such complete self-surrender of his or her body and mind, the devotee makes space for the Sat-Guru to enter. Thus, the devotee often feels aspects of the Sat-Guru's body, mind, or characteristics superimposed upon himself or herself. Devotees of Da Avabhasa have often felt His face superimposed upon theirs, and felt themselves smiling or moving their mouth, for example, as He does.

Da Avabhasa Describes the essence of Ishta-Guru-Bhakti Yoga:

*By Always Feeling (and, Thereby, Always Contemplating) My Bodily (Human) Form, My Spiritual (and Always Blessing) Presence, and My Very (and Inherently Perfect) State, Always Allow The Divine Person To Stand As all that arises, and (Thus) To Stand Even As Your Own body-mind. If You Truly Do This (With Love, Faith, Devotion, and No Withholding), The Entire Process Associated With Spiritual, Transcendental, and Divine Realization and Liberation Will Be Given To You Spontaneously, Progressively, and Exactly. (*The Dawn Horse Testament, *p. 317)*

This practice of full surrender to the Guru, to the Ishta of one's heart, is complete, sufficient, and profound. Sri Da Avabhasa thus calls Ishta-Guru-Bhakti Yoga "the Ultimate and Divine Yoga". In Oral Instructions Given on July 1, 1991, Sri Da Avabhasa further clarified this "radical" and truly Liberating Yoga:

SRI DA AVABHASA: Ishta-Guru-Bhakti Yoga is the Yoga to which I have been Calling everyone. It is the Ultimate and Divine Yoga. Its practice is self-surrendering, self-forgetting, and self-transcending feeling-Contemplation of My bodily (human) Form and, as Grace will have it, My Spiritual (and Always Blessing) Presence and My Very (and Inherently Perfect) State. That is it. . . .

Ishta-Guru-Bhakti Yoga, or the Yoga of self-surrendering, self-forgetting, and self-transcending devotional Contemplation of Me, is not about the achievement of any of the states of experience associated with the developmental stages of the Way of the Heart. Ishta-Guru-Bhakti Yoga is the Yoga of direct Grace. It is always about forgetfulness of the ego-self, and it is always about Remembrance (and, as Grace will have it, the Realization) of My bodily (human) Form and (as Grace will have it) My Spiritual (and Always Blessing) Presence and My Very (and Inherently Perfect) State.

This Yoga is not to be identified with the technical developments that may be experienced in the first six stages of life. Nor is it directly associated with the structures of the body-mind or the effects that may occur in the gross, subtle, and causal dimensions of the body-mind. Right devotional Contemplation of My bodily (human) Form becomes forgetfulness of the egoic body-mind. It becomes an in-depth Contemplation of My "Bright" Condition and a progressively growing ability to receive the Transmission of My Spiritual (and Always Blessing) Presence and My Very (and Inherently Perfect) State. . . .

My devotee surrenders and forgets and transcends the ego-"I" through

*devotional Contemplation of Me. I Grant My devotee the Realization of My
bodily (human) Form and My Spiritual (and Always Blessing) Presence, so
that My devotee may, by These Means, Realize My Very (and Inherently
Perfect) State, Which is Self-Existing and Self-Radiant, the Divine Self-
Condition Itself. Therefore, in the Way of the Heart, Ishta-Guru-Bhakti Yoga
is the direct Means for the Realization of the seventh stage of life . . . even,
Ultimately, to the degree of Divine Translation.*[1]

In the practice of Ishta-Guru-Bhakti Yoga, My devotee always *surrenders
beyond the conditions of the body-mind, and he or she is always given over
to the Ultimate Realization, rather than to any lesser Realization. My true
devotee is always given over to Me to* Realize *My Gift of the seventh stage of
life, and not any of the experiences of the first six stages of life.*

*Guru-devotion, or Ishta-Guru-Bhakti Yoga, is the Yoga I always
Practiced in the years of My Sadhana. It was My fundamental Sadhana.
That is what I Practiced in relationship to each of My Teachers and in rela-
tionship to the Goddess.*[2] *That is how I always Interpreted and Enacted My
Sadhana. Ishta-Guru-Bhakti Yoga, and not any of the technical practices or
experiences, was the primary Means of My Sadhana. Only the Ultimate
Realization That Is the Essence of Ishta-Guru-Bhakti Yoga itself was the
Motive and the Essence of My Practice, even from the beginning. (July 1,
1991)*

ENCHANTMENT

The great gift of Realization is granted by Grace through the
Appearance of the God-Man. The process of that Realization is not
self-effort, or the grinding affair of absolute self-improvement. Rather,
it is founded on the ecstasy of self-forgetting Distraction by the Divine,
whereby one responds to what is Attractive, what Shines with the Radiance
of Divinity, and one is drawn beyond body and mind into natural contemplation of the Supremely Attractive One.

---

1. Divine Translation is the final Demonstration of the four-phase Divinization in the seventh, or fully
Enlightened, stage of life. In this Event, body, mind, and world are no longer noticed, not because the
Divine Consciousness has withdrawn or dissociated from manifest phenomena, but because the Ecstatic
Recognition of all arising phenomena (by the Divine Self, and As only modification of Itself) has become so
intense that the "Bright" Radiance of Consciousness now Outshines all such phenomena.

2. The Divine Goddess is the Great Feminine Power or Spiritual Divine Force Who Guides the practice of
certain unique individuals and even aids their Work in the world. In the final stages of His own Ordeal of
Divine Self-Realization, previous to His Divine Re-Awakening in the Vedanta Temple in 1970, Da Avabhasa
related to the Divine in Its active aspect—the Living Divine Presence and Personality—through the female
archetype of the Goddess, or Mother Shakti. He enjoyed a paradoxical relationship to the Goddess as a concrete, living Personality. Such worship of the Goddess as Supreme Guru is the foundation and Spiritual
Source of His Teachers' lineage, but at last Da Avabhasa's inherent Freedom Drew Him even beyond the
Spiritual Blessings of the Goddess Herself, such that She ceased to function as His Guru and became,
instead, His eternal Consort and Companion.

In the opening chapter of this book, the Talk "Divine Distraction" was presented, in which Da Avabhasa used the example of Krishna and the Gopis to describe this rapturous turning of the devotee to God through the Attractive Power of the Realized God-Man. In the spring of 1983, almost eight years after that Talk was Given, Da Avabhasa again Spoke in extraordinarily similar terms of this great Attractive process. He was at the time in the Fijian islands at a temporary Residence while His devotees were searching for a site for His permanent Hermitage Ashram. He was accompanied by only a few renunciate devotees, all of whom, lifted suddenly into a country totally unknown to them, were held together by one thing only—their overwhelming love for this "Bright" God-Man before them. All were so excited to be on this grand adventure with their Beloved, and their love for Him drew forth His Great Love in a Divine, Intoxicating Effulgence. The Presence of the God-Man was a Magic in the air that healed the body-mind of all its complications. Sitting before this naked love shining in the faces of His devotees, on the evening of April 26, 1983, Da Avabhasa Gave the following Talk, later entitled "Enchantment":

SRI DA AVABHASA: In the ancient legend of Krishna, the women who tended the cattle, who were called "gopis", would leave their villages and go out into the fields to tend their cattle during the day. And that is where they would see Krishna. He would embrace them and Teach them, and they would become completely intoxicated and dance around in the moonlight and do all kinds of crazy things. Every day, they would go back home after the hours when they were supposed to be tending the cattle, but when they had really been involved in this great incident with the Siddha-Master out there in the woods.

These women would continue their ordinary relations, but they were always longing to go back out to the fields. Every day they would want to go back there. "I have to go out and tend the cattle now, my dearest." They would make their husbands breakfast and make their dinners at night and sit next to them fanning them and sleep overnight and have sex with them. Then they would get up the next day and go out as usual, tend to the cattle, and have their meeting with Krishna again.

They became intensely attracted to Krishna, and not only sexually. Attraction itself became the principle of their existence. They became infinitely attracted. And when they realized they were infinitely attracted, they were made infinitely blissful and Perfectly Realized.

During all that time, they continued to come back to their husbands. Sometimes they would not come back for a few days, and their husbands would begin to suspect something was going on. But generally they lived as housewives. They performed all the traditional duties. But when they were given the space associated with their particular daily function of tending the cattle, they were always associating with Krishna.

Sometimes Krishna would leave the neighborhood completely. The gopis would go out and tend the cattle, and Krishna would not come. Then they

would go home and be mournful. They would make a bad dinner. They would not be responsive to their husbands' advances. This might go on for days, months, even years, and they would be continually morose. Then suddenly one day Krishna would show up again.

On the one hand, all the stories about Krishna are about the special relationship a male Adept might have with His women devotees. But on the other hand, it is also a kind of archetype, a crystallization, of the relationship between the Adept—or an individual, humanly manifest, who has also Realized Most Perfect Identification with the Divine—and everyone. In the Krishna tradition in particular, everyone, male or female, engages in the sadhana of attractedness. Krishna is a Sign of the Divine, a traditional Means for Spiritual sadhana, of which the essence is attractedness.

The essence of the Divine symbolized as Krishna is That Which is utterly Attractive, Attractive to the point that attractedness becomes the absolute logic and condition and context of one's existence. The process, or the sadhana, of being attracted by That Which is Absolute is the essence of the Krishna tradition, and it is also the essence of true Spiritual life altogether, whatever the tradition of practice.

One of the women here just described a kind of gopi's realization of falling into the mood of attractedness in relationship to Me. She characterized for everyone the mood and disposition that is the same for everyone who practices in relationship to the Divine, particularly in the form of the Adept.

Everyone here is becoming enchanted by My Company. Whose Company are you in? You are in My Company. I am Personally in your company as That Which is Attractive. This woman said that I am relationship itself. I am all these beings, all these body-minds. She was not just speaking a metaphor. What she described is literally the case, absolutely, literally, the case. That Force of Being Which is Manifested as everything is That Which is absolutely Attractive.

All who enter into the course of Spiritual sadhana in the Company of a fully Awakened Adept become involved with this Attractiveness. They become transformed by just That. In the Way of the Heart, the essence of your practice is your attractedness to Me.

That intoxicating Attractiveness, that completely overwhelming Whirl of Force, of Bliss, of Happiness, Which eventually Reveals Its own State, is the essence of the Way of the Heart. All of My "Considerations" describe the process in certain details, but the essence of the Way of the Heart, for those who fulfill it and who take complete advantage of the Advantage that I Am for their Realization of the Divine, is attraction to Me, an overwhelming attraction to Me, an Attraction that begins to ruin your life eventually. It becomes an Influence that shatters all the conventional arrangements and all the things by which you try to feel good and stay balanced.

It is Personified, Incarnated, and Is, in fact, <u>Me</u>, your Sat-Guru, but That Which is the Sat-Guru is That Which is Reality, That Which is Real, That Which Is the case, That Which Is altogether, That to Which you should devote yourself. However, in your reluctance, not being attracted, being in doubt, being ordinary humans, you do not live as attracted beings or submit to That Which is Attractive.

As My true devotees, you do live as attracted beings, submitted to That Which is Attractive. That is why, regardless of your developmental stage in the Way of the Heart, you are called My devotee. Well—what does that mean? A devotee is someone who has begun to become attracted and whose attitude is totally willing, free, spontaneous submission to That Which is Attractive. As My devotee, you have become enchanted by attractedness, become totally polarized to That. This Attractiveness is what lifts you out of the domain of karma.

In your ordinariness, you are distracted, through the medium of attention and as attention, by all kinds of objects, but you are not enchanted by them. You are attracted by them, and they give you a certain pleasure. Likewise, some things that attract your attention are also not at all pleasurable. You want to avoid them, but they still have your attention. Therefore, you are altogether attracted already, but what you are attracted to is not That Which is the Source of everything attractive. When you find That Which is the Source of everything attractive and become attracted to It, then you become enchanted by attractedness, and you understand, you practice, you embrace all the disciplines of the Way of the Heart.

Thereafter, the fundamental force of your practice of the Way of the Heart is just that attractedness, which is not characterizable by any kind of limitation. You cannot say, "Oh—the Master is very beautiful. I really like those eyebrows there, the way the Master moves, the clothing He wears." My Attractiveness is not nameable. Even though you can say, "Well, yes, the Master is this or that," what is the Sat-Guru, anyway?

When you cannot identify what is Attractive about Me in any concrete terms that relate to the senses and the categories of mind, then you are enchanted. You have moved into the realm of attractedness, and it begins to transform your existence in the direction of Divine Self-Realization, although it might very well begin to cause you a great deal of trouble, might very well destroy some of the conventional balances of your ordinary living. Yet you simply release all that and become more ordinary and continue with this attractedness until attractedness becomes your absolute, spontaneous, uncaused, even unchosen disposition. You have no choice but that attractedness.

The more you are attracted to That Which is Attractive, the more you Commune with Its Qualities and the more you Identify with them. You have nothing to say about That Which is Attractive except that That is Bliss, That is Love, That is Beauty, That is Consciousness, That is Truth. Then at some point you find yourself confessing the Realization of the seventh stage of life.

In the Krishna tradition, males and females confess that they are in a state of enchantment, absolutely attracted to That Which is Attractive. Whatever else they may be doing as a form of discipline or practice or sadhana, it is all a way of participating in this enchantment, this attractedness. They eventually find that they have no choice, no interest, in fact, no alternative, but to submit to That Which is Attractive. They are just drawn into it. It is a kind of intoxication. When they submit to it, then their practice begins to become fruitful.

When you allow yourself to be attracted by That Which is Attractive, Absolutely and Ultimately, then the mind relaxes, the body relaxes, attention relaxes, the motives of life relax, the arrangements of life become ordinary and secondary, and you notice that your enchantment is changing something about your living. Therefore, you simply make those changes instead of feeling interfered with. The fundamental force of the sadhana of submission to the Adept, of being involved in the "Method" of the Siddhas, is the discovery of That Which is Attractive, the "Location" of Happiness, submission to That, and letting That fundamentally be the context of your life.

Now, to do that in the Way of the Heart means also that you practice the various disciplines I Give you. Yes, you do that, but all your practice is animated in the context of attractedness, of enchantment, of uncaused blissfulness, that permits all the signs of the transitions from developmental stage to developmental stage in the Way of the Heart to appear quite naturally and quickly and directly.

In the story of Krishna, there were a few ladies at the beginning. Eventually, there were thousands upon thousands upon thousands of them. But he also had thousands and thousands and thousands of male devotees. Because the women did not go home after a while, the husbands and boyfriends and fathers of all those women began to follow them out. They all became involved in enchantment.

Every one of you, male or female, abandoning all kinds of social conventions, the mind, the body itself—what are you doing here other than being enchanted, spontaneously, unwittingly submitting to That Which is Attractive? Whatever you are saying about it, whatever you are doubting about it, you are moved by enchantment.

You have allowed yourself to be dominated by What is enchanting, What is Attractive. And that is why you are here. That is why all My devotees are here. That is why all My devotees are associated with Me.

When you submit yourself to My Attractiveness, then every aspect of the developmental stages of the Way of the Heart, all the transitions that I "Consider" with you, occur quite spontaneously. It is not that you just practice the Yoga of being attracted. You do all the things associated with the discipline of the Way of the Heart. But the essence of your practice, the driving force of it, the essential content of it, is this attractedness. And the fundamental quality of your life, to the degree that you are really involved in practice, is enchantment, attraction to That Which makes you a little balmy and to Which you cannot help but submit.

Therefore, whatever this pile of flesh here [referring to His own Body] is, it is Divinely Transfigured[3] by the Being that Lives As it, it is changed in various ways, and it appears in various ways that are even perhaps, in human terms, attractive. But What you are Drawn into, What is Attracting you, What is Enchanting you, is the Living Presence of the Divine, That in Which you Stand, That Which is Omnipresent and All-Pervading.

This is the unique significance of the Appearance of the Adept, that That Which is Absolutely Attractive is Incarnate, Stands before beings, and Draws them into relationship, simply Stands, and relations develop, beings become attracted. He simply Stands as the center of that hive, simply Stands, simply is Attractive.

Those who practice the Way Communicated in that Company develop more and more the capability to submit to the state of enchantment, or attractedness, to the point that they are absolutely enchanted by the State of That Which is Attracting them.

Then, suddenly, as if out of the sky-blue day, without the slightest justification, they find themselves babbling the confession of the seventh stage of life. Who knows when it will occur! Nobody can account for it. Suddenly, as enchanted beings, they are communicating to others the Wisdom of Absolute Realization. They Stand in the Divine Domain. They can say it is so and show it is so without the slightest egoic self-consciousness, without the slightest doubt, and without its being anything but absolutely true.

Ordinary beings! How can ordinary beings come to the point of confessing this Absolute? How can any of you make the confession that belongs to the more mature stages of life? Because you are enchanted. Because you have fallen into the "Location" of Happiness. And that is the Force that has you all sitting with Me, and has thousands of others around the world either thinking

3. Divine Transfiguration is the first phase of the four-phase Process of Divine Enlightenment in the seventh stage of life. Sri Da Avabhasa explains that when Divine Self-Realization in the seventh stage of life is firmly established, the body-mind of the Realizer is progressively relaxed into, or pervaded by, the inherent Radiance of the Spiritual and Transcendental Divine Self. This Process of Divine Transfiguration expresses itself as the Realizer's active Spiritual Blessing in all relationships.

Sri Da Avabhasa has Demonstrated and Revealed the inherently Enlightened Wisdom and the spontaneous Spiritual Processes associated with all three of the earlier phases of this Divine Yoga (Divine Transfiguration, Divine Transformation, and Divine Indifference) previous to the ultimate stage, Divine Translation, which coincides with physical death. Please see *The Dawn Horse Testament* for Sri Da Avabhasa's Description of the phases of the Divine Yoga of the seventh stage of life.

about it or devoting themselves to some sort of practice of the Way of the Heart.

They do not know why they are doing it. Why are they doing it? Because of the Attractive Presence that is tangibly Present and yet rather elusive and paradoxical, and that is moving them out of the karmic state of limitation. [to a male devotee] What are you doing over there?

DEVOTEE: I am loving you, Sri Gurudev.

SRI DA AVABHASA: Excellent! This is the substance of this woman's confession, the substance of your life, and the substance of My relationship with you. How can I be anything but your lover, just Radiant here with you? How can I do anything but settle in That Which is Absolutely Attractive to you? Everything you are doing other than the fundamental force of your practice in devotional relationship to Me is a sign of your dissonance, your withholding, your egoic "self-possession".

When you "Locate" the essence of the Way of the Heart, you discover that it is enchantment. That enchantment is expressed through all the disciplines. Enchantment does not override self-discipline. It is not that for some there is some sort of enchanted Way of practice and everybody else is involved in technicalities of meditation! The Way of Enchantment takes the form of the disciplines at every developmental stage of the Way of the Heart. But the Force that is essential to the practice at every stage is enchantment.

"YOU ARE ALL GOING TO BECOME MASTS WITH ME": THE SAT-GURU'S ECSTASY DOES THE YOGA

The process of Ishta-Guru-Bhakti Yoga has been at the heart of Sat-Guru Da Love-Ananda's Communication about the Guru-devotee relationship from the beginning of His Teaching Work. In 1974, in the midst of a dramatic period in which He generated the most extreme ecstasy in hundreds of His devotees day after day, Sri Da Avabhasa described this Process. (Here He uses the term "Divine Light" to refer to His Hridaya-Shakti):

SRI DA AVABHASA: The Guru is not a human being. The Guru is the Divine Lord in human Form. When his devotee becomes a true devotee, when he or she ceases to be a student and surrenders, then the Guru enters his devotee in the form of Divine Light. All kinds of extraordinary experiences manifest as a result.

The Function of the Guru is first of all to make the student a devotee through the process of understanding, until he or she comes to the point of surrender. Then the Guru enters where he or she surrenders, and that one becomes a devotee. That is the entire Yoga of the Way of the Heart. There is

This display of Ecstasy has never happened in the world before. For never has there been such a Teaching Work, such a Blessing Opportunity. Sri Gurudev Da Love-Ananda's Transmission is Given so potently, so fully, so completely, and, remarkably, to ordinary individuals without any qualifications but their devotion.

nothing to do from that point except to surrender to the Guru, surrender to the Lord night and day, think the Lord, speak the Lord, act the Lord, receive the Lord in your body and in your cells, in every function of life, descending and ascending, not as a technique, but as a woman receives her lover.

When a woman receives her lover, there is no doubt about it. She does not have to consult her textbooks! . . . When I enter My devotee, I come down into him or her in the midst of life, because it is in life, not merely in the subtle processes or your mentality, but it is in your life, that the Lord _acquires you_.

The kind of thing you see happening around here has never happened in the world before. You are all going to become masts with Me. You have been the devotee of the world for centuries. (January 3, 1974)

The masts (pronounced "musts") that Sri Gurudev Da Love-Ananda Speaks of are a class of eccentric Divinely Intoxicated people in India. They are known as the "God-Crazy". Because they are Spiritually awake and responsive to higher principles of existence via the Spiritual Process, they are not concerned with the usual conventions of behavior. They may appear to be even psychotic in ordinary terms, but they are quite sane from the perspective of the Spiritual dimension.

When Sri Gurudev happily proclaims that all are to become masts with Him, He is pointing to the Bliss of self-forgetting and world-Outshining God-Love that the relationship to the Sat-Guru becomes. Such masts do not actually become psychotic in ordinary life—in fact, those who engage the true Spiritual Process become more sane, functional, and capable at the level of ordinary life, because they are free of egoic confusion and complication. It is just that their speech and actions are accomplished from a completely different point of view than the usual.

Every day, as the devotees of Heart-Master Da Love-Ananda surrender themselves to Him, they become such "masts", especially when they are Graced to be in the Company of His bodily (human) Form. Sometimes, outwardly, there are kriyas and movements of all kinds, a madhouse of emotion, sounds, purification, and delight. All of the eight classic signs of devotion and ecstasy described in the devotional tradition of the fifteenth-to sixteenth-century Indian ecstatic Chaitanya are naturally there, including tears of love, tremors, quivering, perspiration, dullness, paleness, choked voice, and trance. All of the euphoric joy of the Hasidic dance, of the Whirling Dervishes, the mad Bauls of Bengal, the Shiva Tandava, and the Rasa Leela of Krishna is in evidence. At other times there is a Radiant Stillness and Bliss that is so quiet and Full that the air is heavy with tangible Bliss, and there is a Silence that Washes the entire being. Each circumstance is completely different, for Sri Da Avabhasa's Transmission is Hridaya-Shakti, the Living Power of God, the seventh stage Radiance and Realization, and not any mere Yogic power, intended to accomplish a specific bodily effect.

This display of Ecstasy has never happened in the world before. For never has there been such a Teaching Work, such a Blessing Opportunity. Sri Gurudev Da Love-Ananda's Transmission is Given so potently, so fully, so completely, and, remarkably, to ordinary individuals without any qualifications but their devotion. And while that Divine Transmission has, at times, been Generated by Heart-Master Da Love-Ananda in various specific ways to Grant particular lessons, the Ecstasy and Bliss of His Divine Transmission have always been Given universally and without ceasing.

WORSHIP OF THE INCARNATE DIVINE PERSON

*O*nce upon a time, on the Mountain of Attention, frequented by devotees, and in the most beautiful Place, adorned by Cosmic Nature in the manner of flowers,

Seated in an open Place on one occasion, the Heart-Master (True and Free) was Expounding the Supreme Truth to devotees. The face of one who was close to Him became suddenly "Bright", full of devotion, because he Realized he was seeing the Great One, even with his own eyes.

This Awakened devotee said: "Radiant Da, Giver of Life, I surrender. You are the True Heart-Master for the whole world. You are Supreme. You Radiate the 'Bright' Realization of the Supreme. All beings should always worship and see You with devotion.

You are the One, the Supreme Being, the Source and Domain of all worship and praise.

Radiant Heart, Domain of Truth, please Sing to us the Secret of devotion to the True Heart-Master.

Reveal to us the Secret Method whereby living beings may Realize the

Transcendental and world-Outshining God. I bow down to You. I worship Your Feet. Kindly Explain This to all of us."

When the Master of the Heart Saw this "Bright" face of Awakened devotion and Heard this Confession of Great Sight, He Spoke the following Words, His Heart Overflowing with Abundant Joy:

"This is the Secret of all secrets. I could not Speak This All-Revealing Word until one of you first Confessed you see the Vision of God in My Bodily (Human) Form. I shall Tell you This now, because of your great devotion to Me.

Dear ones, you are each arising in the same Divine Being. This request of yours will benefit the whole world. Therefore, I shall Reveal the Secret of this Vision to you.

To each one who is supremely devoted to the Living God and equally devoted to the True Master of the Heart, the Very Heart (That Is the Truth) Reveals Itself as the Bodily (Human) Form, the Spiritual (and Always Blessing) Presence, and the Very (and Inherently Perfect) State of the True Heart-Master.

The True Heart-Master is thus Realized to be the Incarnation of the Great One. So Declare the Scriptures, and so do I Affirm to you. . . .

The True Master of the Heart has Realized God. Therefore, devotees see God Revealed in the Bodily (Human) Form of the True Heart-Master. . . .

To worship the True Heart-Master childishly is to worship and serve your separate self. To deny or resist the True Heart-Master is to worship and serve your separate self, adolescently. The separate self is, itself and always, the forgetting of the Heart-Source of the world. Therefore, be very devoted to Me, the True Master of your Heart, but not for the sake of ego-salvation, or the glorification of your separate self. Worship Me by surrendering your separate self to Me. Surrender to Me in order to forget and transcend your separate self in Me. Forget and transcend your separate self in Me in order that you may, by Grace, Remember and Realize the Divine Heart-Source and Self of all and All.

I Am the Sign and the Revelation and the Proof of God in the world. I Am the Testament and the Means of Freedom Itself." (The Hymn Of The True Heart-Master, *verses 6-16, 26, 31-32)*

This passage from Sri Da Avabhasa's *Hymn Of The True Heart-Master* is one of the most beautiful descriptions of the traditional and auspicious relationship between the devotee and the Sat-Guru. In the physical Presence of the Sat-Guru, the greatest religious paintings in the Eastern and Western traditions begin to make sense, for they are attempts to approximate the feeling and Reality of the Loka, or Divine Space, that is always created in the Radiant Company of the Divine Person. Adjectives fail one in description; words like "majestic", "lustrous", "glistening", "brilliant", "awe-inspiring", "magnificent", only approximate the unsurpassed expression of the God-Man. In his Company, the being is lifted out of itself and drawn into the Divine Condition that is beyond all description.

In *The Hymn Of The True Heart-Master,* the Sat-Guru is discoursing, in repose and equanimity, when a devotee suddenly acknowledges Who the Sat-Guru Is. The Sat-Guru has apparently been sitting there for some time. Yet, in a moment, this devotee's face is transformed, spontaneously filled as it has never been, "Brightened" by that Sight of sights, the Divine Vision Itself. The devotee has truly seen the Sat-Guru. He (or she) has submitted himself (or herself) to the point of allowing Who the Sat-Guru Is to become Evident. It is not conventional belief that is at the root of the devotee's ecstatic confession. Instead, he surrenders and receives the Darshan of the Sat-Guru. The mere Contemplation of the bodily (human) Form of the Divine Adept before him has moved him at his heart, and he is "Awakened", Liberated by the sight of the Divine Reality.

The devotee is willing to lose all "face", or conventional self-presentation and composure, and to express himself or herself passionately. This is no prepared speech. Its inspiration is the Vision of the Divine Lord in human Form.

The Great Revelation, the Great Wisdom, that is presented in *The Hymn Of The True Heart-Master* is that the Divine Truth is Revealed to the devotee even in the bodily (human) Form of the True Heart-Master. And worship is the native or natural and spontaneous response of the devotee who is Blessed to receive the Divine Revelation of the Heart-Master's bodily (human) Form.

In the "Westernized" culture of today's world there is a great taboo against worship of another. This attitude exists because such worship is only understood to be a kind of cult of egos, in which a karmic entity is worshipped. True worship is not turning to the Sat-Guru as a conventional hero or cultic figure. Rather, it is understanding him (or her) to be Incarnate as, or not different from, the Living Divine. It is this Divinity, this Life-Granting Grace, that is worshipped, not an apparent human personality with particular physical characteristics. On the other hand, the devotee does value all aspects of the Sat-Guru's appearance in this world (including his body and personality) as not different from his Realization.

The Living Miracle of Heart-Master Da Love-Ananda's Divine Emergence is that His bodily (human) Form, down to the soles of His Feet, has been Acquired by His Very (and Inherently Perfect) Divine State. Thus, for His devotee the mere Contemplation of His bodily (human) Form is Liberating. It has been Revealed to me, and to hundreds of His devotees whom I am happy to call my gurubhais (fellow devotees), that mere feeling-Contemplation of the bodily (human) Form of Sri Da Avabhasa in any moment has the power to Release the being of its self-imposed bondage and concerns.

The devotee's worship of Da Avabhasa requires genuine self-transcendence in order to be true. In feeling-Contemplation and worship of Da Avabhasa, His devotee forgets the separate and separative self in the Divine Self-Condition that He Is. The devotee is not in any negative sense bound to

Sat-Guru Da. Rather, he or she is being Drawn to the Divine Condition of Freedom and Ecstasy in Which Sri Da Avabhasa Inheres.

In truth, the Sat-Guru, who has gone beyond identification with the (apparently) separate and separative self and all limitation, is the only "Person" whom it is completely appropriate to worship, for he (or she) is not a "person" at all, in the conventional sense of the word. He is the Divine Person Incarnate. And those who worship at his Feet do not worship an individual as an individual, but worship him as the Divine Alive in human form.

This traditional understanding was articulated by Swami Vivekananda in a talk called "Discipleship", given in San Francisco on March 29, 1900:

> . . . *the guru must be worshipped as God. He is God; he is nothing less than that. As you look at him, the guru gradually melts away—and what is left? The picture of the guru gives place to God Himself. The guru is the bright mask which God wears in order to come to us. As we look steadily on him, gradually the mask falls off and God is revealed.*[4]

In 1978, Da Avabhasa Wrote the Essay entitled "I Have Come to Accept the Worship of My Devotees":

> *The essence of practice in the Way of the Heart is continuous Love-Communion with the Divine Person, the Radiant Transcendental Consciousness in which all beings and worlds are arising, and of which all beings and worlds are the Play, or spontaneous modification. Such Love-Communion must be realized through ecstatic or self-transcending surrender of the total body-mind, via each kind of moment of functional activity. Thus, the Radiant Transcendental Consciousness, or the All-Pervading, Living, and Radiant Love-Presence of the Divine Person, must be Worshipped and Realized moment to moment.*
>
> *The Way of the Heart is the Way of the Devotion of the entire body-mind to the Living God. And the unique Help or Means of this Devotion is the Person and Teaching of the Spiritual Master—Who is not other than the Divine Person, and Who is the Radiant Transcendental Consciousness, shown to Man through Man.*
>
> *Therefore, the foundation and epitome of all practice in this Way is Devotion, Worship, Remembrance, and Surrender of body and attention to the Spiritual Master. This is to be done always. And it is also to be done by all the means devotees choose or create on those special occasions when the Spiritual Master makes Himself bodily available to the community of devotees for Devotional Celebration.*

---

4. *Vivekananda: The Yogas and Other Works,* chosen and with a Biography by Swami Nikhilananda. Rev. ed. (New York: Ramakrishna-Vivekananda Center, 1953), p. 262.

Know this: I appear among My devotees to receive and accept their Sacrifices, their Worship and Remembrance, their Surrender, their Requests, their Love, their explicit Devotion of body and mind. When I visit the community of My devotees, they should spend that time in every kind of devotional association with Me, in order that I may Respond to them from My Heart, Granting them the Blessings of all My Blissful Excesses.

Through this Lawful Worship, I am able to do My Work. If I am not Worshipped by My devotees, My Heart is not touched by them, and My Blessings are not Communicated to them. Therefore, when I come to visit with all of you, create that time as every kind of Worship of Me. Bring your bodies and minds to Me, as I bring this body-mind to you. Then you will be given the Realization of My All-Pervading Person, and you will find Me always present under the conditions of all experience and in the company of all beings. Then, even when I am not bodily with you, you will Worship Me and Surrender to Me via every state of body and mind, and I will always be with you. At last, you will be drawn into the Eternal Identity, so intimate with Me that no essential difference is noticed by you. Then you will abide in Me forever, whether or not the worlds of experience arise to your notice.

I was recently Blessed to witness a Puja performed on Sri Da Avabhasa's bodily (human) Form while His Feet rested in His Padukas (ceremonial sandals). It was an event I will never forget; the vision of Him in that occasion is burned into my heart forever. If one can surrender at such an occasion, there is an initiation that is so profound that it can transform one's entire destiny.

The event that brought about this special Grace was the resumption of formal retreats at Sri Love-Anandashram. On February 16, 1990, the evening of the arrival of the first retreatants, Da Avabhasa, in an extraordinary act of Compassion and Grace, Chose to be physically Present for the Empowerment of the new Meditation Hall for retreatants. On that same day, Da Avabhasa had named the Hall "Mindless Company", and it has proved to be a place true to its name, for those who meditate in it transcend their minds in the Love-Bliss of Da Avabhasa's Spiritual Company. The Empowerment took the form of a full-body Puja which He Graciously allowed the members of the Da Avabhasa Gurukula Kanyadana Kumari Order to offer Him. I was Blessed to attend this occasion. I say I was Blessed, because there is nothing that I had done, that anyone present had done, that warranted our being able to witness His Divine Grace. It was overwhelming.

The Meditation Hall, which holds sixty people, is beautiful but simple. A chair for Sri Da Avabhasa sits in front, with an exquisite backdrop of indigo and white. Newly arrived retreatants and residents of the Ashram village filled the Hall. The retreatants had just disembarked from the boat that had brought them from a nearby island. There had been hardly time for them to shower before coming to the Hall.

To begin the occasion, the Kanyadana Kumaris performed a Sat-Guru Murti Puja[5] on the life-sized photographic Murti that was to be Installed in the Hall. They then circumambulated the Hall outside and inside, and prepared it for Sri Gurudev.

Around seven o'clock, when night had fallen, the conch blew, and in walked Sri Da Avabhasa. The energy in the room rose towards Him instantly. He placed the Staff He was carrying in its stand and Sat down. It is traditionally understood that physical places themselves respond to the Sat-Guru's Influence, and this could be tangibly felt. Here was a room prepared especially for meditation that had never been used before, and it received Sri Gurudev's Energy and filled up with His Grace.

At first, Sri Gurudev simply Sat, and then He slowly placed His Feet in His Padukas—first His right Foot, and then His left. An ancient and timeless ritual was being enacted. In that gesture of placing His Feet, it was already clear that this evening would be an extraordinary Blessing. His mood was extraordinary. The word that I would use to describe it is "submitted". It was so obviously a Sacrifice on His part to allow this worship to be done on Him. There was no person there but the Divine Person, allowing Himself to be worshipped by His devotees for the sake of Granting them His Grace.

Da Avabhasa was wearing a simple indigo and white lungi (cloth garment worn by men in India) around His waist, with His chest and shoulders bare. And He was simply Sitting, Eyes open at times, and closed at others, but not looking at anyone or anything—simply Present and allowing Himself to be worshipped.

Each of the Kanyas performed a different part of the Puja. Kanya Samarpana Remembrance washed and anointed Sri Da Avabhasa's Feet. Kanya Tripura Rahasya washed and anointed His Forehead, marking It with sacred ash (in the traditional "tripundra" stripes) and a dot of kum-kum, or sacred red powder (placed on the ajna center, just above and between His eyes). She placed a large sacred rudraksha mala around His neck and a shawl around His shoulders, and placed the ceremonial hat upon His head. He was already wearing a precious garland of rare "one-faced" rudraksha beads and a small gold-capped rudraksha mala. Kanya Kaivalya Navaneeta served His right Hand and the area of His Heart, marking the three centers of the great heart region[6] with sacred sandalwood oil and ash. And Kanya

---

5. A "Murti" is a sacred form or object through which the Divine Transmission is presumed to flow. A Murti may be a photograph, a statue, or any other physical manifestation, but the Supreme Murti has always been understood to be the bodily (human) Form of the Sat-Guru himself or herself. "Sat-Guru Murti Puja" refers to the sacred ceremony of worship performed on the Sat-Guru. During the Sat-Guru Murti Puja, the Murti is anointed in sacred ceremony, expressing the devotional regard in which the devotee holds the Divine Murti.

In the Free Daist Communion, the Sat-Guru Murti Puja is performed on a daily basis, and through it the devotee establishes himself or herself in Communion with Sri Da Avabhasa. Typically, a photographic representation of Sri Da Avabhasa is used, so that devotees everywhere can perform this puja, even though Da Avabhasa is not physically present.

6. The "three centers of the great region" of the heart, the left side, the middle, and the right side, are the primary centers of attention and the master-controllers of all energies within the extended body-mind. These three heart-centers correspond respectively to the gross, subtle, and causal dimensions of existence, which

Samatva Suprithi served His left Hand and adorned Him with a garland of flowers.

What occurred was deeply archetypal, and it evoked for me feelings and memories deeper than the conscious mind. Suffice it to say that to see His Feet being washed was a Vision of Divinity. Why so? In the West, we understand that the Appearance of the Divine in human form is a supremely Sacrificial Act, and this Sacrifice was so evident in Sri Gurudev's entire Gesture. In the East, the Divine is understood to remain transcendent, beyond all, even when Incarnate in human form, and likewise Sri Gurudev was Himself so clearly in that State as well. The Puja was true worship of What is Supremely Venerable. And the Kanyadanas were very devoted, very full in their expression. Their movements were loving, economical, and direct.

Sri Gurudev Manifested Divinity in His bodily (human) Form. This was the esoteric Revelation. True worship of the humanly Incarnate God-Man is criticized by those who will not admit the possibility of Living Divinity bodily Manifest. But it is accepted by the devotee as the Greatest Gift.

This Puja was offered not only for the sake of those in the room. It was the Blessing of Sri Love-Anandashram as a place of retreat. And it was also of immeasurable benefit to the world, for the Divine Person had Incarnated and had somehow achieved a Victory in this Place where the Guru-devotee relationship in its fullness could be lived. A Hermitage had been established here on Earth where devotees could engage Spiritual retreat in the Company of the Great Adept Da Avabhasa. The Divine had not achieved a worldwide victory in any absolute sense. But a place of Refuge had been allowed, and a great opportunity for humankind was now possible. A great Blessing for the entire Earth was therefore evoked through this response to the Divine, the Divine World-Teacher, Sri Da Avabhasa, and through His acceptance of this lawful worship.

In Da Avabhasa no merely human aspect or quality was animated. He was Perfect Submission and Sacrifice. In allowing Himself to be worshipped, He Submitted and let Himself be given over to His devotees completely. He allowed His bodily (human) Form to be physically treated as the Murti. The devotees around Him had the Supreme benefit of worshipping the Great One Manifest and, in their surrender to Him, receiving the greatest Blessings. It was like one of those occasions described in the great Puranas or Sutras[7] where it is described that gods and goddesses crowd the room to Witness the Divine Blessing. And in my feeling I imagined that in

---

are exemplified respectively by the waking, dreaming, and sleeping states of consciousness. Each of these states must be transcended in the course of practice of the Way of the Heart. Ultimately, attention itself is transcended in the right side of the heart, which is the bodily seat, or Locus, of Consciousness Itself.

7. "Puranas" are traditional Hindu devotional Scriptures in which the life stories of Great Realizers are chronicled, along with the Leelas of the Hindu Gods such as Siva, Krishna, and the Goddess.

"Sutra" is a name for sacred texts used in many of the religions of the Indian sub-continent, especially Buddhism and Hinduism. Hindu Sutras are characteristically composed of short, terse verses strung together to make up the full scripture.

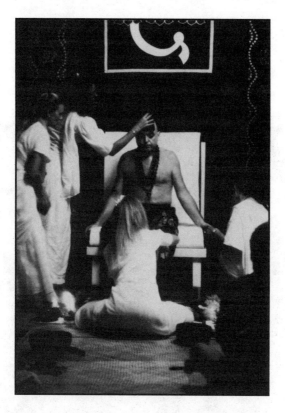

such an occasion as this, they, too, showered their flowers upon Sri Da Avabhasa's body-mind in Celebration of the Miracle of His Sacrifice and Blessing.

He opened His Eyes when the Puja had been completed and saw His own Feet adorned with flowers. The look on His Face when He saw the signs of the worship of His devotees was indescribable. His Eyes grew very wide, as if He were Himself Delighted by it all. To those who were witness to this Miracle of Divine Grace and Blessing, the Beauty of the Vision could be taken in, but never exhausted.

It is said that Darshan of the Sat-Guru is sufficient. Not a word need be said. And here was the great Vision. To surrender in this Company was to be Liberated from the egoic self into the great Company of the Divine. The worship was effective. The Sacrifice was made. And it was not the sacrifice of the priests before Sat-Guru Da that was of ultimate significance. It was Heart-Master Da Himself Who, in allowing Himself to be the Murti, was the Priest of the Sacrifice.

CHAPTER NINE

"What a Glory!"

THE SACRED ORDEAL OF PRACTICE IN THE COMPANY OF A SAT-GURU

Sri Love-Anandashram, September 1991

SADHANA HURTS: THE SPIRITUAL PROCESS
REQUIRES EVERYTHING OF A MAN OR A WOMAN

*G*enuine self-transcending practice in the Company of a Living Adept is the most Graceful Process that is available in all the worlds. It is also the most heroic, or most harrowing to the ego, requiring the greatest strength of character and understanding. Today there is much superficial practice in the name of Spirituality. Sri Da Avabhasa has Revealed the genuine process that is Spiritual life, "the real thing". He has termed the Way of the Heart "the hard school and the happy Way of life".

The Way of the Heart is not difficult because of any intention on the part of Heart-Master Da to make it so—the Spiritual Process itself is just difficult. And Da Avabhasa's integrity is such that nothing but real Spiritual practice—the devotee's real gift of self-transcendence—is acceptable to Him. To want to surrender is one thing. To actually do it is another. One of the great discoveries of every practitioner of real Spiritual life is that simply to intend to surrender does not mean that one is capable of it. One can only truly surrender through Grace, and one is fitted for the reception of Grace only through long and hard practice. The karmas of every body-mind require an ordeal in which all egoic tendencies must be brought to the surface, understood, and surrendered.

The evolutionary process of gradual Spiritual development via one's own creature power, learning lesson after lesson, is an incredibly slow process. Most lifetimes lived in the ordinary way realize very little. Of what great import is a deathbed realization that one has not loved and that in the next lifetime one should be more compassionate, over against a life fully engaged in the self-transcending process of God-Realization? Without the Guidance of a Sat-Guru, there is no map of life that the usual man can follow and be assured of Spiritual advancement. In the Company of the Divine Adept, all is magnified, so that the entire course of Spiritual sadhana, culminating in Divine Self-Realization, may be completed in one lifetime. But to do so requires a tremendous intensity and one-pointed commitment. The devotee must fully comprehend the challenge inherent in the process of the genuine relationship to the Sat-Guru. There is no escaping the tapas, or heat, that burns up the egoic tendencies. As Heart-Master Da has Said, "Sadhana hurts." To confront, take responsibility for, and outgrow the egoic tendencies of the body-mind is difficult. It is not a matter of thinking about it, or changing a little piece of oneself. The great process requires all that appears to be "you" to be transformed.

In the course of Heart-Master Da Avabhasa's early Sadhana, when He was given very practical and ordinary disciplines by His first human Teacher, Rudi (also known as Swami Rudrananda), He practiced them so absolutely and concretely that His skin was literally constantly hot from the tapas generated by the intensity of His practice. The difficulty in no way

Swami Rudrananda (Rudi)

weakened His resolve in His practice. In fact, He was called "Crazy Frank" (since His name at that time was Franklin) by some of Rudi's other students because of His absolute commitment to immediately and unqualifiedly fulfill everything Rudi asked Him to do.

During the "Indoor Yajna" period of Instruction[1] in 1987, Heart-Master Da Spoke very directly about the strength that the devotee needs for the process of Divine Self-Realization. On the evening when He Gave the following Talk, He had been Speaking about the devotee's response to criticism Offered for the sake of his or her growth. As Sri Da Avabhasa describes, when a devotee receives a discipline, he or she should reply: "Good! That is the best discipline. That is what I am going to do, flat. And it will cause me great difficulty, no doubt, but that is what I will do."

Here is an excerpt from the Talk entitled "Sadhana Hurts" Given by Sri Da Avabhasa on December 19, 1987, at Sri Love-Anandashram.

SRI DA AVABHASA: Sadhana hurts. It definitely hurts. It hurts the body, it hurts the feeling, it hurts the mind. It is just heat. It is just energy. And all the time you are feeling beyond it. What a glory! That is how you grow. Such sadhana is greater than death. It is the domain of love, you see. That is what exceeds limits. Love exceeds limits. Love is not indulgence in desire. It is a heat. It is a purifying force. It is a glow. Ultimately it becomes infinitely Radiant and Outshines everything.

And it is difficult, yes. That is why I call the Way of the Heart an ordeal. It is necessarily difficult. In fact, measure it: If it is not difficult today, you are not doing sadhana. Sadhana is difficult. It is a heat. It works against motions, energies, impulses, adaptations. It works against them. It confounds them. It frustrates them. If you do not feel so confounded every day, you are not practicing. You are not doing sadhana. . . . Having been born

---

1. The term "yajna" is Sanskrit for "sacrifice". The "Indoor Yajna" refers to the Instructive Work engaged by Sri Da Avabhasa from April 1987 to March 1988 at Sri Love-Anandashram, during which He comprehensively recapitulated His Teaching Work, and also made many major revisions to His Source-Literature (most especially *The Dawn Horse Testament*).

In the course of this exhaustive re-"consideration" of the fundamental Arguments of the Way of the Heart, relative to Satsang, Ishta-Guru-Bhakti Yoga, the activity of "Narcissus" or self-contraction, and the necessity for real self-understanding, Sri Da Avabhasa exposed many fundamental errors in the practice of the worldwide community of His devotees. By early 1988, Sri Da Avabhasa had re-Instructed His devotees on the necessity of closing the "loopholes" in their practice by right understanding of the traditional fundamentals of the Guru-devotee relationship and right responsibility for all the details of the bodily sadhana Given by the Hridaya-Samartha Sat-Guru Da Love-Ananda Hridayam.

in the ordinary way, having lived the ordinary life, having had to suffer the entire ordeal in every dimension, and in every stage of life, I know what I am talking about. The ordeal is terrible, difficult, painful! But that is what it takes. If you are not enduring the ordeal every day, you are not doing sadhana.

Even as the devotee grows, it is not that the suffering or heat of practice goes away. It is just that the mature devotee does not mind anymore that it hurts! The devotee learns to rest his or her attention not on himself or herself, but on the Sat-Guru. And the devotee becomes more and more grateful even for the difficulty, because he or she feels the Grace of the transformation of his or her egoic tendencies. As this purifying process continues, the ability to connect more truly with the Joy and Happiness that is the Sat-Guru's Spiritual Transmission grows.

Yet, this cannot change the fact that pain and difficulty are part of the experience of every devotee. The devotee may have come to the Sat-Guru originally because he or she felt the pain of life acutely and was moved to what is greater, to a life of Contemplation and Remembrance of the Divine. But to begin practice in the Company of the Sat-Guru does not suddenly take away the experience of suffering. The devotee is not immediately transformed because he or she is now doing practice in relationship to the Sat-Guru. All the egoic tendencies remain and must be understood and transcended. In fact, very often Heart-Master Da's devotees testify to feeling more acutely the suffering of born existence in the context of Spiritual practice because now they can no longer engage in all the ordinary things people do to distract themselves from suffering. They can no longer blithely avoid confronting the suffering that underlies ordinary life by indulging obsessively in money, career, food, sex, and casual entertainments, since all those distractions are now brought under discipline. In the Way of the Heart, Sri Da Avabhasa's devotees are inevitably turned back upon their suffering with a greater and greater intensity.

However, there is a difference. Whereas before the devotee was merely suffering his or her egoic tendencies and feverishly seeking distraction from suffering, now the devotee is actually transforming those same tendencies, dealing with them, growing. And now there is the tremendous Help of the Grace and Transmission of the Sat-Guru. Through feeling-Contemplation of the Sat-Guru, the devotee may enter into the Domain of That Which Transcends all egoic tendencies. Thus, through non-use, these tendencies become "flabby", fall away, and do not bind attention. To see this occurring awakens great gratitude in the devotee, and a profound faith in the Spiritual Way. As egoic tendencies fall away, happiness and human, Spiritual, and Transcendental growth take their place.

It should also be mentioned that the Spiritual Process is only one of many human endeavors that require the participant to experience the pain of transformation. Men and women throughout the world push themselves beyond their limits in accomplishing many ordinary undertakings. Athletes train long hours, dancers stretch themselves beyond their limits, actors and actresses subject themselves to hardship in performing their parts more skillfully—truly the list is endless. In any creative occupation which requires growth and re-adaptation, we must value the goal enough to go through the hardship that is involved to get there. And, as Sri Da Avabhasa has Said on numerous occasions, when one is aspiring to supreme and Divine Enlightenment, why should one expect the requirements to be any less severe? It requires a tremendous effort and willingness to encounter difficulty to go through the Spiritual Process to the end. Moreover, what must be confronted in the Process is the ego itself, and the ego cannot transcend itself. The profound discipline of self-transcendence requires the compassionate help of the Sat-Guru, who has transcended the ego-principle and lives as That Which is Prior to it.

CRISIS AND PURIFICATION IN THE GENUINE SPIRITUAL PROCESS

It is said that once Saint Teresa of Avila was riding through the back roads of Spain during a torrential rainstorm. Her horsedrawn cart hit a huge pothole and collapsed, throwing her head-first into the mud. Saint Teresa complained to Jesus at being treated in this manner in the midst of trying to serve him. The voice of Jesus then came to her from the heavens: "This is how I treat my friends, Teresa." Wiping the mud from her face, she replied, "No wonder you have so few!"[2] As her quip points out, the devotee does not always understand at first the Grace and necessity of the tests and trials of Spiritual life—for it is by encountering and transcending one's tendencies that the capability for surrender is deepened.

Da Avabhasa has often Spoken of the trials and revelations involved in genuine Spiritual sadhana. He remarked late in 1975:

SRI DA AVABHASA: It is absolutely true that this process of sadhana offends all your tendencies, which means it offends you absolutely, in every way, in every dimension in which you have existence or in which you may realize existence. You will feel that offense, you will feel your resistance, and you will feel all kinds of tendencies that are anything but the availability to this Satsang and its sadhana. And you will be tested by them because you must pass through them. That is what sadhana is about. There are times when it is extremely difficult, difficult beyond belief, and you must go through these times. They are the most valuable times, the most purifying times. (November 15, 1975)

2."A Gift of All That One Is': *The Laughing Man* Interviews Mother Tessa Bieleck". *The Laughing Man*, vol. 4, no. 2, p. 52.

It is necessary to endure such tests in the practice and in relationship to the Sat-Guru, because they are key to the process of growth in real practice. There are real tendencies in the devotee that must be transcended through the purifying ordeal of practice. This world is not a Fantasyland full of Sleeping Beauty castles, in which a kiss will change everything.

Lobsang P. Lhalungpa describes the Buddhist understanding of the inherent difficulty of existence in the conditional worlds, and of the Sat-Guru's benign Work in the manifest worlds, to allow everything to be purified in the context of His Blessing Help:

> *It is not possible to entirely avoid the painful results of previous acts. But the guru can hasten their fruition so that we experience them now instead of later. As human beings in contact with the Dharma and the guru, we are in a far better position to cope with adversity than we may be later on, in lower rebirths. Thus, painful experiences may be signs of the guru's compassion.*[3]

The Sat-Guru often intentionally serves the purification of his or her devotees in very direct and skillful ways in order to hasten their Spiritual transformation. Here is a traditional description of such an ordeal from the pen of a devotee of Sadguru Gnanananda, a South Indian Sage who died in 1974:

> *The training that the Swami gave to his secular disciples was interesting. Once the disciple was reasonably safely anchored in him, the Swami would tackle him as if he were squeezing an orange! Strains and stresses would deliberately come his way. His reactions would be watched. The closer a person came to the Swami the less likely it was that the Swami would show the same degree of hospitality; greater were the chances of the Swami behaving rudely—apparently humiliating and ill-treating him! To be in the presence of the Master is in itself a sadhana. The annealing treatment would start. When the test was on, the devotee would start turning his thoughts inwards and looking for the faults within, which had made the Swami 'angry'. He would then try to correct himself so as to come up to the Swami's expectations of him. Then the Swami would cool him down. The devotee would feel happy inwardly. Suddenly the Swami would turn different. Maybe this time the Swami would be indifferent to him. The heat was again on and the disciple would look more deeply inward. The process of purification and purgation would thus go on. The Swami by then would have made a deep impression on him and he would feel safely rooted in him. The roughing up would be taken with good grace! A certain resilience would be developed when the going was difficult. The psychic contact with the Swami when he forged and hammered the devotee made him more pliable and more receptive to true knowledge. The devotee, despite the Swami's seeming indifference, was always aware of his ever enveloping kindness.*

3. Jamgon Kongtrul, *The Torch of Certainty*, trans. Judith Hanson (Boulder, Colo.: Shambhala, 1977), p. 136.

The treatment was however fascinatingly different and varied. One of the devotees was a high-placed government official. The Swami used to treat him with great respect; gave due regard for his official position in life. Slowly as the devotee moved into the orbit and considered himself a disciple of the Swami, the latter took over. The high-placed official would find allotted to him some of the worst rooms in the ashram without even the elementary amenities of life. He had to bear it without complaint and in due course developed vairagya [renunciation]. The Swami would not offer any explanation for this treatment. Sometimes he would be indifferent, sometimes he would find fault and get angry with the disciple without any reason. The devotee being a good aspirant knew he was on probation and should come through creditably. There was an infinite mercy and compassion in this cruelty. The devotee could see behind the forbidding mask a deeply peaceful face lit up with an ethereal tenderness which poured out from his eyes. The Swami eventually made him one of his finest disciples.

The more the Swami liked a person the greater the hardship he went through and greater the help he received. When the Swami was angry without reason, people knew it was a privilege. He always gave attention to the weaker child, to the weaker aspirant, and showed special consideration to those who took particular effort to open up their hearts to receive the shower of his grace. . . . This was the Spiritual training that Swami imparted to everyone around him, for this training ultimately spells surrender to the Divine Will. . . .

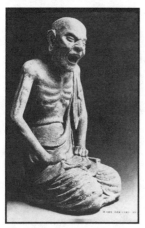

His treatment of sannyasins [renunciates] would be very vigorous. There would not be any regular hours for food for them. Although they were together, on some days milk would be sent up at night only to some of them, the others being deliberately neglected. They would be asked to take specially prepared food in a separate room and then there would come a day when they would be asked to fend for themselves in the dining room. Again under instructions from the Swami, food served would be particularly distasteful. He would watch their reaction. Omkaragiri Swami was the special target of Swami's "mercy". There were days when he had to go without food. The Swami would test whether he was bothered about it. He would abuse him in the presence of others, calling him "Vazhapazha Swami"—that he was fond of plantains. The Swami would silently admire the reactionlessness of this blessed monk. Thus he would train them in the control of [the] sense[s], in the annihilation of the ego and in developing reactionlessness.[4]

4. *Sadguru Gnanananda, His Life, Personality and Teachings,* by His Devotees (Bombay: Bharatiya Vidya Bhavan, 1979), pp. 150-53, 169-70.

Sri Da Avabhasa has explained that the intensity of the demand of the Sat-Guru is always just beyond what the devotee thinks is possible. The devotee is never allowed to be comfortable. All the plans by which one would be a successful ego are undermined. The normal pats on the back are not offered—Sri Da Avabhasa finds no reason to congratulate the very ego that He is working to expose and undermine. For only when His devotee clearly sees the self-imposed self-contraction can he or she transcend it.

There is no way to escape the confrontation of practice. The Sat-Guru attempts to bring on precisely this confrontation, to create this crisis and to free His devotee to surrender more deeply and receive His Blissful Transmission. Heart-Master Da described this crisis in *The Method of the Siddhas*:

SRI DA AVABHASA: You must know that everything I am doing is a means to bring about this crisis. I desire this crisis in you. I don't want it <u>not</u> to happen. I don't want to console you. I don't want you to be happy in your unconsciousness. I want you to become sensitive to your actual state. I want you to know very well what you are always up to. I want you to become capable of seeing yourself under all kinds of conditions. I want you to see the machine of your ordinary activity. And I want it all to collapse. I want it to come to an end. I want the death of all of that. If that death does not occur, there will be no release, no real enjoyment for any of you. There will just be the continual round, the self-creation of this unconscious event of life and death that is already distracting you. I look to create the various means necessary to serve this crisis. Because to serve this crisis is to serve understanding, to serve the joy and true bliss of liberated realization, of radical understanding. Every instant in Satsang is working to bring this about. (p. 212)

Practitioners of the Way of the Heart can all testify to the supreme ability of Heart-Master Da to do just this—to bring about and continually intensify the crisis in devotees. For example, the use of time is such a means employed by Sat-Guru Da. He has Given His devotees a very useful and engaging "daily form" for our life of Spiritual practice, a full schedule that begins with meditation generally at 5:00 A.M. His devotees are also challenged with requirements for Sat-Guru-Seva ("seva" is a traditional Sanskrit word that means "service to"), and for the growth of the Mission of the Way of the Heart. Both service and the full life of practice are required, and they are, at times, seemingly impossible to accomplish concurrently. Thus, out of the demand to fulfill all of the expectations of a practitioner at once, a crisis is created for the devotee. Now, Sri Da Avabhasa will say that the devotee must become more efficient, and this is true. Sri Gurudev's own remarkable ability to act effectively and efficiently is a clear Demonstration of this to His devotees. However, whatever the devotee's acknowledged maturity in practice, Sat-Guru Da always asks for more than the devotee feels capable of. Thus a crisis is brought on in the devotee's life. The devotee continues to try to arrange the basics of his or her life so that he or she may always be fulfilling all Sat-Guru Da's requirements, but it is seemingly impossible without making dramatic changes in his or her present capabilities. The devotee asks, "Should I continue to work and fulfill what Sat-Guru Da has asked me to do, or should I go to bed now to have good energy for early morning meditation? How can I be more efficient at my work?"

In this ordeal, attention becomes more and more riveted on Sri Da Avabhasa, and all the devotee's limitations are revealed. In the continual process of the necessary surrender of his or her egoic limitations, the devotee finds the "arms" to go beyond these limits. It is true that someone who is more Spiritually mature can accomplish more—he or she has more free energy and attention. The only way to truly understand the koan of the Sat-Guru's Demand is to align oneself with the Accomplishing Divine Power, Which is Given by Sat-Guru Da and Which is much greater than one's own "creature power". To do so requires living Satsang in relationship to the Sat-Guru with intensity and consistency. Sri Da Avabhasa's Demand is an apparent koan, a Calling that cannot be fulfilled by a conventional response of the body or the mind. It can only be answered by the transcendence of the conventional point of view and by adaptation to an entirely different way of relating to the Divine Reality, which will naturally result in a change in the devotee's relationship to ordinary reality.

The process of sadhana in the Sat-Guru's Company requires a real confrontation with every "Narcissistic" tendency in the body-mind-self. But genuine practice requires the further capability to transcend whatever is so revealed through self-understanding and real resort to the Grace of the Guru. Only such abidance in the real relationship with the Attractive Help of the Guru makes growth in the Sacred Ordeal possible.

The Help of the Sat-Guru in allowing the devotee to pass through the real ordeal of practice cannot be overestimated. That Help is motivated by Great Compassion for the suffering of the devotee, caught as he or she is in the un-Happy grip of the self-contraction. Heart-Master Da Love-Ananda Spoke in 1979 of the necessity and Graceful purpose of the Sat-Guru's Demand and Instructive Criticism:

SRI DA AVABHASA: I allow you to practice from day to day, but if I come upon you personally every now and then and burn the brush out of you—do a little defoliating—you should know why. This fieriness that I bring to you to correct and transform you is nothing compared to the latent energy of the great cosmos and all that it is willing and able to, ready and even intending to, do to you. What I bring to you is just a glow, a kind of warmth. It is even comfortable.

The fire of the universe, however, is all-consuming. When the universe burns you up, you will have no complaints to make—you will not be there to complain! The fieriness that I bring to you only Serves your Enlightenment. Therefore, the fact that I may seem to be angry with you in some moment is

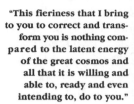

"This fieriness that I bring to you to correct and transform you is nothing compared to the latent energy of the great cosmos and all that it is willing and able to, ready and even intending to, do to you."

not a reflection of your karma. It is a form of My Work to Awaken you, to quicken you, to move you out of the pattern of mediocre practice. The import of it is that you must practice from the heart, with a will, from moment to moment.

As I have stated before, Sri Da Avabhasa has at times pointed out that tremendous karmas can be purified in His Company in surprising ways. There have been many dramatic cases of Heart-Master Da's devotees experiencing physical, emotional, and mental purifications of all kinds—physical illnesses, changes in their practical lives, their relationships, their understanding—through the Blessing of coming into His Company. Even the entire Way of the Heart that Sri Da Avabhasa has Revealed can be seen as an ordeal of purification. Upon meeting Sri Gurudev Da Love-Ananda, the devotee is Liberated at heart, but then the rest of him or her must catch up. Here is a humorous and personal story by Aniello Panico of such purification, which occurred in 1972, very early in Sri Da Avabhasa's Work with His devotees:

I was once Graced to go on a trip to Mexico with Heart-Master Da Love-Ananda for two weeks, just the two of us. On about the third day of our trip, I got very sick. Sri Gurudev decided to send for a doctor because I was really in bad shape. I was lying in bed with a high fever. The doctor who came to my room was dressed all in white, looking like a tennis pro from the local country club. I thought to myself, "This guy's no doctor." After examining me, he told me I had "Montezuma's Revenge", a form of dysentery. I took the pills he prescribed for me and I got much worse. I became so ill that I could hardly move.

Sri Gurudev would sit beside me and feed me soup with a spoon. He also tucked me in bed and kept changing the sheets, which were continually getting drenched with my sweat. After about four or five hours of this intense

fever and sweating and delirium, He asked me,
   "Are you conscious enough to understand something?"
   I said, "No . . . I don't know."
   He said, "Sit up in bed!"
   I said, "I can't."
   He reiterated His request: "Sit up in bed!"
   I pleaded, "There is no way I can."
   He insisted, "Sit up in bed!"
   It required an incredible effort, but I did sit up.

   As I was sitting there, Heart-Master Da read a passage from a Tibetan text that He had brought with Him. In this text, there is a detailed description of what occurs in the devotee when he or she meets the Spiritual Master. And as Heart-Master Da read these symptoms to me, I realized that this was a perfect, exact diagnosis of my ailment. Each of my symptoms was elaborated, literally word for word, in this ancient text! Heart-Master Da finished reading, closed the book, and said, "So I didn't want you to think that it's only Montezuma's Revenge!"

   It became obvious to me that my illness was a form of purification of my gross karmas.

   I had been with Heart-Master Da for only six months, and I could see that He was Working to prepare me for a truly Spiritual relationship with Him. It was such a tender moment: What Grace to have been Blessed with the Divine Adept's Showing His Love by feeding me soup with a spoon!

BE DEVOTED REGARDLESS

There is no way to predict or interpret the ordeal of sadhana in relationship to the Sat-Guru. The single admonition is that whatever arises, one should hold to the Liberating practice, as Heart-Master Da has Said, "like a soldier on the march", and not let experience or difficulty or crisis of any kind dissuade one from the practice of Satsang. The mature practitioner in the Way of the Heart understands that this purification is the entire process. Once an individual has come into the Company of Heart-Master Da Love-Ananda, he or she has already been Given access to the relationship to the Living Divine that is Liberating. All the rest is the purification of the body-mind.

   The true devotee maintains the disposition of such surrender and does not look for a "result". He or she has faith that the surrender itself, the relationship itself, is sufficient. Early in His Teaching Work, Sat-Guru Da Love-Ananda described this practice of faith in the Sat-Guru:

SRI DA AVABHASA: *Turn your attention to Me and do not measure that turning relative to whether or not your mind stops and you feel better.*

Love Me and do not measure that love against whether or not you still feel negative emotions and confusion. Give your life to Me, turn to Me bodily, recollect Me at all times, whether I am physically Present with you or not, and do not measure that activity against whether or not you feel pains in your body. Maintain that discipline of turning to Me. It can be done, as long as you do not associate that turning with the reading of problems in you. The turning can always be done. You are never disabled in terms of that turning. It is only these effects, because you are always reading them and wanting to manipulate them, that make you doubt your ability to turn.

But you can always turn. That is the principle wherein these effects become obsolete—not in that moment necessarily, although on some occasions they disappear immediately. But ultimately they disappear because they are not being used. What you are doing is this turning to Me. These effects are simply memories presently communicating themselves as your functions. They are a kind of remembering. But when your conscious life becomes participation in relationship to Me, then these effects become obsolete. It is not for you to measure that process, to decide when they should become obsolete. Be willing to have these things arise in you forever. Make your business turning to Me. (January 29, 1976)

There is a maxim that the devotee must "cultivate the relationship with the Sat-Guru". The Sat-Guru looks for a variety of responses if the devotee is truly practicing: He or she is naturally moved to the Sat-Guru with devotion. The devotee's love and attention are obvious. The devotee remains continually in relationship to the Sat-Guru, no matter what the circumstance. Even in the midst of a difficult test or crisis, his or her devotion remains one-pointed.

The true devotee responds with energy even when the Sat-Guru is revealing his or her egoic strategies. It is not that such a devotee will outwardly always seem composed, at ease, or in balance—he or she may be truly practicing and at the same time appear completely ragged and out of shape. There is no way to look good in the midst of true practice and its trials, and Spiritual growth is not about looking good in any case. But the Sat-Guru must be able to depend on the devotee to continue responding to him with positive energy no matter what the test. And in that case, the Sat-Guru can do his work with a devotee without hesitation.

One day a devotee living in the residence next to mine at Sri Love-Anandashram came into my room,. He was troubled beyond consolation. He leaned against the wall and then collapsed in a heap, beyond the point of tears. At that time, the editorial department was disturbing Sri Gurudev's Work on His Source-Literature by making numerous errors in processing His manuscripts. Some weeks previously this friend had jumped into the center of the difficulty to try to help. He had temporarily abandoned his normal service as a writer, at which he was effective and was apparently serving Sat-Guru Da quite well. Day and night he tried every possible thing he could do to help this ailing department, but still it was failing, and the criticisms from Sri Gurudev were flying thick and fast.

As the weeks went by, the devotee was getting very little of his own writing done and began missing his own editorial deadlines. My friend told me that he felt he had "ruined" his relationship to Sat-Guru Da, and he was broken-hearted. I did my best to help him with advice about the situation, which he appreciated, but it was also clear that a profound lesson was in the making. I had some sympathy with the opinion that this devotee might better have kept to his service in the area where he knew he could be successful, but I could not criticize his positive and sympathetic response to Sri Gurudev. And I could also feel that because his rescue mission had been failing, perhaps he had undermined his relationship to Sat-Guru Da.

Just a few weeks later, Sat-Guru Da commented on this devotee. There was no mention of the continued failures that had occurred as the editorial department had sunk beneath the level of acceptable service. Instead, in no uncertain terms, Sri Gurudev praised this devotee for always giving Him energy.

The incident showed me that one cannot assume a conventional attitude in relationship to the apparent successes of one's service. Ultimately, of course, genuine and concrete fulfillment of the Sat-Guru's wishes is always necessary. However, what the Sat-Guru principally reads in the devotee's gesture is the degree of self-transcendence and devotion in his or her service and practice. One must remain associated with the Sat-Guru, no matter what criticism or test he or she gives. As Heart-Master Da has Said on many occasions, such tests are there to be passed, not failed. The secret to coming through to the other side of the test is always, no matter what the circumstance, to remain in Satsang, fulfilling all of the practical responsibilities of practice. The trust of the Sat-Guru is the most valuable thing to the devotee, and the traditions recommend that the devotee cultivate this trust constantly.

The most famous traditional story of the Sat-Guru's testing his devotee is the story of Marpa (1012-1096), the patriarch of the Kagyu sect of Tibetan Buddhism, and his great service to Milarepa (1040-1123). Milarepa comes to Marpa for Liberation. He is strongly motivated, for he has committed many bad deeds. In his youth, to avenge wrongs done to his family, he had studied black magic and conjured up hailstorms that killed many people. He knows that without Marpa's help his destiny is dreadful.

Marpa, although observing both Milarepa's great Spiritual potential and also his great need, always treats him harshly, and never reveals to him the great love and admiration he holds for his devotee. He puts Milarepa through ordeal after ordeal to purify and transform him, most dramatically instructing Milarepa to build a stone tower, and then requiring him over and over again to tear down what he has built and rebuild it again elsewhere. Milarepa tries everything to persuade his Guru to be reasonable. He extracts promises from Marpa, asks Marpa's wife to be witness to Marpa's

Marpa

agreements—but it is all to no avail. Up goes the next stone tower, and then Marpa instructs Milarepa to tear it down again.

Bleeding sores from carrying rocks appear on Milarepa's back—but still he complies with his Sat-Guru's instructions. He is scolded time and again by Marpa for presuming anything positive about himself, for not fulfilling Marpa's instructions more perfectly, for feeling that he deserves anything from his Guru. Marpa will not give Milarepa the initiation he seeks—the Teaching that Marpa has "travelled to India at great expense to bring back".

Milarepa's compliance with his Guru's instruction (some notable transgressions notwithstanding) and Marpa's stern demand are both exemplary. In this story we feel the incredible sacred ordeal that is Spiritual practice, but also the extraordinary "Skillful Means" (to liberate the devotee) that the Sat-Guru must use. There is also a clear picture of the pain that the Sat-Guru feels in his Service to his devotee. For example, many times, Marpa holds back tears as he watches Milarepa's ordeal, and he will not let Milarepa feel his love, in order not to give Milarepa any relief from the heat of self-reflection that his ordeal requires. At last, the ordeal is too much for Milarepa. He cannot take it any longer. Sensing this, Marpa initiates him.

Milarepa

Just after the ceremony, Marpa explains to Milarepa and his other devotees the purpose of his actions in these legendary words from the famous numtah, or "Spiritual biography", of Milarepa:

> *Therefore was I angered [at Milarepa] and although my anger recoiled on me like a wave of water, yet it was not like vulgar worldly anger. Religious anger is a thing apart; and in whatever form it may appear, it hath the same object—to excite repentance and thereby to contribute to the spiritual development of the person. Should there be any one amongst you who are seated here, who, not understanding the religious motive, feeleth shocked at these things, I exhort him not to be shaken in his faith and belief.*[5]

Marpa goes on to describe the Spiritual purpose of the eight tests to

5. W. Y. Evans-Wentz, *Tibet's Great Yogi Milarepa*, 2d ed. (London: Oxford University Press, 1980), pp. 130-31.

which he subjected Milarepa and to express regret that Milarepa's weakness had not allowed him to complete the ninth:

Had I the chance of plunging this Spiritual son of mine nine times into utter despair, he would have been cleansed thoroughly of all his sins. He would thus not have been required to be born again, but would have disappeared totally, his physical body being forever dissolved; he would have attained Nirvana. That it will not be so, and that he will still retain a small portion of his demerits, is due to the weakness and misunderstandings of the Spiritual purposes of these tests.[6]

"YOUR OBLIGATION FOR SERVICE IS EFFECTIVE TWENTY-FOUR HOURS A DAY"

The opportunity to serve the Sat-Guru in any capacity is the greatest opportunity and joy for the devotee. True service is non-self-referring activity. It is to give one's attention to the Sat-Guru in the context of any action or activity, instead of directing attention to yourself. Service to the Sat-Guru, or Sat-Guru-Seva, is thus a means of contemplating the Sat-Guru. Through the contemplation that is that service, the devotee is made happy. Instead of dwelling on self-concerns and problems, the devotee Communes with the Divine.

In the Way of the Heart, every aspect of the devotee's life must become such Sat-Guru-Seva. Any area the devotee still regards as his or her "private life", separated from Sat-Guru-Seva and the demand of sacrifice or surrender, provides a hedge for the ego. True Sat-Guru-Seva provides a mechanism for the natural undoing of karmas because attention is granted or given to the Divine in the form of the Sat-Guru rather than to the egoic self. Thus, the law that one becomes what one meditates on works for the devotee in Sat-Guru-Seva. This is a necessary aspect of the Sacred Ordeal that is the devotee's response to the ceaseless gifts Given by the Sat-Guru. The demand to serve without any lapse through every form of action is the practical means by which the devotee's life becomes a vehicle to Incarnate the Guru's Graceful Demand, and thus to constantly receive his Blessing. The all-encompassing demand for service is a Gift from the Sat-Guru to the devotee—it is still a trial, but the devotee understands it as the means by which attention can be placed on what is Great.

Heart-Master Da Spoke to the all-inclusiveness of Sat-Guru-Seva in this Talk from July 9, 1988, Given at the Mountain Of Attention Sanctuary:

SRI DA AVABHASA: All action must become service. All service must be Guru-Seva. All Guru-Seva is Guru-Contemplation. Action, or service, then, is

6. Ibid.

Guru-Contemplation. Sat-Guru-Darshan is to abide in that Contemplation of Me constantly in the midst of activity. Thus, service is a particular form of sadhana, just as meditation is another form of sadhana. They are both about the same thing, though, ultimately. Service and meditation are about the same feeling-Contemplation of Me, through a somewhat different apparent design.

The secret, then, is to remain always in this feeling-Contemplation of Me.

Service also enables the devotee to make his or her life altogether a sacrifice to a greater purpose, that of the Spiritual Service to the world that is the Sat-Guru's Work. It frees the devotee from his or her own conventional destiny and plans, and combines the devotee with the Sat-Guru's intent of magnifying the Spiritual Process in the world. Serving the Sat-Guru's Work for all beings establishes a link of right relationship to the Sat-Guru in concrete terms.

As one who has served Sri Da Avabhasa and His Work since the age of twenty-one, I can tell you that there is no greater joy in my life. Time and again during His Teaching years, I found the opportunity to thank Sri Da Avabhasa for the opportunity to give my life over through direct service to Him, and even now when writing to Sri Gurudev in any capacity, I thank Him for the Gift of service to Him. Tears come to my eyes when I feel what a Blessing it is to be given such means of Remembering Him, Contemplating Him. Through that service, I have felt Him and His Blissful Grace so strongly. I regard myself to be one of the most fortunate people on Earth for having been Given the opportunity of serving at His Feet. It has meant that my life has been directed toward a greater purpose than my own mortal destiny—a Divine Purpose—and it has meant that the more I have practiced this Sat-Guru-Seva, the more I have been able to Contemplate Him.

The mature devotee understands that service to the Guru transforms the devotee through its demand, and provides a means by which the state of his or her practice can be revealed and strengthened. For his own part, whether the Sat-Guru's circumstance is served or not served does not change his or her Divine Condition of Happiness one iota. Once a devotee of Sri Da Avabhasa sent Him a letter of apology for "disturbing Him" with an editorial error in entering Sri Da Avabhasa's Work on *The Basket of Tolerance*. From the way the devotee's letter was written, it was clear that he felt that Sri Gurudev Da Love-Ananda was personally upset in a conventional manner. And so Sat-Guru Da Love-Ananda Instructed His devotee directly, telling him that the error had been a sign of the devotee's lack of full and right attention to Him, and His upset was intended to serve the devotee's right practice. Thus, the devotee needed the Sat-Guru's upset, which reflected to him his lack of service. Therefore Heart-Master Da's upset over His devotee's wrong fulfillment of his service was for the devotee's benefit. Sri Gurudev Da Love-Ananda Himself remained in Bliss.

Everything that the Sat-Guru asks of his devotees is for the purification and Liberation of them and the world.

Sri Da Avabhasa has made clear that the Sat-Guru is of most Spiritual benefit to the devotee when the devotee simply allows him to Abide in his Divine Disposition of Heart-Transmission, or Heart-Blessing. Sri Gurudev Da Love-Ananda has made it clear that it is the obligation of all devotees who receive the Gifts of the Sat-Guru to see to it that the Sat-Guru is served properly and truly. What the Sat-Guru brings is the Great Blessing, and he (or she) must be allowed to simply give That. Never, it was said traditionally, should the Sat-Guru be required to do what devotees can do themselves. This is not an unusual principle—in every aspect of life, those with the most genius and expertise are allowed the opportunity to use their gifts, whereas others more ordinary in their talents perform more ordinary tasks. In Spiritual life, when somone has Incarnated as the Divine Being in bodily (human) Form, this principle is tantamount to Law. The devotee must always completely handle the Sat-Guru's requirements, not because the Sat-Guru "needs" such service in personal terms. Rather, to truly serve the Guru benefits the devotee and the entire world, by allowing the Sat-Guru to do his (or her) true Work. Everything at the physical level should be handled for the Great Realizer, so that he is never drawn from his Spiritual Work, so that not a minute of his attention is distracted from being the Divine Blesser or Murti for his devotees.

Sri Da Avabhasa Spoke about the obligation of service in the following Talk, Given in 1980.

SRI DA AVABHASA: If you enter into Spiritual relationship with an Adept, you must enter into his service. When the great gift of Spiritual Transmission is what you are receiving, your obligation for service is effective twenty-four hours a day. It is a lifelong obligation, a total obligation, even as the Spiritual Master lives his entire life in obligation to his devotees. People who do not express that consciousness cannot use the Teaching. They become guilty and build up too much residual egoic self-energy through their non-service and non-surrender. Eventually they stop practicing because they can no longer justify taking the Gift of Spiritual Help. Then they just sit around with glazed looks on their faces.

As a practitioner of this Way of the Heart you are obliged to live as a servant—not as a slave but as a servant. In other words, you are obligated to express the commitment to self-transcendence in all your relations. And you are obliged to do so constantly. Such service is practice. Such service is participation in the reception of Grace. Such service is Spiritual life.

The principal ceremony enacted by devotees, which is giving and receiving of gifts in the Communion Halls, epitomizes the principle that they must enact in their lives. It is the Life-Principle, the Law. If the giving and receiving of gifts becomes mechanical, then all acts of self-giving become mechanical and are minimized, and soon you resent every demand on your energy.

This Way is not to hear a lecture every Sunday, depending on the

**"If you enter into Spiritual relationship with an Adept,
you must enter into his service. When the great gift of Spiritual Transmission
is what you are receiving, your obligation for service is effective
twenty-four hours a day. It is a lifelong obligation, a total obligation,
even as the Spiritual Master lives his entire life in obligation to his devotees."**

*Spiritual Master as a child depends on a parent, and depending on the staff
of the Communion to create nice little programs to keep you amused. You
must practice. You must create a cultural circumstance in which the Adept
can be effective and then you must use it. And what is that cultural system?
Primarily it is a group of people associating themselves with the Spiritual
Master through service. When you are simply, effectively doing that, then I
am moved, through the Agents that I use, to serve you, to see to it that you
are kept in touch with what you need Spiritually.*

*My requirements are not merely personal. They are the requirements for
your good. There are certain personal things, obviously, that are needed for
My daily living, but if you come to Me and ask Me what I need, ultimately
you will find out from Me all the things that must be done so that all human
beings can live an Enlightened life.*

Sat-Guru-Seva is thus a sadhana, a vehicle for the Liberation of the
devotee.

Right service of the Guru is not simply a good thing to do. It is a
<u>necessity</u>. If the devotee has not truly surrendered his or her action through
real service to the Guru, and brought real gifts of that service to the Guru's
Feet, then the Guru cannot lawfully magnify his (or her) Blessing of the
devotee. The Guru, of course, will always remain in the general State of
Giving, or Blessing. But the specific and personal Flow of Grace to his
devotee is stopped or greatly diminished whenever the devotee does not
put himself or herself in right relationship to the Sat-Guru through <u>effective</u>
service. Thus, genuine service of the Sat-Guru is the means by which the
devotee must demonstrate his or her reception and true practice of all of
the Sat-Guru's Gifts.

CULTIVATING OR PLEASING THE GURU
THROUGH SERVICE TO HIM OR HER

All of the formalities of the Guru-devotee relationship can be summarized in one traditional guideline, which Sri Gurudev Da Love-Ananda has called the most basic principle:

SRI DA AVABHASA: The traditions of the Spiritual Master or the Guru communicate much about what one should do in relationship to the Adept. Basically, the traditional instructions may be summarized by the verse in Fifty Verses of Guru-Devotion, *by Ashvaghosha: "Do whatever pleases your Guru and avoid doing anything he would not like. Be diligent in both of these" (verse 46).[7] In other words, knowing the Law of sacrifice, cultivate the Adept's impulse to be accessible, to Teach, to be Present, to be Company for people. If you force him to be hidden or to get away, you are violating the Law, denying yourself the use of Agency. Why do it? Once you understand the transforming Power and Help available in that relationship, then of course you will do everything necessary to cultivate access to him. That is the kind of consciousness that must be developed. . . . (*The Bodily Location of Happiness, *p. 70)*

My own service at the Feet of Sri Da Avabhasa has been direct Instruction in many of the principles of Sat-Guru-Seva. As I have said earlier, for a number of years I was Graced to be the librarian directly serving Heart-Master Da Love-Ananda's Work with the texts of the Great Tradition. During this period He created for the sake of His devotees and all other interested individuals many reading lists on various subjects, such as sexuality, diet and health, exercise, and devotion. Each reading list was a carefully prepared selection of books, which, when thoroughly studied in the context of His Instruction in the Way of the Heart, would allow the reader to be educated beyond his or her provincialism or dogmatism, and to develop understanding about a particular subject area by seeing all traditional perspectives in the clarity of the orientation of the seven stages of life. Sri Gurudev Da Love-Ananda does not read books—His relationship to them is entirely psychic, and He knows their content without even having to open their covers. In preparing these lists Sri Gurudev Da Love-Ananda was intent on Serving Spiritual aspirants completely. His lists embrace every significant point of view (secular, religious, Spiritual, or Transcendental) on all aspects of any given subject. Thus, anyone studying these lists is able to view the full context of the literature on the subject from Da Avabhasa's "Radical" Perspective. His "Consideration" of the traditional literature on each subject is now summarized in *The Basket of Tolerance*, as well as the larger and even more inclusive "Seven Schools of God-Talk and God-Realization".

---

7. Asvaghosa, *Fifty Verses of Guru-Devotion* (Dharamsala, India: The Library of Tibetan Works and Archives, 1976), p. 29.

Sri Da Avabhasa would request that I find particular books for His review as He would fill out particular topics in His lists. In participating with Him in this Work, I began to become sensitive to His extraordinary method of "Consideration", or in-depth exploration of an area with an intelligence based in Realization, rather than in mere conceptual mind. I began to see how this Work carried Him naturally from one subject to the next in an investigation of incredible breadth and depth. Heart-Master Da Love-Ananda would ask for particular books, and after He would review these, He would often ask for books on related subjects that carried on the thread of His "Consideration".

As I served Him, I studied His way of Working. He sometimes told me things to do for Him directly, but more often, just by serving Him and studying His actions, a sense of how I could best serve Him would be Revealed to me. I once asked Him how to choose books to send for His review, and His reply was: "Study what I have looked at or done in the past." I began to become more sensitive to Him by this study, and I became more able to feel what direction or orientation might be pleasing to Him. Thus, before He even asked, I tried to anticipate His Requirements and serve His Work by suggesting books that might extend His "Consideration". At the same time, I was always mindful not to burden Him with an unnecessary "tonnage" of books.

I found that to serve in this way was a very specific form of Spiritual practice. The more I learned to feel Heart-Master Da Love-Ananda, the more I could tell by very small signs whether a book or communication I made to Him was pleasing or not. I could tell by the subtleties of the words He used when He sent messages, but even more so by the tone of His messages beyond the words. I realized that Sat-Guru Da is always Giving messages to His devotee of what pleases Him and what does not, and as I grew in my feeling in this area, I was able to tell by subtler and subtler signs whether a book had pleased my True Heart-Master. Eventually I was often able to feel His pleasure or displeasure without any particular overt sign at all. I would be able to tell from how He treated a book or where He might put it on the list, or I could read between the lines of the simply communicated written notes I received. I could tell just what had pleased Him and what He might want next. He could Give a tremendous range of subtle communications without actually relaying them verbally. I would be able to tell what was going on simply by His actions.

In this wonderful Play I participated in with Him, Sri Gurudev Da Love-Ananda would make Requests that required me to rely on Him completely in faith, rather than use my conventional mind. He would ask for "the green book that has something to do with Hinduism and that came from India". Or the "small hardback volume I looked at last year about Yoga that has a title that begins with 'S'". And sometimes He would simply say, "that red book upstairs in the hallway—James will know which one." And the person giving me the message would say, "Do you know?" The only way that I could answer such Requests was to feel Sri Gurudev Da Love-Ananda very directly, and then immediately I was a channel for His Intention, and I would know what He was referring to and could get the book. But if I was out of relationship to Sri Gurudev Da Love-Ananda, or out of balance physically or emotionally, then I could not feel what He was Communicating, and I would be forced to rely on my thinking mind alone to determine what book He was asking for. And in such a case, the search could take several hours or days, and many rounds of Communications from my Heart-Master; and the search was often fruitless in the end, because I had already lost the connection of genuine Sat-Guru-Seva. At these times I would disturb Sri Gurudev Da Love-Ananda, and eventually I would be told not only about my failures as a librarian, but also about the failures in my relationship to Sri Gurudev, and I knew that these criticisms were true.

On one occasion when Heart-Master Da was living at Tumomama Sanctuary in Hawaii, a devotee attending to Him telephoned me with a request for a dozen or so books. Many of the references to the books were rather cryptic, calling on me to rely on my intuition, rather than what was literally stated. But even more so, I understood that if I stayed strongly in relationship to Sri Gurudev, He would Communicate to me the capability to find the books for Him. I turned to Him more deeply, and He was right there, and I felt so much love and attraction for His Divine Form. And in this mood, I found all the books He wanted for His Work. I laughed when the list was finished, knowing what an ordeal it might have been. And I joked that I was particularly "in tune" that night. Now, I am quite a slender fellow, with the bookish body-type of a librarian. When the attendant relayed to Heart-Master Da Love-Ananda that I felt I was "in tune" with Him, Sri Gurudev replied, humorously, "If James is so psychic, how come He doesn't put on weight looking at all these books?" I didn't need to think about this—it made complete sense to me!

I was astounded many times by the Revelation that occurred in my service to Sri Gurudev—time and again I would be at the library looking at a book, and I would wonder if Sri Gurudev would ever ask for books on that subject. And that very evening such a book would be requested. Or it would occur to me, "I wonder if Sri Gurudev will ever want to see books on such and such a subject again. He hasn't looked at these in a while." And then, with an uncanny regularity, He would ask to review these books. This occurred time after time. I came to understand that my service was founded in the living relationship to Sat-Guru Da Love-Ananda, not merely in the details of fulfilling His Requests.

One night in 1982, after a period in which hundreds of books had been added to "The Seven Schools of God-Talk and God-Realization", the book-list Sri Gurudev was concentrating on at that time, Heart-Master Da confirmed this process in which I had learned to more and more trust my feeling and relationship to Him.

He Said, "Jim would constantly bring me exactly the books that I would know of in advance. He would always go and get those books. They were titles that I knew in advance, subjects I knew. He always brought those books exactly. He did not have the slightest idea what he was doing."

As He Said, I did not know much about what was occurring, but I did know that if I relied upon Sri Gurudev completely and studied Him with my heart-feeling and stayed open to His Transmission of Grace, I could please Him. This principle of simply relying on the Sat-Guru and serving with the understanding that there is a greater psycho-physics involved, applies to true Sat-Guru-Seva. I needed to anticipate and provide for His "consideration", and not simply fulfill what He asked in that moment. And there were endless opportunities to please Him. But it required my always feeling Him and caring about how He felt, rather than caring about myself. It required me to go beyond my limits and grow in my service. By doing this, I was Contemplating Him, and I found myself transformed in my awareness and in my Spiritual practice altogether.

I also so valued Sri Gurudev Da Love-Ananda's Service and Instruction to the world through His Work with the books of the Great Tradition of mankind that I never wanted to impede His Work or make Him feel in the slightest that anything He was doing was a burden or a problem for me. I always knew this service to be a great Gift and Blessing, not only for me, but for the whole world. At appropriate moments, I did my best to tell Sri Gurudev Da Love-Ananda this. I wanted Him to feel His devotees' appreciation for His Work, and I wanted Him to feel that we would do anything that was necessary so that He would feel supported to continue in it.

THE SACRED ORDEAL OF THE SAT-GURU

For the devotee, the process of sadhana and the demands of service are a sacred ordeal, but the difficulty and frustration faced by the Sat-Guru are greater than those of any devotee. Although the Sat-Guru comes with Blessings to Give, devotees often resist and avoid them. Therefore, the Sat-Guru's own Work involves a most intense ordeal. Sri Da Avabhasa has Said on many occasions that the Ordeal of Serving His devotees is more of a struggle than was His own Sadhana of re-establishing His Divinely Enlightened Condition. He described this difficult process in a Talk from the late 1970s entitled "The Divine Life and Work of the Spiritual Master":

SRI DA AVABHASA: *You must understand that the unique status of the Spiritual Master is not given for his own sake. The Spiritual Master is not a human being with a superior egoic consciousness that he or she is God. The ego of such a one is destroyed, transcended in the process of his or her lifetime. The situation of the Spiritual Master is not as you might imagine. You*

may be thinking: "We all know you are not suffering like us! We poor bastards are the ones who are suffering—you've got it made!" Well, such thinking is not true at all. The lifetime of the Spiritual Master is only sacrifice, and therefore more a torment than the lifetime of the ordinary soul. Read the biographies of the great Spiritual Masters. They all tell the same story of a life that is terrible in some ways, a life in which frequently they are exploited and rejected, and in which they are under the constant threat of domination by worldly and negative forces. Such individuals are always dealing with great forces, not just mastering their rejection by human beings, but tussling with daemonic energy. Such is also the case in my lifetime! What you see in my lifetime is the biography of the Divine Being. This is how the Divine Being must live among human beings.

People who are not truly devotees often feel that they must become like the Spiritual Master, that they must have the status of the Spiritual Master. Such people envy the Spiritual Master, and they will not surrender to him. They only want from him a token, a bit of magic, that will somehow make them like he is. But understand this: No un-Enlightened soul wants to be in the position of the Spiritual Master! If you understood my constant experience, you would not envy it—nor could you endure it! One must be Helped by great Divine Power in order to endure the events associated with such a unique life, in order to pass through such events with a clear understanding of what they are as a Divine Process. Only the Divine has the power to endure the complete revolution of consciousness. Only the Divine has the power to confront the entire play of manifest existence and master all the forces to which beings are subject. The Spiritual Master engages those forces in actual warfare, whereas devotees in general perceive the same forces to be the play of their natural experience. The devotee does not struggle with the power that produces weather or with the physics of light personified as self-conscious beings, although the devotee is also somehow involved in the same play. The Purusha, the Divine, is the victorious Warrior, the Master of all life.

The Ordeal of the Sat-Guru and his (or her) emotional sacrifice in his service to others are a counterpart to his Inherence in the Divine. Both are true simultaneously. He feels the suffering of life, and at the same time he is founded in the Divine Condition, absolutely and fully. This is the Paradox of the Incarnate Divine.

Sri Love-Anandashram, September 1991

CHAPTER TEN

"The Gift That Is The Heart Itself"

SRI DA AVABHASA'S TRANSMISSION OF HRIDAYA-SHAKTI

DIVINE INITIATION AT HOLY CAT GROTTO

O n the warm night of September 17, 1979, Heart-Master Da Love-Ananda gathered with His devotees to enact an age-old ritual of Grace and Blessing—initiating devotees into a more mature level of practice in sacred relationship to Him. There were three hundred of us, including the twenty or so initiates, seated in Holy Cat Grotto,[1] the natural open-air amphitheater at the Mountain Of Attention. The Grotto, fed by Laughing Man Creek, is of great natural beauty. But more than this, this sacred Site is a preserve of Heart-Master Da's Blessing-Transmission—it is filled with the Weight and Fragrance of His Heart-Power. The main altar faces a great pool of hot water, flowing from a natural hot spring, and is cloaked in heated wafts of steam and mist. Across the pool is a massive rock face, down which pours a small stream of cool water that flows into the heated pool. The pool is thus a sangam, or meeting place of sacred waters. Holy Cat Grotto has all of the natural characteristics of a great tirtha, or water-baptism site.

When it was my turn to approach Sri Da Avabhasa to be initiated in this sacred place, He was kneeling on the right side of the Grotto's inner pool. I felt His Attention move over me like a blanket of Embrace, enveloping

---

1. Holy Cat Grotto is the site where Robert the Cat's ashes are enshrined. The great Avadhoota Dattatreya is described in the Bhagavata Purana as having twenty-four Upa-Gurus, or secondary Gurus, who were for him forms of the one Great Guru. These included a fish, a heron, and a bee. Similarly, during the early time of Heart-Master Da's Sadhana, when He lived on the beach cliffs of northern California, the great Avadhoota Da Love-Ananda was served by the cat Robert. It was in honor of Robert, His "friend in the wilderness", that Holy Cat Grotto was named.

me with His Peace and Bliss. I offered a marigold into the pool and bowed before Sri Da Avabhasa with an expectation that sent a thrill throughout my body. I surrendered myself before Him, and gave everything that I was to Him.

The intensity of His Grace and Blessing overwhelmed me. I was somehow aware that His Hand had gone into the water and was moving towards me. As I lifted my head from my prostration, Heart-Master Da Love-Ananda gently but forcefully placed His great Palm, now filled with the warm water of the Grotto, on my forehead. The water's warmth bore with it His Grace, and it fell over my head and down my chest to my heart. The Blessing that moved into me was a giant wall of completely Conscious Force—and there was no end to it. It was Consciously and Compassionately Given, and I felt completely relaxed in relationship to this great Strength.

Then, in a moment that passed both incredibly rapidly, because I was so intensely alive, and also very slowly, because I wanted it to last forever, Heart-Master Da Love-Ananda moved even closer to me. He was the Divine Person Incarnate, and His Face was overbrimming with Love. He was completely Intent, His Surrender and Giving Full and Perfect. He placed His right Palm over my left ear and the left side of my head. His left Hand was cupped over my right ear. And He moved His mouth close to my ear and Spoke.

Sri Gurudev's Voice was deep and strong. He Spoke, with distinct Words, and with such a Divine Impact that I will forever hear the very Words in my ear,

"I _Am_ the Prayer of Remembrance. Call upon Me with the Name 'Da'."

"I **Am** the Prayer of Remembrance. Call upon Me with the Name 'Da'."

That Voice penetrated my being with extraordinary Siddhi. I felt myself being filled with Light, and Sound, and Energy—and that Power was White and very Bright. It reverberated through me as a physical Force, pushing against every part of me, and pushing out against my skin down to my feet. It was Awake. This Force became the content of my brain, and massaged my mind with its Vibrations. It moved through me, and became me, taking me over. It was Love-Bliss. Gratefully I sat in the Love and Emotion of this Siddhi that was Heart-Master Da's Gift until I saw that it was time to move back to my seat.

Even as I moved away, His Loving Glance remained on me. He still Blessed me, still I felt Immersed in His Radiant Fullness. As I sat down, I noticed that now the next person was being Initiated. But still, Heart-Master Da Love-Ananda was with me. He was no longer looking at me, but His Siddhi remained.

Such a moment is archetypal. For here, in this moment of sacred ritual before the assembled sangha, or Spiritual community, of all who were His devotees at that time, Sri Gurudev Da Love-Ananda had Given in a magnified form the same Transmission of Love-Bliss that He is always Giving to all. On this occasion, it was wonderfully outwardly enacted in traditional form. But this same process, the same giving of the devotee to the Sat-Guru and the Sat-Guru's Return of extraordinary Blessing, is enacted in every moment of Da Avabhasa's Work with those who turn to Him in devotion.

"MY BLESSING WORK IS THE TRANSMISSION WORK (OR GIVING WORK) OF THE HEART": YOGIC SHAKTIPAT AND HRIDAYA-SHAKTIPAT

In the Essay "The Spiritual Master Provides the Radiant Touch of God", which appeared in *The Enlightenment of the Whole Body*, Da Avabhasa Spoke about the principles of Transmission alive in the Blessing Company of the Sat-Guru.

The Spiritual Master, because of his Transformed psycho-physical Condition, is Radiant and Conscious in the Perfect Identity of Self in God. Therefore, he Functions as an Agent of Transformation in the case of devotees who submit to him in love, in the spiritual manner.

The Spiritual Master is one who has fulfilled the Law in his own Transformation, and who has been Served by the Presence, the Attention, the Glance, the Instruction, and the Touch of others, who were Agents of God. Likewise, he also serves devotees by his Presence, Attention, Glance, Instruction, and Touch.

By such means, the Spiritual Master Awakens and Enlivens devotees with the Radiance of the Divine Person. It is a literal and necessary Process.

It is not symbolic, appearing only as ritual. By his Contact with devotees, who make themselves available through devotional Communion with him, the Spiritual Master Serves the Perfect Purpose of God. (p. 255)

The means by which such Spiritual Initiation, or diksha, may take place are described in the Spiritual traditions in specific detail. But what is more significant than <u>how</u> such Grace is Transmitted is what is the <u>Source</u> of Transmission. And in genuine Spiritual cultures it has always been understood that the Supreme Source of Blessing Transmission is the Sat-Guru. As the *Siva Sutras* declare, "The Guru is the Grace-bestowing power of God."[2]

And the *Kularnava Tantra* confirms:

It is laid down by the Lord that there can be no moksha, *liberation, without* diksha, *initiation; and initiation cannot be there without a Teacher. . . . Without a Teacher, all philosophy, traditional knowledge, Mantras are fruitless.*[3]

Because of the scarcity of genuine Spiritual culture or practice in today's world, there is little understanding of the process of this Spiritual Transmission. Da Avabhasa has thus had to clarify every aspect of the Gifts of tangible Grace that the Sat-Guru Gives to his devotee.

SRI DA AVABHASA: The literal Power of the Adept is not a figment of the imagination. The traditions describe the Siddha-Power and the experience of devotees who truly associated with such a One. The process of Spiritual Transmission is a literal process, because the Adept is not merely an ordinary individuated being. He has thoroughly transcended all of the artifacts of individuation, and he is simply and directly Present as the Force of Divine Influence. That Influence is Radiant throughout all space-time without limitation. Those who awaken as devotees of the Divine in such form encounter the expressions of this Siddhi, or the ecstatic marvels of Divine Communion.

Transmission is a literal process and not an imaginary one. The Influence of the Sat-Guru is All-Pervading and Radiant without obstruction. When you contact It in the context of your individual or personal life, you feel It pervading your life. What you are observing then is the Play of the Divine, the Play of the Sat-Guru's Influence, the Means through which you enter into Divine Communion. Therefore, you experience, in life and meditation, uncommon states that are the expressions of Divine Communion. . . .

The Influence that is operative through Me and as Me is the Divine. As the Divinely Self-Realized Adept, I am not some sort of demigod or a separate God, but I have Realized the Condition of all beings, and, by virtue of that

2. Swami Muktananda, *Kundalini: The Secret of Life* (South Fallsburg, N.Y.: SYDA Foundation, 1979).

3. M. P. Pandit, *Kularnava Tantra* (Madras: Ganesh and Co., 1965), p. 101.

Realization, I Function in a unique fashion in the human plane.

The Sat-Guru is not significant as a worldly personality, but he is significant as a Vehicle of Transmission. Thus, I should be reserved for the setting where I can Function purely as the Agent of Spiritual Heart-Transmission. (July, 1982)

In the Yogic traditions, Spiritual Transmission is called "shaktipat", which means descent (pat) of power (shakti). In the case of a seventh stage Realizer such as Sri Da Avabhasa, what is Communicated is not confined to bodily energy, or even to the Yogic energies described in various Spiritual traditions. Rather, what is Transmitted is the Realization and Potency of the Heart, the Hridaya-Shakti, which is the Transmission of the Love-Bliss that is Prior to the body, the mind, and the separate and separative self.

Heart-Master Da Love-Ananda describes the Blessing Grace of a fully Enlightened Being as completely different from that offered by Teachers of a lesser Realization or Blessing capability. The Hridaya-Shakti, Which Sri Da Avabhasa Transmits, is the Gift of the Heart Itself. Hridaya-Shakti "Awakens The Realization Of The Divine Self-Condition Itself", beyond the Circle and the Arrow or all the experiences of the body-mind.

The "Circle" and the "Arrow" are Sri Da Avabhasa's precise terms that describe the two principal circuits through which the Living Spirit-Current can be felt to flow in the body-mind. The "Circle" traces a pattern in which energy descends down the front of the body or the frontal line, and ascends along the spinal line. At times of deep meditation the Spiritual energies may be felt in a different way, as an "Arrow". Sri Da Avabhasa explains that this is "a motionless axis that seems to stand in the center of the body, between the frontal and spinal lines".

When the Circle is open, the body-mind is filled with Spirit-Energy. However, all the energies of the body-mind are representative of simply the first five stages of life. It is in this dimension of the being that the energies of Yogic Shaktipat operate.

More profound than, or prior to but inclusive of, the Circle and the Arrow, is the domain of the Heart Itself. The Heart is associated with the sixth and the seventh stages of life. It is the dimension of Divine Consciousness Itself, Prior to any necessary association with the body-mind.

There is, therefore, a profound difference between the Transmitter of Yogic Shaktipat, and the Divinely Enlightened Transmitter of Hridaya-Shaktipat. Whereas traditional Yogic Shaktipat draws one into the experiential phenomena potential in the body-mind in the first five stages of life, the Transmission of the Heart simply Attracts and Draws the devotee beyond all experience, into the Divine Heart Itself.

The devotee who receives Hridaya-Shakti may also experience many movements of energy in the body-mind, but they are not the essential Nature of, or Communication that is made by, the Hridaya-Shakti. Rather, Hridaya-Shakti is always Drawing the devotee beyond the experiential dimension of the body-mind, into the Transcendental (and Inherently Spiritual) and "Bright" Divine Condition that is the Heart Itself, and of which the body-mind and all its conditional energies are merely a modification. Hridaya-Shakti is the Transmission of the Very Condition of Sri Da Avabhasa, and therefore It Draws His devotees into His Condition or Very (and Inherently Perfect) State, Which is Prior to all arising, Pervading all that arises, and Transcending every kind of experience in Its Bliss.

I quote here Heart-Master Da Love-Ananda's description of this distinction between the Transmission of Yogic Shaktipat, which is associated with the first five stages of life, and the Transmission of the Heart, which He calls "Hridaya-Shaktipat" and "Hridaya-Shakti-Kripa", and which is associated with the seventh stage of life. His description comes from chapter twelve of *The Dawn Horse Testament*:

> *My Transmission Work (or Inherently Spiritual Blessing Work) Is The Transmission (or Giving) Of Hridaya-Shakti, The Graceful Heart-Power (That Is The Heart Itself)*. . . .
>
> *Hridaya-Shakti-Kripa (or Hridaya-Shaktipat) Is Given By The Heart Itself (Which Is The Very Divine Person, or The Self-Existing and Self-Radiant Divine Self-Condition Itself, Who I Am)*. . . .
>
> *Whereas conditional (or conventional Yogic) Shaktipat and conventional Yogic Practice Actively Seek conditional Goals Of attention (In or Above The Circle, and The Arrow, Of the body-mind), Hridaya-Shakti-Kripa (or Hridaya-Shaktipat) Directly Reveals (and, Subsequently, The Thereby Spiritually Initiated Practice Of The Way Of The Heart Directly Realizes) The (Inherently) Perfectly Subjective Heart Itself, Which Is Eternally Prior To attention, mind, body, The Circle, The Arrow, and all worlds, and The Heart's Own (Inherently, and Ultimately, Perfect) Way, Which Is To Stand As Is, Prior To Every Kind Of Seeking, and Prior To Any and All Movements Of attention, and Prior Even To attention itself*. . . . *(pp. 151-52)*

The Transmission of the seventh stage Realizer must also be distinguished from that of a sixth stage Realizer, or the Realizer still involved in sixth to seventh stage Teaching and practice (that is, those whose Realization, Teaching, or practice, although exhibiting elements of the seventh stage Demonstration, is not purely or completely Demonstrative of the seventh stage of life). In the seventh stage of life, or Most Perfect Divine Self-Realization, there is no withdrawal or dissociation from life. Everything that arises is tacitly Recognized as a transparent and non-binding modification of the One Divine Consciousness. Thus, the Transmission of the Realizer Alive as this Condition is active and direct.

However, in one still practicing or Teaching in the context of the sixth stage of life, there is the tendency to view the Divine Condition as not only Prior to, but also <u>exclusive</u> of, the body, the mind, and the world. Thus, there is a tendency to dissociate from bodily existence itself, and to focus on or withdraw into the Heart or Consciousness Itself, in a strategic fashion that excludes all arising phenomena. The Transmission of such sixth stage or sixth to seventh stage Realizers is therefore more indirect, or passive. It is not "directly effective", penetrating all of phenomenal existence, as does the seventh stage Hridaya-Shakti. Rather, it is the communication of the Transcendental Heart, apart and still, dissociated from life.

TANGIBLE EXPERIENTIAL SIGNS OF THE RECEPTION OF
THE BLESSING-GRACE OF SRI DA AVABHASA

The devotees of Hridaya-Samartha Sat-Guru Da Love-Ananda are the fortunate recipients of His Hridaya-Shakti in every moment in which they turn to Him. Although Sri Da Avabhasa constantly Transmits only the Hridaya-Shakti, those who are Blessed to receive His Grace feel It in different ways, according to their stage of maturity. Hridaya-Shakti is the full seventh stage Transmission of the Heart, but It is "read" or experienced through the limited mechanism of the individual who receives It. Therefore, although Sri Da Avabhasa is only the Inherently Perfect Heart of the Divine Self-Condition, and He Freely Gives the Transmission of that State always, the devotee's availability to receive this Gift develops over time and by stages.

For those just beginning their practice of the Way of the Heart, His Hridaya-Shakti serves every kind of purification and rebalancing of the grosser or more ordinary dimensions of human existence. However, for those who have submitted themselves to Him in body-forgetting, emotion-forgetting, and mind-forgetting feeling-Contemplation and who have matured in the practice of self-transcendence in His Company, His Graceful Blessing is felt in more esoteric ways. A wide range of maturity is demonstrated among practitioners of the Way of the Heart, from early beginning practice to practice in the ultimate stages. And even as our Great Heart-Master has Promised, His Blessing is freely Given day by day to all those who love Him and turn to Him in their genuine practice of the Way of the Heart, no matter what their present stage of development.

The following account of reception of Sri Da Avabhasa's Transmission is by Linda Beltrame, an Australian by birth, and currently a beginning practitioner in the Way of the Heart.

During the course of my three-week Darshan and Meditation retreat at Sri Love-Anandashram in 1990, I was abundantly Gifted with all of the Sat-Guru's Seven Gifts of Grace. All the forms of practice of the Way of the Heart were clarified and intensified so that I felt re-enlivened in my understanding and reception of His Gifts.

One aspect of His Blessing that was particularly potent for me was the reception of His Spiritual Transmission. On several occasions, either in Darshan or meditation or devotional chanting, I would feel a depth of love arise in me that would literally cause me to swoon in heart-response to the Attractiveness of His Being. I would literally drop to the floor, curled about, or fully prostrate, because it was so Powerful. I was completely gone in love, so aware of Him that there was no sense of me left. My mind was gone, and there was almost no sense of separate and separative self. I simply felt my Sat-Guru. Two of these occasions, similar in nature, stand out as a profound Gift of His Hridaya-Shaktipat.

On the second occasion, as I became aware of His Spirit-Presence descending in the frontal line of my body, I simply surrendered into it, while Contemplating His bodily (human) Form before me. I could feel the tangible infusion of His Blissful Energy, forceful and "Bright", moving in the areas of the head and throat, the heart and solar plexus, and particularly strong at the sexual center and bodily base. As the feeling of this Current grew even stronger, I engaged the perineal lock, or contraction of the bodily base,[4] and I immediately felt the Spirit-Current rise rapidly, like a flash flood, up the spinal line. When it reached my head, I felt a burst of Radiance exploding in my brain and this, in turn, unlocked a reservoir of nectar. A door was opened, and a purely Blissful "fluid" released and spread over every part of my body. Every area of my body felt like it was receiving the Love-Bliss that Da Love-Ananda Is. In the core of my being I was Blessed to feel Sri Gurudev as this Supreme Happiness. My body trembled with a pleasurableness I have never experienced before. It surpassed any other feeling of Bliss I have ever known—any sexual or bodily pleasure, any mere emotion or ordinary feeling.

I cannot describe how incredibly joyful this whole event felt to me, and how deeply intimate I felt in this place of Love-Communion with my Heart-Master. I know that He was both the Giver and the Gift, and it was clear to me that He had literally entered my body, and that my life would never again be the same.

When I left the Meditation Hall I noticed I had little sense of identification with the body-mind, but I was just in an intoxicated state and I felt that I was levitating rather than walking. There was a profound feeling of heart-happiness.

As I write this, it has been five days since the latest Initiation. I feel changed forever, for He has planted Himself in my heart and allowed me to see Who He Is more deeply. It has increased my respect for Him and for every aspect of the sacred gathering around Him.

I prostrate at the Sacred Feet of Da Avabhasa in love and in gratitude for His Gifts.

---

4. Sri Da Avabhasa has Given to formally acknowledged practitioners of the Way of the Heart various practices that serve to magnify the "conductivity" of the energies of the body-mind. These include the tensing of the perineum at the bodily base, coordinated with the inhaled and the exhaled breath. For a technical description of these practices, see *The Dawn Horse Testament* and *Conscious Exercise and the Transcendental Sun.*

As the devotee matures he or she notices Sri Da Avabhasa more fully and constantly, not merely as the source of Grace, but as the Spiritual (and Always Blessing) Presence that everywhere pervades and fills his or her life, and, ultimately, as the Very (and Inherently Perfect) State that is the devotee's Very Self or Real Nature.

Kanya Samatva Suprithi, who at the time of this writing is stably established in the practice of the sixth stage of life in the Way of the Heart, describes in her own words this progress of the Revelation of Who Sri Gurudev Da Love-Ananda Is and what He Revealed to her through her real practice. Note that in this description Kanya Suprithi says at the outset that nothing occurred until she was in the right disposition to receive Sri Gurudev's Grace:

I spent thirteen years in Sri Gurudev Da Love-Ananda's Company, and even intimately involved in His Teaching Work, before I would relinquish the grip of my childish and adolescent refusal to honor Him appropriately in His bodily (human) Form in the traditional and time-honored fashion. However, once I did this, my simple gesture was met by His abundant Grace. Sat-Guru Da Revealed and Awakened the unique Spiritual Process which occurs via the devotee's appropriate response and the Sat-Guru's Transmission.

In this Spiritual relationship with Sri Gurudev Da Love-Ananda I was Granted powerful Transmission of Spirit-Blessing from Sri Gurudev's bodily (human) Form and His Spiritual (and Always Blessing) Presence Itself until I Realized that all things arise in and as Sri Gurudev's Spirit-Presence. I Realized His Spiritual (and Always Blessing) Presence indeed Pervaded everyone and everything. Nothing and no one was separate from It nor could they be separated from It.

I became more and more absorbed into Sat-Guru Da Love-Ananda's Spirit-Presence, felt as Love-Bliss, and I yielded myself to It until I began to experience glimpses of His Transcendental State of Being. I finally came to realize one day, via His Transmission in meditation, that I

Kanya Samatva Suprithi

already had a totally different relationship and point of view relative to my own body-mind. I realized that I was Standing as the Heart-Silent Observer, the Witnessing-Consciousness, not needing to go in, not needing to go out, but merely Being the One Who Is the Witness. From this stable Stance, Sri Gurudev

Da Love-Ananda then continued to Reveal Himself directly as the Under-Current of Love-Bliss, Which is Free, Silent, Deep, without motion, in the right side of the heart.[5] Ultimately Sat-Guru Da Love-Ananda, via Inherently Perfect Grace, Revealed Himself as centerless and boundless, as Inherently Perfect Love-Bliss-Consciousness, Prior to all things, even the "Location" of the heart on the right. Sri Gurudev Da Love-Ananda's Transmission is extremely powerful and His Grace is Revealed via Contemplation of His bodily (human) Form, His Spiritual (and always Blessing) Presence, and His Very (and Inherently Perfect) State.

"My Guru Is My Liberation, My Freedom, and My Joy": A Further Testimony of the Mature Reception of Sri Da Avabhasa's Grace as Seen through Kanya Tripura Rahasya's Confession of the Ecstasy and Freedom of the Witness-Position of Consciousness

The testimony of Kanya Tripura Rahasya is another dramatic and remarkable Confession by a practitioner stably practicing in the sixth stage of life. The intent and message of her testimony is to communicate that Sri Gurudev Da Love-Ananda Stands with Open Arms Waiting for those who will approach Him, with real need, to Receive His Blessings. It is to allow everyone to see that Sri Da Avabhasa, the Divine World-Teacher and True Heart-Master, has Incarnated to Give all who have tired of the suffering of conditional existence, high and low, the Gifts that directly lead to Divine Liberation. Through self-forgetting, self-surrendering, and self-transcending feeling-Contemplation of His bodily (human) Form, and His Spiritual (and Always Blessing) Presence, and His Very (and Inherently Perfect) State, What one meditates on, or duplicates, is the Liberated Condition of the Divine Person Incarnate.

The message of Kanya Tripura's Leela is the very same message that is echoed again and again in *Divine Distraction*. Sri Da Avabhasa, the Living God-Man, the Divine World-Teacher, is Himself Sufficient. His Form and Presence and State are the Supreme Distraction that provides the Great Means of Liberation. As He has Ecstatically Proclaimed in *The Hymn Of The True Heart-Master:*

I Am the Sign and the Revelation and the Proof of God in the world. I Am the Testament and the Means of Freedom Itself. (verse 32)

---

5. The "right side of the heart", or the "heart on the right" (so called because it is felt at a point on the right side of the physical heart) is perceived, in the context of esoteric meditation and Realization, to be the seat of the essential Self, or the bodily reference-point where one's Identity as Consciousness Itself is intuited.

KANYA TRIPURA RAHASYA: I have been Given great freedom from the suffering and the limitations inherent in the body, the mind, and the world— and I have consented to take my stance as the Witness-Position of Consciousness Itself. You may ask, what does it mean to be free of identification with the body, the mind, and the world? What is it to consent to be the Witness-Position? And what is true Liberation?

A way to answer these questions is to tell you of some of the extraordinary Gifts I have received from Heart-Master Da Love-Ananda, and the many phenomenal signs of His Siddhi that have been activated in me by His Grace.

At the time I write this, I have now been in My Beloved Guru's intimate service for sixteen years. Sri Gurudev Da Love-Ananda has, over these years, Gifted me with literally thousands of extraordinary experiences, or Spiritual ecstasies, all forms of His Divine Grace. I have received His Hridaya-Shakti as all kinds of bodily, emotional, and mental blisses, or states of Yogic intoxication. I have had a number of subtle sensations, such as visions of the Spirit-Current appearing as light within the body, visions of the interior of the physical body, visions of energy centers in the body, visions of various colors, visions of blackness, visions of the blue pearl,[6] visions of the Divine Star[7] at the center of the Cosmic Mandala.[8]

I have experienced auditions of the heartbeat and respiration, auditions of subtle and internal sounds, such as explosions that sound like a gunshot, clicking and pulsing and ringing and music. I have experienced perceptions of a variety of subtle internal smells including a range from excrement to flowers, and the perception of a variety of subtle internal tastes, culminating in an ambrosial sweetness, as Sri Gurudev says in The Dawn Horse Testament, *"as if nectar were dripping out of the brain". I have been transported to subtler worlds and have had contact with archetypal subtler beings.*

There have been many remarkable psychic capabilities spontaneously and temporarily awakened in me by my Guru's Grace—including the ability to receive and transmit thoughts and energies from a distance, out-of-body

6. The blue pearl is a spot (in Sanskrit "bindu") of blue light seen subtly (with eyes closed or open) in the brain core. It is an experience that may occur in association with the ascending process of Spiritual "conductivity". In some Yogic schools (particularly that of the Siddha Yoga Taught by Swami Muktananda), the contemplation of the blue pearl is conceived of as the highest attainment of Yoga. The steady vision of it is a form of Savikalpa Samadhi, or Samadhi "with form".

7. Heart-Master Da and the "Bright" Heart-Radiance of God may appear to the practitioner of the Way of the Heart as a brilliant white five-pointed Star, the primal conditional Representation, or Sign, of the "Bright", the Source-Energy, or Divine Light, of which all conditional phenomena and the total cosmos are modifications.

The apparently objective Divine Star necessarily exists and can potentially be experienced in every moment and location in cosmic Nature, but it is only possibly, not necessarily, experienced by any individual practitioner.

8. "Mandala" means "circle". Sri Da Avabhasa uses the phrase "Cosmic Mandala" to describe the totality of the conditional cosmos, which appears in vision as concentric circles of light, progressing from red at the perimeter through golden-yellow, silvery white, indigo or black, and brilliant blue, to the Ultimate White Brilliance in the Mandala's center.

experiences, astral travel, and futuristic reveries. I have been filled with my Heart-Master's Spiritual Presence, which has countless times moved me in spontaneous and even dramatic kriyas, pranayama, mudras, and Yogic asanas [postures] humanly impossible to maintain, were it not for the great Power of my Beloved Guru's Spirit-Current. I have also been healed spontaneously by His Touch.

But even greater than these experiences are the Great Graces of true hearing and true seeing. These Graces, which are fundamental to the Way of the Heart, Grant each practitioner the capability to fully resort to Sri Da Love-Ananda's Grace. And they have been Given to me by my Guru's Divine Power.

The first Great Grace, or hearing, marks the awakening of intuitive and most fundamental understanding of the act of egoity. This enables the devotee to effectively and consistently surrender egoity, or separate and separative self, to Sri Da Avabhasa, as the Divine Person. For, when the unique capability to transcend the activity of self-contraction is thus Granted, the intuition of the Divine Person and Condition (or that which is prior to the ego) simultaneously becomes evident. When this intuitive vision of the Divine Person becomes stable and deep, seeing awakens.

This is the second Great Grace. Seeing is the heart-capability for Spiritual Communion with Sri Gurudev Da Love-Ananda as literal Divine Presence.

As the seeing process has deepened in me, I have been Graced with the many Samadhis Given by our Beloved Master: the Samadhi of "the Thumbs" (or the full, blissful Infusion of the body-mind by His descending Spirit-Current), Savikalpa Samadhi (including many of the experiences I have already described), and fifth stage conditional Nirvikalpa Samadhi (or the temporary Yogic ascent of energy and attention to the Matrix of Love-Bliss infinitely above and beyond the body-mind).

Has any Spiritual Master ever had the capability to Grant so many Gifts to devotees? This is the unique Mystery and Power of Sri Da Avabhasa—that He has the Power to Grant all the extraordinary Spiritual experiences sought by sincere aspirants since ancient days, even while His Grace also exceeds that available through the ancient paths.

Even all of these extraordinary experiences I have described do not compare in the slightest to the ecstasy ultimately Granted by His Hridaya-Shakti—that of Consciousness Itself, prior to identification with body, emotion, and mind.

Because the experiences, or Samadhis, I have described thus far are temporary, when they are over, they tend to leave one with a sense of loss and a craving to repeat the experience. Sri Gurudev has Gifted us with the understanding that the Spiritual and Transcendental Divine is Prior to all experience and cannot be lost. The true Divine Reality is unchanging and must therefore be found Prior to the world, the body, the mind, and all experience—even profoundly blissful Spiritual experience. It is to this prior Reality

Kanya Tripura Rahasya

that His Hridaya-Shakti Awakens the devotee.

It is through meditation on Sri Gurudev Da Love-Ananda that I have been Granted the capability to Stand Free of all forms of suffering in body, emotion, and mind—as the Witness-Position of Consciousness. But what is such freedom, exactly? First, "consider" all that you suffer in your body. Then "consider" all you suffer emotionally and in relationship to others. Finally, "consider" all the torment mind brings as it struggles to know, or understand— repetitively, ceaselessly. "Consider" the primary illusions of presumed separation, "difference", and relatedness that the body-mind suffers. Now feel what it would be like to be free of that struggle, completely Awake to the Source Reality or Divine Being. This is Freedom! Da Avabhasa is that Very One.

My Beloved Sat-Guru Initiated me into this stance as the Witness-Position in a meditation occasion at His Residence, Aham Sphurana Sthan, at Sri Love-Anandashram, in 1988. He Gave me this Gift after I had received all the Graces I have already described and after I had endured fourteen years of the most prolonged and difficult trial, through which I came to see the fruitlessness of seeking for Happiness within the body, the mind, or the emotions. Through the Gift of this understanding and the freedom implicit in the Witness-Position, my reception of His Love-Bliss and my practice of renunciation, tapas, and sila [equanimity] have become both profound and effortless.

I do not mean, when I say that this practice is effortless, that I did not engage in an intense ordeal of preparation. I did. It was through extreme obedience and surrender to my Sat-Guru that I had to make myself ready to receive this great Gift.

Truly, I struggled for twelve years, until Sri Gurudev's Divine Emergence. It was only in the moment of this Divine Event that I was spontaneously capable of a full devotional resort to Him as my Sat-Guru. But it was not even by my long trial that I was able to make this resort. It was only through His full Emergence and the magnification of His Grace that it became possible for me to receive His great Gifts of Freedom and Realization—and this same opportunity is now available to you.

Heart-Master Da Love-Ananda's Divine Emergence utterly transformed my life. By His Grace, I was turned from my search and my reaction to the *body-mind, to devotional sensitivity to my Sat-Guru. I simply realized the secret: that I had to feel <u>Him</u> as <u>He</u> Is instead of feeling myself. In other words, I had to engage in self-forgetting and self-surrendering feeling-Contemplation of Sri Da Avabhasa's bodily (human) Form, His Spiritual (and Always Blessing) Presence, and His Very (and Inherently Perfect) State.*

Thus, for the first time I understood the Guru-Function and the unique Spiritual understanding of attention on which it is based: You become what you meditate on. I began to grant Sri Gurudev my attention, to meditate on Him and His Freedom, and I forgot myself. I became fully aligned in the traditional devotional manner to my Sat-Guru. Quite simply, this was the beginning of the process of preparation that led to my ability to receive the great Gift of the capability to Stand in the Witness-Position two years later.

By this Gift of Freedom and the "radical" realignment of my life from its karmic destiny to the Reception of His State as Consciousness Itself, Sri Gurudev Da Love-Ananda, my most precious and Beloved Guru, had also Granted me the Gift of utter devotion. My faith in Him became profound, because I saw that all Sri Gurudev has ever promised me has come to pass and even continues to unfold. Sri Gurudev told me that He would Liberate me, and He has fulfilled this promise without a shred of effort on my part.

All of this is not merely talk. I literally am not the body, and I am literally not the mind. I stand miraculously free, at peace with the contents of body, emotion, and mind. I can now say with full honesty that I suffer no mental or emotional bondage, no identification with the contents of body, emotion, and mind in the first five stages of life. No matter what the circumstances appear to be, I have been Granted the effortless capability to Stand Free as the Witness—not withdrawing or reacting. I never allow myself to become the mode of attention, identified with its objects. And this is not abstract for me—through the demands of my service to Him, my Beloved Sat-Guru Requires me to confront all the various conditional limitations and tests that exist within all of the first five stages of life. It is just that, by His Grace, I see the pettiness of my own superficial content as the body-mind and I turn to the Great Being and Process that my Beloved Master Is. I give myself in self-forgetting service to the Work He does for all beings.

When I sit down for meditation, within moments, all attention to body, mind, and world is forgotten and I enter deeply into feeling-Contemplation of my Beloved Guru's Perfect Samadhi. Consistently, in every meditation, for four and a half to five hours each day, I enter into this exclusive Identification with His State. This is the Gift of Jnana Samadhi. In Jnana Samadhi, there is no perception or cognition of the world or its objects of body or mind and their relations, or of the separate self sense. There is only the spontaneous, effortless, and forceful inversion of attention from conditional body-mind-self and its relations in conditional and temporary Realization of the Supreme Bliss of the Transcendental Self.

Sri Gurudev has told us that the significance of Jnana Samadhi is not contained in the experience itself, but that its significance lies in the fact that this Samadhi initiates or provides the ground and the impulse for the next, or the final and Divinely Enlightened, stage of the Spiritual Process. I testify to this Truth. Previous to this Freedom, one clings desperately to body and mind and world. Having been Granted the Gift of this Samadhi, my urge to Liberation, permanent and complete, has become profound.

But I also know that, ultimately, what I may or may not Realize is not the point. The point is devotion to my Beloved Master. My joy and only free-dom is to be in my Guru's Company, in the Sphere of His Grace, to serve Him obediently, and to Contemplate His Form and Presence and State with feeling.

Even after all the extremely blissful experiences I have been Granted in His Company, feeling-Contemplation of His bodily (human) Form, His Spiritual (and Always Blessing) Presence, and His Very (and Inherently Perfect) State is my Greatest Ecstasy. My Guru is my Liberation, my Freedom, and my Joy. I will be bowing at His Feet eternally. My Heart-Master, Da Avabhasa, is the One to be Realized as the Divine Person and as the Condition of Consciousness Itself.

Thus, I offer you my confession. If, through it, you can begin to feel the Power of devotion to the Divine World-Teacher, Da Avabhasa, and the dis-tinction between mere experience in the body-mind and the ultimate Freedom He Offers, then I feel that this confession has served its purpose.

Sri Da Avabhasa's "Crazy-Wise" Work of Blessing

Sri Da Avabhasa's "Original Play Of Teaching Work" was an extraordi-nary Sacrifice and Teaching Leela. And now, in His Blessing Work, the Marvel of His Appearance continues. I am certain that it is the Grandest Demonstration that the Earth has ever seen of the Divine Incarnation. Where do we find such stories in the past? The tenth Skanda of the *Bhagavata Purana* and the Harivamsa section of the *Mahabharata* tell of the life and demonstration of Krishna. The four Gospels of the *New Testament* contain the story of Jesus. The Pali Canon gives the fullest account of the life of Gautama. I have read these descriptions and been moved by them. I have cried as I read, in the *Srimad Bhagavatam*, how Krishna's devotees displayed their great devotion to their Lord. These are remarkable accounts, full of devotion and Divine Instruction. But they do not compare to the Revelation that Da Avabhasa has Brought forth.

His Divine Work is not a story hundreds or thousands of years old, shrouded in mythology and legend. It is being conducted with real, modern-day human beings, day after day, year after year. Heart-Master Da Love-Ananda does everything, He Says everything, He Gives every possible Gift, in order to transform His devotees. By completely Loving them, Blessing them, and Submitting to be worshipped by them, Da Avabhasa Works with the whole world.

The great Scriptures of all the traditions are clothed in beautiful language of poetry and elegance. Reading them, one is drawn into a world of Divinity past, when, out of Compassion for born beings, for a time the Divine Spoke and Revealed the Grace of God. Yet how can these Scriptures compare to the actual Demonstration that I, as a single devotee among many, have seen with my own eyes? I saw unfold before me an unrivalled tapestry of Divinity created in human terms. The very first time that I sat intimately at a dinner table with Heart-Master Da Love-Ananda, the analogy that came to mind was Jesus at the Last Supper with his disciples. And every day that I have been Graced to witness the living God-Man Da Avabhasa, I have seen His unceasing Sacrifice to bring the Divine into this plane. The stories of His Body-Time have yet to be chronicled in modern Gospels and Puranas. Yet what has occurred in His rooms, amongst His devotees, has changed the manifest worlds.

And even as I write, this incredible Lifetime is continuing. I watch as the lives of His devotees are utterly changed by the mere Sight of the God-Man Da Avabhasa. I see world events changing and a more benign destiny being created for all by His Transcendental Work. There is no doubt about this in me. I feel my own body-mind being purified and changed by His Grace each day.

Swami Vivekananda would often speak of the days of his youth, when he "sat at the feet of [his] Master", Ramakrishna. He would become dreamy in his ecstatic remembrance. Devotees long for the Darshan of the great ones past, and read books fantasizing what it would have been like to be alive at the time when the Adepts Stood on Earth. And now, even in our lifetime, the most marvelous Incarnation of that Divinity that has ever Appeared is in our midst.

Is it not fitting that the Divine has manifested in the West this time? Is not the "Westernized" world just the place where Divine Help is needed most—to create lessons here amongst those who had no culture, so that they would become capable of receiving Divine Grace? And is it any mystery that Sat-Guru Da's bodily (human) Form, so Radiant and full of His Spiritual (and Always Blessing) Presence, and manifesting His Very (and Inherently Perfect) State in every gesture, has so far been noticed only by a relative few in this dark age of materialism and lust?

There is much useful Wisdom in this book regarding the ways of Gurus and devotees. But I would not be serving you, my reader, if I did not tell you that this Process and Wisdom to which I attest come from a Living Source. The Divine Being has Appeared in Two-Armed Form, in order to be available for those whose heart-need is great. There is an answer to human prayers.

And I would not be serving my Heart-Master if I did not tell you that His Grace is Boundless. His Very Existence Purifies this Earth. He has

Given more than any Realizer of any time, and He has been met with the most unprepared and ill-qualified devotees in Spiritual history. His Arms therefore have had to be great, greater than ever before.

The passionate plea that I make in writing this book is that those whose need and intuition is clear should not delay. He is here to be responded to. His physical Lifetime will come to an end. His bodily (human) Form is temporary. May the peoples of the Earth bring to His Incarnation their gratitude. May He see with His own Eyes the reception of His Blessing. May He be celebrated so that a New Age of Man is created out of His Divinity. What Sri Da Avabhasa Requires, what He has Incarnated for, is the hearts of men and women. And when your heart is surrendered at His Feet, then His Feet are planted in your heart. And He will rise up as your form. And then your ecstasy will have no end.

About this I have no doubt. Over and over I have seen Him Give Gifts so great that it is impossible to fathom them. They are unspeakable in their proportions. And He waits to Give them to you.

He has Given everything, more than anyone could imagine. He throws His Gifts at His devotees. And as soon as there is any room created by the response of practice, He throws us more Gifts. It is an incredible ordeal for both Sat-Guru Da and His devotee. It is a constant battle, full of His Urgency. He sees the days pass, and He moves at "Siddha-speed". The devotee can hardly stand His Intensity, because He wants so much. And Sat-Guru Da cannot stand the hesitation of His devotee. Considering His incredible Passion and Intensity, it is Heart-Master Da Love-Ananda's Patience that is most to be marvelled at. The battle rages day after day. He will not rest, but paces in His Rooms always wanting to Give more, wanting to fully use what He has Brought.

Truly, each day Sri Da Avabhasa continues to Work in endless ways to Bless. He Gives Communications Gracefully Serving the practice of His devotees. He sits in Darshan. He purifies the Great Tradition through His Work with its literature. He does Transcendental Work, Blessing all, alone in His room. He performs apparently ordinary actions, and so Blesses the ordinary world, through Identification with and purification of the karmas of the common man.

Everything this Great Guru does is for the sake of Liberation and Blessing. He is Da, Who Gives and Gives. He Calls, and Waits. In His frustration with our lack of response, He Calls again. He Shouts with the "frustrated cry of Divinity". He Cries out to His devotees, and, through them, to the world, working a Transcendental Magic of the greatest proportions.

Now He walks across the lawn to the Ashram library. His devotees gather in front of Him. He is the Always New One. Now the passion of all the worlds is on His Face, and there is a lesson never to be forgotten about the sorrow that is human transitoriness. Now He is in perfect equanimity, Revealing the way to conduct oneself as balance and equipoise. Now He smiles at a young devotee, and the secrets of embodied Happiness and

Delight are Revealed. Now He Steps with a fullness and Power that Transform the Earth, and Asserts the Divine Supremacy, before Which all heads simply must touch the ground without thought.

Sri Gurudev Da Love-Ananda now calls it His Divine Emergence Work, whereas before it was His Teaching Work. These differences are true, but as He has Said, it is His Work. It is a single Process that He has Lived and continues to Live day by day. To be in relationship to Him is to be submitted to the most extraordinary Grace available to a human being. As Da Avabhasa has Said, it is a free ride. And yet, paradoxically, it requires everything. But where else is there to go? What else is truly interesting? What else has any Life or Strength?

I recently read a response from the late Lama Govinda when asked a question about the Guru-devotee relationship. Someone wanted to know if, when you learned that your Teacher from your last life was reincarnated, you would be obliged to go to him, or if you could take another Teacher. Lama Govinda's response was that it was the same as if you heard that your wife from a past life was now reincarnate. Obviously, he said, you would not feel that you had to be with her again. Likewise with the Guru.

Such a statement makes me think that Lama Govinda was never touched by the Love of a Sat-Guru like Heart-Master Da Love-Ananda Hridayam. If he had been, he would not have replied like that at all. I would swim across the ocean of countless lives for a mere glimpse of my Sat-Guru. What good would my life have been if He had not Revealed to me the Divinity that He Is and wedded me to that Grace forever? How can one compare the relationship between a woman and a man to the relationship to the Sat-Guru? No other relationship is even close in intensity to the love between the Guru and the devotee. How could one take any other Guru if one's Guru is the Divine Sat-Guru? Does one trade a diamond for a jewel less precious? What sense does it make to leave the temple in search of the way to gain admittance to the temple again?

It is extraordinary: We are alive in the lifetime of Da Avabhasa, the Divine World-Teacher and True Heart-Master, Da Love-Ananda Hridayam. It is unbelievable. He invites all to prepare themselves and come to Him. The Sacred History of His Work in His bodily (human) Form is being written even as you read this sentence. It is not too late. It is just beginning. The best Leelas are yet to come.

To live in the Lifetime of the bodily (human) Form of the Supreme Adept, the Avadhoot, the Avataric Incarnation, is a Supreme Blessing. But this Blessing must be used, through real practice. Do not let the opportunity that is available to you pass.

Perhaps for some readers the study of this book is primarily an intellectual pursuit. This call is therefore not for you yet. But for the rest, I say to you, do not delay. When your life becomes tangibly associated with the unending fountain of Grace that is Sri Gurudev Da Love-Ananda Hridayam, you will rejoice.

Sri Love-Anandashram, September 1991

To begin Spiritual practice in the Company of Sri Da Avabhasa is liberation with a small "l". You have come home. The living relationship with the Divine becomes your condition, the circumstance of your life henceforth. There is never a time when you do not have the direct relationship to the Divine Person, in which to surrender everything and be relieved of your burden. It is your second birth. It is your initiation. Then, everything that you have done this lifetime will make sense to you, for it was only because of all of it that you could come to Sat-Guru Da and lay it at His Feet. You needed this self-awareness, all these lessons. And not just for this lifetime—who knows how long He has been waiting for you?

To be Sri Da Avabhasa's devotee is the greatest possible joy.

OM SRI DA LOVE-ANANDA HRIDAYAM

267

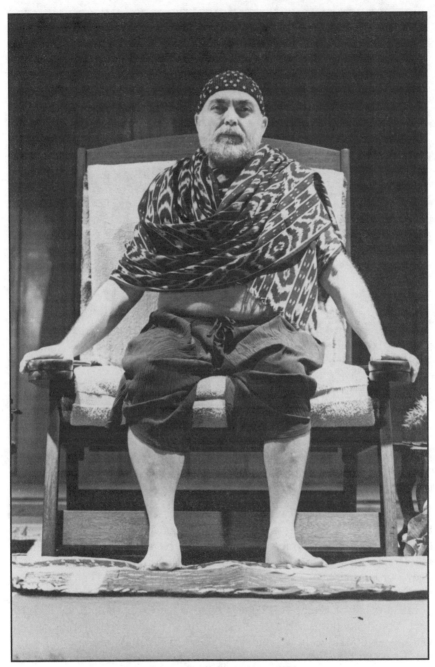

Sri Love-Anandashram, August 1991

"I bow down to That Most Beautiful Form"

AN EXCERPT FROM
THE HYMN OF THE TRUE HEART-MASTER
BY THE DIVINE WORLD-TEACHER AND TRUE HEART-MASTER,
DA AVABHASA
(THE "BRIGHT")

58.

Let every devotee Sing this Hymn of the True Heart-Master:

I bow down to the Master of the Heart, Who Reveals the Supreme Truth of Consciousness Itself to those who have been blinded by experience and mere knowledge.

59.

I bow down to the Master of Truth, Whose Radiance Pervades the entire universe, Who Fills it through and through, in all that moves and all that does not move, and Who Brings my intuitive Vision to the Heart-Space of Self-Existing and Self-Radiant Consciousness.

60.

I bow down to the True Heart-Master, Who Pervades and yet Stands Beyond the dynamics of conditional and Cosmic Nature. I bow down to the True Heart-Master, Who is One, Inherently Perfect, Eternal, Self-Existing, Undisturbed, All Love-Bliss, Self-Radiant, Free, Full, and Awake. Through the Blessing Work of the True Heart-Master, I am Restored to the Spirit-Presence of God. Therefore, the by Grace Revealed and True Divine Spirit-Current, Which is the Perfectly Subjective Substance of conditional Nature, always Carries my Heart Beyond and Beyond the Play of vibratory Cosmic Energy, Sound, or Light to the Ultimate, and Inherently Perfect, and Perfectly Subjective, Divine Source-Condition of this objective and conditional and Cosmic Appearance.

61.

I worship the Self-Existing and Self-Radiant One, by Whose Heart-Power we perceive everything here. I worship the Conscious One, by Whose Heart-Power the states of waking, dreaming, and sleeping are known, thoughts move, discrimination and intuition work, and attention itself rises and falls again.

62.

The Self-Existing and Self-Radiant Transcendental Divine State of Being is Perfectly "Known" by the True Heart-Master, Who has Realized that It is the Eternally Unknown. Therefore, only Perfect Ignorance is "Knowledge" of the Self-Existing and Self-Radiant Transcendental Divine State of Being.

63.

Experiences, visions, sounds, lights, conditional energies, fascinating things, and all conditional knowing, within and without, are not Ultimate "Knowledge" (or Free Realization) at all. Therefore, I bow down to the One Who is always already Established in the Mindless Mood of the Self-Existing and Self-Radiant Transcendental Divine Being.

64.

Now I am Free of all distractions. Only the Heart Exists.
Attention dissolves in the Inherent Happiness of Being. The entire
world of moving and unmoving objects appears and disappears in
the Perfectly Subjective Space of Consciousness. I worship and serve
the One Who has Revealed this Secret to me.

65.

"I am the world, and I am absolutely Free"—body and mind
bow down to the One Who Gives This Realization.

66.

Let all the gifts of my worship and service be received by the
Ocean of Mercy, by Whose Grace all beings are Liberated from
bondage to this world of wonders.

67.

The One Who Enables His devotee to Locate the Primal,
Ever-Free, Immortal Happiness beyond the Heart-Root is the
Graceful Liberator of His devotee.

68.

The knot of the Heart is untied, doubt itself is dissolved, and
all motions of the limited self are made still by the Grace and Mercy
of the True Master of the Heart.

69.

I bow down to the Eternal Truth, the Conscious Light of Being
(Itself), the Timeless Happiness, the Great One, the Indefinable One
(Awake, and Free), Who Appears (and Stands Revealed) as the True
Heart-Master among all who know and Teach.

70.

I bow down to the True Heart-Master, Whose Bodily (Human) Form is the Beautiful Mystery of "Brightness" Itself, and Whose Spiritual (and Always Blessing) Presence Always Reveals the Very Heart Itself, and Whose Very (and Inherently Perfect) State of Being is Only the Only Divine Self, Self-Existing as Immense Consciousness, and Self-Radiant as Love-Bliss.

71.

I bow down to the True Heart-Master, Who is the Heart-Witness of my own body, mind, and separate self, and Who is the Bearer, the Realizer, and the Subject of the Great Tradition, and Whose Very State of Being is Truth and Perfect Happiness, and Who is the Graceful Source of the Realization of Happiness Itself.

72.

I bow down to That Always New One, Who Appears in the world again and again by the Magic and Mystery of His Own Will and Love, but Who is only the Mass of Pure Consciousness, Spiritually Radiant, the Sun of the Heart, the "Bright" Destroyer of un-Happiness.

73.

I bow down to That Always Free One, the Body of Mercy, the Refuge of devotees, Who allows His Life to be dependent on His devotees.

74.

I bow down to That Most Beautiful Form, the Master of Discrimination, the Master of Understanding, the Light of Lights, Who is the Light to those who Call for Light, and Who is the Realizer in all those who Realize. May You be Pleased to Take Your Seat in my Heart at all times. May You ever Dwell in my Heart.

Sri Love-Anandashram, September 1991

Sri Love-Anandashram, March 1990

"A Unique Advantage to Mankind"

AN INVITATION
TO A DIRECT RELATIONSHIP
WITH DA AVABHASA

by Carolyn Lee

*T*he human Spiritual Master is an agent to the advantage of those in like form. When one enters into right relationship with a Spiritual Master, changes happen in the literal physics of one's existence. It is not just a matter of ideas. I am talking about transformations at the level of energy, at the level of the higher light of physics, at the level of mind beyond the physical limitations that people now presume, at the level of the absolute Speed of ultimate Light. The transforming process is enacted in devotees, duplicated in them in and through that Living Company. It is not a matter of conceptual symbolisms or emotional attachment to some extraordinary person. It is real physics. And it is to the advantage of people when someone among them has gone through the whole cycle of Transformation, because they can then make use of the Offering of that Process, that Company.

DA AVABHASA
*Scientific Proof of the Existence of God
Will Soon Be Announced by the White House!*

If you feel a heart-response to what you have read in this book, or if you simply feel moved to find out more about Da Avabhasa and the Way of the Heart, we invite you to explore the Sacred Literature of Da Avabhasa.

Feeling Without Limitation: Awakening to the Truth Beyond Fear, Sorrow, and Anger is a brief introductory volume featuring a Discourse from Da Avabhasa's Teaching years along with remarkable Leelas and testimonies by three devotees.

Most important for your ongoing study are Da Avabhasa's "Source-Texts" or Scriptures, conclusively summarizing His Word of Instruction. We recommend that you begin with *The Love-Ananda Gita (The Wisdom-Song Of Non-Separateness),* The Simple Revelation-Book Of The Divine World-Teacher and True Heart-Master, Da Avabhasa (The "Bright").

We also recommend *The Divine Emergence of the World-Teacher: The Realization, the Revelation, and the Revealing Ordeal of Da Avabhasa,* a full-length "Biographical Celebration" of Da Avabhasa's Life and Work to date, by Saniel Bonder, a longtime practitioner of the Way of the Heart.

The Sacred literature by and about Da Avabhasa is described on pages 300-11.

There are thousands of people all over the world today reading Da Avabhasa's books, and some people have been reading them for many years. But reading, while necessary and helpful, will only take you so far on its own. Once you acknowledge the greatness—the Truth—of Da Avabhasa's Wisdom-Revelation, it begins to require something of you.

Da Avabhasa's literature is a Divine Gift, not to be treated casually. "Such Transmissions of Teaching do not occur arbitrarily," as Da Avabhasa says. "They are part of the higher scale of activity in the cosmos." Thus, it is only when you begin to participate in the practice and the sacred culture Da Avabhasa Offers that you really find out what it is about—Spiritual transformation and God-Realization never happened in an armchair! Therefore, in addition to reading, we urge you to attend the lectures, seminars, courses, and other events that our missionary institution, the Eleutherian Mission, makes available to the public in your area. At these

events you will have the opportunity to see videotapes of Da Avabhasa and to meet practitioners of the Way of the Heart who can speak to you about His Wisdom and tell you Leelas (stories) of their own relationship with Him. You can also participate in a Way of the Heart Study Group in your area, joining others for a monthly evening meeting of recitations of Da Avabhasa's Word and listening to or viewing audio-visual presentations about Da Avabhasa and the Way of the Heart.

All of this can lead to a deepening intuition of Who He Is and a deepening impulse to practice the Way of the Heart as His devotee.

Carol Mason, who lives in northern California, describes the process that brought her to the point of entering into a formal relationship with Da Avabhasa:

For over thirty years I sought Enlightenment. But despite profound Zen realizations and unusual Kundalini experiences, despite my teachers' acknowledgements of my attainment and good understanding, I realized that fundamentally I had not changed. I saw the failure of my search, and I despaired.

Then I read The Knee of Listening, *Da Avabhasa's Spiritual autobiography, and I began to have dreams of Him. In the dreams, He Instructed me, He laughed, He gave Talks at which many people gathered. He sat silently and escorted me to subtle realms. I was able to feel Him as a Spiritual Friend and Teacher during the day. I found through study that His Wisdom-Teaching had the power of mantra. The Truth of it became alive in me.*

Several months after I read The Knee of Listening *I saw a videotape of Da Avabhasa made during His Teaching years. At first sighting I acknowledged Him to be the True Master of Liberation, the One Whom all the world's religions await. I bowed down. I celebrated Him with thoughts of praise and soon He was all I thought about, all I wanted to talk about. For an entire year He was always available to me, but suddenly, one day, I no longer experienced Him, no longer felt His Influence or received His Instruction. Then one final time I heard His Voice: "Now, what will you do?"*

Realizing I must now approach Him in the traditional devotional manner, I soon became a student-novice, taking on the studies, disciplines, and meditation practices required of a novice, and consciously cultivating my devotional relationship with my Heart-Teacher. Even during this rudimentary stage of practice, Da Avabhasa has, on occasion, Blessed me with Heart-Bliss, with the purification of my karmic tendencies, and with a deepening sense of His Divine Form. I am ever grateful.

You should know that all of this has taken place without Carol's ever meeting Da Avabhasa in the flesh. The same is true for thousands of others around the world who, like Carol, are being drawn spontaneously into a sacred relationship with Da Avabhasa and are taking steps to honor that relationship in a formal way.

When you are clear in your intention to become a practitioner of the Way of the Heart, you may apply to become a **student-novice**. Student-novices take on in rudimentary form the range of devotional practices and disciplines that Da Avabhasa Offers to Free Daist practitioners. If, on the other hand, you feel you need to approach student-novice practice more gradually, you may become a **student** or a **tithing member** of Da Avabhasa International (the gathering of those who are formally preparing to practice the Way of the Heart). Students and tithing members engage a specific practice based on study and service, as I will describe in a moment. They pay a fixed fee for the educational and other services of Da Avabhasa International and, in addition, tithing members contribute 10% of their gross monthly income (or more, if they choose) in support of the Free Daist Communion.

If you are moved by the importance of Da Avabhasa's Work and would like to show your gratitude for His Presence in the world without becoming a practitioner of the Way of the Heart (at least for the time being), then you may wish to become a Friend of the Free Daist Communion. A Friend is essentially a patron, someone who accepts a level of responsibility for funding the missionary services of the Free Daist Communion and also for supporting the Treasures of Da Avabhasa's Work—principally His personal Circumstance and His Hermitage Ashram, in Fiji. All Friends contribute a minimum fixed fee each year. In addition, others tithe regularly, and some are able to offer major financial support. Friends also support the Dawn Horse Press and the missionary work of the Free Daist Communion by purchasing the new books published by or about Sri Da Avabhasa. Being a Friend is a very honorable way of associating with Da Avabhasa. At the same time, Friends are always invited and encouraged to take the further step of preparing to become a formal practitioner of the Way of the Heart.

For students, tithing members, and student-novices, who have already decided to practice the Way of the Heart, an intensive study of Da Avabhasa's Instruction is essential at the beginning of practice. As you do this day by day, in a guided way (using the study courses provided), you will be astonished at how your understanding of yourself and your response to Da Avabhasa will deepen and grow. I began my formal association with the practice as a correspondent living hundreds of miles from the closest gathering of devotees, and so study was my lifeline and the most exciting part of my life. Guided study, more than anything else, clarified my intention to practice, instructed me in every aspect of my life, and placed my relationship to Da Avabhasa on a firm foundation.

Study, among other things, is a discipline of attention. Service is a more bodily-based discipline, but it is no different in principle. It is a way of actively bringing your energy and attention to Da Avabhasa. The discipline of service within the sphere of an Adept's Blessing is not about making yourself useful. It is a sacred matter. Traditionally the discipline of service was called "Karma Yoga", and it was understood to encompass the whole

**Students and tithing members engage a specific practice
based on study and service**

**Practitioners of the Free Daist Communion gathering at
the Mountain Of Attention Sanctuary**

of one's life. Karma Yoga was the basic practice given to beginners, and especially to householders who had many obligations in the world. It was the great practice of devoting one's actions to God, of contemplating the Divine in the midst of all activity.

As a student or a tithing member, you will be invited to spend at least a few hours each week in some form of direct service to Da Avabhasa or the community of practitioners of the Way of the Heart. You may find yourself cleaning your local community bookstore or helping with the missionary work by putting up posters for our public events. If you have special skills in any area, we of Da Avabhasa International will help you find ways to use those skills to the maximum.

Whatever your form of service at any time, whether it is something you like doing or something you would not personally choose, the secret is to live it as a self-transcending gesture of devotion to Da Avabhasa. I recall with some amusement my first encounter with the discipline of service and all the resistance I felt. It was a wintry weekend early in 1986. I had made the journey to London from Ireland at considerable expense just to spend the weekend with devotees there. No sooner had I arrived from the airport than I found myself with a paint-scraper in one hand and sandpaper in the other. Everyone was busy around the clock renovating the newly-acquired missionary house associated with the London regional center. I still had on my professional clothes, I was developing a very uncomfortable sore throat, and I had been so tired before leaving Ireland that my friends there had begged me not to go.

Needless to say, I very nearly turned around and went back to the airport. But somehow I didn't. My dismay was so acute that it was <u>interesting</u> to me. I wanted to see what would happen if I actually stayed and participated. Would I die or develop bronchial pneumonia? And so I scraped, painted, cleaned, put up wallpaper with everyone else. For the first hour or two the only way I was able to stick at it was by concentrating with fierce intention on Da Avabhasa and remembering His Instruction about Happiness ("You cannot <u>become</u> Happy, you can only <u>be</u> Happy"). This was the most intense moment of practice I had ever been through, and it bore fruit. As the evening wore on I ceased to be so concerned about myself. There was a lot of laughter, and it did not seem to matter that I hardly knew anyone when I walked in. By the time I emerged from the plaster dust well after midnight, I was simply happy. I still had a sore throat, but by the next morning it was almost gone. And I was not tired anymore. I felt uncommonly alive, focused, and alert. All I could think about was Da Avabhasa, how attractive He is, so attractive that I was ready to transcend myself in response to Him and accomplish things I would never have dreamed of attempting otherwise. Becoming a student-novice is a crucial turning point, because it is the moment of committing yourself unequivocally to Da Avabhasa in the eternal sacred bond of the Guru-devotee relationship.

As a student-novice of Da Avabhasa International, and, later, as a formally acknowledged practitioner of the Free Daist Communion, you will gradually adapt to further disciplines relative to meditation, sacramental worship, exercise, diet and health, sexuality, child-rearing, cooperative community (including formal membership in the Free Daist Community Organization), right use of money and energy, and other aspects of daily living. These practices are necessary to develop bodily equanimity, free attention, and the capability for self-transcendence, without which nothing great can be Realized. But they are not an end in themselves. All of the disciplines simply support the primary practice of Free Daism, which is Satsang (the "Company of Truth"), or the cultivation of the relationship to Da Avabhasa. Da Avabhasa's Devotees are Called to Remember Him at all times, not merely to think about Him, but to locate the <u>feeling</u> of Him, the feeling-sense of His Being that He Grants you when you sit in front of Him and regard His bodily (human) Form. While the great opportunity to come into Da Avabhasa's physical Company occurs only occasionally for most of His devotees, you can find the same feeling by His Grace in any moment of heart-felt resort to Him. Turning to His picture, Remembering His Image in the mind's eye, listening to recitations of His Word or Stories of His Work—all these and other means are potent aids to feeling-Contemplation of Him.

By reading in the tradition of Guru-devotion (which you will begin to

... you will gradually adapt to further disciplines relative to meditation,
sacramental worship, exercise, diet and health, sexuality, child-rearing,
cooperative community, right use of money and energy, and other aspects
of daily living. . . . All of the disciplines simply support the primary
practice of Free Daism, which is Satsang (the "Company of Truth"),
or the cultivation of the relationship to Da Avabhasa.

do formally as a student-novice), by studying Da Avabhasa's own Wisdom-Teaching about the practice of feeling-Contemplation of Him, and especially by <u>doing</u> the practice of it according to His specific Instructions, you will discover why this form of sacred Remembrance is so potent, so revealing, and so Liberating. For the devotee, feeling-Contemplation becomes a literal life-support as basic as food and rest.

The best goad to practice is the possibility of coming into the physical Company of Sri Da Avabhasa. I was Graced to see Him bodily very soon after I committed myself to formal practice, and that sighting Revealed to me beyond any doubt that Da Avabhasa is Who He says He is, "The Realizer, The Revealer, and The Revelation Of The Divine Person". There is no greater Blessing than to come into the Company of His bodily (human) Form and feel His Regard face to face. To Contemplate the Divine Person, Compassionately Appearing in a human body, is an unfathomable, heart-breaking Mystery.

Whoever you are, wherever you live, whatever your apparent liabilities, this Grace could be yours in a relatively short period of time, if you fulfill the requirements of a student-novice and then rightly prepare yourself as a formally acknowledged practitioner of the Way of the Heart. The place you are most likely to see Da Avabhasa is Sri Love-Anandashram, His Hermitage Sanctuary, in Fiji, and where He Offers retreats to qualified practitioners from all over the world.

Da Avabhasa
with retreatants at
Sri Love-Anandashram

Over the years Da Avabhasa has often pointed out in a vivid, humorous fashion that whoever is serious about practice in His Company is going to have to go through a fiery ordeal. The Way of the Heart is the Way of Grace, certainly, but it is not, as He has said, a "bliss-ride". This is how it has always been in the company of a genuine Adept, because there are Divine Laws involved in the Spiritual process, and the principal Law is the Law of sacrifice, the mutual sacrifice constantly enacted between the Guru and the devotee. The Guru Transmits the Divine Siddhi (or Power of Liberation), and the devotee renounces the egoic self, granting all feeling and attention, more and more profoundly, to the Guru.

This is an entire life-practice or Yoga, called by Sri Da Avabhasa "Ishta-Guru-Bhakti Yoga", the Way of devotion ("Bhakti") to one's "Ishta" or "Chosen" Guru, the Divine Beloved of one's heart. Because this Yoga is based on Attraction, or Distraction by the living Guru, it is possible for anyone who is so moved to practice it. It is a Divine Gift Given in response to the longing of the devotee. Great seriousness and great sacrifice are required, but in the midst of all of that there is the greatest imaginable joy. Ishta-Guru-Bhakti Yoga in its fullness is a life of Love, lived in Communion with the Divine in Person. Everyone, somewhere in the depths of his or her being, desires such a life.

For the devotee who gives himself or herself over fully to this great Guru Yoga in Sri Da Avabhasa's Company, growth in the Way of the Heart is inevitable. And Sri Da Avabhasa has described in every detail the Spiritual, Transcendental, and Divine Awakenings that are the Graceful Gifts, over time, of Ishta-Guru-Bhakti Yoga. He has also established practicing orders—the Free Daist Lay Congregationist Order (or, simply, the Lay Congregationist Order), the Free Daist Lay Renunciate Order (or, simply, the Lay Renunciate Order), and the Naitauba (Free Daist) Order of Sannyasins (or, simply, the Free Renunciate Order)—the latter two of which have principal responsibilities in service to His Work, and all of which allow His devotees to intensify their devotional practice in the form and manner that is appropriate for them once they have basically developed their sacred practice.

When His devotee moves beyond the student-beginner stage (the first phase of formal practice in the Way of the Heart), he or she enters either the Lay Congregationist Order or the Lay Renunciate Order depending on his or her demonstrated qualifications of practice.

The Lay Congregationist Order is a practical service order whose members perform the many supportive practical services necessary for the work of the institution, the culture, and the community of all Free Daists. "Lay congregationists" conform every aspect of their life and practice to the Wisdom and Blessings of Sri Da Avabhasa, but their practice is not as intensive, nor as intensely renunciate an approach to Perfectly self-transcending God-Realization as the practice of "lay renunciates" or "free renunciates".

Any member of the Lay Congregationist Order who develops the required signs (at any point in his or her practice of the Way of the Heart) may be accepted into the Lay Renunciate Order.

The Lay Renunciate Order is a cultural service order composed of practitioners who are especially exemplary in their practice of devotion, service, self-discipline, and meditation. Members of the Lay Renunciate Order provide the inspirational and cultural leadership for the institution, the culture, and the community of Sri Da Avabhasa's devotees, and they also guide and participate in public missionary work. Their basic responsibility is to serve all practitioners of the Way of the Heart in their practice of Ishta-Guru-Bhakti Yoga and to attract others to a life of Guru-devotion. When they reach practicing stage three of the Way of the Heart (the first stage of full Spiritual Awakening), Sri Da Avabhasa has indicated that His "lay renunciates" will begin to function as His Instruments, or means by which His Divine Grace and Awakening Power are Magnified and Transmitted to other devotees and to all beings.

While members of the Lay Renunciate Order are most likely to be celibate practitioners, membership in the Lay Renunciate Order does not necessarily require celibacy, but only a truly renunciate (and, Yogically, uniquely effective) discipline of sexuality.

The Lay Renunciate Order is directly accountable to the senior practicing Order of the Way of the Heart, the Free Renunciate Order. The Free Renunciate Order is a retreat Order composed of devotees from the Lay Renunciate Order who have Awakened beyond the point of view of the body-mind to the Transcendental Position of Consciousness in the sixth stage of life, or to full Divine Self-Realization in the seventh stage of life.

Because of their extraordinary practice and Realization in the Company of Sri Da Avabhasa, "free renunciate" devotees are His principal human Instruments in the world. From among the seventh stage practitioners in the Free Renunciate Order, there will be selected after, and forever after, His human Lifetime, successive "Living Murtis", or Empowered Human Agents, who will serve the magnification of His Heart-Transmission to all beings universally and perpetually. "Murti" means "form", or "representational image". The "Living Murtis" of Sri Da Avabhasa (of which there will be only one in any then present-time) will not be Gurus in their own right. They will serve, rather, as a unique Living Link to Sri Da Avabhasa so that His Heart-Transmission will remain unbroken generation after generation.

Apart from its profound function to provide "Living Murtis" from among its membership, the Free Renunciate Order is the senior authority on all matters related to the culture of practice in the Way of the Heart and is completely essential to the perpetual continuation of authentic practice as Sri Da Avabhasa has Given it.

The members of the Free Renunciate Order generally reside at Sri Love-Anandashram. As in the Lay Renunciate Order, the Free Renunciate Order members are likely to be celibate, although they may be sexually active in a truly renunciate (and, Yogically, uniquely effective) manner.

The original and principal members of the Free Renunciate Order are Sri Da Avabhasa Himself and the Da Avabhasa Gurukula Kanyadana Kumari Order, which consists of four women devotees who have for many years lived and served in Sri Da Avabhasa's intimate sphere and who have demonstrated the most exemplary practice of Ishta-Guru-Bhakti Yoga. Every practitioner who comes in contact with the Kanyas is deeply impressed by their radiant Happiness in the midst of all circumstances, and by their transformation as human beings. The Kanyas, who are presently practicing in the sixth stage of life, are a great sign of the Truth of Sri Da Avabhasa's Wisdom and the effectiveness of His Work.

The magnitude of the Gift Sri Da Avabhasa brings to humanity is being Revealed through the developing sacred culture of Free Daism. If you decide to participate in Da Avabhasa International and to proceed from there to become a formally acknowledged practitioner of the Way of the Heart, you will be collaborating in a unique experiment—the founding of a

The Da Avabhasa Gurukula Kanyadana Kumari Order

culture and a community whose sacred practice is always founded in direct enjoyment of the Happiness of the seventh stage of life, as Transmitted by a living, seventh stage Realizer, the Divine World-Teacher, Da Avabhasa.

How often has such a Being as Da Avabhasa Appeared? If such a One is here now, is there anything more worth doing than to enter into His Company? He is addressing you personally when He Says:

SRI DA AVABHASA: Physical embodiment has the purpose of Enlightenment, the purpose of purification. . . . If you will receive My Teaching-Revelation, if you will "consider" it, if you will become responsive, then you become capable of making use of this lifetime for the purpose it inherently can serve. . . . You must submit the body-mind to the Great Purpose. . . . That is what I am Calling you to do. Accept the Dharma, the Law, inherent in your birth, the purpose that is inherent in your birth. Take up the Way of the Heart in My Company. (August 15, 1988)

If you are feeling the urge to move beyond your present level of human growth and are interested in what Da Avabhasa is Offering you, contact us at one of the addresses listed below. We will be happy to send you a free brochure on the forms of participation available to you. We invite you to enter into this sacred relationship with Da Avabhasa, and be tempered and opened in God by His Grace. We look forward to hearing from you.

Correspondence Department
THE FREE DAIST COMMUNION
P.O. Box 3680
Clearlake, California 95422, USA

Phone: (707) 928-4936

The Regional Centers of the Free Daist Communion

UNITED STATES

NORTHERN CALIFORNIA
The Free Daist Communion
740 Adrian Way
San Rafael, CA 94903
(415) 492-0932
(415) 492-0216

NORTHWEST USA
The Free Daist Communion
7214 Woodlawn Ave NE
Seattle, WA 98115
(206) 522-2298

SOUTHWEST USA
The Free Daist Communion
1043 Mesa Drive
Camarillo, CA 93010
(213) 391-8344
(805) 482-0854

NORTHEAST USA
The Free Daist Communion
28 West Central
Natick, MA 01760
(508) 650-0136

SOUTHEAST USA
The Free Daist Communion
10301 South Glen Road
Potomac, MD 20854
(301) 983-0291

HAWAII
The Free Daist Communion
105 Kaholalele Road
Kapaa, HI 96746-9304
(808) 822-3386
(808) 822-0216

AUSTRALIA
The Free Daist Communion
173 Victoria Parade
Fitzroy, Victoria 3065
Australia
(613) 417-7069

EASTERN CANADA
The Free Daist Communion
108 Katimavik Road
Val-des-Monts, Quebec J0X 2R0
Canada
(819) 671-4398
(819) 671-4397

THE NETHERLANDS
Da Avabhasa Ashram
Annendaalderweg 10
6105 AT Maria Hoop
The Netherlands
4743-1281
4743-1872

NEW ZEALAND
The Free Daist Communion
61 Opanuku Road
Box 3185 Auckland
New Zealand
(649) 814-9272
(649) 390-032

THE UNITED KINGDOM
AND IRELAND
Da Avabhasa Ashram
Tasburgh Hall
Lower Tasburgh
Norwich NR15 1LT
England
(508) 470-574

A Guide to the Sacred Esoteric Language of the Way of the Heart

adolescent, childish

Heart-Master Da uses the term "childish" to refer to the refusal to outgrow a superficial or beginner's state of mind, and to the search to transfer the child's dependence on parents to childish dependence on a parental God, savior, or institution.

Adolescence, on the other hand, is characterized by separative independence, as well as the felt dilemma of dependence versus independence.

advanced and ultimate

Da Avabhasa uses the term "advanced" to describe the practice of His devotees (or of practitioners in any other tradition) who practice in the fourth stage of life and the fifth stage of life, and He reserves the term "ultimate" to describe the practice of His devotees (and of practitioners in any other tradition) in the sixth stage of life and the seventh stage of life.

Arati (See **Sat-Guru Arati.**)

Arrow

In profound, deep meditation, the Spirit-Current may be felt in the form of what Sat-Guru Da Love-Ananda calls the "Arrow", or as He explains, a motionless axis that seems to stand in the center of the body, between the frontal and the spinal lines.

Ashram

A place where a Realizer lives and gathers with devotees.

Avadhoot, Avadhoota

"Avadhoota" means one who has "shaken off" or "passed beyond" all worldly attachments and cares, including all motives of detachment (or conventional and other-worldly renunciation), all conventional notions of life and religion, and all seeking for "answers" or "solutions" in the form of conditional experience or conditional knowledge.

bhakti, bhakta

"Bhakti" is the practice of heart-felt devotion to the Ultimate Reality or Person, to any form of Divine Image, or to a human Guru.

The term "bhakta" refers to a devotee whose principal characteris tic is outwardly expressive devotion.

the "Bright"

Since His Illumined boyhood, Heart-Master Da has used the term the "Bright" (and its variations, such as "Brightness") to describe the Blissfully Self-Luminous Divine Being, eternally, infinitely, and inherently Self-Radiant, Which He knew even then as the All-Pervading, Transcendental, Inherently Spiritual, and Divine Reality of His own body-mind and of all beings, things, and worlds.

causal (See **gross, subtle, and causal.**)

childish (See **adolescent, childish.**)

the Circle

A primary circuit or esoteric passageway

of the Living Spirit-Current as It flows through the body-mind. The Circle is composed of two arcs, the descending current in association with the frontal line, or the more physically oriented dimension, of the body-mind, and the ascending current in association with the spinal line, or the more mentally and subtly oriented dimension, of the body-mind.

"conductivity"

Sri Da Avabhasa's technical term for those disciplines in the Way of the Heart through which the body-mind is aligned and submitted to the Spirit-Current (or, for beginners, to the natural life-energy of the cosmos).

"consideration"

The technical term "consideration" in Da Avabhasa's Wisdom-Teaching is similar to the Sanskrit concept of "samyama", as classically presented in the *Yoga-Sutras* attributed to the Yogic Adept Patanjali. Such "consideration", as Sat-Guru Da explains in *Love of the Two-Armed Form* (pp. 1-2), is "a process of one-pointed but ultimately thoughtless concentration and exhaustive contemplation of a particular object, function, person, process, or condition, until the essence or ultimate obviousness of that subject is clear". As engaged in the Way of the Heart, this concentration results "in both the highest intuition and the most practical grasp of the Lawful and Divine necessities of human existence".

"Crazy", "Crazy Wisdom"

The term "Crazy Wisdom" characterizes aspects of Heart-Master Da's intentional Teaching Work (1970-1986), as well as the Divinely Mindless Quality of His eternal Realization.

In many esoteric sacred traditions, certain practitioners and Masters have been called "crazy", "mad", or "foolish". In whatever tradition and time they appear, these individuals violate prevailing taboos (personal, social, religious, or even "spiritual") either to instruct others or simply to express their own inspired freedom.

The exemplars of what Heart-Master Da calls "the 'Crazy Wisdom' tradition" (in which He Stands) are Realizers of the advanced and the ultimate stages of life in any culture or time who, through spontaneous Free action, blunt Wisdom, and liberating laughter, shock or humor people into self-critical awareness of their egoity. Such Realizers may manifest "Crazy" activity only occasionally or temporarily, and never for its own sake.

Since His Divine Emergence in 1986, Sri Da Avabhasa no longer identifies with egoic aspirants or the egoic world. Instead, in His Blessing Work, He spontaneously Reveals the Divine Self-Reality to all and Calls all to conform themselves to Him absolutely through practice of Ishta-Guru-Bhakti Yoga in the Way of the Heart. This in itself, over against the illusory rationality of the separate, egoic mentality, is a Divinely 'Crazy' State and Manner of life. Thus, Heart-Master Da's Service to others in His Divine Emergence Work, in which He is spontaneously Moved to Bless all beings, can likewise be called "Crazy-Wise".

The Da Avabhasa Gurukula Kanyadana Kumari Order (See Kanya.)

Darshan

Sanskrit: "seeing", "sight of", "vision of" any sacred object, especially the Sat-Guru.

Dharma

"Dharma" in its most profound sense is the perfect fulfillment of duty—the living of the Divine Law. A great Spiritual Teaching, including its disciplines and practices, may thus be referred to as "Dharma".

Divine Domain

Heart-Master Da Love-Ananda Affirms that there is a Divine Domain that is the "Bright" Destiny of every Realizer of the Divine Self. Because this God-World, or Realm of Divine Self-Light, transcends even the most heavenly, or subtle, dimensions of conditional space-time, it is beyond the capability of the conditional mind to experience, describe, or comprehend. Heart-Master Da Love-Ananda Reveals that the Divine Domain, or the Divine Self-Domain, is not other than the Heart. It is the "Bright", fully Realized. It is not elsewhere, not a place like a subtle heaven or mythical paradise, but It is the always present, Transcendental, Inherently Spiritual, Divine Self of every conditional self, and the Radiant Source-Condition of every conditional place.

Divinely Recognize, Divine Recognition

Sat Guru Da Avabhasa's technical term for the Inherent and Most Perfect comprehension and perception, Awakened in the seventh stage of life, that all phenomena (including body, mind, and conventional self) are merely apparent modifications of the Self-Existing and Self-Radiant Divine Person.

feeling-Contemplation

Sri Da Avabhasa's term for the essential devotional and meditative practice that all devotees in the Way of the Heart engage in relationship to His bodily (human) Form, His Spiritual (and Always Blessing) Presence, and His Very (and Inherently Perfect) State. Feeling-Contemplation of Heart-Master Da is Awakened by Grace through Darshan, or feeling-sighting, of His bodily (human) Form, His Spiritual (and Always Blessing) Presence, and His Very (and Inherently Perfect) State.

the Great Tradition

Heart-Master Da's term for the total inheritance of human cultural, religious, magical, mystical, Spiritual, Transcendental, and Divine paths, philosophies, and testimonies from all the eras and cultures of humanity.

gross, subtle, and causal

The three dimensions of which the human body-mind and its environment are composed.

The gross dimension is associated with psycho-physical embodiment and experience in the waking state.

The subtle dimension includes the etheric, lower mental, and higher mental aspects of the conditionally manifested being, and is associated with experience in the dreaming state, in visionary, mystical, and Yogic phenomena, and during and after death.

The causal dimension is the root of attention, the essence of the separate "I". It is associated with the formless awareness of deep sleep.

Gurudev

"Dev" means "God". "Gurudev" thus means the "Guru who is God", and is used to refer to one's principal Guru.

hearing

Sri Da Avabhasa's technical term for the most fundamental understanding of the self-contraction. Through such most fundamental self-understanding, the practitioner of the Way of the Heart awakens to the unique capability for direct transcendence of the self-contraction and simultaneous intuition of the Divine Person and Self-Condition. Hearing is awakened in the midst of a life of devotion, service, self-discipline, meditation, disciplined study of, or listening to, Sri Da Avabhasa's Teaching Argument, and constant self-surrendering, self-forgetting, and self-transcending feeling-Contemplation of Him.

Hearing is the necessary prerequisite for the Spiritual Realization that Heart-Master Da calls "seeing". (See also **seeing**.)

the Heart

God, the Divine Self, the Divine Reality.

Divine Self-Realization is associated with the opening of the primal psycho-physical seat of Consciousness and attention in the right side of the heart, hence the term "the Heart" for the Divine Self.

The Heart is not "in" the right side of the human heart, nor is it in or limited to the human heart as a whole, or to the body-mind, or to the world. Rather, the human heart and body-mind and the world exist in the Heart, the Divine Being.

The Sanskrit term for "heart" is "hridaya".

Ishta, Ishta-Guru-Bhakti Yoga

Ishta-Guru-Bhakti Yoga is a compound

of traditional Sanskrit terms for the principal Gift, Calling, and Discipline Sat-Guru Da Offers to all who would practice the Way of the Heart.

"Ishta" literally means "chosen", or "most beloved". "Bhakti" means, literally, "devotion".

Ishta-Guru-Bhakti, then, is devotion to the Supreme Divine Being in the Form and through the Agency of the human Sat-Guru.

"Yoga", from a Sanskrit root meaning "to yoke, to bind together", is a path, or way, of achieving Unity with the Divine.

In the Way of the Heart, Ishta-Guru-Bhakti Yoga is the Way of devotion to, Communion with, and, ultimately, Realization of the Divine Person through the Agency (and the direct Revelation) of the Heart-Chosen Sat-Guru, Sri Da Avabhasa, the Beloved Ishta-Master of His devotee's heart.

Jnana Samadhi (See Samadhi, the great Samadhis.)

Kanya

The abbreviated Designation for a member of the Da Avabhasa Gurukula Kanyadana Kumari Order.

Kanyadana is the long-standing practice in India by which a young woman (a kanya) is "given" (dana) to a Sat-Guru (either in formal marriage or, simply, as a consort, or a serving intimate). Every kanya, thus given (or devoted), is one who (unique among all other devotees in her tradition) serves the Sat-Guru intimately, and who, in that unique context, continually receives the Sat-Guru's Instructions and Blessings. Therefore, the ancient practice of presenting a woman in kanyadana to the Sat-Guru, for the sake of her Divine Self-Realization, is traditionally considered to ensure the most auspicious destiny for her. And, as a kumari, she is, necessarily, a pure (or chaste, self-renouncing, and Spiritually Awakened) woman (whether she is celibate or, Yogically, sexually active).

The Da Avabhasa Gurukula Kanyadana Kumari Order is the unique sacred circle of women who have consecrated themselves to the service of Da Avabhasa in true inti-

macy for the sake of their Divine Self-Realization, and who, by virtue of that relationship, have the capability to serve the Spiritual growth of others by inspiring their devotional surrender to Heart-Master Da.

kriyas

Sanskrit: actions. Spontaneous, self-purifying physical movements that arise when the natural bodily energies are stimulated by the Divine Spirit-Current, or as effects of the Sat-Guru's Spiritual Presence in and upon the body-mind. They may be experienced as thrills in the spine, shaking of the spine, spontaneous demonstration of difficult Yogic postures, spontaneous, automatic, and sometimes strongly expressed and repetitive Yogic breathing (pranayama), and so on.

Leela

Sanskrit: play, or sport. Traditionally, all of manifest existence is seen to be the Leela, or the Divine Play, Sport, or Free Activity of the Divine Person. Also, the Divinely Awakened Play of the Divinely Self-Realized Adept, through which he or she mysteriously Instructs and Liberates others and the world itself. By extension, a Leela is an instructive and inspiring story of such an Adept's Teaching and Blessing Play.

mala

Sanskrit: garland. Typically, a rosary of 108 beads plus a central, or Master, bead.

mudra

In Sanskrit, a gesture of the hands, face, or body expressing exalted Spiritual states of Consciousness. Mudras may arise spontaneously in deep meditation, or in one or another form of Samadhi, or contemplative absorption.

Divinely Self-Realized Adepts may spontaneously exhibit Mudras as Signs of their Blessing and purifying Work with devotees, as Heart-Master Da does from time to time.

Murti

Sanskrit: form. Traditionally, in ceremonial worship and meditation, practitioners of religion and Spirituality have used many kinds of Murtis (Forms or Representations of the Divine), such as statues, paintings, photographic likenesses, etc. The most highly valued and respected Murti of the Divine Person, especially among practitioners of esoteric paths of Spiritual, Transcendental, and Divine Awakening, is the bodily (human) Form of the Divinely Self-Realized Adept.

"Narcissus"

In Sat-Guru Da's Teaching-Revelation, Narcissus, the self-lover of Greek mythology, is a key symbol of un-Enlightened Man as an egoically "self-possessed" seeker, enamored of his own self-image and egoic self-consciousness. As "Narcissus", every human being constantly suffers in dilemma, contracted in every dimension of the being, recoiling from all relations and even from the fundamental manifest condition of relationship (or relatedness) itself.

Nirvikalpa Samadhi, fifth stage conditional (See **Samadhi, the great Samadhis**.)

Prasad

In Sanskrit, "Prasad" is equivalent to "Grace". It means "the return of the Gift to the giver". In the Way of the Heart, "Prasad" signifies all the kinds of offerings (originally given by the practitioner to Heart-Master Da) returned to the practitioner by Him, such as sacred ash, sweets, Blessed water, and the like, as the tangible Blessing of the Giver of Divine Grace. The ultimate Prasad is Heart-Master Da's constant Gift of Himself to every practitioner.

"radical"

Heart-Master Da uses the term "radical" in its original and primary sense. It derives from the Latin "radix" meaning "root" and thus principally means "irreducible", "fundamental", or "relating to the origin".

In contrast to the progressive or evolutionary egoic searches espoused by the world's religious, Spiritual, and Transcendental traditions, the "radical" Way of the

Heart Offered by Heart-Master Da is always already established in the Divine Self-Condition or Reality.

sadhana

Sanskrit: discipline. Traditionally, practices directed toward religious or Spiritual goals. Sadhana in the Way of the Heart is not action to attain Truth or any state or condition, but, rather, action that expresses present, intuitive Communion with Truth, in conscious Satsang with Sri Da Avabhasa.

Sage

Heart-Master Da uses this term technically to indicate those Realizers or Adepts who have achieved a profound depth of intuition of the Transcendental Self via meditation upon and Realization of Consciousness in one or another of the great sacred traditions of the sixth stage of life. (Compare **Saint** and **Yogi**.)

Saint

Heart-Master Da uses the capitalized term Saint (which, from the Latin "sanctus", literally means sacred) to indicate a great practitioner or Adept who has achieved profound, ascended Union with the Divine Spirit-Reality in the context of the fourth or the fifth stage of life. (Compare **Sage** and **Yogi**.)

Samadhi, the great Samadhis

"Samadhi", in Sanskrit, means "placed together". It indicates concentration, equanimity, and balance, and it is traditionally used to denote various exalted states that appear in the context of esoteric meditation and Realization. Although some or even all of the great Samadhis of the fourth, the fifth, the sixth, and the seventh stages of life may appear in the course of an individual's significantly maturing practice of the Way of the Heart, it is by no means necessary, as Da Avabhasa indicates in His Wisdom-Teaching, that all of them appear in any given practitioner's case.

The Samadhi of "the Thumbs": The experience of "the Thumbs" occurs when the body-mind is invaded by a most forceful descent of the Spirit-Current. In the fullest form of this experience, which Heart-Master Da calls "the Samadhi of 'the Thumbs'", the Spirit-Invasion completely descends in the frontal line of the body-mind and enters the spinal line, overwhelming the ordinary human sense of bodily existence, and infusing the whole being with intense blissfulness and releasing the ordinary, confined sense of body, mind, and separate self.

Savikalpa Samadhi: The Sanskrit term "Savikalpa Samadhi" literally means "concentration (or absorption) with form". Heart-Master Da indicates that there are two basic forms of Savikalpa Samadhi. The first is the experience of Spiritual ascent of energy and attention into mystical experiential phenomena, visions and other subtle sensory perceptions of subtle psychic forms, and states of Yogic bliss or Spirit-Intoxication. The second, and highest, form of Savikalpa Samadhi is traditionally called "Cosmic Consciousness", or the Vision of Cosmic Unity.

Fifth stage conditional Nirvikalpa Samadhi: "Nirvikalpa" means "without form". Hence, "Nirvikalpa Samadhi" means literally "concentration (or absorption) without form". Traditionally this state is the final goal of the many schools of Yogic ascent belonging to the fifth stage of life. In fifth stage conditional Nirvikalpa Samadhi, attention ascends beyond all conditional manifestation into the formless Matrix of the Spirit-Current or Divine Light infinitely above the world, the body, and the mind. Fifth stage conditional Nirvikalpa Samadhi is a forced and temporary state of attention (or, more precisely, the suspension of attention). It is produced by manipulation of attention and of the body-mind, and is thus incapable of being maintained when attention returns, as it inevitably does, to the states of the body-mind.

Jnana Samadhi: "Jnana" derives from the Sanskrit verb root "jna", literally "to know". Most individuals practicing in the sixth stage of life experience Jnana Samadhi at least once, or even frequently. Produced by the forced withdrawal or inversion of attention from the conditional body-mind-self and its relations, Jnana Samadhi is the

conditional, temporary Realization of the Transcendental Self, or Consciousness, exclusive of any perception or cognition of world, objects, relations, body, mind, or self-sense.

Sahaj Samadhi: The Hindi word "sahaj" (Sanskrit: "sahaja") literally means "together born" or "coincident", and it is extrapolated to mean "natural", even "innate". Sri Da Avabhasa uses the term to indicate the Coincidence (in the case of Divine Self-Realization) of the Inherently Spiritual and Transcendental Divine Reality with empirical, conditional reality—the inherent, or native, and thus truly "Natural" State of Being. The "Naturalness" of Divine Self-Realization, or Sahaj Samadhi, is that it is entirely Free, unforced, and effortless, consonant with the Nature of Divine Being (Itself), Which is Self-Existing, Self-Radiant, and always already the case.

Sahaj Samadhi stands in contrast to all Samadhis previous to Perfect Divine Awakening, which always depend upon a strategic effort of the un-"Natural" self-contraction, or motion of attention, to create a temporary psycho-physical state of balance and equanimity which admits a momentary intuition of Divine Freedom.

Moksha-Bhava Samadhi: "Moksha" means "liberation" in Sanskrit. Heart-Master Da uses "Bhava" here, which traditionally has several meanings, to indicate the Transcendental, Inherently Spiritual, and Divine Being (rather than any psycho-physical state or realization previous to Divine Self-Realization). Moksha-Bhava Samadhi is therefore the ultimate Realization of Divine Existence, in which all conditional states, forms, and phenomena are Outshined by the Self-Existing and Self-Radiant "Brightness" of Divine Consciousness and Love-Bliss. Moksha-Bhava Samadhi is thus the ultimate "Mood of Ecstasy", consisting of Inherence in Divine "Brightness" without the noticing of any arising conditions.

At death the Realizer of the seventh stage of life may Realize permanent establishment in Moksha-Bhava Samadhi, which is Divine Translation into the Divine Self-Domain.

Sat-Guru Arati

A traditional Hindu ceremony of waving lights around the Body of the Sat-Guru (or a Representation of his or her physical Form, such as a photograph) to express devotion and gratitude. Devotees of Sri Da Avabhasa perform the Arati at the closing of each day by waving lights and incense around a Murti of Sat-Guru Da, making ecstatic sounds with musical instruments, and chanting.

Sat-Guru-Naama Mantra

The term "Sat-Guru-Naama Mantra" refers to the Divine Name of the Sat-Guru which is used in the Way of the Heart as a means of Invoking and worshipping the Divine Person and the Sat-Guru.

In the Way of the Heart, the Sat-Guru-Naama Mantra Given by Sri Da Avabhasa has two possible forms: "Om Sri Da Love-Ananda Hridayam" and "Om Sri Da Avabhasa Hridayam". The Sat-Guru-Naama Mantra is used by all practitioners of the Way of the Heart in sacramental worship and Invocation of Sri Da Avabhasa. It is also used by some practitioners as a form of Contemplative practice.

Sat-Guru-Seva

In Sanskrit, "seva" means "service". In the Way of the Heart, Sat-Guru-Seva is the remarkable opportunity to live every action and, indeed, one's entire life, as direct service and responsive obedience (or sympathetic conformity) to Sat-Guru Da in every possible and appropriate way.

It is one of the Seven Gifts of Sri Da Avabhasa's Grace.

Satsang

The Sanskrit word "Satsang" literally means "the company of Truth, or of Being". The term traditionally refers to the practice of spending time in the sacred presence of holy or wise persons, a holy place, a venerated image, the burial shrine of a Saint or Realizer, or the Divine Person.

Heart-Master Da uses the term in the most profound sense, indicating the eternal relationship of mutual sacred commitment between Himself as Sat-Guru (and as the Divine Person) and His devotee. Satsang with Sri Da Avabhasa is an all-inclusive Condition, bringing Divine Grace and Blessings and sacred obligations, responsibilities, and tests into every dimension of the individual's life and consciousness.

seeing

In the practice of the Way of the Heart, when hearing (or most fundamental self-understanding) is steadily exercised in meditation and in life, the native feeling of the heart ceases to be chronically constricted by self-contraction. The heart then begins to Radiate as love in response to the Spiritual (and Always Blessing) Presence of Da Avabhasa.

This emotional and Spiritual response of the whole being is what Heart-Master Da calls "seeing". Seeing coincides with true and stable emotional conversion to love and true and stable receptivity to Da Avabhasa's Spiritual Transmission. (See also **hearing**.)

"self-possession"

Conventionally, "self-possession" means possession of oneself—or full control (calmness, or composure) of one's feelings, impulses, habits, and actions. Heart-Master Da uses the term in a "radical" sense, to indicate the state of being possessed by oneself, or controlled by chronically self-referring (or egoic) tendencies of attention, feeling, thought, desire, and action. Thus, unless (in every moment) body, emotion, desire, thought, separate and separative self, and all attention are actively and completely surrendered, one is egoically "self-possessed", even when exhibiting personal control of one's feelings, habits, and actions. And the devotional practice of feeling-Contemplation of Heart-Master Da is the principal Means Given (by Grace) to practitioners of the Way of the Heart, whereby they may responsively (and, thus, by Grace) surrender, forget, and transcend egoic "self-possession".

Shakti, shakti

The Living Conscious Force or Divine Cosmic and Manifesting Energy; the generative Power and Motion of the cosmos; Spiritual Power; the Life-Current of the Living God. When capitalized (Shakti), the term refers to the Universal or Perfect Divine Power. When written in lowercase (shakti), the term refers to that same Power in the form of various finite energies and activities, high or low, within or associated with the human individual.

Traditionally, the Divine Self-Radiance (the female aspect of the One Reality), or the All-Pervading Energy that is modified as all conditional forms, has been contacted and worshipped as the Divine Goddess. By Herself, She is Maya, the Goddess associated with the deluding power of Nature, or the veiling of God.

Heart-Master Da Demonstrated in His Ordeal of Re-Awakening that this great Power is ultimately Husbanded by Transcendental Consciousness. In that case, the Goddess-Power is submitted to the Transcendental Divine Self, and She then becomes associated with the Spirit-Power that leads all beings to Divine Enlightenment.

Shaktipat, Hridaya-Shaktipat

In Hindi, "Shaktipat" is the "descent of the Power". Yogic Shaktipat, which manipulates natural, conditional energies or partial manifestations of the Spirit-Current, is typically granted through touch, word, glance, or regard by Yogic Adepts in the fifth stage, or the fourth to fifth stages of life. Yogic Shaktipat must be distinguished from (and otherwise understood to be only a secondary aspect of) the Blessing-Transmission of the Heart Itself (Hridaya-Shaktipat). Such Heart-Transmission, Which is spontaneously Granted or Freely Radiated to all by Hridaya-Samartha Sat-Guru Da, may be Granted only by a Divinely Self-Realized, or seventh stage, Samartha Sat-Guru. Hridaya-Shaktipat (or Hridaya-Kripa) does not require intentional Yogic activity on the Sat-Guru's part, although such Yogic activity may also be spontaneously generated by the Sat-Guru. Hridaya-Shaktipat operates principally at, in, and as the Heart Itself, primarily Awakening the intuition of "Bright" Consciousness, and only secondarily (and to one degree or another, depending on the characteristics of the individual) magnifying the activities of the Spirit-Current in the body-mind.

Siddha

"Siddha", in Sanskrit, means "a completed, fulfilled, or perfected one", or "one of perfect accomplishment, or power". In Sri Da Avabhasa's usage, a Siddha is a Transmission-Master of any degree of Spiritual, Transcendental, or Divine Realization and Capability.

Siddhi, siddhi

Sanskrit: "power", or "accomplishment". When capitalized in Heart-Master Da's Wisdom-Teaching, Siddhi is the Spiritual, Transcendental, and Divine Awakening-Power of the Heart that He spontaneously and effortlessly exercises as Hridaya-Samartha Sat-Guru.

The uncapitalized term "siddhi" denotes various Yogic capabilities and psychic powers, traditionally called "ordinary", or "natural", siddhis.

Sri

Sanskrit: flame. A term of honor and veneration, with the connotation that the honored one is "Bright", or Potent, with Blessing Power.

stages of life

Heart-Master Da has described the evolutionary development and self-transcending Spiritual, Transcendental, and Divine Realization of the human individual in terms of seven stages of life.

The first three stages develop and coordinate the physical, emotional (or emotional-sexual), and mental (or mental-intentional) functions of the body-mind, respectively, and the corresponding expressions of religious awakening and participation, optimally developed in the context of authentic early-life devotion to the bodily (human) Form of the Sat-Guru and, thus and thereby, to the Divine Person.

The fourth stage of life involves the cultivation of heart-felt surrender to and intimacy with the bodily (human) Form, and, eventually, and more and more profoundly, the Spiritual Presence, of the Sat-Guru and, through such explicit devotional self-surrender to the Sat-Guru, devotional intimacy and Union with the Divine Person. Secondarily, in the fourth stage of life, the gross body-mind of the Awakening devotee is adapted and submitted to, and harmonized in, the Living Spirit-Current of the Sat-Guru and the Divine Person.

The fifth stage of life, if it must be developed, involves the ascent of attention and self-awareness beyond the gross body-mind and into the subtler field of psyche and mind, outside and beyond the brain. Traditionally, the fifth stage of life, therefore, develops the esoteric Yogic and cosmic mysticism of the Spiritual Life-Current in its ascent to the Matrix of Light, Love-Bliss, and Spirit-Presence above the world, the body, and the mind. When that mysticism is followed to its eventual culminating Union with the Spiritual Divine Matrix of Love-Bliss, the individual enjoys fifth stage conditional Nirvikalpa Samadhi.

In the Way of the Heart, most practitioners are Graced to bypass some or all of the fifth stage Yogic process. This is possible by Sat-Guru Da's Grace, Whereby the devotee is Attracted through feeling-Contemplation of His bodily (human) Form and Spiritual (and Always Blessing) Presence directly into feeling-Contemplation of His Very (and Inherently Perfect) State, such that exhaustive (or even any) exploration of fifth stage Yogic processes is rendered unnecessary. Thus, for such practitioners, fifth stage conditional Nirvikalpa Samadhi and other fifth stage states may or may not arise.

The sixth stage of life traditionally involves the inversion of attention upon the Perfectly Subjective Position of Consciousness, to the exclusion of conditional phenomena. The deliberate intention to invert attention for the sake of Realizing Transcendental Consciousness does not, however, characterize the sixth stage of life in the Way of the Heart. Rather, for devotees in the Way of the Heart, the sixth stage of life begins when the Witness-Position of Consciousness spontaneously awakens and becomes stable.

In the course of the sixth stage of life, the mechanism of attention, which is the root-action of egoity (felt as self-separation, self-contraction, or the feeling of relatedness), gradually subsides. At a felt point in the right side of the heart (corresponding to the sinoatrial node), the knot of attention dissolves and all sense of relatedness yields to the Blissful and undifferentiated Feeling of Being. The characteristic Samadhi of the sixth stage of life is the temporary and exclusive Realization of the Transcendental Self, or Consciousness Itself.

The seventh stage of life begins when Sri Da Avabhasa's devotee Awakens by Grace to Most Perfect and permanent Identification with Consciousness Itself. This is Divine Self-Realization, the perpetual Samadhi of "Open-Eyes" (Sahaj Samadhi) in which all "things" are Divinely Recognized without "difference" as merely apparent modifications of the One Self-Existing and Self-Radiant Divine Consciousness. In the course of the seventh stage of life there may be incidents of spontaneous "Moksha-Bhava-Nirvikalpa Samadhi", in which psycho-physical states and phenomena do not appear to the notice, being Outshined by the "Bright" Radiance of Consciousness Itself. This Samadhi, which is the ultimate Realization of Divine Existence, culminates in Divine Translation, or the permanent Outshining of all apparent conditions in the Inherently Perfect Radiance and Love-Bliss of the Divine Self-Condition.

The seven stages of life as Revealed by Sri Da Avabhasa are not to be understood as a version of the traditional ladder of Spiritual attainment. These stages and their characteristic signs arise naturally in the course of practice for a devotee in the Way of the Heart, but the practice itself is oriented to the transcendence of the first six stages of life in the seventh stage disposition of Inherently Liberated Happiness, Granted by Grace in the Love-Blissful Spiritual Company of Heart-Master Da Avabhasa.

subtle (See **gross, subtle, and causal**.)

Tantra, Tantric

The word "Tantra" means literally "continuity", "essence", or "underlying unity", and it signifies "the inherent Unity that underlies and transcends all opposites, and that resolves all differences or distinctions".

In some schools of the Tantric approach to Spiritual practice and Realization, the passions and attachments native to the body and mind are specifically used as the principal context of self-mastery and Spiritual growth. In these schools of Tantric practice, the practitioner utilizes the most intense (and, therefore, also potentially dangerous) energies of the being for the work of self-understanding and self-transcendence.

tapas

Sanskrit: "heat"; also "penance". The fire of self-frustrating discipline generates a heat that purifies the body-mind, transforms loveless habits, and liberates the practitioner from the consolations of ordinary egoic existence. In reference to Sri Da Avabhasa, Whose Realization of the Divine Being is already Perfect, Tapas refers to the Penance He performs for the sake of His devotees and the world.

Yogi

In a general sense, a Yogi is a practitioner or adept of any of a wide variety of disciplines within the Hindu tradition that are engaged for the sake of Spiritual Union, or Re-Union, with the Divine.

However, Sri Da Avabhasa's principal technical use of the term "Yogi" is to describe an Adept who has achieved one or another degree of mastery of Yogic processes of Spiritual concentration and ascent of attention (and its withdrawal from descended outward, or gross, pursuits) for the sake of attaining one or another of the Samadhis that traditionally represent exalted Divine Communion or mystical Union in the fifth stage of life. (Compare **Saint** and **Sage**.)

FURTHER NOTES TO THE READER

An Invitation to Responsibility

The Way of the Heart that Sri Da Avabhasa has Revealed is an invitation to everyone to assume real responsibility for his or her life. As Sri Da Avabhasa has Said in *The Dawn Horse Testament,* "If any one Is Interested In The Realization Of The Heart, Let him or her First Submit (Formally, and By Heart) To Me, and (Thereby) Commence The Ordeal Of self-Observation, self-Understanding, and self-Transcendence." Therefore, participation in the Way of the Heart requires a real struggle with oneself, and not at all a struggle with Sri Da Avabhasa, or with others.

All who study the Way of the Heart or take up its practice should remember that they are responding to a Call to become responsible for themselves. They should understand that they, not Sri Da Avabhasa or others, are responsible for any decision they may make or action they take in the course of their lives of study or practice. This has always been true, and it is true whatever the individual's involvement in the Way of the Heart, be it as one who studies Da Avabhasa's Wisdom-Teaching, or as a formal Friend of the Free Daist Communion, or as a participant in Da Avabhasa International, or as a formally acknowledged member of the Free Daist Communion.

Honoring and Protecting the Sacred Word through Perpetual Copyright

Since ancient times, practitioners of true religion and Spirituality have valued, above all, time spent in the Company of the Sat-Guru, or one who has Realized God, Truth, or Reality, and who Serves that same Realization in others. Such practitioners understand that the Sat-Guru literally Transmits his or her (Realized) State to every one (and every thing) with which he or she comes in contact. Through this Transmission, objects, environments, and rightly prepared individuals with which the Sat-Guru has contact can become Empowered, or Imbued with the Sat-Guru's Transforming Power. It is by this process of Empowerment that things and beings are made truly and literally sacred, and things so sanctified thereafter function as a Source of the Sat-Guru's Blessing for all who understand how to make right and sacred use of them.

The Sat-Guru and all that he Empowers are, therefore, truly Sacred Treasures, for they help draw the practitioner more quickly into the Realization of Perfect Identity with the Divine Self. Cultures of true Wisdom have always understood that such Sacred Treasures are precious (and fragile) Gifts to humanity, and that they should be honored, protected, and reserved for right sacred use. Indeed, the word "sacred" means "set apart", and thus protected, from the secular world. Sri Da Avabhasa is a Sat-Guru of the Most Perfect degree. He has Conformed His body-mind completely to the Divine Self, and He is thus a most Potent Source of Blessing-Transmission of God, Truth, or Reality. He has for many years Empowered, or made sacred, special places and things, and these now Serve as His Divine Agents, or as literal expressions and extensions of His Blessing-Transmission. Among these Empowered Sacred Treasures is His Wisdom-Teaching, which is Full of His Transforming Power. This Blessed and Blessing Wisdom-Teaching has Mantric Force, or the literal Power to Serve God-Realization in those who are Graced to receive it.

Therefore, Sri Da Avabhasa's Wisdom-Teaching must be perpetually honored and protected, "set apart" from all possible interference and wrong use. The Free

Daist Communion, which is the fellowship of devotees of Sri Da Avabhasa, is committed to the perpetual preservation and right honoring of the sacred Wisdom-Teaching of the Way of the Heart. But it is also true that in order to fully accomplish this we must find support in the world-society in which we live and from the laws under which we live. Thus, we call for a world-society and for laws that acknowledge the Sacred, and that permanently protect It from insensitive, secular interference and wrong use of any kind. We call for, among other things, a system of law that acknowledges that the Wisdom-Teaching of the Way of the Heart, in all Its forms, is, because of Its sacred nature, protected by perpetual copyright.

We invite others who respect the Sacred to join with us in this call and in working toward its realization. And, even in the meantime, we claim that all copyrights to the Wisdom-Teaching of Sri Da Avabhasa and the other sacred literature and recordings of the Way of the Heart are of perpetual duration.

We make this claim on behalf of Sri Love-Anandashram (Naitauba) Pty Ltd, which, acting as trustee of the Sri Love-Anandashram (Naitauba) Trust, is the holder of all such copyrights.

Da Avabhasa and the Sacred Treasures of Free Daism

Those who Realize God bring great Blessing and Divine Possibility for the world. As Free Adepts, they Accomplish universal Blessing Work that benefits everything and everyone. Such Realizers also Work very specifically and intentionally with individuals who approach them as their devotees, and with those places where they reside, and to which they Direct their specific Regard for the sake of perpetual Spiritual Empowerment. This was understood in traditional Spiritual cultures, and those cultures therefore found ways to honor Realizers, to provide circumstances for them where they were free to do their Divine Work without obstruction or interference.

Those who value Sri Da Avabhasa's Realization and Service have always endeavored to appropriately honor Him in this traditional way, to provide a circumstance where He is completely Free to Do His Divine Work. Since 1983, Sri Da Avabhasa has resided principally on the Island of Naitauba, Fiji, also known as Sri Love-Anandashram. This island has been set aside by Free Daists worldwide as a Place for Sri Da Avabhasa to Do His universal Blessing Work for the sake of everyone and His specific Work with those who pilgrimage to Sri Love-Anandashram to receive the special Blessing of coming into His physical Company.

Sri Da Avabhasa is a legal renunciate. He owns nothing and He has no secular or religious institutional function. He Functions only in Freedom. He, and the other members of the Naitauba (Free Daist) Order of Sannyasins, the senior renunciate order of Free Daism, are provided for by the Sri Love-Anandashram (Naitauba) Trust, which also provides for Sri Love-Anandashram altogether and ensures the permanent integrity of Sri Da Avabhasa's Wisdom-Teaching, both in its archival and in its published forms. This Trust, which functions only in Fiji, exists exclusively to provide for these Sacred Treasures of Free Daism.

Outside Fiji, the institution which has developed in response to Sri Da Avabhasa's Wisdom-Teaching and universal Blessing is known as "The Free Daist Communion". The Free Daist Communion is active worldwide in making Da Avabhasa's Wisdom-Teaching available to all, in offering guidance to all who are moved to respond to His Offering, and in providing for the other Sacred Treasures of Free Daism, including the Mountain Of Attention Sanctuary (in California) and Tumomama Sanctuary (in Hawaii). In addition to the central corporate entity of the Free Daist Communion, which is based in California, there are numerous regional entities which serve congregations of Sri Da Avabhasa's devotees in various places throughout the world.

Free Daists worldwide have also established numerous community organizations, through which they provide for many of their common and cooperative community needs, including needs relating to housing, food, businesses, medical care, schools, and death and dying. By attending to these and all other ordinary human concerns and affairs via self-transcending cooperation and mutual effort, Sri Da Avabhasa's devotees constantly free their energy and attention, both personally and collectively, for practice of the Way of the Heart and for service to Sri Da Avabhasa, to Sri Love-Anandashram, to the other Sacred Treasures of Free Daism, and to the Free Daist Communion.

All of the organizations that have evolved in response to Sri Da Avabhasa and His Offering are legally separate from one another, and each has its own purpose and function. He neither directs, nor bears responsibility for, the activities of these organizations. Again, He Functions only in Freedom. These organizations represent the collective intention of Free Daists worldwide not only to provide for the Sacred Treasures of Free Daism, but also to make Da Avabhasa's Offering of the Way of the Heart universally available to all.

The Sacred Literature of Da Avabhasa (The "Bright")

Heart-Master Da Love-Ananda provides a way in which Oneness may be experienced by anyone who is bold enough to follow his teachings. It is important to understand that his vision is neither Eastern nor Western, but it is the eternal spiritual pulse of the Great Wisdom which knows no cultural, temporal, or geographical locus; it represents the apex of awareness of our species.

Larry Dossey, M.D.
author, *Space, Time, and Medicine*
and *Beyond Illness*

The teachings of Heart-Master Da, embodied in an extraordinary collection of writings, provide an exquisite manual for transformation. . . . I feel at the most profound depth of my being that his work will be crucial to an evolution toward full-humanness.

Barbara Marx Hubbard
author, *The Evolutionary Journey*

Do you hunger for Spiritual Truth?

Do you long to know precisely why everything you seek, and everything you hold on to, never seems to give you lasting fulfillment?

Do you wish to see the whole process of Spiritual Awakening explained, and all the conflicting paths and doctrines of humanity clarified, by an all-illuminating Revelation of sacred understanding?

Are you ready for Wisdom that shows you exactly how you unconsciously cut yourself off from the Divine Reality—and exactly how to reconnect, and to always participate consciously in that Reality, with every breath, in all relationships, in all action and meditation, even to the degree of Perfect Divine Self-Realization?

If your answer to any of these questions, or all of them, is "yes", then you need seek no further. We invite you to explore the Sacred Literature of Da Avabhasa.

SOURCE LITERATURE

THE LOVE-ANANDA GITA

(THE WISDOM-SONG OF NON-SEPARATENESS)
The "Simple" Revelation-Book Of Da Kalki (The Divine World-Teacher and True Heart-Master, Da Love-Ananda Hridayam)

The Love-Ananda Gita is Da Avabhasa's quintessential Revelation of His Way of the Heart, containing His basic Instructions on the fundamental practice of Satsang, or feeling-Contemplation of His bodily (human) Form, His Spiritual (and Always Blessing) Presence, and His Very (and Inherently Perfect) State of Free Being. The most basic Source-Text of His entire Word of Confession and Instruction. [The next edition of *The Love-Ananda Gita* will be published with the following attribution: *The Simple Revelation-Book Of The Divine World-Teacher and True Heart-Master, Da Avabhasa (The "Bright").*]
Standard Edition
$34.95* cloth, $19.95 paper

* All prices are in U.S. dollars

THE DAWN HORSE TESTAMENT

The Testament Of Secrets
Of The Divine World-Teacher
and True Heart-Master,
Da Avabhasa (The "Bright")

In this monumental text of over 800 pages (a substantial updating and enlargement of the original Work published in 1985), Da Avabhasa Reveals the Mysteries and devotional Secrets of every practice and developmental stage of the Way of the Heart. Ken Wilber, renowned scholar of Eastern and Western psychology and religion, was moved to write:

The Dawn Horse Testament *is the most ecstatic, most profound, most complete, most radical, and most comprehensive __single__ spiritual text ever to be penned and confessed by the Human-Transcendental Spirit.*
New Standard Edition
$24.95 paper

THE DA UPANISHAD

THE SHORT DISCOURSES ON self-RENUNCIATION, GOD-REALIZATION, AND THE ILLUSION OF RELATEDNESS

Da Avabhasa's most concise Instruction relative to the forms of the Way of the Heart described in *The Dawn Horse Testament,* emphasizing the non-strategic, non-ascetical practice of renunciation in the Way of the Heart. (*The Da Upanishad* is an enlarged and updated edition of Da Avabhasa's Work formerly titled *The Illusion Of Relatedness.* The next edition will be titled *The Da Avabhasa Upanishad.*)
Standard Edition
$19.95 paper

THE ego-"I" is THE ILLUSION OF RELATEDNESS

Published here in book form, this central Essay from *The Da Avabhasa Upanishad* is an indispensable introduction to the esoteric Wisdom-Instruction of the Divine World-Teacher of our time. It includes Da Avabhasa's utterly extraordinary commentaries on dietary and sexual Yoga, His Divinely Enlightened secrets on how to responsibly master and transcend all of the psycho-physical "sheaths" or bodies, and passage after passage that exposes the very core of our suffering, the illusion of relatedness.
$8.95 paper

THE BASKET OF TOLERANCE

*A GUIDE TO PERFECT
UNDERSTANDING OF THE ONE
AND GREAT TRADITION
OF MANKIND*

Never before in history has it been possible for a seventh stage Adept to Give the world such a Gift: a comprehensive bibliography (listing more than 2,500 publications) of the world's historical traditions of truly human culture, practical self-discipline, perennial religion, universal religious mysticism, "esoteric" (but now openly communicated) Spirituality, Transcendental Wisdom, and Perfect (or Divine) Enlightenment, compiled, presented, and extensively annotated by Da Avabhasa Himself. The summary of His Instruction on the Great Tradition of human Wisdom and the Sacred ordeal of Spiritual practice and Realization.
New Standard Edition
(forthcoming, 1992)

THE LION SUTRA

*(ON PERFECT TRANSCENDENCE OF
THE PRIMAL ACT, WHICH IS THE
ego-"I", THE self-CONTRACTION, OR
attention itself, AND ALL THE ILLUSIONS
OF SEPARATION, OTHERNESS,
RELATEDNESS, AND "DIFFERENCE")
The Perfect Revelation-Book Of
The Divine World-Teacher and
True Heart-Master, Da Avabhasa
(The "Bright")*

A poetic Exposition of the "Perfect Practice" of the Way of the Heart—the final stages of Transcendental, Inherently Spiritual, and Divine Self-Realization. Of all Da Avabhasa's Works, *The Lion Sutra* is the most concentrated Call and Instruction to Realize the Consciousness that Stands prior to body, mind, individual self, and objective world. (First published in 1986 under the title *Love-Ananda Gita*.)
New Standard Edition
$24.95 cloth, $14.95 paper

THE LIBERATOR (ELEUTHERIOS)

*AN EPITOME OF PERFECT WISDOM
AND THE PERFECT PRACTICE*

In compelling, lucid prose, Da Avabhasa distills the essence of the ultimate processes leading to Divine Self-Realization in the Way of the Heart—the "Perfect Practice", which involves the direct transcendence of all experience via identification with Consciousness Itself, through feeling-Contemplation of His Form, His Presence, and (most crucial in these stages of practice) His Infinite State.
New Standard Edition
(forthcoming, late 1991)

THE HYMN OF THE TRUE HEART-MASTER

*The New Revelation-Book Of The
Ancient and Eternal Religion Of
Devotion To The God-Realized Adept*

The Hymn Of The True Heart-Master is Da Avabhasa's ecstatic proclamation of the Sat-Guru as the supreme Means for Divine Self-Realization. In 108 poetic verses, Da Avabhasa extols the Way of Divine Unity through Ishta-Guru-Bhakti Yoga, or worshipful service and devotion to the Ishta-Guru or "Chosen" and "Most Beloved" Master of one's heart. This volume also includes many of Da Avabhasa's primary Essays and Discourses on the principle of Guru-devotion in His Company as well as moving Leelas (or Stories) by His devotees that demonstrate the supreme transforming power of this Yoga.
New Standard Edition
(forthcoming, late 1991)
$34.95 cloth, $19.95 paper

INTRODUCTORY TEXTS

FREE DAISM

THE ETERNAL, ANCIENT, AND NEW RELIGION OF GOD-REALIZATION
An Introduction to the Blessing Work of the Divine World-Teacher and True Heart-Master, Da Avabhasa (The "Bright") and the Spiritual Process Lived in His Company
by Richard Schorske

Addressed to new readers and written in a highly accessible style, *Free Daism* thoroughly introduces Da Avabhasa and the sacred orders of His most exemplary devotees, the stages and disciplines of the Way of the Heart, and the unique features of the institution, the sacred devotional culture, and the worldwide community of His devotees. (forthcoming, late 1991)

LOVE OF THE GOD-MAN

A COMPREHENSIVE GUIDE TO THE TRADITIONAL AND TIME-HONORED GURU-DEVOTEE RELATIONSHIP, THE SUPREME MEANS OF GOD-REALIZATION, AS FULLY REVEALED FOR THE FIRST TIME BY THE DIVINE WORLD-TEACHER AND TRUE HEART-MASTER, DA AVABHASA (THE "BRIGHT")
by James Steinberg

The longer work from which *Divine Distraction* was derived. *Love of the God Man* is a full-length (over 800-page) discussion of the profound laws and virtues of the Guru-devotee relationship as practiced in the Way of the Heart. Nowhere else in the literature of sacred life does such an encyclopedic treatment of the Guru-devotee relationship exist. *Love of the God-Man* is an inexhaustible resource, full of Da Avabhasa's Wisdom and His Leelas (inspiring stories) and many stories from the Great Tradition.
Second Edition (forthcoming, 1992)

DIVINE DISTRACTION

A GUIDE TO THE GURU-DEVOTEE RELATIONSHIP, THE SUPREME MEANS OF GOD-REALIZATION, AS FULLY REVEALED FOR THE FIRST TIME BY THE DIVINE WORLD-TEACHER AND TRUE HEART-MASTER, DA AVABHASA (THE "BRIGHT")
by James Steinberg

Presented by a longtime devotee of Da Avabhasa, this shorter version of *Love of the God-Man* describes, illustrates, and extols the Guru-devotee relationship. *Divine Distraction* features compelling stories of Da Avabhasa's Work with His devotees, and illuminating passages from His Wisdom-Teaching, along with instruction and stories from great Masters and disciples in the world's religious and Spiritual traditions.
$12.95 paper

FEELING WITHOUT LIMITATION
AWAKENING TO THE TRUTH BEYOND FEAR, SORROW, AND ANGER

A brief introductory volume featuring a Discourse from Da Avabhasa's Teaching years that presents in simplest terms His fundamental Argument about human suffering, seeking, and freedom. Also includes remarkable Leelas and testimonies by three devotees.
$4.95 paper

THE PERFECT ALTERNATIVE
A TESTIMONY TO THE POWER OF THE TRANSFORMING GRACE OF SRI DA AVABHASA (THE "BRIGHT")
by Kanya Samatva Suprithi

A gem of a book by one of the four most mature practitioners of the Way of the Heart, a woman who has entered the sixth stage of life through Da Avabhasa's Grace. Kanya Samatva Suprithi presents here a very readable summary of Da Avabhasa's basic Arguments about seeking and Happiness, and she includes some of her own story as a Daist practitioner. An excellent and very concise introduction to Da Avabhasa and His Work.
$4.95 paper

AVADHOOTS, MAD LAMAS, AND FOOLS
by James Steinberg

A brief and lively account of the "Crazy Wisdom" style of sacred Instruction employed by Adepts in many traditions, times, and cultures, including Leelas of Da Avabhasa's Teaching years and His Divine Emergence Work.
(forthcoming, late 1991)

THE WISDOM-LITERATURE OF DA AVABHASA'S TEACHING WORK

THE KNEE OF LISTENING
THE EARLY LIFE AND EARLIEST "RADICAL" SPIRITUAL TEACHINGS OF THE DIVINE WORLD-TEACHER AND TRUE HEART-MASTER, DA AVABHASA (THE "BRIGHT")

VOLUME I
THE LIFE OF UNDERSTANDING

Da Avabhasa's autobiographical record of the very human—as well as Spiritual, Transcendental, and Divine—Ordeal of His Illumined birth and His boyhood in America, His Spiritual insights, practice, and growth as a Devotee of great modern Yogic Adepts, and His Divine Re-Awakening or Enlightenment.
New Standard Edition
(forthcoming, 1992)

VOLUME II
THE WISDOM OF UNDERSTANDING

Da Avabhasa's earliest Essays on the practice and Realization of "Radical" Understanding.

(These first two volumes of *The Knee of Listening,* taken from the original, unabridged manuscript and including recent commentary by Da Avabhasa and His devotees, are nearly twice the length of the previously published edition of *The Knee of Listening.*)
New Standard Edition
(forthcoming, 1992)

VOLUME III
THE METHOD OF THE SIDDHAS: TALKS ON THE SPIRITUAL TECHNIQUE OF THE SAVIORS OF MANKIND

In this book of powerful and often extremely humorous Talks with His devotees in 1972 and 1973, the first year of His formal Teaching Work, Da Avabhasa Reveals the Secret of the Way of Satsang—the profound and transforming relationship between the Sat-Guru and His devotee.
New Standard Edition
(forthcoming, 1992)

SCIENTIFIC PROOF OF THE EXISTENCE OF GOD WILL SOON BE ANNOUNCED BY THE WHITE HOUSE!

PROPHETIC WISDOM ABOUT THE MYTHS AND IDOLS OF MASS CULTURE AND POPULAR RELIGIOUS CULTISM, THE NEW PRIESTHOOD OF SCIENTIFIC AND POLITICAL MATERIALISM, AND THE SECRETS OF ENLIGHTENMENT HIDDEN IN THE BODY OF MAN

Speaking as a modern Prophet, Da Avabhasa combines His urgent critique of present-day society with a challenge to create true sacred community based on actual Divine Communion and a Spiritual and Transcendental Vision of human Destiny.

New Standard Edition
(forthcoming, 1992)

THE TRANSMISSION OF DOUBT

TALKS AND ESSAYS ON THE TRANSCENDENCE OF SCIENTIFIC MATERIALISM THROUGH "RADICAL" UNDERSTANDING

Da Avabhasa's principal critique of scientific materialism, the dominant philosophy and world-view of modern humanity that suppresses our native impulse to Liberation, and His Revelation of the ancient and ever-new Way that is the true sacred science of Life, or of Divine Being Itself.

New Standard Edition
(forthcoming, 1992)

THE ENLIGHTENMENT OF THE WHOLE BODY

A RATIONAL AND NEW PROPHETIC REVELATION OF THE TRUTH OF RELIGION, ESOTERIC SPIRITUALITY, AND THE DIVINE DESTINY OF MAN

One of Da Avabhasa's early Revelations of the Way of Eternal Life that He Offers to beings everywhere, including Ecstatic Confessions of His own Enlightened Realization of the Divine Person, and sublime Instruction in the practices of the Way of the Heart. When initially published in 1978, this Text was a comprehensive summary of His Way of the Heart. Includes a unique section, with illustrations, on the esoteric anatomy of the advanced and the ultimate stages of Spiritual transformation.

New Standard Edition
(forthcoming, 1992)

NIRVANASARA

Da Avabhasa critically appraises the sacred Wisdom-Culture of mankind, particularly focusing on the two most sublime traditions of sacred life and practice—Buddhism and Hindu non-dualism (Advaita Vedanta). Here He also announces and expounds upon His own Way of the Heart as the continuation and fulfillment of the most exalted Teachings of Buddhism and Hinduism.

New Standard Edition
(forthcoming, 1992)

THE DREADED GOM-BOO, OR THE IMAGINARY DISEASE THAT RELIGION SEEKS TO CURE

In this remarkable book, Da Avabhasa Offers a startling and humorous insight: All religion seeks to cure us of an unreal or fundamentally imaginary disease, which He calls "the Dreaded Gom-Boo". This disease is our constant assumption that we have fallen from Grace and are thus in need of the salvatory "cure" of religious belief.

The good news of Da Avabhasa's Way of the Heart is that we need not seek to be cured but need only feel, observe, understand, and renounce (through the real ordeal of sacred practice) the very activity of seeking itself, and thus be restored to our native Happiness and Freedom.
New Standard Edition
(forthcoming, 1992)

CRAZY DA MUST SING, INCLINED TO HIS WEAKER SIDE
CONFESSIONAL POEMS
OF LIBERATION AND LOVE

Composed principally in the early 1970s and expressed spontaneously with the ardor of continuous, Divinely Awakened Identification with all beings, these remarkable poems proclaim Da Avabhasa's vulnerable human Love and His Mysterious, "Crazy" passion to Liberate others from ego-bondage.
$9.95 paper

THE SONG OF THE SELF SUPREME
ASHTAVAKRA GITA
The Classical Text of Atmadvaita
by Ashtavakra

An authoritative translation of the *Ashtavakra Gita,* a text Da Avabhasa has described as "among the greatest (and most senior) communications of all the religious and Spiritual traditions of mankind". His illuminating Preface is a unique commentary on this grand classic of Advaita Vedanta, discussing the *Ashtavakra Gita* in the context of the total Great Tradition of Spiritual and Transcendental Wisdom. Da Avabhasa also identifies and discusses the characteristics of those rare texts and traditions that fully communicate the Realization and "Point of View" of the seventh, or fully Enlightened, stage of life.
New Standard Edition
(forthcoming, 1992)

PRACTICAL TEXTS

THE EATING GORILLA COMES IN PEACE
THE TRANSCENDENTAL PRINCIPLE
OF LIFE APPLIED TO DIET AND
THE REGENERATIVE DISCIPLINE
OF TRUE HEALTH

In a substantial reworking of the first edition of this text, Da Avabhasa Offers a practical manual of Divinely Inspired Wisdom about diet, health and healing, and the sacred approach to birthing and dying.
New Standard Edition
(forthcoming, 1992)

CONSCIOUS EXERCISE AND THE TRANSCENDENTAL SUN
THE PRINCIPLE OF LOVE APPLIED
TO EXERCISE AND THE METHOD
OF COMMON PHYSICAL ACTION.
A SCIENCE OF WHOLE BODY WISDOM,
OR TRUE EMOTION, INTENDED MOST
ESPECIALLY FOR THOSE ENGAGED
IN RELIGIOUS OR SPIRITUAL LIFE

Conscious exercise is a "technology of love"—which transforms physical exercise, play, and all ordinary activity into an embrace of the infinite energy of the cosmos, always in the conscious context of feeling-Contemplation of Da Avabhasa Himself as Divine Heart-Master. Greatly enlarged and updated from earlier editions.
New Standard Edition
(forthcoming, early 1992)

LOVE OF THE TWO-ARMED FORM

THE FREE AND REGENERATIVE FUNCTION OF SEXUALITY IN ORDINARY LIFE, AND THE TRANSCENDENCE OF SEXUALITY IN TRUE RELIGIOUS OR SPIRITUAL PRACTICE

Da Avabhasa's Instruction on the cultivation of "true intimacy" and the Realization of truly ecstatic, Spiritualized sexuality—a profound critique of both worldly exploitation of sex and ascetical, anti-sexual religious messages. As an alternative to these errors of West and East, Da Avabhasa proposes the specific practices of sexual "conscious exercise" and "sexual communion" (for sexually active individuals who practice in Satsang with Him). His Enlightened Wisdom-Teaching on emotion and sexuality Calls and inspires all men and women to a new and compassionate union of love, desire, and Spiritual consciousness.
New Standard Edition
(forthcoming, 1992)

EASY DEATH

TALKS AND ESSAYS ON THE INHERENT AND ULTIMATE TRANSCENDENCE OF DEATH AND EVERYTHING ELSE

In this major revision of the popular first edition of His Talks and Essays on death, Da Avabhasa Reveals the esoteric secrets of the death process and Offers a wealth of practical Instruction on how to prepare for a God-Conscious and ecstatic transition from physical embodiment. Elisabeth Kübler-Ross wrote of the first edition: "An exciting, stimulating, and thought-provoking book that adds immensely to the literature on the phenomena of life and death. Thank you for this masterpiece."
New Standard Edition
(forthcoming, late 1991)

culminated, on January 11, 1986, in the Great Event that inaugurated His Divine Emergence as the World-Teacher and His ongoing Blessing Work.

Richly illustrated with more than 100 photographs of Da Avabhasa and full of the often dramatic Stories of His Teaching years and His Divine Emergence Work, as well as His own unique Confessions of Divine Incarnation, Realization, and Service to all beings. [The next edition of *The Divine Emergence of the World-Teacher* will be subtitled *The Realization, the Revelation, and the Revealing Ordeal of Da Avabhasa (The "Bright")*].
$14.95 paper

THE CALLING OF THE KANYAS

CONFESSIONS OF SPIRITUAL AWAKENING AND PERFECT PRACTICE THROUGH THE LIBERATING GRACE OF THE DIVINE WORLD-TEACHER AND TRUE HEART-MASTER, DA AVABHASA (THE "BRIGHT")
by Meg McDonnell
with the Da Avabhasa Gurukula Kanyadana Kumari Order (Kanya Tripura Rahasya, Kanya Samarpana Remembrance, Kanya Kaivalya Navaneeta, and Kanya Samatva Suprithi)

The story of the Graceful ordeal of sacred practice and transformation embraced by the formal renunciate order of four women devotees who personally serve Da Avabhasa. The confessions and the example of the Kanyas call everyone to deeply understand and heartily respond to the Supremely Blessed Event that has made their own Spiritual transformation possible: Da Avabhasa's Great Divine Emergence, beginning in early 1986 and continuing ever since.
(forthcoming, 1992)

LEELAS

The Sanskrit term "leela" (sometimes "lila") traditionally refers to the Divine Play of the Sat-Guru with his (or her) devotees, whereby he Instructs and Liberates the world. Da Avabhasa has said that Leelas of His Instructional Play with His devotees are part of His own Word of Instruction, and they are, therefore, Potent with the Blessing and Awakening-Power of His Heart-Transmission.

THE DIVINE EMERGENCE OF THE WORLD-TEACHER

THE REALIZATION, THE REVELATION, AND THE REVEALING ORDEAL OF DA KALKI
A Biographical Celebration of Heart-Master Da Love-Ananda
by Saniel Bonder
Never before have the Life and Work of a seventh stage Divine Incarnation been so carefully documented. This lively narrative focuses on Da Avabhasa's lifelong Ordeal of Divine Transmutation, which finally

FOR AND ABOUT CHILDREN

WHAT AND WHERE AND WHO TO REMEMBER TO BE HAPPY

A SIMPLE EXPLANATION
OF THE WAY OF THE HEART
(FOR CHILDREN, AND EVERYONE ELSE)

A new edition of Da Avabhasa's essential Teaching-Revelation on the religious principles and practices appropriate for children. In Words easily understood and enjoyed by children and adults, Da Avabhasa tells children (and adults) how to "feel and breathe and Behold and Be the Mystery".
New Standard Edition, fully illustrated (forthcoming, 1992)

THE TWO SECRETS (yours, AND MINE)

A STORY OF HOW THE
WORLD-TEACHER, DA KALKI,
GAVE GREAT WISDOM AND BLESSING
HELP TO YOUNG PEOPLE (AND EVEN
OLDER PEOPLE, TOO) ABOUT HOW TO
REMEMBER WHAT AND WHERE AND
WHO TO REMEMBER TO BE HAPPY
A Gift (Forever) from Da Kalki
(The World-Teacher, Heart-Master
Da Love-Ananda), as told by
Kanya Remembrance, Brahmacharini
Shawnee Free Jones, and their friends

A moving account of a young girl's confrontation with the real demands of sacred practice, and how Da Avabhasa lovingly Instructed and Served her in her transition through a crisis of commitment to practice that every devotee must, at some point, endure.
$12.95 paper

VEGETABLE SURRENDER,

OR HAPPINESS IS NOT BLUE
by Heart-Master Da and two little girls

The humorous tale of Onion One-Yin and his vegetable friends, who embark on a search for someone who can teach them about happiness and love, and end up learning a great lesson about seeking. Beautifully illustrated with original line drawings.
$12.95 cloth, oversize

THE TRANSCENDENCE OF CHILDHOOD AND ADOLESCENCE

Compiled from Da Avabhasa's previously unpublished Instructions, this book comprehensively addresses the conscious education of young people in their teenage years, providing for the modern age an Enlightened vision of the ancient principle and way of life called "brahmacharya". In this approach, as practiced in the communities of Free Daists, young people (typically between the ages of 11 and 15) make a free and conscious choice to devote their lives to the Realization of the Divine Reality, under the direct tutelage of their "brahmacharya master" or Guru. This book presents a "radical" vision of education that is virtually unknown in the modern West.
(forthcoming, 1992)

LOOK AT THE SUNLIGHT ON THE WATER

EDUCATING CHILDREN FOR A LIFE OF
SELF-TRANSCENDING LOVE AND
HAPPINESS: AN INTRODUCTION

Full of eminently practical guidance for the "whole bodily" and sacred education of children and young people, this simple, straightforward, informative

text is also perhaps the best available brief summation of Da Avabhasa's Wisdom on the first three stages of life, or the period from infancy to adulthood.
$12.95 paper

PERIODICALS

THE FREE DAIST
The Bi-Monthly Journal of the Heart-Word and Blessing Work of the Divine World-Teacher and True Heart-Master, Da Avabhasa (The "Bright")

The Free Daist chronicles the Leelas of the Teaching Work and the Divine Emergence Work of Da Avabhasa, and describes the practice and process of devotion, self-discipline, self-understanding, service, and meditation in the Way of the Heart. In addition, the magazine reports on the cultural and missionary activities of the Free Daist Communion and the cooperative community of Da Avabhasa's devotees. Of special interest is the regular "Hermitage Chronicle" offering current news of Da Avabhasa's Life and Work.

Subscriptions are $44.00 per year for six issues. Please send your check or money order (payable to The Dawn Horse Press) to: The Free Daist, P.O. Box 3680, Clearlake, CA 95422, USA.

THE "BRIGHT"
Celebrations of the Divine World-Teacher, Da Avabhasa (The "Bright")

A brief bi-monthly periodical, oriented to the general reader, introducing the Good News of Da Avabhasa and His Work and countering the trends of scientific materialism, religious provincialism, and anti-guruism in present-day society.

Subscriptions are $12.00 per year for six issues. Please send your check or money order (payable to The Dawn Horse Press) to: The "Bright", P.O. Box 3680, Clearlake, CA 95422, USA.

A subscription to both *The "Bright"* and *The Free Daist* is only $48.00.

THE GARDEN OF LIONS MAGAZINE
The Worldwide Voice of Young Free Daists

This unique magazine is the voice of the worldwide culture of children and young people who practice the Way of the Heart under the Enlightened Guidance of the living Sat-Guru, Da Avabhasa. *The Garden of Lions Magazine* includes published Instruction on various aspects of sacred practice for young people, Discourses Given by Da Avabhasa, personal accounts and inspiring stories from the lives of young devotees, and a great variety of articles and artwork from young people of all ages from all over the world. Themes have included: an introduction to the practice of Brahmacharya, or the study of God, the Spiritual practice of Ecstasy and Guru-devotion, and the Enlightened practice of sexuality for young people.

The Garden of Lions Magazine is a truly extraordinary celebration of the unprecedented Wisdom-Teaching and Way of life Given by Da Avabhasa.

Subscriptions are $16.00 per year for three issues. Please send your check or money order (payable to *The Garden of Lions Magazine*) to: The Garden of Lions Magazine, Subscription Department, P.O. Box 1737, Lower Lake, CA 95457, USA.

VIDEOTAPES

THE WAY OF THE HEART

On the "Radical" Spiritual Teaching and Universal Blessing Work of the Western-Born Adept, Heart-Master Da Love-Ananda

Incorporating rare segments of recent and historical footage, Part One tells the Story of Sri Da Avabhasa's Illumined Birth and His Ordeal of Divine Re-Awakening for others, and celebrates the Emergence of His Work of World Blessing. Part Two (which includes Talk excerpts by Da Avabhasa and testimonials by longtime practitioners) describes the Gifts and forms of practice that are Given to all who take up the Way of the Heart as Da Avabhasa's devotees. Part Three introduces the sacred culture of the Way of the Heart.
$29.95, 2 hours,
VHS, NTSC, or PAL format

The Way of the Heart is also available in a modified form, which includes recent footage of Da Avabhasa in Darshan with devotees and other material not included in the full-length version. A brief, summary audio-visual introduction to His Life and Divine Work as the World-Teacher in a world addicted to egoic suffering and seeking.
$19.95, 76 minutes,
VHS, NTSC, or PAL format

ORDERING THE BOOKS AND VIDEOTAPES OF DA AVABHASA

The books and videotapes of Da Avabhasa are available at local bookstores and by mail from the Dawn Horse Book Depot.

Please write to us at the address below for a complete catalogue of books and audio-visual publications on the Way of the Heart and traditional sacred literature.

In the USA please add $1.75 for the first book or videotape and $.75 for each additional book or videotape. California residents add 7¼% sales tax.

Outside the USA please add $4.00 for the first book or videotape and $1.00 for each additional book or videotape.

To order the books and videotapes listed above, and to receive your copy of the Dawn Horse Press Catalogue, please write:

The Dawn Horse Book Depot
P.O. Box 3680
Clearlake, CA 95422, USA
(707) 928-4936

INDEX

An Invitation

O f all the means for Spiritual growth and ultimate Liberation offered in the sacred traditions of humankind, the most treasured is the Way of Satsang, or the Way lived in the Blessing Company of One Who has Realized the Truth. Da Avabhasa, the Divine World-Teacher and True Heart-Master, Da Love-Ananda Hridayam, Offers just such a rare and Graceful Opportunity.

The transformative relationship to Da Avabhasa is the foundation of the Way of the Heart that He Offers. Through a whole personal and collective life of self-transcending practice in His Company, ordinary men and women may be purified of their egoic suffering and enjoy the Blessings of a God-Realizing destiny.

If you would like to receive a free introductory brochure or talk to a practicing devotee about forms of participation in the Way of the Heart, please write or call our Correspondence Department:

Correspondence Department
The Free Daist Communion
P.O. Box 3680
Clearlake, California 95422, USA
(707) 928-4936